CAPTURING THE REVOLUTION

The United States, Central America,
and Nicaragua, 1961–1972

Michael D. Gambone

PRAEGER

Connecticut
London

Library of Congress Cataloging-in-Publication Data

Gambone, Michael D., 1963–
    Capturing the revolution : the United States, Central America, and
Nicaragua, 1961–1972 / Michael D. Gambone.
        p.   cm.
Includes bibliographical references and index.
    ISBN 0–275–96594–5 (alk. paper) — ISBN 0–275–97305–0 (pbk. : alk.
paper)
    1. Latin America—Politics and government—1948–.   2.
Revolutions—Latin America—History—20th century.   3. Latin
America—Foreign relations—United States.   4. United States—Foreign
relations—Latin America.   5. Central America—Politics and
government—1951–1979.   6. Nicaragua—Politics and
government—1937–1979.   7. Alliance for Progress.   I. Title.
    F1414.2.G356   2001
    972.805′2—dc21   00-069858

British Library Cataloguing in Publication Data is available.

Library of Congress Catalog Card Number: 00-069858
ISBN: 0–275–96594–5
        0–275–97305–0 (pbk.)

First published in 2001

Praeger Publishers, 88 Post Road West, Westport, CT 06881
An imprint of Greenwood Publishing Group, Inc.
www.praeger.com

Printed in the United States of America

The paper used in this book complies with the
Permanent Paper Standard issued by the National
Information Standards Organization (Z39.48–1984).

10   9   8   7   6   5   4   3   2   1

For
Audrey Philcox
A good Christian woman
and a gentle soul

Contents

Tables

Acknowledgments

This book represents the effort and assistance of a great many individuals. I am most indebted to a host of archivists, without whose advice and support this work would not have progressed. I would like to offer my sincere thanks to Maura Porter and June Payne at the John F. Kennedy Library; Regina Greenwell, Bob Tissing, Linda Seelke, Matt Hanson, Deidre Doughty, Dan Gardner, and Charlaine Burgess at the Lyndon B. Johnson Library; and Pat Anderson at the Nixon Presidential Materials Staff of the National Archives and Records Administration. Last, it is also important to recognize John Kissinger and Jennifer Allen at Alvernia College for keeping me fed with what must have seemed like an endless flow of books, articles, and documents.

Outside funding also managed to keep this project alive over the past three years. I would like to extend my gratitude to the University of Texas for its Moody Research Grant and the Development and Research Committee at Alvernia College for its research support. Their generous support made the extensive travel necessary for this book possible. Thanks must also go to Lynn Clapham and Mary Brown for their hospitality and gourmet cooking during my visit to Boston.

Work cannot occur without support at home. Throughout the entirety of this project my wife Rachel has provided not only moral and spiritual support, but has also served as a sounding board for many of its ideas. Her knowledge undoubtably saved many a good idea and produced others still during the early draft stages of the manuscript. In the latter part of the writing process, she managed to provide me with the time necessary to finish, taking care of our young cub and newest addition, Michael.

Abbreviations and Acronyms

AID	Agency for International Development
ANC	Accion National Conservadora
ANSESAL	Salandoran National Security Agency
CABEI	Central American Bank for Economic Integration
CACM	Central American Common Market
CASP	Country Analysis and Strategy Paper
CGT	Confederacion General de Trabajo (General Confederation of Workers)
CIA	Central Intelligence Agency
CIEP	Council on International Economic Policy
CINCARIB	Commander-in-Chief, Caribbean
CNT	Confederacion Nacional de Trabajadores (National Confederation of Workers)
CONDECA	Consejo de Defensa Centro Americana (Central American Defense Council)
DLF	Developmental Loan Fund
ECLA	Economic Commission for Latin America
EEC	European Economic Community
EXIM	Export–Import Bank
FAN	Fuerza Aérea de Nicaragua
FAR	Fuerzas Armadas Rebeldes
FER	Frente Estudiantil Revolucionario
FOA	Foreign Operations Administration
FRS	Frente Revolucionario Sandino
FSLN	Frente Sandinista de Liberacion Nacional
FTM	Federacion de Trabajadores de Managua (Managua Worker's Federation)
GN	Guardia Nacional
IADB	Inter-American Development Bank
IAN	Agrarian Reform Institute
IBRD	International Bank for Reconstruction and Development
ICA	International Cooperation Administration
IDA	International Development Association
IDB	Inter-American Defense Board

IFC	International Finance Corporation
IIC	Integration Industries Convention
IMF	International Monetary Fund
INFONAC	Instituto de Fomento Nacional (National Development Agency)
JCS	Joint Chiefs of Staff
LAFTA	Latin American Free Trade Association
MAAG	Military Advisory and Assistance Group
MAP	Military Assistance Program
MDAP	Military Defense Assistance Program
METASA	Metales y Estructuras, S.A.
MR	Movilizacion Republicana
MR-13	Movimiento Revolucionario 13 de Noviembre
MSP	Mutual Security Program
NAC	National Advisory Council
NATO	North Atlantic Treaty Organization
NEP	New Economic Policy
NIE	National Intelligence Estimate
NSAM	National Security Action Memorandum
NSC	National Security Council
NSDM	National Security Decision Memorandum
NSSM	National Security Study Memorandum
OAS	Organization of American States
ODECA	Organizacion de Estados Centroamericanos
OECD	Organization of Economic Cooperation and Development
OISP	Overseas Internal Security Program
OPS	Office of Public Safety
PCT	Partido Conservador Tradicionalista
PGT	Communist Guatemalan Workers Party
PLI	Partido Liberal Independiente
PLN	Partido Liberal Nacionalista
PMA	Policia Militar Ambulante
PRD	Partido Revolucionario Dominicano
PSC	Partido Social Cristiano (Social Christian Party)
PSN	Partido Socialista Nicaragüense
ROCAP	Regional Office for Central America and Panama
SALT	Strategic Arms Limitation Treaty
SFG	Special Forces Group
SIECA	Secretariat for Economic Integration
SNIE	Special National Intelligence Estimate
SPTF	Social Progress Trust Fund
UFCO	United Fruit Company
UNO	Union Nacional Opositora
USARCARIB	United States Army Caribbean
USMC	United States Marine Corps
USOM	United States Operations Mission
WTIS	World Trade Information Service

Introduction

In 1961, revolutionary fervor spread around the globe, challenging any one nation or ideology to capture it. Throughout the underdeveloped world, the collapse of old colonial empires heralded approaching upheaval. By 1960, all of French West Africa and French Equatorial Africa was free. All told, seventeen African nations would emerge from the chaos that followed Europe's scramble out of the continent between 1960 and 1961 alone.[1] In Southeast Asia, the final resolution of French withdrawal proceeded as guerrilla war embroiled both Laos and Vietnam.[2] Throughout Latin America, old authoritarian regimes suffered under the strain of restive populations intent on socioeconomic and political reform. Between 1956 and 1960, ten military governments were toppled in Latin America, while popular democratic movements enjoyed their greatest resurgence since World War II.[3]

What was the best means to prevent the spread of revolution? This was a question asked in capitals throughout the Western world in 1961. Should the symptoms of trouble—instability, strikes, political agitation, low-intensity war—be addressed first? Or should the root causes, the social and economic underpinnings of revolution, find first priority. Would it be of benefit to build barriers against revolution or attempt to "capture" the desires, expectations, and energy that drove it?

In the years following World War II, the United States devoted enormous energies to answering these questions. Explicit was the desire to build both a shield against instability and prevent its precursors. The latter intent was clearly apparent at the Bretton Woods Conference in 1944, where U.S. representatives worked to refashion the structure of international finance around the World Bank, a measure designed to encourage multilateral trade, interdependence, and peace. Their hope was to avoid autarky and rival regional economic systems that had severely undercut global stability in the 1930s and contributed to the world war. However, Bretton Woods failed to anticipate the breakdown of American–Soviet relations in the aftermath of World War II. Faced with the onset of the Cold War, policy makers were forced to develop an increasingly intricate set of programs to address the issue of instability. One such effort was the Marshall Plan in 1947, a series of loan, grant, and assistance programs designed to "capture" or preempt instability by removing its economic foundations. These were later reinforced by U.S. support for Western European economic integration, a process that eventually led to the European Economic Community. In the meantime, dedicated American policies were also constructed to shield Western Europe from outright symptoms of instability. U.S. military assistance followed in the wake of insurgency in Greece and Turkey in 1947. Two years later, the North Atlantic Treaty Organization integrated the defense of Western Europe and its allies.

By the 1950s, the regional focus of these policies changed, although their basic mechanisms remained largely intact. Faced with the increasing restiveness of underdeveloped nations and open Soviet support for "wars of national liberation," Washington redrew its efforts to both "capture" revolutionary activity and shield against it. The Eisenhower administration would create such new agencies as the Developmental Loan Fund (1957), the International Development Association (1960) and, in Latin America, the Inter-American Development Bank (1959).[4] Throughout, the intent was to sponsor productive, pro-American development in lieu of instability and potential Communist inroads throughout the world. Accompanying this, however, Eisenhower also prepared a mailed fist, heavily promoting American military assistance to the Third World through the Mutual Security Program as well as approving frequent interventions by the Central Intelligence Agency in potential hot spots.[5]

The new Kennedy administration maintained continuity with the past when crafting policies to circumvent revolution. It maintained the American article of faith that military, political, and economic assistance, coupled with selective instances of intervention, would allow the United States to prevail over global instability. The young policy makers present in 1961 believed that free markets bolstered by a strong dollar and mentored by the World Bank could produce not only greater prosperity, but a dynamic entrepreneurial environment that would foster democracy. Similarly, anti-Communism, reinforced by U.S. military assistance and the American nuclear umbrella, would allow for the requisite stability necessary for free economic and political systems. The final product of introducing these institutions would be a linear progression of development toward new, modern, liberal states. The future of the Third World, as they saw it, would thus resemble Western Europe, rebuilt with U.S. assistance, protected by U.S. nuclear power, and aligned with American ideals.

The new Kennedy administration departed from the past to the extent that it realized the vast complexity of this task and the need to integrate both American and local institutions into one viable response to revolution. Somehow, Washington would have to effectively marry U.S. resources and knowhow with the dozens of disparate underdeveloped nations clamoring for stability, prosperity, and reform. The formidable challenge of 1961 was to recraft policy that had succeeded in Europe to fit entirely new political, military, and socioeconomic environments throughout the Southern Hemisphere.

Latin America offered U.S. policy makers a likely place to begin. Long considered by Washington to be a primary sphere of U.S. influence, the hemisphere had undergone significant changes as a result of the Great Depression and World War II. The international financial crisis of 1929 had removed the last vestiges of non-U.S. economic influence from Latin America and encouraged local industrial development. While this sector had surged (particularly in steel, autos, and consumer products) in the 1940s and 1950s, it had still not resolved the basic dependency of most Latin American economies on primary commodities. How could these structural problems be reconciled with local demands for modernization and the expectation of the industrialized nations of the world that the flow of cheap raw materials would continue uninterrupted? Moreover, how could growth be channeled to meet the increasing expectations of Latin American citizens for higher wages, better housing, and improved living standards?[6] Similarly, the Allied triumph against fascism in 1945 had served as a political point of departure in Latin America. Bolstered by the defeat of Hitler and the Allies' endorsement of the "Four Freedoms" (freedom of speech, freedom of religion, freedom from want, freedom from fear), advocacy of liberal democracy heavily influenced the Latin American political discourse of the postwar period. Students, labor unions, peasant organizations, and a few regimes interested in weathering this trend embraced the principle of popular, participatory democracy. The days of authoritarian, oligarchical government seemed numbered in many countries, a reality driven home by the collapse of the Batista regime in 1959. Effectively capturing this intricate array of problems and expectations posed one of the greatest foreign-policy challenges faced by the United States in 1961. In practice, it would require a program of a greater conceptual and financial scale than the Marshall Plan.

For their own part, Latin Americans saw great possibilities and great dangers at the start of the 1960s. Postwar economic development had introduced entirely new industrial and manufacturing sectors into the hemisphere. Foreign capital had begun to return, prompted by the respective economic "miracles" of Europe and Japan. However, deep, systemic social problems had accompanied progress. Urban populations exploded after 1945, creating shortages of housing, medical care, and schools. Unused arable land vanished, consumed by burgeoning export agriculture. Infrastructure, particularly electrical power generation, failed to keep pace with residential, commercial, or industrial growth. Trade deficits and balance-of-payment difficulties, especially after primary commodity prices began to decline in the 1950s, claimed increasing portions of national budgets. A generation of Latin Americans, led by Argentine Raul Prebisch, believed that modernization would lead to more "mature," stable economies and stave off encroaching socioeconomic instability. Although Prebisch and his cohort could offer few specific programs to achieve this modernization, their general ideas dovetailed nicely with those of a young American president who appeared prepared to countenance their demands for greater tariff protections, more access to U.S. markets, and equitable global commodity prices. At the start of the period, it appeared that real progress and, perhaps equally important, real assistance and trade from the developed world, would define a new status quo in Latin America.[7]

The political future of the hemisphere seemed equally unsettled. Castro's successful revolution against Batista highlighted similar vulnerabilities in Nicaragua, Guatemala, Bolivia, and the Dominican Republic. In 1961, Cuba served as both an alternative paradigm to old authoritarianism and an open protagonist of its own version of popular revolution.[8] Conversely, on the right, the 1960s offered the dark possibility that reactionary dictatorship could construct a durable alternative to populist democracy. Armed and advised by the United States in opposition to Communist insurgencies, these regimes began the formation of new states defined by their access to and use of Western managerial techniques and modern military doctrine.[9]

NEW DEPARTURES IN SCHOLARSHIP

Explaining these events as they unfolded during the 1960s has occupied two generations of historians. Scholars have embraced the dichotomy of revolution and response and created an enormous body of work that has approached both topics from an impressive number of angles. Historians have studied revolutionary ideology as it evolved within the intellectual history of Latin America. They have addressed revolutionary leadership by reconstructing the biographies of its protagonists. They have examined the military as an institution to discover the internal motives that promoted its intervention in civilian affairs.[10] Thousands of additional pages have been devoted to explaining the host of institutions created to contend with revolution. Scholars have addressed the Inter-American Development Bank, the Mutual Security Program, and the Central American Common Market.[11] They have broken apart assistance to Latin America from the perspective of the American agencies involved, as well as the U.S. and Latin American policy makers themselves.[12]

Fueling this scrutiny has been the declassification of thousands of linear feet of documents contained in federal archives relevant to the 1960s, a process that has opened up new areas of investigation into the Kennedy, Johnson, and Nixon administrations.[13] Research once focused on the crises of the decade, particularly regarding Cuba, Berlin, and the Vietnam War, has begun to broaden its examination of American foreign policy at the global and regional levels. Historians of Latin America have benefited from an accumulation of data generated by the Inter-American Development Bank and the Alliance for Progress, and from access to collections contained in the United States and archives abroad.

Modern scholarship reflects the benefit of this work. American diplomatic historians have succeeded in expanding the historical context of post–1945 American foreign policy. In *Guns and Butter*, Diane Kunz explores the difficulties confronted by the United States within the rapidly changing postwar global economic system of the 1960s. Her work juxtaposes the challenge of maintaining American global security commitments abroad with an unsuccessful struggle to develop an international economic policy worthy of the myriad problems of trade deficits, foreign aid, and currency stability.[14] Recent scholarship has also offered international-relations paradigms outside the traditional context of U.S. hegemony. Steven J. Stern has expanded the conceptual boundaries of this topic by linking local Latin American rural work patterns and the evolution of labor movements with the world economic system.[15]

Contemporary examinations of Latin American history have made similar progress. Scholarship has been able to move beyond the initial proposals made by the dependency school thirty years ago to a more intricate understanding of Latin American political economy and economic-development policy. Hindsight and greater access to documentation have allowed authors to better evaluate some of the growth models proposed in the 1960s (e.g., import substitution industrialization), as well as the degree to which development was politicized by rival internal faction within Latin American society.[16] Today we are better able to understand many of the internal dynamics that affected Latin American revolution. Recent documents released by the Lyndon Baines Johnson Library, for example, point to a much more significant Chinese sponsorship of dissidents in South America.[17] The cumulative effect of this historical work has been to add many additional layers of understanding to local revolution and the indigenous response.

Two significant limits have emerged in the course of this study. The first is relevant to studies of the nature of revolution in Latin America. The subject itself invites analysis of a complex mosaic of causation. Yet too often historians attempt to explain revolution as a function of a specific cause: as part of the Cold War conflict, as part of regional animosities, as part of internal factionalism, or as part of a personal crusade. Each of these issues is rich in its own history and valuable, but hamstrung by the absence of perspective and a clear understanding of priority within the larger confines of the historical narrative.

A second limit exists with regard to our understanding of efforts to "capture" revolution in Latin America. Again, the study of this history has been handicapped by its focus on single protagonists. On too many occasions, historians have overdrawn the role of the American state and the relatively small circles of individuals who formulated policy at the expense of linking these actors to any external context. As Michael H. Hunt has observed, academic study often reverts to an effort to either vindicate or criticize the United States as a primary protagonist in a rather insular examination of international relations.[18] Authors engaged in the debate between orthodox and revisionist scholarship of American intentions have often neglected integrating the study of U.S. foreign policy with its recipients. Historians, particularly those who study Latin America, have only recently begun to analyze the intermixing of perceptions, plans, and actual policies of participants on both sides of the foreign-policy equation.[19]

This book proposes to integrate the issues of revolution and response into a more holistic study of the United States and Latin America. It will introduce the issue of revolution from the international level, in the context of the Cold War, and carry it downward through intervening layers of national, regional, and local application. All the while, it will seek out points at which the various concepts of revolution overlapped, rebounded, and influenced the final definition of the idea. Soviet influence in Latin America during the 1960s, for example, is axiomatic. However, the various filters that communism traveled through, be they Nicaraguan, Cuban, or Bolivian, substantially changed what form of revolution communism inspired. Nor was communism the only fountainhead of revolution. Grassroots movements designed to challenge the status quo proliferated throughout Latin America during the 1960s.

The same degree of integration is necessary when examining efforts to "capture" revolution in Latin America. No one single level of assistance or intervention is adequate to understand the response to instability. International agencies such as the World Bank and the International Monetary Fund blanketed the hemisphere by the 1960s. The United States advocated its own sponsorship through a host of civilian and military agencies. These were combined with regional and local institutions through the auspices of the Alliance for Progress. At the bottom of this vast pyramid were the labor unions, merchants associations, churches, political parties, and civic associations attempting to address the problem of revolution and its precursors. All of these respective layers must be addressed collectively in order to evaluate their goals, comparative influence upon each other, and effectiveness.

This multilayered approach will begin with the United States. For obvious reasons, it is impossible to discard America from any serious examination of the hemisphere. For the entirety of the 1960s, the United States assumed a contested but primary role in the political, military, and economic affairs of the hemisphere. In order to avoid sweeping generalizations of this particular actor, it is important to understand the epistemology of American policy and the eventual products of this thought, and, perhaps more important, to test policy against a broad spectrum of global, regional, and local environments. In this manner, the reader will have a better means to judge its effectiveness and evaluate the degree (or degrees) of U.S. influence upon Latin America.

Central America will serve as an intermediate level of analysis. The five nations of the isthmus fall within an area of traditional U.S. interests dating back to the nineteenth century. Central America also provides a coherent unit of comparative analysis that may be used to test both major revolutionary trends and the responses crafted to meet them. An analysis of this region will address Soviet influences upon revolutionary activity, Castro's attempt to export his own brand of rebellion, and local revolutionary movements such as the FSLN. Conversely, Central America also contains practical examples of U.S. assistance, local development policies, and collective economic and security programs.[20] Incorporating this regional approach may create a greater degree of Central American distinctiveness in the historical narrative, a process that will take into account the diverse nature of the five nations, internal frictions between them, and uncontrollable factors (e.g., the unforeseen problems of the Central American Common Market) that often militated against the intentions of both U.S. and Central American policy makers.[21]

Nicaragua will occupy the final rung of this analysis. In recent years, the country has attracted considerable scholarship, prompted by the historical interest of a generation of historians inspired by the Sandinista revolution.[22] As is the case with U.S. and Latin American histories, the study of Nicaragua has also begun to press forward into the 1960s, the benefactor of greater access to primary sources. This has led historians to examine the successive post–Somoza Garcia regimes and devote considerable attention to the issues of political and military stability and development. A continuation of this work will allow the tandem topics of revolution and response to be pressed forward to a level of detail far beyond the international and regional approaches noted earlier. It will juxtaposition the grand ideas of the Alliance for Progress against important Nicaraguan internal developments, a path that will lead the historian and the reader through indigenous political maneuvering, personal rivalries, and Nicaragua's own many separate aspirations. It may also shed light on the degree to which the Somoza regime acted as an appendage of American policy or as its own distinct entity in the 1960s.[23]

Before beginning this effort, it is important to establish the historical context for the events that would transpire in the 1960s. More specifically, it is critical to provide some degree of exposition for the ideas of revolution and response before introducing them in the year 1961. This presentation will briefly place the story in the earliest portion of Latin America's past.

THE REVOLUTION DEFINED

Sudden conflict in the service of change has defined Latin American history for centuries. It met Cortez in the accumulating rebellion that diminished the Aztecs and prepared the path toward the valley of Mexico. It preceded Pizarro in the form of a civil war that divided the great Inca empire. It left its mark on the internecine bloodshed immediately following the conquest of Peru, eventually producing a blood feud that cost the latter conquistador his life.[24]

As colonial Latin America evolved, so to did the forms of strife within it. In many instances, it was the product of institutional conflict, from the friction produced in battles over jurisdiction. As the decades passed, the creole came to resent and rebel against the authority of the peninsulare. The church bridled at the control exercised by royal appointees and learned early on that popular violence could be used as a means to checkmate secular authority. The periodic *tumultos* scattered throughout the colonial period, perhaps the most famous being that which occurred in Mexico City in 1624, reflected a basic cognizance within the clergy that sedition could serve its purposes.[25] For the subdued native populations of Spanish America, revolt and rebellion were often the product of the rate of change forced upon local culture by the pace of later Bourbon reforms. Revolution, when it did come, served more often as a means to slow change rather than to increase its tempo.[26]

The Age of Enlightenment added its own complex layer of new political ideology to the older distinctions of race, privilege, and religion. Although the concepts expressed by Locke, Rosseau, and Jefferson failed to reach the vast majority of Spanish Americans by the time of the French Revolution, they did significantly influence a generation of leaders, from Francisco Miranda, the "morning star of Spanish America," to Simón Bolívar, who served at the center of the challenge to Spanish monarchy. The Enlightenment proposed models of a utopian republic, with all its alternative mechanisms of reconstructing political power once it was captured from the crown. Latin Americans as widely separated in their vision of this new utopia as Bolívar and Francisco de Paula Santander agreed in principle that the sovereignty of the people, regardless of its actual form, was the foundation of the new Latin America. Perhaps even more important, the very concept of governance based upon public consent and the broad militarization of formerly disenfranchised social groups (particularly the mestizo majority in many countries) had begun to nurture a nascent form of nationalism, what Bolívar described as commonly held "patriotic ideals," lending Latin Americans a sense that revolution had become a consensual act with the concurrent expectation of greater participation in post-Independence governance.[27]

The nineteenth century saw the nature of conflict in Latin America change yet again. In part, this stage of evolution was the product of the external pressures of the Industrial Revolution, which demanded a reordering of Latin American resources toward export-oriented economies. Latin American society found itself subordinated to foreign interests. This process saw the creation of a professional security apparatus to preserve stability and encourage new capital, alterations in civil law to encumber the public with obligations to the state, and the displacement of rural populations from arable land. Combined, these changes produce widespread resentment that sometimes exploded into open rebellion. Nicaragua's passage of vagrancy laws and laws permitting the conscription of Indians for public labor led to the so-called War of the Comuneros in 1881, a conflict that eventually cost 5,000 lives.[28]

In another sense, the nineteenth century also saw war employed to shape the political reconstruction of post-Independence Latin America. War between Peru and Gran Colombia in 1830 saw the end of the latter's grasp on Venezuela and Ecuador. For all its desire to avoid conflict, Buenos Aires was compelled by pressure from the public and elements of the military to intervene against the Brazilian occupation of its sister province, the Banda Oriental. Within the Central American isthmus, the creole elites who survived the post-Independence period scrambled to rebuild their region in a new, unified image. It was a short-lived project. The collapse of the United Provinces of Central America in 1841 resulted in years of internecine war dedicated to somehow reconstructing stability under the auspices of individual caudillos, such as Rafael Carerra (1839–1865) and Justo Rufino Barrio (1873–1885) of Guatemala and José Santos Zelaya of Nicaragua (1893–1910). The sponsorship of exile armies within the borders of rival Central American nations became an embedded, bitter tradition that persisted well into the twentieth century.[29]

The new century saw the pace of change introduced during the post-Independence era accelerate. In the new modern age, Latin America found itself fully integrated into the global system of capital, a process that offered the enormous benefit of profits drawn from the commercial networks of multinational corporations, but at the cost of creating a vast, disenfranchised urban and rural proletariat. As the demands of modern capitalism placed additional stressors on Latin American society, host governments in the hemisphere compensated by modernizing and internationalizing their militaries, and soliciting military assistance from Germany, France, Great Britain, and the United States. The bloody repression that pervaded the first half of the twentieth century, particularly in Central America and the Caribbean, served as a testament to the effectiveness of these foreign advisory missions.

The ascendancy of the United States as the primary power in the Western Hemisphere placed additional, unprecedented pressures on Latin America. Not content with the quiet manner of commercial and financial influence that the British had brought to bear on Latin American affairs throughout the nineteenth century, American policy dedicated itself to redrawing the legal, cultural, and social substance of the region. Theodore Roosevelt's corollary to the Monroe Doctrine dealt not only with the question of Latin American indebtedness but also with the self-indulgence lifestyle of local elites who had produced it. The high-handed nature of this new hegemon rankled many Latin Americans and held portents for a backlash against U.S. power.[30]

Revolution was also internationalized in the new modern age. Drawing from sources throughout the world, Latin Americans dissidents explored Marxism–Leninism, Socialism, Christian Democracy, and a host of alternative means to replace the status quo.[31] In doing so, they recreated ideology in a form suited to their own particular needs. Augusto César Sandino recast antiimperialism, nationalism, and Marxism in his prolonged rural guerrilla war against the United States in the 1920s and early 1930s, and a new generation subsequently redeveloped them a quarter century later.[32]

The study of Latin American revolution in the 1960s must be considered in the preceding context, as a late chapter in a history of conflict spanning five centuries. It is impossible to study the decade without including the heavy burden placed upon it by past tradition and long-established practice. The bitter conflicts that pervaded Central America after World War II, the endemic plotting, assassination attempts, and sponsorship of exile armies, hearkened back to a time when *personalismo* and long-established individual hatreds defined the basic course of war in the region.[33]

This is not to say that Latin American revolution suffered from a lack of any contemporary influences during the 1960s. The deployment of nuclear weapons to Cuba certainly transformed the fundamental nature of the Cuban revolution as a threat to Latin America.[34] In fact, the Cuban Missile Crisis itself was emblematic of the latest historical event layered upon the many eras of Latin American warfare: the Cold War. The Cold War was the final step toward internationalizing Latin American revolution. It made any armed challenge to the hemispheric status quo not simply a disruption of capitalism or a threat to regional stability, but a component of a global bipolar conflict between superpowers. Latin Americans soon discovered that they were encompassed by the global imperatives of the United States and the Soviet Union. By 1962, Castro's revolution had become an appendage of Soviet strategic policy. Conversely, Latin America and its wealth of natural resources had existed as a component of American Cold War planning since the mid-1950s.[35]

The challenge to the contemporary historian is to discern the impact of the past on revolutionary movements in the 1960s and establish the importance of modern factors that created their own unique influence during the decade. What formed revolutionary intent in 1961? To what extent did traditional animosities within the Latin American nations define revolution? To what extend were these submerged with the Cold War? What was the eventual outcome once local and global priorities were intersected?

In many respects, the history of Central America and Nicaragua in the 1960s serves as a valuable means to begin deciphering this story. The isthmus itself was ripped apart by revolutions after 1945. Fed by the high expectations for greater political freedom and prosperity that followed World War II and spurred on by the leadership of such figures as José Figueres, Fidel Castro, Carlos Fonseca Amador, and Yon Sosa, a diverse array of revolutionary movements sprang up throughout the region.

Similarly, during the postwar period the Somoza regime in Nicaragua struggled mightily to preserve itself against a revolutionary tide that had accounted for the demise of contemporary dictatorships in Guatemala, Cuba, and El Salvador. For years, the family successfully maintained a balancing act between the expectations of the ruling elite, the general population, and its own interests, while accepting World Bank reforms and U.S. military assistance. Yet it was never able to adapt quickly enough to completely stave off the specter of revolution. Once economic reforms began to take hold in the late 1950s, Castro's Cuba emerged to offer a new challenge to the Somoza regime. Others soon followed. Within Nicaragua itself a vital Christian Democratic movement began to take shape at the end of the decade, led by a young generation of Nicaraguans impatient with the political deal making that characterized the country's stratified political system. Finally, the decade also saw the reemergence of Sandinismo, separable from Cuban Marxism by its reliance on Nicaragua's historical past, but definitely influenced by it. As these challenges multiplied, the successors to Anastasio Somoza Garcia found themselves hard pressed to concoct policies necessary for the regime's survival.[36]

CAPTURING THE REVOLUTION

As the nature of revolution evolved, efforts to prevent it adapted accordingly. Throughout most of the periods discussed, simple coercion was the method of choice used by Spanish viceroys and their later successors in the post-Independence era. In this context, leaders maintained order by using military and police powers as a blunt instrument to terrorize a population into compliance with state policies. Arguably, this tradition persisted far into the twentieth century as witnessed in post–1954 Guatemala, Chile after the 1973 coup against Allende, and El Salvador during its civil war in the 1980s.

Despite the longevity of these trends, the twentieth century did bring important changes to the methodology of resisting revolution. In the aftermath of World War II, policy makers sought not simply to react to instability but also to prevent its root causes. In Latin America as well as the United States, this conventional wisdom focused on the social, political, and economic underpinnings of dissent, making the case that once these problems were effectively addressed, stability would follow. The policy maker's goal, and in some respects his holy grail, was to decipher the requisite combination of military, political, and economic inputs necessary to engineer a modern country.

This structuralist approach was expressed by the nation-building theories of Walt W. Rostow, Max F. Millikan, and Adolf Berle and defined by the considerable success of the Marshall Plan (1947) in Western Europe. It shaped security policy for the next quarter century.[37] Consequently, the advisory missions from the United Nations, the World Bank, and the United States that proliferated throughout the world during the 1940s and 1950s attempted to recreate the Western European success story for a global array of new client nations in the Third World. In practice, however, this proved to be an extremely difficult goal from the very start. It was problematic in part because the various sponsors could never agree upon the appropriate means to pursue any one policy area. The Eisenhower administration battled constantly with the United Nations regarding the form economic development should take, preferring "hard" (short-term, high-interest) loans to "soft" (long-term, low-interest) loans or outright grants. Although the United States began to mitigate this position by the end of the 1950s, the basic friction that existed between sponsor agencies muddled efforts to reconstruct the non-Communist world.

Almost from the very start, Latin Americans contested U.S. Cold War priorities. American policy makers foremost sought security to counter what they perceived as a growing Communist threat to the hemisphere. In the 1950s, the United States primary military mission was the reinforcement of collective regional security under the auspices of the 1947 Rio Pact. Through the auspices of the Military Defense Assistance Program, dozens of military advisory missions were dispatched throughout the region to train and modernize the Latin American military for hemispheric defense. These efforts were supplemented by internal security assistance (e.g., the Overseas Internal Security Program) that helped rebuild and update police capabilities to combat subversive activity.[38]

In contrast, Latin Americans bridled at the low priority Washington assigned to postwar economic assistance for the hemisphere. They resented the extractive nature of U.S.–Latin American economic relations, one which had provided the United States with raw materials for commerce and strategic stockpiles (e.g., 65% of its bauxite) without reciprocal assistance for Latin American economic development.[39] Latin American policy makers such as Pedro Beltran argued that technical aid via the Point Four Program (1949) was useful, but fell far short of the massive, comprehensive projects then available for European recovery. As time wore on, attacks on American capitalism increased. Juan Peron of Argentina lost few opportunities to denounce an economic status quo dominated from the north. In Central America, American multinational corporations such as the United Fruit Company became lightning rods for local discontent.[40]

Faced with persistent U.S. footdragging as the 1950s wore on, Latin Americans began to construct their own departures from the contemporary economic system. Individual nations began to solicit capital investment from the recovering economies of Europe. Britain, France, Germany, and Italy eagerly responded, offering their new clients commercial credit on terms far better than the United States. Nations such as Nicaragua, which were ostensibly closely held within the American economic orbit, saw a dramatic change in their trade structure. Between 1951 and 1960, the U.S. share of Nicaraguan imports declined from 72.2 to 52.7 percent.[41] Collectively, local policy makers began to organize, creating the Economic Commission for Latin America in 1950 and pursuing a series of regional integration plans designed to construct the Central American Common Market and the Latin American Free Trade Association.[42]

From a much broader perspective, it appeared that the backlash initiated by American intervention at the start of the century had matured as it spread. For two decades, roughly from the start of World War II to the conclusion of the Eisenhower administration, American policy makers had attempted to reinforce U.S. control of the hemisphere by institutionalizing a broad spectrum of hemispheric affairs. By introducing itself into military affairs through the Rio Pact, inter-American relations via the Organization of American States (1948), and eventually economic development through its late-coming sponsorship of LAFTA and the CACM, the United States permeated virtually every facet of Latin American life.[43] From the perspective of the U.S. policy maker, these were proactive responses necessitated by the Cold War and, to an extent, by Latin American demands for greater attention. For many Latin Americans, however, the United States had become an intrusive, paternalistic power whose constant presence was something to dilute, if not avoid.

Such was the situation as it existed at the start of the 1960s. The challenge to the newly arrived Kennedy administration was twofold: First, it had to devise an effective means to halt the spread of Communism in Latin America, at that time a threat primarily identified with Castro's Cuba. The second half of the U.S. mandate was more difficult. In order to appropriately recapture leadership in the hemisphere,

Kennedy's brain trust had to face the accumulating expectations of Latin America, a process that not only required recognition of economic growth and stability, but also contained some tolerance of self-determination. Reflecting upon this dilemma thirty-seven years ago, Albert O. Hirschman remarked that American policy makers needed to understand that reform might never be entirely peaceful, nor did revolution always have to be violent.[44] How could the United States, for example, divine the difference between legitimate political reform and a Communist cat's-paw? The paradox confronting the United States was the need to sacrifice a certain degree of power in order to create a degree of stability.

Central America faced a similar set of problems at the start of the 1960s. Its stability was threatened by the stated objective of the Castro regime to spread revolution to the region. Skirmishes between guerrilla columns and Honduran, Nicaraguan, and Costa Rican forces peppered the isthmus in the early years of the decade. Open political conflict often accompanied rural war. In countries throughout Central America, students, unions, and fringe political parties took their case to the newspapers and the streets. Salvadoran student protests in 1960 were met with a bloody crackdown. During the 1963 Nicaragua elections, the Somoza regime responded to demonstrations with a greater degree of restraint. Conversely, Central American stability was sometimes threatened by the military itself. The Ydigoras government in Guatemala, for example, bore an unexpected cost for its close alignment with Washington in 1960, when junior officers rebelled against both rampant corruption and official support of Cuban exiles training for the Bay of Pigs invasion.[45] Security policy therefore had to face in two directions, one that placated the military with large budgets, modern equipment, and constant vigilance, the other addressing the growing rebel threat in the countryside.

Central American economic integration faced a similar balancing act. It offered the tantalizing possibility of new markets and future regional growth, but also exposed many more unanswered questions. What were the best means to shift an untrained, predominantly rural labor force into a manufacturing economy? How could individual countries modernize their infrastructures without bankrupting their treasuries? The Central American Common Market, still in its infancy at the start of the 1960s, faced far greater complexities. How would it address the economic imbalances that existed between more industrialized members (e.g., Nicaragua and Guatemala) and those who still lagged behind their neighbors (e.g., Honduras and El Salvador)?[46] How would it integrate industry on a regional scale? What conditions could it place on capital investment?

For its own part, Nicaragua entered the 1960s still reeling from the aftershocks of Anastasio Somoza Garcia's 1956 assassination and subsequent challenges to his family's power. Exiles invasions threatened the country from its northern and southern borders. Political parties in opposition to the regime multiplied. Many old stalwarts in the Somozas' own Liberal Party openly questioned their ability to lead and prepared to challenge them in the upcoming 1963 presidential election. Overlaying this period of crisis was a significant decline in coffee and cotton prices, a trend that severely limited Managua's ability to assuage challenges as the elder Somoza had, with official and unofficial patronage. Although Luis and Anastasio "Tachito" Somoza Debayle inherited the institutions constructed by their father, particularly the *Guardia Nacional*, they did not enjoy the same degree of loyalty that had bolstered the regime for years. On the eve of the Alliance for Progress, their mission was to reinvent themselves as well as their response to revolution.

For every party concerned, capturing the revolution in Latin America necessitated policies that could reconcile complex, often contradictory issues. The times presented a challenge that did not beg the absolutes normally associated with the Cold War era. Centuries of traditional practice, the hybridization of ideology, contemporary market trends, the personal agendas of both U.S. and Latin American leaders, and many other factors blurred the lines distinguishing disagreement from rebellion or reform from repression.[47] The pursuit of clarity derived from these factors became the defining mission of a decade.

NOTES

1. Kevin Shillington, *History of Africa* (New York: St. Martin's Press, 1995), 374–394; Ronald Oliver and J. D. Fage, *A Short History of Africa* (New York: Penguin Books, 1995), 221; Wilfred Cartey and Martin Kilson, *The Africa Reader: Independent Africa* (New York: Vintage Books, 1970), 59–120.

2. George C. Herring, *America's Longest War: The United States and Vietnam, 1950–1975* (New York: McGraw-Hill, 1996), 72–79; Joseph Buttinger, *Vietnam: A Political History* (New York: Praeger, 1968), 454–459; Denis Warner, *The Last Confucian* (New York: Macmillan, 1963), 194–223.

3. John H. Coatsworth, *Central America and the United States: The Clients and the Colossus* (New York: Twayne, 1994), 90–121; Cole Blasier, *The Giant's Rival: The USSR and Latin America* (Pittsburgh: University of Pittsburgh Press, 1987), 75–92.

4. For the early stages of this process, see Dean Acheson, *Present at the Creation: My Years in the State Department* (New York: W. W. Norton, 1969); John Lewis Gaddis, *The United States and the Origins of the Cold War, 1941–1947* (New York: Columbia University Press, 1972), 1–31; Melvyn P. Leffler, *A Preponderance of Power: National Security, the Truman Administration and the Cold War* (Stanford: Stanford University Press, 1992), 55–99.

5. An excellent survey of this period is contained in Douglas S. Blaufarb, *The Counterinsurgency Era: U.S. Doctrine and Performance, 1950 to the Present* (New York: The Free Press, 1977). For more recent studies of covert U.S. activity in the 1950s, see Nick Cullather, *Secret History: The CIA's Classified Account of Its Operations in Guatemala, 1952–1954* (Stanford: Stanford University Press, 1999); Mary Ann Heiss, *Empire and Nationhood: The United States, Great Britain, and Iranian Oil, 1950–1954* (New York: Columbia University Press, 1997).

6. Max F. Millikan, *Income Stabilization for a Developing Democracy* (New Haven, Conn.: Yale University Press, 1953); Max F. Millikan and Walt W. Rostow, *A Proposal: Key to an Effective Foreign Policy* (New York: Harper and Brothers, 1957); Walt W. Rostow, *The United States in the World Arena: An Essay in Recent History* (New York: Harper and Row, 1960). See also Samuel P. Huntington, *The Soldier and the State: The Theory and Politics of Civil–Military Relations* (Cambridge: Belknap Press of Harvard University Press, 1957); Samuel P. Huntington, *Political Order in Changing Societies*. New Haven, Conn.: Yale University Press, 1968).

7. One of the earliest and best examples of scholarship on this topic is David Green, *The Containment of Latin America: A History of the Myths and Realities of the Good Neighbor Policy* (Chicago: Quadrangle Books, 1971). See also Pedro G. Beltran, "Foreign Loans and Politics in Latin America," *Foreign Affairs* 34 (1956): 297–304; Eduardo Santos, "Latin American Realities,"

Foreign Affairs 34 (1956): 245–257; Tulio Halperin Donghi, *The Contemporary History of Latin America* (Durham, N.C.: Duke University Press, 1993), 247–260.

8. Jorge I. Dominguez, *Cuba: Order and Revolution* (Cambridge: Belknap Press of Harvard University Press, 1978); Walter LaFeber, *Inevitable Revolutions: The United States in Central America* (New York: W. W. Norton, 1984); Steven G. Rabe, *Eisenhower and Latin America: The Foreign Policy of Anti-Communism* (Chapel Hill: University of North Carolina Press, 1988).

9. Philipe C. Schmitter, ed., *Military Rule in Latin America: Functions, Consequences, and Perspectives* (London: Sage, 1973); David Collier, ed., *The New Authoritarianism in Latin America* (Princeton: Princeton University Press, 1979); Frederick M. Nunn, *The Time of the Generals: Latin American Professional Militarism in World Perspective* (Lincoln: University of Nebraska Press, 1992).

10. Brian Loveman, *For la Patria: Politics and the Armed Forces in Latin America* (Wilmington, Del.: Scholarly Resources, 1999); Richard J. Bloomfield and Gregory F. Treverton, eds., *Alternative to Intervention: A New U.S.–Latin American Security Relationship* (Boulder, Colo.: Lynne Rienner, 1990); Tad Szulc, *Fidel: A Critical Portrait* (New York: Avon Books, 1986); Richard Gott, *Guerrilla Movements in Latin America* (New York: Doubleday, 1971); Willard F. Barber and T. Neale Ronning, *Internal Security and Military Power: Counterinsurgency and Civic Action in Latin America* (Columbus: Ohio State University Press, 1966).

11. Victor Alba, *Alliance Without Allies: The Mythology of Progress in Latin America* (New York: Praeger, 1965); John M. Hunter, "Latin American Integration and the Alliance." *Current History* 53 (1967): 257–265; Simon G. Hanson, *Dollar Diplomacy Modern Style: Chapters in the Failure of the Alliance for Progress* (Washington, D.C.: Inter-American Press, 1970); Jerome Levinson and Juan de Onis, *The Alliance That Lost Its Way: A Critical Report on the Alliance for Progress* (Chicago: Quadrangle Books, 1970); Albert O. Hirschman, *A Bias for Hope: Essays on Development and Latin America* (New Haven, Conn.: Yale University Press, 1971); R. Peter DeWitt, *The Inter-American Development Bank and Political Influence* (New York: Praeger, 1977); David E. Apter, *Rethinking Development: Modernization, Dependency, and Postmodern Politics* (London: Sage, 1987); L. Ronald Scheman, ed., *The Alliance for Progress: A Retrospective* (Westport, Conn.: Praeger, 1988).

12. Mark T. Gilderhus, "An Emerging Synthesis? U.S.–Latin American Relations since the Second World War," *Diplomatic History* 16 (1992): 429–452; Franz Schurman, *The Foreign Politics of Richard Nixon: The Grand Design* (Berkeley, Calif.: Institute of International Studies, 1987); Walt W. Rostow, *Eisenhower, Kennedy, and Foreign Aid* (Austin: University of Texas Press, 1985); Burton I. Kaufman, *Trade and Aid: Eisenhower's Foreign Economic Policy, 1953–1961* (Baltimore: Johns Hopkins University Press, 1982); Robert A. Packenham, *Liberal America and the Third World: Political Ideas in Foreign Aid and Social Science* (Princeton, N.J.: Princeton University Press, 1973).

13. For a recent discussion of the current limits to this research, see Steven G. Rabe, "John F. Kennedy and Latin America: The 'Thorough, Accurate, and Reliable Record' (Almost)," *Diplomatic History* 23 (1999): 539–552.

14. Diane B. Kunz, *Guns and Butter: America's Cold War Economic Diplomacy* (New York: The Free Press, 1997). See also Duncan Green, *Silent Revolution: The Rise of Market Economics in Latin America* (London: Cassell, 1995); Abraham F. Lowenthal, ed., *Exporting Democracy: The United States and Latin America, Themes and Issues* (Baltimore: Johns Hopkins University Press, 1991); G. John Ikenberry, David A. Lake, and Michael Mastanduno, eds., *The State and American Foreign Economic Policy* (Ithaca, N.Y.: Cornell University Press, 1988). For a very early sample of this type of scholarship, see Robert Warren Stevens, *Vain Hopes, Grim Realities: The Economic Consequences of the Vietnam War* (New York: New Viewpoints, 1976).

15. Frederick Cooper, Florencia E. Mallon, Steve J. Stern, Allen F. Isaacman, and William Roseberry, *Confronting Historical Paradigms: Peasants, Labor, and the Capitalist World System in Africa and Latin America* (Madison: University of Wisconsin Press, 1993). See also William

Roseberry, Lowell Gudmundson, and Mario Samper Kutschbach, eds., *Coffee, Society, and Power in Latin America* (Baltimore: Johns Hopkins University Press, 1995).

16. William R. Cline and Enrique Delgado, eds., *Economic Integration in Central America* (Washington, D.C.: The Brookings Institution, 1978); Victor Bulmer-Thomas, *The Political Economy of Central America since 1920* (New York: Cambridge University Press, 1987).

17. See, for example, Central Intelligence Agency, Intelligence Information Cable, "Chinese Communist Party Advice to Latin American Communist Revolutionary Leaders," 25 June 1964, Lyndon Baines Johnson Library, National Security File, Country File, Latin America, Box 2.

18. Michael H. Hunt, "The Long Crisis in U.S. Diplomatic History," *Diplomatic History* 16 (1992): 115–116.

19. Michael A. Genovese, *The Nixon Presidency: Power and Politics in Turbulent Times* (Westport, Conn.: Greenwood Press, 1990); Michael R. Beschloss, *The Crisis Years: Kennedy and Khrushchev, 1960–1963* (New York: Edward Burlingame Books, 1991); John Robert Greene, *The Limits of Power: The Nixon and Ford Administrations* (Indianapolis: Indiana University Press, 1992); Warren I. Cohen and Nancy Bernkopf Tucker, eds., *Lyndon Johnson Confronts the World: American Foreign Policy, 1963–1968* (New York: Cambridge University Press, 1994); Diane B. Kunz, ed., *The Diplomacy of the Crucial Decade: American Foreign Relations during the 1960's* (New York: Columbia University Press, 1994); Joan Hoff, *Nixon Reconsidered* (New York: Basic Books, 1994); H. W. Brands, *The Wages of Globalism: Lyndon Johnson and the Limits of American Power* (New York: Oxford University Press, 1995); Robert Dallek, *Flawed Giant: Lyndon Johnson and His Times, 1961–1973* (New York: Oxford University Press, 1998).

20. John E. Findling, *Close Neighbors, Distant Friends: United States Central American Relations* (Westport, Conn.: Greenwood Press, 1987); James Dunkerley, *Power in the Isthmus: A Political History of Modern Central America* (New York: Verso, 1988); John A. Booth and Thomas W. Walker, *Understanding Central America* (Boulder, Colo.: Westview Press, 1989); Louis W. Goodman, William M. Leogrande, and Johanna Mendelson Forman, *Political Parties and Democracy in Central America* (Boulder, Colo.: Westview Press, 1990); Robert A. Pastor, *Whirlpool: U.S. Foreign Policy toward Latin America and the Caribbean* (Princeton, N.J.: Princeton University Press, 1992); Frederick S. Weaver, *Inside the Volcano: The History and Political Economy of Central America* (Boulder, Colo.: Westview Press, 1994); Michael L. Krenn, *The Chains of Interdependence: U.S. Policy toward Central America, 1945–1954* (Armonk, N.Y.: M. E. Sharpe, 1996). For an important examination of Central America from the perspective of neodependency, see Gabriel Kolko, *Confronting the Third World: United States Foreign Policy, 1945–1980* (New York: Pantheon Books, 1988). See also Robert A. Packenham, *The Dependency Movement: Scholarship and Politics in Development Studies* (Cambridge: Harvard University Press, 1992).

21. Carlos Rangel, *Del Buen Salvaje al Buen Revolucionario* (Caracas, Venezuela: Monte Avila Editores, C.A., 1977), 306; Coatsworth, *Central America and the United States*, 97–99; Morris H. Morley, *Washington, Somoza, and the Sandinistas: State and Regime in U.S. Policy toward Nicaragua, 1969–1981* (New York: Cambridge University Press, 1994), 2–3, 6–8.

22. Two excellent examples have been produced: Michel Gobat, "Against the Bourgeois Spirit: The Nicaraguan Elite Under United States Imperialism" (Ph.D. diss., University of Chicago, 1998); Richard Grossman, "'Hermanos en la Patria': Nationalism, Honor and Rebellion: Augusto Sandino and the Army in Defense of the National Sovereignty of Nicaragua, 1927–1934" (Ph.D. diss., University of Chicago, 1996).

23. Robert Kagan, *A Twilight Struggle: American Power and Nicaragua, 1977–1990* (New York: The Free Press, 1996), 3; Morley, *Washington, Somoza, and the Sandinistas*, 35; Eduardo Crawley, *Nicaragua in Perspective* (New York: St. Martin's Press, 1979), 123–133; Thomas W. Walker, ed., *Revolution & Counterrevolution in Nicaragua* (Boulder, Colo.: Westview Press, 1991); Margaret Randall, *Sandino's Daughters: Testimonies of Nicaraguan Women in Struggle* (New Brunswick, N.J.:

Rutgers University Press, 1995); Mark Everingham, *Revolution and Multiclass Coalition in Nicaragua* (Pittsburgh: University of Pittsburgh Press, 1996).

24. John A. Crow, *The Epic of Latin America*, 4th ed. (Berkeley and Los Angeles: University of California Press, 1992), 92–106.

25. Ibid., 319–328.

26. Ward Stavig, "Ethnic Conflict, Moral Economy and Population in Rural Cuzco on the Eve of the Thupa Amaro II Rebellion," *Hispanic American Historical Review* 68 (1988): 737–770; Jan Szeminski, "Why Kill the Spaniard? New Perspectives on Andean Insurrectionary Ideology in the Eighteenth Century," in *Resistance, Rebellion, and Consciousness in the Andean Peasant World*, ed. Steven Stern (Madison: University of Wisconsin Press, 1987), 166–192.

27. Halperin Donghi, *The Contemporary History of Latin America*, 1–41; Forrest McDomald, *Novus Ordo Seclorum: The Intellectual Origins of the Constitution* (Lawrence: University Press of Kansas, 1985), 57–96; Crow, *The Epic of Latin America*, 398–514. See also John Lynch, *The Spanish American Revolutions, 1808–1826* (New York: W. W. Norton, 1986), 1–37.

28. Bulmer-Thomas, *The Political Economy of Central America since 1920*, 1–24; John A. Booth and Thomas W. Walker, *Understanding Central America* (Boulder, Colo.: Westview Press, 1989), 29. See also John H. Coatsworth and Alan M. Taylor, eds., *Latin America and the World Economy since 1800* (Cambridge: Harvard University Press/David Rockefeller Center for Latin American Studies, 1998).

29. Gambone, *Eisenhower, Somoza, and the Cold War in Nicaragua*, 106–111; Ralph Lee Woodward, *Central America: A Nation Divided* (New York: Oxford University Press, 1985), 92–119. See also Daniel Castro, ed., *Revolution and Revolutionaries: Guerrilla Movements in Latin America* (Wilmington, Del.: Scholarly Resources, 1999).

30. This contrast between British and American foreign policy is best drawn in Friedrich Katz, *The Secret War in Mexico: Europe, the United States and the Mexican Revolution* (Chicago: University of Chicago Press, 1981). See also LaFeber, *Inevitable Revolutions*.

31. Gérard Chaliand, ed., *Guerrilla Strategies: An Historical Anthology from the Long March to Afghanistan* (Berkeley and Los Angeles: University of California Press, 1982); Sheldon B. Liss, *Radical Thought in Central America* (Boulder, Colo.: Westview Press, 1991); Eric Selbin, *Modern Latin American Revolutions* (Boulder, Colo.: Westview Press, 1991); Matt D. Childs, "An Historical Critique of the Emergence and Evolution of Ernesto Che Guevara's *Foco* Theory," *Journal of Latin American Studies* 27 (1995): 593–624. For studies on the theology of revolution, see Ernesto Cardenal, *The Gospel in Solentiname* (Maryknoll, N.Y.: Orbis Books, 1976); Deane William Ferm, *Third World Liberation Theologies* (Maryknoll, N.Y.: Orbis Books, 1986); Curt Cadorette, *From the Heart of the People: The Theology of Gustavo Gutiérrez* (Oak Park, Ill.: Meyer Stone Books, 1988); Margaret E. Crahan, "Religion and Politics in Contemporary Latin America," in *Security in the Americas*, ed. Georges Fauriol (Washington, D.C.: National Defense University Press, 1989); Ronaldo Muñoz, *The God of Christians* (Maryknoll, N.Y.: Orbis Books, 1990); Edward A. Lynch, *Religion and Politics in Latin America: Liberation Theology and Christian Democracy* (Westport, Conn.: Praeger, 1991).

32. Jeffrey L. Gould, "Notes on Peasant Consciousness and Revolutionary Politics in Nicaragua, 1955–1990," *Radical History Review* 48 (1990): 65–87; Steven Palmer, "Carlos Fonseca and the Construction of Sandinismo in Nicaragua" *Latin American Research Review* 23 (1988): 91–109.

33. See Charles D. Ameringer, *The Caribbean Legion: Patriots, Politicians, Soldiers of Fortune, 1946–1950* (University Park: Pennsylvania State University Press, 1996).

34. See Richard E. Welch, *Response to Revolution: The United States and the Cuban Revolution, 1959–1961* (Chapel Hill: University of North Carolina Press, 1985).

35. See Cole Blasier, *The Giant's Rival: The USSR and Latin America* (Pittsburgh: University of Pittsburgh Press, 1987). For a primary source that discusses U.S. Cold War plans for Latin America see NSC 5509, Draft report prepared by the National Security Council, 2 March 1955, in U.S. Department of State, *Foreign Relations of the United States, 1952–1954, The American Republics.* Vol. 4 (Washington, D.C.: U.S. Government Printing Office, 1983), 182. For a recent account of the impact of the Cold War in Central America, see Cullather, *Secret History.*

36. Rose J. Spalding, *Capitalists and Revolution in Nicaragua: Opposition and Accommodation, 1979–1993* (Chapel Hill: University of North Carolina Press, 1994); Mark Everingham, *Revolution and Multiclass Coalition*; Knut Walter, *The Regime of Anastasio Somoza, 1936–1956* (Chapel Hill: University of North Carolina Press, 1993); Saul Landau, *The Guerrilla Wars of Central America: Nicaragua, El Salvador & Guatemala* (New York: St. Martin's Press, 1993); Walker, *Revolution & Counterrevolution in Nicaragua.* A classic in the field remains Richard L. Millett, *Guardians of the Dynasty* (Maryknoll, N.Y.: Orbis Books, 1977).

37. Robert A. Packenham, *Liberal America and the Third World: Political Ideas in Foreign Aid and Social Science* (Princeton, N.J.: Princeton University Press, 1973); Wilfred L. David, *The Conversation of Economic Development: Historical Voices, Interpretations, and Reality* (Armonk, N.Y.: M. E. Sharpe, 1997).

38. Aaron Bank, *From OSS to Green Berets: The Birth of the Special Forces* (Novato, Calif.: Presidio Press, 1986); Robert H. Holden, "Constructing the Limits of State Violence in Central America: Towards a New Research Agenda," *Journal of Latin American Studies* 28 (1996): 435–459; Michael McClintock, *The American Connection: State Terror and Popular Resistance in Guatemala* (London: Zed Books, 1995); Michael McClintock, *Instruments of Statecraft: U.S. Guerrilla Warfare, Counter-Insurgency, Counter-Terrorism, 1940–1990* (New York: Pantheon Books, 1992); Richard H. Immerman, *The CIA in Guatemala: The Foreign Policy of Intervention* (Austin: University of Texas Press, 1982); Michael T. Klare, *Supplying Repression: U.S. Support for Authoritarian Regimes Abroad* (Washington, D.C.: Institute for Policy Studies, 1977).

39. Gambone, *Eisenhower, Somoza, and the Cold War in Nicaragua*, 19.

40. David Green, *The Containment of Latin America: A History of the Myths and Realities of the Good Neighbor Policy* (Chicago: Quadrangle Books, 1971); David Rock, *Argentina, 1516–1982: From Spanish Colonialism to the Falklands War* (Berkeley and Los Angeles: University of California Press, 1988).

41. Gambone, *Eisenhower, Somoza, and the Cold War in Nicaragua*, 64.

42. Ibid., 21, 46–49.

43. For a recent study, see Gerald Horne, "American Empire and Culture Imperialism: A View from the Receiving End," *Diplomatic History* 23 (1999): 463–478.

44. Albert O. Hirschman, *Journeys toward Progress: Studies of Economic Policy-Making in Latin America* (New York: Twentieth Century Fund, 1963), 251–275.

45. Dunkerley, *Power in the Isthmus: A Political History of Modern Central America*, 445–448.

46. Cline and Delgado, *Economic Integration in Central America*, 19–33.

47. Thomas J. McCormick, "Something Old, Something New: John Lewis Gaddis' 'New Conceptual Approaches,'" *Diplomatic History* 14 (1990): 427. See also David S. Painter, "Explaining U.S. Relations with the Third World," *Diplomatic History* 19 (1995): 525–548.

"radical nationalism" could come under the influence of communism.[7] In this setting, old hands in Washington saw a repeat of the "popular front" strategy utilized with considerable success in both Europe and Asia prior to World War II. Contemporaries saw the developing situation in Cuba as proof positive that nationalism, however well intentioned, could rapidly devolve toward the Soviet orbit.

With all this said, the Kennedy administration faced a number of critical decisions in 1961. Precisely what could the United States do to head off revolutionary reactionism in the Third World? How could the United States avoid simply reacting to Communist provocations and regain the initiative in this conflict? What resources would this effort require? How best could it be organized? Before any of these questions could be answered, it was important for policy makers to understand the nature of change throughout the world, its distinct characteristics, and its evolution. At the start of the 1960s, academics, diplomats, and an array of experts attempted to decipher the origins of revolution to discover its contemporary form.

CYCLES OF REVOLUTION IN CENTRAL AMERICA

The post–1945 history of Central America is a story of revolutionary upheaval and counterrevolutionary repression. In truth, a great deal of the history of the isthmus contained elements of opposition and reaction. After the region gained its independence from Spain, internal affairs largely devolved into a series of conflicts more defined by geography, heritage, or *personalismo* than any particular ideology. In Nicaragua, for example, Liberal interests tended to cluster around the city of Leon, while opposing Conservatives inhabited Granada. Family animosity carried forward the feuds that erupted as local interests collided.[8]

By the early twentieth century, however, this dichotomy had undergone an important evolution. The discovery of viable export crops, primarily coffee and bananas, accelerated the pace of state formation to the point that the "liberal," positivist regimes of the nineteenth century began to assemble the basic tools of a modern nation: professional militaries, a civil service, and a nascent financial sector. Costa Rica pursued this construction even further, dedicating state programs to public health, sanitation, and national insurance and creating a model for other parts of Central America to emulate.[9] As educational systems improved throughout the region and a managerial class began to appear in the service of export agriculture, participation in national affairs broadened and expectations began to focus on true political and social reform.[10] In 1924, for example, Victor Raul Haya de la Torre founded the American Popular Revolutionary Alliance, an organization that devoted itself to using the democratic process to achieve economic and social justice.[11] Labor organization also expanded in the 1920s. According to Ralph Lee Woodward, by 1928, trade union membership in Central America approached almost 5,000 members.[12]

The Great Depression largely ended these hopes. The failure of export-led agriculture prompted political and economic retrenchment as ruling elites struggled to maintain solvency in a collapsing global economy. In this new era, the professional militaries of the past became, according to Marvin Goldwert, a new "third political force" posed against the traditional Liberal–Conservative oligarchy, or, more simply, vehicles to national power.[13] After 1930, coups in Guatemala, Honduras, and El Salvador installed a generation of officers in what became long-standing and repressive dictatorships. In Nicaragua, Anastasio Somoza Garcia coupled the assassination of Augusto César Sandino with a campaign that openly undercut the power of president Juan Batista Sacasa. By 1937, he had gained complete control of his country.[14]

Bloody repression followed in nearly every Central American nation. In El Salvador, a peasant uprising against local landlords was brutally quashed by the Maximiliano Hernandez Martinez regime, resulting in the deaths of thousands. Somoza actively pursued and liquidated the Sandinista leadership that had survived the death of their leader. Labor unions, student organizations, and opposition political parties suffered much the same fate in the 1930s.

But reform did not die. In fact, new political parties built upon de la Torre's concept of "popular democracy" began to grow. In 1934, the Cuban Revolutionary Party– *Autentico* was founded. During the 1930s its leaders dedicated themselves to rebuilding organized labor and addressing fundamental problems of working conditions and collective bargaining.[15] In Venezuela, Romulo Betancourt and a generation of student reformers created Accion Democratica, an organization devoted to "economic nationalism, agrarian democracy, and social justice, ardently debating possible means whereby the country [may] recover and strengthen a regime of public liberties."[16]

Perhaps the most important boon to popular reform was World War II. The war years were defined by the Atlantic Charter and its promise to "respect the right of all peoples to choose the form of government under which they will live," which many in Central Americans saw as a mandate against the continuation of dictatorship in the region.[17] More important, the war brought thousands of American servicemen to Central America, individuals who made the concept of freedom a living reality.

These developments galvanized urban labor, students, and political opponents of Central American dictatorship. In 1944, coalition organizations, backstopped by a young generation of military officers, succeeded in overthrowing both Jorge Ubico in Guatemala and Hernandez Martinez in El Salvador. Anastasio Somoza Garcia also found himself under siege by war's end, the target of labor protests and a restive generation of *Guardia* officers who identified themselves as supporters of constitutional reform and an apolitical military.[18]

The vehicle carrying this movement forward into postwar Central America was the Caribbean Legion. Founded in 1947, it was the product of civil conflict in Costa Rica and Rafael Trujillo's repressive policies in the Dominican Republic. Its purpose, as promoted by José "Don Pepe" Figueres was to simply rid Central America and the Caribbean of dictatorship. The Legion's first target was the Picado government of Costa Rica in 1948, to be followed, according to Figueres, by strikes against Somoza and Trujillo. The substantial number of Dominican and Nicaraguan exiles in the Legion appeared eager to comply.[19]

Ultimately, the Caribbean Legion succeeded only in Costa Rica, where, reinforced by arms from the Arevalo government in Guatemala, it managed to remove Teodoro Picado from power. Efforts to unseat the regimes in Nicaragua and the Dominican Republic proved futile and, in the former's case, sparked an internecine conflict between Figueres and Anastasio Somoza that peppered Central America with exile raids for most of the 1950s.

More important, the Legion's activities provoked a sharp backlash on the part of the United States. Reversing a policy that initially condemned dictatorship after World War II, American leaders, concerned about maintaining influence within the hemisphere, gravitated toward stringent condemnation of anti-communism in Latin America. The Truman administration's final NSC report on Latin America stressed "first and foremost an orderly political and economic development which will make the Latin American nations resistant to the internal growth of communism and to Soviet political warfare."[20] When Dwight D. Eisenhower assumed office in 1953, Washington's primary concern was to prevent Soviet intrusion into its traditional sphere of influence. In part, this meant increased support for internal security under the Military Assistance Program. Arms shipments under the MAP and technical assistance for the Overseas Internal Security Program soon followed to militaries throughout the region.[21] American attention also focused on governments perceived to be sympathetic to the Communist Bloc. The House Select Committee on Communist Aggression claimed in 1954, for example,

The Communist penetration of Guatemala could be accurately evaluated only as one portion of Communist activity everywhere. The vast international network of Communist aggression does not minimize the role assigned by it to the Central American beachhead; on the contrary it highlights the special significance of the Communist campaign in Guatemala as particularly aimed against the United States.[22]

Little more than a year after Eisenhower's inaugural, an American-sponsored coup removed the Arevalo government, replacing it with the more pliable leadership of Carlos Castillo Armas. Some 17,000 Guatemalans were arrested in the purge that followed his return.[23]

It appeared that the heyday of reactionary dictatorships had returned. Reinforced by American aid and increasing demand from recovering economies in Japan and Western Europe, Central America enjoyed an export boom in the mid-1950s. However, in truth, American assistance served only to prolong the conflict between old regimes and a growing body of new opposition. Little, if any, of the economic bounty enjoyed by countries like Nicaragua, Guatemala, or El Salvador found its way toward the population at large. Violence, long a tragic normality, proliferated as U.S. assistance refined and improved the ability of Central American states to root out and crush dissidents. The torture and imprisonment of rebels like Pedro Joachim Chamorro soon became part of the currency of rebellion in Central America.[24]

Under these deteriorating conditions, dictatorships began to bog down as the decade ended. Anastasio Somoza Garcia was gunned down by a poet, Rigoberto Lopez Perez, in September 1956. Castillo Armas suffered a similar fate in 1957, after three years of erratic and repressive governance.[25] But it was the developing revolution in Cuba that captured the attention of many Latin Americans, and later, the world.

Cuba symbolized both the traditional form of revolution and its evolution in Latin America. The violent overthrow of a corrupted despot was a time-worn concept, as was the sanctuary that Mexico provided Castro and his followers. However, what differed from the past was the composition of the rebels themselves. The two Castro brothers, Alfredo Guevara, Che Guevara, and a number of revolutionary cadres were the product of the university.[26] In his famous opening statement to the tribunal that would judge his guilt after the abortive Moncada barracks raid in 1953, Fidel Castro embraced his chosen profession: the law.[27] But what set Castro apart from the revolutionaries of the postwar period was his dogged refusal to pursue his goals through cooperation with existing elites. Unlike Accion Democratica's temporary alliance with the Venezuelan military in 1945 or the infamous "Pact of the Generals" between Anastasio Somoza Garcia and his Conservative Party counterpart Emiliano Chamorro five years later, Castro embraced the principle of popular revolution without compromise. By eliminating the old order from participation in revolutionary leadership, he hoped to avoid this past taint and capture the imagination of the people at large. Before the tribunal that sent him to prison in 1953, Castro warned that they "should entertain no doubt as to the people's will to fight."[28] In 1959, this prediction appeared to have come true, spawning a generation of revolutionaries bent on attaining power through the masses.

Accompanying the Cuban revolution was another trend that represented an important political point of departure in Latin America. In the late 1950s and early 1960s, Christian Democracy emerged as a major political force in Central and South America. Rooted in the Pontifical Commission for Latin America created by Pius XII in 1958 and *Mater et Magistra* (1961), it represented a shift in the Vatican's attitude toward the church's social duty and a growing body of thought that disparaged both communism and capitalism. Christian Democrats believed that communism's inherent economic determinism denied the value of the individual, while within capitalism, communities saw their social linkages displaced by unbridled, individual material competition.[29]

In place of these systems, Christian Democrats proposed a "communitarian society," one in which moral, economic, and cultural rights would form the basis for priority and policy. In order to reach these goals, they pursued social reform through direct action, undertaken by a partnership between the church and the state, and focusing on such fundamental needs as housing, health care, wages, and the vote.[30] A more radical offshoot of this ideology, which would become known as liberation theology, also established roots in the rural communities throughout the hemisphere.[31] In these places, young priests such as Ernesto Cardenal used the gospels to teach *campesinos* the value of self and the virtue of resistance.[32]

As a political movement, Christian Democracy enjoyed substantial appeal among the growing body of Latin Americans who were disenchanted with the existing order, particularly young intellectuals who had tired of sterile debate between old factions and saw the futility of confrontation with security forces within their countries. In contrast, Christian Democracy offered a chance to regain relevancy in the popular mind by promoting direct answers to commonplace problems. Rather than simply chafing under the institution control of dictatorship, it offered opposition groups in countries like Nicaragua one of the most coveted ingredients of the political discourse: the initiative.

By the conclusion of the 1950s, the old, reactionary regimes of the past faced two formidable alternatives to the status quo. From Cuba, Fidel Castro excited the minds of dissidents throughout Central America and the Caribbean with his triumph over the Batista regime. More significant, he appeared more than willing to provide training and assistance to any leader willing to risk a chance at popular rebellion. Christian Democracy provided a peaceful alternative to Castroism. As a movement, its incrementalist approach to reform was appealing to those interested in minimizing internal disruption or, perhaps more important, alienating the United States. This latter point would become increasingly important as Castro began his shift toward the Soviet sphere of influence after 1960.

Deciphering the intent and direction of this latest revolutionary cycle became a consuming task for Americans watching the region. It also presented a delicate and dangerous balancing act for policy makers. How could the United States cultivate grass roots reform that challenged existing governments, but counteracted the possibility of another Cuba? How could American aid differentiate between legitimate dissidents and radical revolutionaries? Most importantly, how could Washington recapture the perception of regional leadership from Havana?

CONSTRUCTING THE ALLIANCE FOR PROGRESS

The election of John F. Kennedy marked, according to Joseph Tulchin and Knut Walter, "a true disposition to export democracy and the conviction that democratic government was infinitely exportable and adaptable."[33] Douglas Dillon remarked in 1961:

This is a revolutionary task, but we are no strangers to revolution. . . . The fruits of the American revolution have not yet been extended to all our people. Throughout the hemisphere millions still live with hunger, poverty, and despair. They have been denied access to the benefits of modern knowledge and technology. And they now demand those benefits for themselves and for their children. We cannot rest content until these just demands are met.[34]

Unfortunately, events already set in motion by the Eisenhower administration briefly overcame any coherent attempt to address the problem of instability, anti-Americanism, or Communist advances in Latin America. The Bay of Pigs disaster of April 1961 was neither of the administration's making nor completely indicative of its approach to revolution. It did, however, focus Washington on two salient features absent from American policy: the need to take a less reactionary stance regarding the problems of Latin American development and the need to develop proper mechanisms to ensure its success.[35]

According to John Lewis Gaddis, the Kennedy administration perceived itself as the defender of diversity.[36] As Dean Rusk noted in 1961: "We believed that any country that was independent and secure, concerned about the needs of its own people, and cooperative in the international arena helped the interests of the United States."[37] In principle, the new president appeared much more willing to consider diversity in a political spectrum that excluded open alliance with the Soviet bloc. At the outset of his term, the United States was willing to support national sovereignty to the extent that it would not supplement communism.

Even this freedom had limits, however. While Walt Rostow commented that America would not require "all societies at all times accept democratic values as their aspiration and move uninterruptedly toward its achievement," he conversely explained that it was in America's interest "that the societies of Eurasia, Africa, and Latin America develop along the lines broadly consistent with our own concepts of individual liberty and government based on consent."[38]

But how best to achieve "lines broadly consistent" with democracy? When he assumed office, Kennedy brought with him a host of Marshall Plan veterans who saw foreign aid as a holistic concept. Adolf Berle, Lincoln Gordon, and Walt Rostow all returned to public service convinced that the greatest mistake of the preceding decade had been what Rostow called the "piecemeal" approach taken by the Eisenhower administration, noting that foreign aid policy had "neither a defined forward objective nor the fresh capital to move towards it."[39]

In this context, the development theories of MIT economist Max F. Millikan and Rostow enjoyed perhaps the most traction in administration circles. In their 1957 book, *A Proposal: Key to an Effective Foreign Policy*, the authors argued that "well-conceived programs of common action" could promote not only economic benefits, but a sense of united purpose, confidence, and progress.[40] What was needed most from the United States was a long-term commitment of funding, time, and attention. Other notable minds within the Kennedy circle readily concurred. In a paper titled "A Positive Approach to Economic Aid," John Kenneth Galbraith urged, "The prospect of very substantial economies in the more purposeful use of aid, in a tighter assessment of outlay in relation to performance, in better administration, and in insuring that assistance is not wasted because the decisive obstacles to advance have not been removed."[41] To overcome "decisive obstacles," Galbraith recommended "a firm contract" between the United States and aid recipients, one that established planning objectives, appropriate milestones, and the means to achieve them.[42]

Collectively, these advisors offered what the United States had sought throughout the 1950s, a direction that was proactive rather than reactive, something that offered a response to communism that was not strictly ideological. In 1961, it appeared that America was prepared to endorse what Albert O. Hirschman called the "program approach" to foreign aid, one that prepared for "laying the groundwork for a substantial and steady flow of aid through a meeting of the minds between donor and recipient."[43] All that remained were the particular details.

For the Kennedy administration, the Alliance for Progress represented America's first opportunity to translate development theory into operational policy. In the words of Arthur Schlesinger, the United States faced a crisis in Latin America, one which "if ignored, might end by transforming the southern half of the hemisphere into a boiling and angry China, but which, if approached in a strong and comprehensive way, might not still be beyond our power to affect."[44] During the 1960 campaign, candidate Kennedy had offered conspicuous attention to the need for an "Alliance for Progress" in the Americas. In the weeks following his election, a task force appointed by the president elect and led by Adolf Berle consulted extensively with both U.S. experts and Latin Americans who were close to the issue of regional development. Pedro Beltran, then Prime Minister of Peru, president Lleras Camargo of Colombia, and former president of Costa Rica José Figueres all contributed in the months that followed.[45]

A definitive statement on this issue appeared only a few weeks after Kennedy's inauguration. On 13 March 1961, before an audience of Latin American diplomats and members of Congress, the president staked out the common ground between the inhabitants of the Western Hemisphere: "The revolutions which gave us birth ignited, in the words of Thomas Paine, 'a spark never to be extinguished.' And across vast, turbulent continents these American ideals still stir man's struggle for national independence and individual freedom." Kennedy reminded his listeners that, in the present day, "millions of men and women suffer from the daily degradations of hunger and poverty" with growing discontent. He explained that "our unfulfilled task is to demonstrate to the entire world that man's unsatisfied aspiration for economic and social justice can best be achieved by free men working within a framework of democratic institutions."[46] To meet this need, he proposed the creation of "massive planning effort" for Latin American growth, one that combined aid, economic integration, and social reform.[47] One week later, in a special message to Congress, Kennedy called for a series of reforms to American aid policy, stressing "our moral obligations as a wise leader and good neighbor in the interdependent community of free nations," and, more important, the immediate need for a long-term monetary commitment to foreign assistance.[48]

The president's key advisors followed closely in the wake of these dramatic statements with their own interpretations of development. In Latin America, Rostow saw the possibility of the political and economic "take-off" he had envisioned almost a decade earlier. He argued that countries such as Argentina, Venezuela, Brazil, and Colombia constituted perfect candidates for an "economic development decade."[49] Other officials saw derivative political benefits in this process, specifically in creation of more pluralistic constituencies. The State Department's Bureau of Intelligence and Research, for example, believed that broad economic development would spark a "middle class revolution" that would in turn break apart the landed oligarchy's hammerlock on economic and political institutions.[50] Lincoln Gordon argued that economic preconditions in Latin America, while not ideal, were sufficient to promote both liberal democratic development and economic growth.[51]

Early in Kennedy's term, for example, American officials contemplated forging links between Christian Democrats and the Alliance for Progress. This approach carried a number of advantages. Christian Democracy offered a clear third alternative to either the old, vested interests of Latin America's traditional oligarchs or leftists attempting to follow the path blazed by Fidel Castro. By embracing a leader such as Chilean Christian Democrat Eduardo Frei, the policy community in Washington saw a chance to win the popular Latin American imagination away from Castro.[52]

One dissenting voice appeared from within the State Department regarding this plan. In a 1962 memo to the president, Roger Hilsman pointed out the potential risks of tying the alliance too closely to the Catholic church. He agreed that both the church and the *Alianza* promoted the idea of rapid progress toward solving social problems. What concerned him was anti-American sentiment prevalent among clerics, something the United States should not embellish with assistance that was "too materialistic" and "concentrated in governmental and secular institutions." Hilsman advised caution and recommended that programs "be measured realistically only on a national basis."[53]

As this discussion progressed, the final catalyst for the alliance formed during the meeting of American states at Punta del Este, Uruguay, in August 1961. The event was, in Kennedy's words, "a demonstration of the capacity of free nations to meet the human and material problems of the modern world."[54] For American policy makers, however, it represented a pressing need for concrete commitments. Some within the administration saw a need to maintain the perception that the United States had finally committed itself to the underdeveloped world. Adolf Berle suggested an "enlargement of the education–information–propaganda effort."[55] In more practical terms, Kennedy administration officials contemplated an aid plan that would send $1 billion to Latin America in 1961, triple the 1960 figure and more than double the annual average between 1950 and 1960.[56] Chester Bowles recommended quick action regardless of the figure, before the consensus surrounding the Act of Bogata dissipated.[57] Special counsel to the president Richard N. Goodwin pressed for the United States to create a "special fund" for Latin America by at least 1962 and to begin "soundly conceived plans and projects" to flesh out the alliance.[58]

The actual meeting at Punta del Este evolved into a study in contrasts. During the course of deliberations, the administration went to great lengths to assure those assembled that the United States was prepared "to improve and strengthen democratic institutions through the application of self-determination by the people."[59] Throughout, the vast array of economic and social reforms discussed were directly linked to the future prospect of political progress. In its final published preamble, the Charter of Punta del Este stressed the assembled nations' commitment to building a broad "framework of personal dignity and political liberty."[60]

For their own part, Latin Americans wanted definitive commitments on the subject of economic assistance. Argentina, Uruguay, and Chile all expressed interest in a Latin American common market. Brazil pressed for American support of an international coffee agreement. Although Bolivian diplomats continually sided with the Cuban delegation on matters of politics, they sent out feelers to determine the possibility of price supports for the tin market.[61]

In the end, the conference produced a wide-ranging set of more specific proposals that included a regional common market, commodity price stabilization, and social reform.[62] It also resulted in a rather unexpected commitment from the U.S. delegation. Throughout the meeting, Treasury Secretary C. Douglas Dillon, the head of the U.S. delegation, had dueled with his Cuban counterpart Che Guevara about the nature and sincerity of America's commitment to the alliance, and made the remarkable commitment of $20 billion to the alliance over the next decade. Dillon reported at the conclusion of the conference that the "final result is, I think, everything we could have hoped for and the alliance for progress has now been fully and successfully launched."[63]

On balance, Punta del Este was a victory for Latin America. The participating countries won from the United States a declaration that included support for ninety-four separate social and economic issues, ranging from adequate per capita income to improved life expectancies.[64] For their own part, the United States received in return a condemnation of Soviet influence in Cuba and a generalized commitment from conference participants to democratic reform and social justice. The unfolding dilemma for

Washington was the fact that its pledge of $20 billion in aid was a definable and measurable quantity, while the Latin American portion of the bargain was not.

Regardless, during fall 1961, the regional reaction to Punta del Este was almost overwhelmingly positive. Late in the year, Kennedy traveled to Venezuela and Colombia and was met by cheering crowds that numbered in the tens of thousands.[65] Colombian president Alberto Lleras Camargo reportedly asked Kennedy in Bogota, "Do you know why those workers and *campesinos* are cheering you like that? It's because they believe you are on their side."[66] In statements to the press, Lleras Camargo lauded the president for awakening "great hope" in the Alliance for Progress.[67] Overall, the event proved to be remarkably different from the disastrous "goodwill" tour taken by Richard Nixon only three years earlier.

NICARAGUAN DEMOCRACY IN THE "STATE OF TRANSITION"

At the start of the 1960s, Nicaragua was the cause for both hope and caution. In 1959, while Castro triumphed in Cuba, Nicaragua saw a recession in which the country's gross national product declined by 3 percent and did not recover its losses a year later. Cotton, which had been the most productive export earner in the 1950s, suffered through the worst harvests the country had seen in half a decade. These economic difficulties were exacerbated by a population explosion, increasing at an estimated 3.6 percent a year. The U.S. embassy reported in July 1960, "There does not appear to be another commodity boom on the horizon which will give the Nicaraguan economy the tremendous impetus that it experienced in the past decade."[68]

Political troubles accompanied this decline. In the wake of his father's death in 1956, Luis Somoza Debayle had proclaimed a new era in Nicaragua and pledged to "modernize and reorganize" his government.[69] As president in his own right, Somoza Debayle relaxed press censorship and released all political prisoners held since 1950. Throughout, the elder brother emphasized the transitory nature of his government, describing it as a "buffer" between the old regime and a new democracy.[70] In a July 1960 press conference Somoza claimed, "Whenever the political parties proceed in peace and in conformity with the law, they would not encounter obstacles."[71]

Somoza's efforts could not forestall significant changes in the basic nature of the Nicaraguan political climate. As in most of Latin America, the concept of rebellion underwent an important evolution in Nicaragua during the 1950s. It was changed by what scholars later identified as the "generation of 1940." When Luis Somoza stepped into his father's shoes in 1957, the bulk of Nicaragua's new dissidents were young, university trained, and significantly dissatisfied with the political status quo. Pedro Joachim Chamorro was perhaps the best known and most active among this new group. The younger Chamorro was at the forefront of attempts to build an anti-Somoza coalition from elements of the Liberal Independent Party, the Social Christian Party, and a number of the country's moribund trade unions.[72] He had also embraced violent rebellion on occasion. Chamorro was arrested for participating in the so-called April conspiracy against Somoza in 1954, and, after a short prison sentence, returned to his country at the head of a rebel column in 1959. Chamorro took full advantage of relaxation of restriction on the Nicaraguan press by publishing his account of prison a year later in *Diario de un Preso*.[73]

In the meantime, the Somozas found their government under siege from armed exile groups determined to replicate Castro's success in Cuba. After 1956, rebel columns marched against Managua from sanctuaries in both Honduras and Costa Rica. Richard Millett has estimated that between 1959 and 1961 there were twenty-three armed uprisings against the regime. In total, Luis Somoza spent four of his five years as president governing under martial law.[74]

The end product of this situation was the prospect of a highly contested presidential election in 1963. Roger Hilsman, director of the State Department Bureau of Intelligence and Research, noted at the end of 1962, "In Nicaragua a non-violent termination of the Somoza political dynasty through free elections will be hard to achieve. As the lid is loosened a real explosion may develop."[75] Of particular concern was the prospect that Communists would be able to influence the electoral process through their control of labor unions such as the Confederacion General de Trabajo and the Federacion de Trabajadores de Managua.[76] A resurgence of the Partido Socialista Nicaragüense, arguably the oldest Communist organization in the country, and the appearance of the Movilizacion Republicana also worried embassy officials in Managua, particularly in the case of the latter, which many Americans saw as the "intellectual front" for communism in Nicaragua.[77] Communist student groups were also active at the University of Nicaragua, providing sanctuary for armed dissidents and an ongoing forum for critics of the regime. Faculty of the school were periodically denounced in even the anti-Somoza *La Prensa* for their leftist sympathies.[78]

The most important challenge to the political status quo, however, came not from the far left, but from the ranks of Nicaragua's traditional parties. Since 1944, the Partido Liberal Independiente had opposed the regime in Managua. Led by Dr. Alejo Icaza, it saw meaningful political reform only in wresting power from the Somozas. An alliance of the Independent Liberals and the traditional Conservative Party in 1959 marked their first formal collaboration against the family since 1936.[79] Although it eschewed violence, PLI leaders warned American officials in early 1962 that there were limits to stopping the PLI rank and file from "pouring out into the streets."[80]

The Partido Conservador Traditionalista also saw its ranks and purpose renewed with the death of the elder Somoza. Formed during World War II when Nicaraguan conservatives split over the issue of continued cooperation with the Somoza regime, it became the vehicle of Emiliano Chamorro's campaign against the Somozas. The party was tainted by the 1950 *Pacto de los Generales* and disbanded after PCT leaders, including Chamorro, were implicated in a 1954 assassination attempt against Somoza. The old PCT structure was finally destroyed in 1959 after its leadership sponsored a series of failed military coup attempts against Managua.[81]

By 1960, leadership of the party fell to Dr. Fernando Agüero Rocha, a prominent figure in a 1954 assassination attempt against Anastasio Somoza Garcia and the boycott of the Luis Somoza Debayle's 1957 election. Agüero was a key leader in the Christian Democratic Popular Movement of the late 1950s and was part of the youth group that was able to wrest control of the PCT at the party's 1960 convention.[82] Heavily influenced by the Christian Democratic movement in Nicaragua, the PCT pursued, according to Thomas Walker, "a program of proselytism among the masses."[83] Under Agüero's guidance, the party adopted a social reform platform that was "the product of the suffering, of the meditation, and of the frustration of many generations of Nicaraguans."[84] He ridiculed the Somozas:

The incessant violation of human rights, the control over the transmission of the spoken word, and the conversion of some tribunals of justice into repressive dependencies of the Executive have recently been aggravated by the persecution of opposition leaders who are necessary for the organization of the political Parties.[85]

Agüero argued that the growth of communism in Nicaragua was the result of government policy, not Havana's influence. The party's 1960 political manifesto demanded three basic reforms: a new electoral law, reorganization of the *Guardia Nacional*, and OAS supervision of the presidential election.[86] The one issue that handicapped the PCT by 1963 was a growing disenchantment with what many members considered Agüero's own *personalismo*. As a consequence, many defected to a splinter party, the Partido Social Cristiano.[87]

Dissent within Luis Somoza's own party, the Partido Liberal Nationlista, also clouded the political landscape after 1960. Signs of disillusionment with the regime had appeared as early as 1959, when a faction known as the Bloque del Norte made as unsuccessful bid to hold direct elections for representatives to the party's Grand Convention and the National Executive Committee. Somoza appointees openly lamented the failure of this effort and the "window dressing" amendments subsequently made to PLN statutes by the regime.[88]

Internal animosity exploded into an open, ongoing controversy when Somoza announced his support for Foreign Minister René Schick as the Liberal candidate for president in January 1962. In an interview with the Somoza paper *Novedades*, Schick claimed that he was "a good standard bearer of Nicaraguan union because I do not hate anybody."[89] Many within Somoza's administration took exception to the decision. An early front runner for the nomination, Minister of Government Julio Quintana, bitterly opposed Schick. Quintana questioned whether Schick possessed a constituency in either the party or the general public and publicly stated that none of the Somozas had ever succeeded in imposing a candidate upon the Nicaraguan people without Liberal approval. Quintana threatened to take his supporters within the PLN to a floor fight at the party's national convention in 1962.[90] For its own part, the American embassy reacted with alarm at the prospect, noting that "there are just enough Liberals, who are so determined to have a change that they will not support a Somoza-tainted Liberal candidate, to keep the Agüero bandwagon well supplied with inspiring motive power."[91]

As it unfolded, the election campaign of 1962–1963 was a bumpy ride for Nicaragua. In March, the PCT was able to mobilize thousands in support of its platform. An estimated 20,000 people turned out in Granada to condemn the regime and demand free elections before the onset of communism.[92]

Despite this pressure, Luis Somoza successfully stonewalled PCT efforts to include meaningful third-party supervision of the elections. Repeatedly, he simply refused to accede to Conservative demands that the Organization of American States preside over national elections, citing the unnecessary cost of such an exercise and, via the government organ *La Hora*, in a cunning appeal to local anti-Americanism, noted that U.S. Marines had been the last foreign agency to control such a process. At best, Somoza appeared willing to allow a few observers, but never considered complete OAS supervision of the event.[93]

Somozas' management of the contest within his own party proved more costly to the regime. Quintana's efforts to discredit the Schick decision continued unabated through spring 1962. Prior to the PLN's national plebiscite in March, Senator Alejandro Abaunza Espinoza, a party elder statesman, denounced the Schick nomination as a "gigantic fraud." In the meantime, members of Somoza's own cabinet, such as Agriculture Minister Enrique Chamorro, added their voices to a chorus of complaints. At the PLN convention in May, Quintana used a controversy over a procedural ruling to dramatically stalk off the floor with more than two dozen supporters in tow.[94]

Violence also marred the election period. In October 1961, Agüero managed to avert an assassination attempt.[95] In April 1961, a National Guardsman was killed in a border skirmish, marking the start of a year of short, sharp battles between the *Guardia* and armed exiles.[96] Additional rebel groups reported crossing the border from Costa Rica during much of the summer of 1962.[97] That July, members of the PCT occupied the deputies' gallery in Managua to protest elections rules. An estimated 30,000 people turned out in the streets in support and clashed with police afterward.[98]

Throughout the campaign, American policy makers struggled with the problem of mitigating the effects of these controversies. The embassy maintained its distance from the contenders as well as its open preference of a reformable political status quo. It recognized that both Liberals and Conservatives were deadlocked in their mutual distrust. Ambassador Aaron Brown himself was dubious about the trustworthiness of either party: "When both sides agree to negotiate, at least in present circumstances, such willingness, in both cases, seems to be predicated on their separate intention to gain advantage over the other side, rather than on any compelling desire to meet each other's requirements half way." In a report to the State Department early in 1962, he noted that what was most needed was a means to hold political debate "without passion."[99] The ambassador saw the problem in the need to replace *caudillismo*—originating from either the Somoza or Chamorro families—with a genuine political discourse that could tolerate debate and sidestep personal invective.[100]

For his own part, Brown searched for a middle ground in Nicaragua's political arena, somewhere between the Conservative desire for the complete elimination of the Somozas and the Somozas' desire to ignore third-party supervision.[101] He advocated American support for self-help projects as a means to move the country toward meaningful political and economic reforms. The embassy, for example, lauded tax reform and school construction efforts as positive signs of improvement.[102] To move this process along, Brown wanted to expedite AID assistance to the country, an effort that was often stalled by bureaucratic delays. In a letter to Lansing Collins, director of the Office of Central American Affairs, he complained "that this is a typical case where the U.S. Government, theoretically trying to do good, succeeds only in spreading the impression that it is hopelessly permeated with unsympathetic and bumbling bureaucrats."[103]

In their attempt to portray the United States as an objective neutral power, American policy makers also wanted to avoid any possible allusion that Washington actively supported the Somozas, "providing the least opportunity for either the government or the opposition to take advantage of our actions for partisan political purposes."[104] The embassy consistently recommended, for example, that military visits by flag officers, warships, or training missions be kept at an "bare minimum." Brown also pressed for a curtailment of military deliveries to Nicaragua.[105] This did not prevent the delivery of six jet trainers that were immediately used to overfly Managua as part of Armed Forces Day in May 1962.[106]

The ambassador believed that this activity offered an opportunity to exercise American leverage. State Department officials, for example, floated a trial balloon regarding OAS supervision in May 1962. In a private meeting with Anastasio Somoza, Assistant Secretary of State for Inter-American Affairs Edwin Martin recommended that OAS observers would put the burden of proving fraud on the Conservatives. Neither Somoza nor Ambassador Sevilla-Sacasa, however, were prepared to concede the point, instead referring to the support for rural schooling provided by the Alliance for Progress and ongoing concerns about Communist activity in the country.[107]

Nor did this course of action prevent unexpected collisions between Nicaraguan political leaders and the Kennedy administration. During the summer of 1962, Adolf Berle was contacted by PCT leader Fernando Agüero to discuss the possible formation of a "transitional government" or a small junta to oversee political reforms and the national election.[108] At the time, Berle was not an active member of the administration, having departed service after leading two task forces on Latin America in 1960 and 1961. His discussion mortified foreign-service officers because it was publicly misconstrued as official U.S. policy.[109] In the aftermath, Aaron Brown blandly commented from Managua,

Perhaps I should shrug my shoulders and refrain from comment on the larger matter of Mr. Berle's role in all this, irrespective of the substance of his suggestions. On reflection I suspect that I don't need to tell you how I feel about it and in any case I have to leave it up to you and Ed (Martin) to keep on with the neutralization work.[110]

As the United States groped toward a means to influence Nicaraguan politics, the Somozas pursued their own plans to defuse criticism of the regime. One constant refrain was that they would adhere to the constitution and the principle of democracy. Luis Somoza noted with pride in 1960 that Nicaragua had conducted its first municipal elections in more that twenty years.[111] During a press conference reported in *Novedades*, Luis Somoza cited the best way to fight communism:

What we are going to do is expose communism in all its false principles, in all its tricks and demagogy, so that the public realizes the truth. Thus we will leave them without followers. It is the best way to fight them. Because to make arrests or to discharge people, etc., . . . can lend itself to injustices. Therefore we are acting with great caution.[112]

The younger Somoza went so far as to publicly claim that the next president would determine the next head of the *Guardia*.[113]

Anastasio "Tachito" Somoza Debayle's metamorphosis during the political battles of 1961–1962 was a story that encouraged U.S. officials and deeply worried opponents. During the vehement debates over the conduct of the election and the selection of a PLN candidate, many observers noted that Anastasio consistently adopted more moderate positions than his brother.[114] He endorsed tax reform, for example, as "the best and only way to fight communism."[115] In June 1962, he announced the formation of an "Electoral Police Corps" whose function would be "simply keeping order to avoid clashes and violent incidents between members of the parties who go to the polls."[116] But perhaps his most important undertaking was a series of trips to the United States and around the world that received constant attention in the Nicaraguan press. While in America, Somoza addressed a dinner of West Point alumni in New York to note the continuing warm relations between the two countries. The speech was later placed in the *Congressional Record* by Congressman Daniel J. Flood.[117]

Massive, carefully orchestrated demonstrations of public adoration accompanied Somoza's return to Nicaragua. After returning from his three-week visit to the United States in early 1962, thousands greeted the general at Managua airport and lined the road for his motorcade to Cathedral Square.[118] From his perch in the PCT, Fernando Agüero denounced these proceedings as a transparent effort to both demonstrate U.S. support for the Somoza family and polish Tachito's image for the upcoming presidential contest in 1967.

In the end, these efforts did provide breathing space for the Somoza family. Most important, they led the American country team in Nicaragua to adopt what amounted to a wait-and-see approach to the election. A cable to the State Department in January 1962 commented,

Throughout this intrigue the Embassy perceives much self-seeking on the part of all concerned; a certain superiority on the part of the President to out-maneuver both his foes and his friends; a possibility that appearances to the contrary, Minister Schick may not ultimately be the Liberal candidate; and lastly, that there is yet no evidence that the President and his brother are not in earnest when they say the election will be free and honest within more or less reasonable concepts of the term.[119]

Aaron Brown believed that the Somozas had managed to meet the minimum litmus test of a political debate "without passion." The ambassador took the mass rallies in support of the sitting government with the requisite grain of salt. He was encouraged, however, by the degree of tolerance demonstrated by the regime regarding the PCT's own well-attended meetings. The embassy report concluded on an upbeat note:

Assuming, however, as we do, that the transition toward a democracy is in the long-range interest of the people and closest to our long-range interests here, we think that the only way to start the transition is to begin. Even with all of the inevitable stresses and strains which we are now observing here, we think that it is advantageous that the start is at last being made.[120]

The final election was anticlimactic at best. As the regime's public relations campaign rolled forward, splits within the opposition movement blossomed into open conflict over election strategy. In January 1962, Conservative leader Fernando Agüero dismissed efforts of PCT and other opposition groups to form a united opposition, deciding to go it alone.[121] This move dismayed fellow conservatives and members of the Social Christian Party who saw an electoral coalition as the only chance to win against a Somoza-backed candidate. When Agüero finally decided to abstain from the election in December, a decision that stunned the party rank and file, many of the smaller splinter parties followed suit.[122]

The embassy noted in January 1963 that, with the self-destruction of the PCT, the election outcome had become a "foregone conclusion" and that "most Nicaraguans—including oppositionists as well as pro-Government elements—appear to be at least resigned to this prospect, if not happy about it."[123] Good economic news also arrived to aid the regime. Reports of bumper crops of coffee and cotton assuaged local worries concerning the longevity of the recession and prospects for the future.[124] The final vote tally granted 167,352 votes to René Schick and a mere 13,755 to token PCN candidate Diego Manuel Chamorro Bolaños. Both the OAS and the U.S. embassy served as observers, although embassy officials later admitted that the accuracy of the preliminary and final vote count "will never be known."[125]

CONCLUSIONS

In rhetorical terms, the Alliance for Progress was a master stroke. It placed the new Kennedy administration firmly in the camp of Latin American nations that had lobbied for a greater policy priority for more than fifteen years. The duration of the proposal itself committed Washington to a "decade of development," and its very scale heartened governments throughout the hemisphere.

Unfortunately, formulating a workable policy from a series of broad claims proved problematic in the early stages of the alliance. Most of the administration's experts agreed that a comprehensive approach to assistance was an absolute. Utilizing the experiences gained from similar assistance efforts in Western Europe in the late 1940s and a faith in contemporary academic theories of development, they believed that socioeconomic, political, and military development aid could be integrated in a manner conducive to stability and progress. However, proceeding from that point, consensus diminished. Left unanswered in the heady days of 1961 was exactly how this integrated approach would be programmatically translated. Encouraging economic growth was a tangible goal. But how best to "export" democracy? More important, unresolved at the start of the Alliance for Progress was the final role Latin Americans would assume as part of these U.S. proposals. The issues of membership and responsibility in collective organizations such as the Central American Common Market were fairly well defined, but the exact nature of the U.S.–Latin American partnership within specific country programs was much less so. A dawning realization for both U.S. and Latin American officials in 1961 was the degree of effort and time necessary to make the Alliance for Progress a practical hemispheric policy.

As the policy debate in Washington attacked these questions, existing entrenched interests in Central America maintained their grip on the isthmus. Military and military-dominated governments in Guatemala, El Salvador, Honduras, and Nicaragua all continued to emphasize the threat of Castro-inspired revolution, encouraged by a decade of American military assistance and the Kennedy administration's own support of the paramilitary invasion of Cuba. American investors also drew great solace from the fact that new U.S. policy apparently would not interfere with their status. Concessions demanded as part of U.S. support for the Central American Common Market abolished provisions for local monopoly ownership of new industry. The United Fruit Company retained its extensive agricultural holdings in Guatemala. In Honduras, UFCO, with the support of the American embassy, successfully lobbied to protect company acreage from land-reform programs sponsored by the Villeda Morales administration (1957–1963).[126]

This control, as officials in Washington full well understood, was problematic in Central America. Military dominance of governance offered few assurances of stability. The breakdown that came from within the Guatemalan military after 1960 indicated serious divisions regarding the nation's future direction. The same type of conflict was apparent in the short-lived October 1960 coup conducted by a coalition of reformist military officers and civilians in El Salvador. Meanwhile, beneath this military layer of internal conflict, popular revolutionary movements simmered. The absence of meaningful land reform and the expansion of coffee and cotton plantations in Honduras provoked increasing instances of peasant unrest in the northern parts of the country.

In Nicaragua, there was little doubt as to the form or substance of democracy. René Schick held the office of the president, but in the eyes of the general population the Somozas retained uncontested power over the nation. The American embassy was somewhat tentative regarding the issue of who was in control. Aaron Brown remarked in September 1963,

In the face of General Somoza's politicking it was generally considered [in Nicaragua] that Schick would have a major confrontation with Tacho about it, and we share that view. Something like that now appears to have occurred, and for one reason or another the General *seems* to have decided to accede to the President's wishes, although it is too early to say this for sure. If appearances are borne out in fact, public opinion will recognize it in due course.[127]

Brown recognized that there was no absolute separation between the Somozas and Schick. But, he was also not sure he wanted a "divorce" between the new president and the old regime, staking his optimism on the belief that progress had been made to the extent that opposition characterizations of Somoza as a "cruel rapacious ogre" and Schick as a "puppet" had not been justified.[128]

Brown's somewhat grasping evaluation is a good reflection of the basic difficulty faced by American policy makers tasked with promoting reform in the earliest stages of the Alliance for Progress. The embassy team rightly worried that too close an association with the Somoza family would cultivate the perception of de facto U.S. support for its leadership. Unfortunately, when Brown opted for a lower-profile approach to the government in Managua, relying instead on attempts at quiet persuasion, he sacrificed a great deal of American leverage.

For their own part, the Somoza brothers demonstrated an increasing sophistication in their orchestration of both internal Nicaraguan affairs and U.S.–Nicaraguan relations. Luis Somoza's conduct of the Liberal Party nomination process and the general election itself represented an interesting—and successful—balancing act among fellow party rivals, Fernando Agüero Rocha's Conservative Party, and the American embassy. Anastasio Somoza's carefully planned role as a statesman and the unlikely "good cop" within the family was equally impressive to the extent that it embellished local perceptions regarding American support of the regime and the sop it offered Aaron Brown.

What the Somoza regime failed to do, like its counterparts in Central America, was to address the root causes of dissent in Nicaragua. The 1963 presidential contest was, in the longer term, a Pyrrhic victory. Agüero's boycott of the final election represented a political coup, but one that did not bode well for the future legitimacy of the Schick government. The absence of a legitimate political outlet for regime opponents encouraged their further radicalization. This number included members of the family's Liberal Party, such as Julio Quintana, as well as the fringe elements of the Nicaraguan left. As a whole, they would make both attempts at legitimate political reform and service to the regime increasingly difficult in the future.

NOTES

1. "Program for the Decade of Development," 22 March 1961, John F. Kennedy Library (hereafter JFK), Teodoro Moscoso Papers, Box 1.

2. Warren I. Cohen, *The Cambridge History of American Foreign Relations: America in the Age of Soviet Power, 1945–1991*, Vol. 4 (New York: Cambridge University Press, 1993), 81–120; Stephan Haggard, *Pathways from the Periphery: The Politics of Growth in Newly Industrializing Countries* (Ithaca, N.Y.: Cornell University Press, 1990), 51–99. For an example of the German economic "miracle," see Ralf Dahrendorf, *Society and Democracy in Germany* (New York: W. W. Norton, 1967), 397–411. For an example of the American security commitment to Southeast Asia, see Ronald H. Spector, *Advice and Support: The Early Years, 1941–1960* (Washington, D.C.: Center for Military History, 1983).

3. Michael R. Beschloss, *The Crisis Years: Kennedy and Khrushchev, 1960–1963* (New York: Edward Burlingame, 1991), 41.

4. Letter, José Figueres to Peter R. Nehemkis, 16 December 1960, JFK, Jack N. Behrman Papers, Box 1.

5. John H. Coatsworth, *Central America and the United States: The Clients and the Colossus* (New York: Twayne, 1994), 96–100.

6. SNIE 80-62, 17 January 1961, in U.S. Department of State, *Foreign Relations of the United States, 1961–63, The American Republics* (hereafter *FRUS*), Vol. 12 (Washington, D.C.: U.S. Government Printing Office, 1996), 211.

7. Ibid.

8. Ralph Lee Woodward, *Central America: A Nation Divided* (New York: Oxford University Press, 1985), 92–119; John Lynch, *The Spanish American Revolutions, 1808–1826* (New York: W. W. Norton, 1986), 333–340.

9. Woodward, *Central America*, 214–215. Political reforms made more tentative but steady progress. See Fabrice Edouard Lehoucq, "The Institutional Foundations of Democratic Cooperation in Costa Rica," *Journal of Latin American Studies* 28 (1996): 329–355.

10. Michael F. Jiménez, "From Plantation to Cup: Coffee and Capitalism in the United States, 1830–1930," in *Coffee, Society, and Power in Latin America*, ed. William Roseberry, Lowell Gudmundson, and Mario Samper Kutschbach (Baltimore: Johns Hopkins University Press, 1995),

38–64; Adrian J. English, *Armed Forces of Latin America: Their Histories, Development and Military Potential* (London: Jane's, 1984), 327; Ciro F. S. Cardoso, "Central America: The Liberal Era, c. 1870–1930," in *The Cambridge History of Latin America*, ed. Leslie Bethell (New York: Cambridge University Press, 1983).

11. Charles D. Ameringer, *The Caribbean Legion: Patriots, Politicians, Soldiers of Fortune, 1946–1950* (University Park: Pennsylvania State University Press, 1996), 1–3.

12. Woodward, *Central America*, 209.

13. Marvin Goldwert, *The Constabulary in the Dominican Republic and Nicaragua: Progeny and Legacy of United States Intervention* (Gainesville: University of Florida Press, 1962), 46–47.

14. Michael D. Gambone, *Eisenhower, Somoza, and the Cold War in Nicaragua, 1953–1961* (Westport, Conn.: Praeger, 1997), 112–115.

15. Jorge I. Dominguez, *Cuba: Order and Revolution* (Cambridge: Belknap Press of Harvard University Press, 1978), 54–76, 84–109.

16. John D. Martz, *Accion Democratica: Evolution of a Modern Political Party in Venezuela* (Princeton, N.J.: Princeton University Press, 1966), 125; Judith Ewell, "Venezuela Since 1930," in *The Cambridge History of Latin America*, vol. 8, ed. Leslie Bethell (New York: Cambridge University Press, 1991); John D. Martz, "Petroleum: The National and International Perspectives," in *Venezuela: The Democratic Experience*, ed. John D. Martz and David J. Myers (New York: Praeger Special Studies, 1986). See also Terry Lynn Karl, "Petroleum and Political Pacts: The Transition to Democracy in Venezuela," *Latin American Research Review* 22 (1987): 63–94; Philip B. Taylor, *The Venezuelan Golpe de Estado of 1958: The Fall of Marcos Pérez Jimenez* (Washington, D.C.: Institute for the Comparative Study of Political Systems, 1968); Robert J. Alexander, *The Venezuelan Democratic Revolution: A Profile of Romulo Betancourt* (New Brunswick, N.J.: Rutgers University Press, 1964).

17. Stephen J. Valone, ed., *Two Centuries of U.S. Foreign Policy: The Documentary Record* (Westport, Conn.: Praeger, 1995), 84–85.

18. Jeffrey L. Gould, "For an Organized Nicaragua: Somoza and the Labor Movement," *Journal of Latin American Studies* 19 (1987): 353–387; Richard L. Millett, *Guardians of the Dynasty* (Maryknoll, N.Y.: Orbis Books, 1977), 204–207.

19. Ameringer, *The Caribbean Legion*, 11–60; Charles D. Ameringer, *Don Pepe: A Political Biography of José Figueres of Costa Rica* (Albuquerque: University of New Mexico Press, 1978), 31–85.

20. Richard H. Immerman, *The CIA in Guatemala: The Foreign Policy of Intervention* (Austin: University of Texas Press, 1982), 11.

21. NSC 5623/1, "U.S. Policy Toward Latin America," 25 September 1956, Dwight D. Eisenhower Library (hereafter DDE), White House Office of the Special Assistant for National Security Affairs, Records: 1952–1961, NSC Series, Policy Papers Subseries, Box 18; Walter LaFeber, *Inevitable Revolutions: The United States in Central America* (New York: W. W. Norton, 1984), 98–105.

22. U.S. Congress, Select Committee on Communist Aggression, *Report of the Subcommittee to Investigate Communist Aggression in Latin America* (Washington, D.C.: U.S. Government Printing Office, 1954), DDE, White House, NSC Papers, OCB Central File Series, Box 73.

23. James Dunkerley, *Power in the Isthmus: A Political History of Modern Central America* (New York: Verso, 1988), 435. See also Stephen Schlesinger and Stephen Kinzer, *Bitter Fruit: The Untold Story of the American Coup in Guatemala* (New York: Doubleday, 1982).

24. Donald C. Hodges, *Intellectual Foundations of the Nicaraguan Revolution* (Austin: University of Texas Press, 1986), 164–167; Jaime Morales Carazo, *Mejor que Somoza cualquier cosa!* (Mexico: Compañia Editorial Continental, S.A., 1986), 89–95. See also Patricia Taylor Edmisten, *Nicaragua Divided: La Prensa and the Chamorro Legacy* (Pensacola: University of West Florida Press, 1990).

25. Dunkerley, *Power in the Isthmus*, 335–342.

26. Tad Szulc, *Fidel: A Critical Portrait* (New York: Avon Books, 1986), 135–147, 197.

27. Fidel Castro, "History Will Absolve Me," in *The Selected Works of Fidel Castro, Revolutionary Struggle, 1947–1958*, Vol. 1, ed. Rolando E. Bonachea and Nelson Valdés (Cambridge: MIT Press, 1972), 164–165.

28. Ibid., 177.

29. Curt Cadorette, *From the Heart of the People: The Theology of Gustavo Gutiérrez* (Oak Park, Ill.: Meyer Stone Books, 1988), 1–29; Deane William Ferm, *Third World Liberation Theologies* (Maryknoll, N.Y.: Orbis Books, 1986), 3–56; Ronaldo Muñoz, *The God of Christians* (Maryknoll, N.Y.: Orbis Books, 1990), 15–36.

30. Thomas W. Walker, *The Christian Democratic Movement in Nicaragua* (Tuscon: University of Arizona Press, 1970), 1–15; Edward A. Lynch, *Religion and Politics in Latin America: Liberation Theology and Christian Democracy* (Westport, Conn.: Praeger, 1991), 71–72.

31. Margaret E. Crahan, "Religion and Politics in Contemporary Latin America," in *Security in the Americas*, ed. Georges Fauriol (Washington, D.C.: National Defense University Press, 1989), 107–116.

32. See Ernesto Cardenal, *The Gospel in Solentiname* (Maryknoll, N.Y.: Orbis Books, 1976).

33. Joseph Tulchin and Knut Walter, "Nicaragua: The Limits of Intervention," in *Exporting Democracy: The United States and Latin America, Themes and Issues*, ed. Abraham F. Lowenthal (Baltimore: Johns Hopkins University Press, 1991), 127.

34. Arthur M. Schlesinger, Jr., *A Thousand Days: John F. Kennedy in the White House* (Boston: Houghton Mifflin, 1965), 761–762.

35. "Weighing the Damage from the Cuban Debacle," *Business Week*, 29 April 1961, 26–27.

36. John Lewis Gaddis, *Strategies of Containment: A Critical Appraisal of Postwar American National Security Policy* (New York: Oxford University Press, 1982), 198–205.

37. Dean Rusk, *As I Saw It* (New York: W. W. Norton, 1990), 398.

38. Gaddis, *Strategies of Containment*, 203.

39. Memorandum to the President from Walt W. Rostow, "Crucial Issues in Foreign Aid," 28 February 1961, JFK, National Security File, Meetings and Memoranda, Box 324; Diane B. Kunz, *Guns and Butter: America's Cold War Economic Diplomacy* (New York: The Free Press, 1997), 126–127.

40. Max F. Millikan and Walt W. Rostow, *A Proposal: Key to an Effective Foreign Policy* (New York: Harper and Brothers, 1957), 22. See also Albert O. Hirschman and Richard M. Bird, *Foreign Aid: A Critique and a Proposal* (Princeton, N.J.: Princeton University Press, 1968), 3–14.

41. John Kenneth Galbraith, "A Positive Approach to Economic Aid," 1 February 1961, JFK, National Security File, Subjects, Box 297.

42. Ibid.

43. Hirschman and Miller, *Foreign Aid*, 4–5.

44. Schlesinger, *A Thousand Days*, 186.

45. This group included Arthur Whitaker from the University of Pennsylvania and Robert Alexander from Rutgers University, and Arturo Morales-Carrion, Secretary of State for Puerto Rico. Interview with Lincoln Gordon, 10 July 1969, Lyndon B. Johnson Library, Oral History Collection, 1–8.

46. "Address of the President at a White House Reception for Latin American Diplomats, Members of Congress and Their Wives," 13 March 1961, JFK, Arthur Schlesinger Papers, White House File, Subject Files, 1961–64, Box WH 14.

47. Scope Paper, United States Delegation to the Special Meeting of the Inter-American Economic and Social Council, Punta del Este, Uruguay, 6 July 1961, JFK, Treasury, Office of International Affairs, Box 11; Schlesinger, *A Thousand Days*, 191–194.

48. Office of the White House, "Special Message on Foreign Aid," 22 March 1961, JFK, NSF, Subjects, Box 297.

49. Memorandum to the President from Walt W. Rostow, "The Idea of an Economic Development Decade," 2 March 1961, JFK, NSF, Regional Security, Box 215.

50. "The Role and Trend of Public Opinion in Latin America: 1961," 16 February 1962, USIA Research and Reference Service; U.S. Department of State, Bureau of Intelligence and Research, "The Basic Imbalance between Urban and Rural Areas in Latin America," Intelligence report no. 8449, 17 April 1961, JFK, Arthur Schlesinger Papers, White House Files, Subject Files, 1961–64, Box WH-14.

51. Lincoln Gordon, "The Alliance at Birth: Hopes and Fears," in *Exporting Democracy: The United States and Latin America, Themes and Issues*, ed. Abraham F. Lowenthal (Baltimore: Johns Hopkins University Press, 1991), 74.

52. Lynch, *Religion and Politics in Latin America*, 67–77; Benjamin Keen and Mark Wasserman, *A History of Latin America* (Boston: Houghton Mifflin, 1988), 348–349.

53. Memorandum, Roger Hilsman (Bureau of Intelligence and Research) to Dean Rusk, 12 October 1962, JFK, Schlesinger Papers, White House File, Subject Files, 1961–64, WH-14.

54. Text of the message of President John F. Kennedy to the Inter-American Economic and Social Conference, Punta del Este, Uruguay, 5 August 1961, JFK, President's Office File, 1961–63, Countries, Box 121a.

55. Report of the President's Task Force on Latin America, 7 July 1961, JFK, President's Office File, 1961–63, Countries, Box 121a.

56. Memorandum, the Secretary of the Treasury (Dillon) to President Kennedy, 1 August 1961, *FRUS*, 47.

57. Memorandum, Undersecretary of State (Bowles) to Secretary of State Rusk, 25 July 1961, *FRUS*, 44.

58. Memorandum, the President's Assistant Special Counsel (Goodwin) to President Kennedy, 28 September 1961, *FRUS*, 64.

59. U.S. Agency for International Development, Bureau for Latin America, *The Charter of Punta del Este* (Washington, D.C.: U.S. Government Printing Office, 1961), 1; Office of the White House Press Secretary, Text of the Message of President John F. Kennedy to the Inter-American Economic and Social Conference, Punta del Este, Uruguay, 5 August 1961, JFK, President's Office Files, Countries, Box 121a.

60. U.S. Agency for International Development, *The Charter of Punta del Este*, 4.

61. Report from the Representative to the United Nations (Adlai Stevenson) to President Kennedy, 27 June 1961, *FRUS*, 31; Edward C. Burks, "Dillon Predicts Aid of 20 Billion to Latin America," *New York Times*, 8 August 1961, 1, 3.

62. Scope Paper; William O. Walker, "Mixing the Sweet with the Sour: Kennedy, Johnson, and Latin America," in *The Diplomacy of the Crucial Decade: American Foreign Relations during the 1960's*, ed. Diane B. Kunz (New York: Columbia University Press, 1994), 50–52.

63. Cable, Dillon to Rusk, 17 August 1961, JFK, President's Office Files, Countries, Box 121a.

64. Robert A. Pastor, *Whirlpool: U.S. Foreign Policy toward Latin America and the Caribbean* (Princeton, N.J.: Princeton University Press, 1992), 175.

65. Juan de Onis, "Kennedy, on Visit, Hails Venezuela as Aiding Liberty," *New York Times*, 17 December 1961, 1.

66. Schlesinger, *A Thousand Days*, 767.

67. Juan de Onis, "Lleras Says U.S. Awakens Hopes," *New York Times*, 19 December 1961, 2.

68. Cable, Embassy (Managua) to State, 5 July 1960, National Archives and Records Administration (hereafter NARA), Records Group 59 (hereafter RG 59), General Records of the Department of State, Central Decimal File, 1960–1963, Box 1529, 817.00/7-560.

69. "Somoza Sure of Winning," *New York Times*, 4 February 1957, 3.

70. "Managua for Amnesty," *New York Times*, 16 June 1957, 13; Cable, Embassy (Managua) to State, 20 June 1958, NARA, RG 59, 1950–1959, Box 2979, 717.11/6-2057.

71. Cable, Managua to State, 12 July 1960, NARA, RG 59, General Records of the Department of State, Central Decimal File, 1960–1963, Box 1527, 717.00/7-1260.

72. Beverley and Zimmerman, *Literature and Politics*, 64–69; Ameringer, *The Caribbean Legion*, 1–10; Ameringer, *Don Pepe*, 31–45.

73. Patricia Taylor Edmisten, *Nicaragua Divided: La Prensa and the Chamorro Legacy* (Pensacola: University of West Florida Press, 1990), 34–35.

74. Millett, *Guardians of the Dynasty*, 224–225; David Close, *Nicaragua: Politics, Economics, and Society* (London: Pinter, 1988), 26.

75. Memorandum from the Director of the Bureau of Intelligence and Research (Hilsman) to the Assistant Secretary of State for Inter-American Affairs (Martin), 19 December 1962, *FRUS*, 126.

76. Letter, Wymberly De R. Coerr (Deputy Assistant Secretary of State for Inter-American Affairs) to Katherine W. Bracken (Director, Office of Central American and Panamanian Affairs), 11 April 1962, NARA, RG 59, General Records of the Department of State, Bureau of Inter-American Affairs, Office of Central American and Panamanian Affairs (ARA/OAP), Subject and Country Files, Lot Files, 65D159, 66D131, Box 5.

77. Cable, Embassy to State, 11 May 1962, NARA, RG 59, State Department Decimal File, 1960–1963, Box 1527, 717.11/5-1162.

78. Cable, Managua to State, 7 June 1962, NARA, RG 59, State Department Decimal File, 1960–1963, Box 2354, 817.432/6-762; Cable, Embassy (Managua) to State, 11 May 1961, NARA, Records Group 286 (hereafter RG 286), Records of the Agency for International Development, Office of Public Safety, Latin America, Country File, Nicaragua, Box 90.

79. "Somoza Foes Unite," *New York Times*, 26 February 1959, 14.

80. Cable, Embassy to State, 25 January 1962, NARA, RG 59, State Department Decimal File, 1960–1963, Box 1527, 717.00/1-2562.

81. Henry Wells, ed., *Nicaragua Election Factbook*. (Washington, D.C.: Institute for the Comparative Study of Political Systems, 1967), 20; Cable, Managua to State, 13 December 1960, NARA, RG 59, State Department Decimal File, 1960–1963, Box 1528, 717.00/12-1360.

82. Walker, *The Christian Democratic Movement in Nicaragua*, 28–29.

83. Ibid.

84. Enrique Alvarado Martinez, *El pensamiento politico nicaragüense: de los ultimos años* (Managua: Editorial y Lit. Artes Graficas, 1968), 21–30.

85. Cable, Embassy to State, 9 August 1960, NARA, RG 59, State Department Decimal File, 1960–1963, Box 1527, 717.00/8-960.

86. Ibid.

87. Wells, *Nicaragua Election Factbook*, 20.

88. Cable, Embassy (Managua) to State, 9 June 1960, NARA, RG 59, 1960–1963, 717.00/6-960.

89. Cable, Managua to State, 2 November 1961, NARA, RG 59, State Department Decimal File, 1960–1963, Box 1528, 717.00/11-261.

90. Cable, Embassy (Managua) to State, 25 January 1962, NARA, RG 59, 717.00/1-2562.

91. Ibid.

92. Cable, Managua to State, 2 March 1962, NARA, RG 59, 1960–1963, 717.00 (W)/3-262.

93. Cable, Embassy to State, 12 July 1960; Cable, Embassy (Managua) to State, 9 August 1960, NARA, RG 59, 1960–1963, 717.00/8-960; Cable, Embassy to State, 27 October 1961, NARA, RG 59, 1960–1963, 717.00/10-2761; Cable, Embassy to State, 13 December 1960, NARA, RG 59, 1960–1963, 717.00/12-1360.

94. Cable, Embassy to State, 31 May 1962, NARA, RG 59, 1960–1963, 717.00/5-3162.

95. Cable, Managua to State, 10 October 1961, NARA, RG 59, 1960–1963, 717.00/10-1961.

96. Cable, Managua to State, 28 April 1961, NARA, RG 59, 1960–1963, 717.00 (W)/4-2861.

97. Cable, Managua to State, 13 July 1962, NARA, RG 59, 1960–1963, 717.00 (W)/7-1362.

98. Cable, Managua to State, 11 July 1962, NARA, RG 59, 1960–1963, 717.00/7-1162.

99. Cable, Embassy to State, 25 January 1962, NARA, RG 59, 1960–1963, 717.00/1-2562.

100. Ibid.

101. Ibid.

102. Cable, Managua to State, 8 March 1962, NARA, RG 59, 1960–1963, 817.00/3-862.

103. Letter, Aaron S. Brown to Lansing Collins (Director, Office of Central American and Panama Affairs), 13 September 1963, NARA, State Department Lot Files, 66D131, Box 6.

104. Cable, Managua to State, 8 March 1962, NARA, RG 59, 1960–1963, 817.00/3-862.

105. Letter, Jeffrey C. Kitchen to William P. Bundy, 22 August 1961, NARA, RG 59, 1960–1963, 717.5811/8-2261; Cable, Managua to State, 4 April 1962, NARA, RG 59, 1960–1963, 717.56/4-362.

106. Letter, John M. McIntyre (Officer in Charge of Nicaragua Affairs) to Aaron S. Brown, 29 June 1962, NARA, RG 59, 1960–1963, 717.5622/6-2962.

107. Memorandum of Conversation, "General Somoza Calls to Discuss Forthcoming Election in Nicaragua," 2 May 1962, NARA, RG 59, 1960–1963, 717.00/5-262.

108. Attachment, Letter, Aaron S. Brown to Katherine W. Bracken, 9 August 1962, NARA RG 59, 1960–1963, State Department Lot Files, 65D159, 66D131, Box 5.

109. Letter, Edwin Martin to Chester Bowles (Acting Secretary of State), 19 July 1962, NARA, RG 59, 1960–1963, 717.00/7-1962.

110. Letter, Aaron S. Brown to Katherine W. Bracken, 9 August 1962.

111. Cable, Managua to State, 9 May 1960, NARA, RG 59, 1960–1963, 717.00/5-960.

112. Cable, Managua to State, 11 May 1962, NARA, RG 59, 1960–1963, 717.11/5-1162.

113. Memorandum of Conversation, "Comments by General Somoza on Possible Future Political Developments," 15 June 1961, NARA, RG 59, 1960–1963, 717.00/6-1561.

114. Cable, Managua to State, 27 October 1961, NARA, RG 59, 1960–1963, 717.00 (W)/10-2761.

115. Cable, Managua to State, 27 July 1962, NARA, RG 59, 1960–1963, 717.00/7-27621.

116. Cable, Managua to State, 28 June 1962, NARA, RG 59, 1960–1963, 717.00/7-27621.

117. Cable, Managua to State, 6 April 1962, NARA, RG 59, 1960–1963, 717.00(W)/4-662.

118. Cable, Managua to State, 2 March 1962, NARA, RG 59, 1960–1963, 717.00 (W)/3-262.

119. Cable, Embassy to State, 25 January 1962, NARA, RG 59, 1960–1963, 717.00/1-2562.

120. Ibid.

121. Walker, *The Christian Democratic Movement*, 34–35.

122. Wells, *Nicaragua Election Factbook*, 30.

123. Cable, Embassy to State, 4 January 1963, NARA, RG 59, 1960–1963, 717.00/1-463.

124. Ibid.

125. Cable, Embassy to State, 6 February 1963, NARA, RG 286, 1960–1963, Box 90.

126. Victor Bulmer-Thomas, *The Political Economy of Central America since 1920* (New York: Cambridge University Press, 1987), 171–174; Coatsworth, *Central America and the United States*, 96–109; Dunkerley, *Power in the Isthmus*, 536–537.

127. Letter, Aaron S. Brown to V. Lansing Collins (Director, Office of Central American and Panamanian Affairs), 12 September 1963, NARA, RG 59, 1960–1963, State Department Lot Files, 66D131, Box 6. Emphasis in original.

128. Ibid.

CHAPTER 2

The Challenge of Guerrilla War

Those who have never had the opportunity to surrender, never had the valor to rebel.

Pedro Joachim Chamorro

John F. Kennedy entered office in 1961 intent on restoring U.S. military capability to meet a broad array of Cold War challenges. These ranged from the new threat of ballistic missiles to "brushfire" wars in the Third World. In the aftermath of the Cuban revolution, Central America and the Caribbean appeared particularly vulnerable to the latter threat. Consequently, U.S. officials attempted to craft military assistance that would effectively counter wars of rebellion and shape host militaries into more moderate institutions. As these policies evolved, it became increasingly apparent that both identifying local revolutionary threats and creating leverage adequate to the task of military reform would be a much larger task than originally anticipated.

MILITARY AFFAIRS IN THE COUNTERINSURGENCY ERA

For most Americans living in 1961, there was an important sense that the Cold War had taken a new and dangerous direction against their country. This perception of insecurity had begun after news of Sputnik broke across the world four years earlier. A near state of panic ensued as politicians and the public alike demanded to know how American technology had been bested by Communist Russia. Despite Eisenhower's best efforts to reassure Americans that the softball-sized satellite posed no immediate threat to the United States or its security, a precedent had been set. The public discourse of the late 1950s is littered with constant references to the "gaps" that existed between Communist military capabilities and those at home.

For those charged with maintenance of American military affairs, the times also held a very tangible sense of caution. While most observers within the defense community dismissed the Soviet nuclear threat, there was a growing realization within this circle of policy makers that nuclear parity might prove a greater threat to stability than strategic superiority. Parity, and the threat of "mutually assured destruction," promised a greater reliance on existing conventional weapons and promised the greater likelihood of a war waged by mass armies.[1]

American ground forces were very poorly prepared for this contingency. The 1950s were lean years for the branches of the military thought to be obsolescent in the new nuclear age. Army general Maxwell Taylor sardonically described the times as his service's "Babylonian captivity," a period in which training, new equipment, and readiness were sacrificed to support the "dogma" surrounding nuclear weapons and the United States Air Force.[2] In real terms, American ground forces had measurably dwindled, in the case of the Army from 998,000 personnel in 1957 to 862,000 by 1960, creating significant concerns that it could not meet conventional challenges abroad.[3]

The United States was equally unprepared to address the unconventional conflicts that threatened global stability at the start of the 1960s. The blurring of the line that separated soldiers from civilians was not new to the history of warfare. However, the very nature of the post–1945 world introduced some important changes to its basic practice. Unconventional war in the Third World took on a new importance for Americans when, at the 1956 Soviet Twentieth Party Congress, Nikita Khrushchev announced his support for "wars of national liberation."[4] The Russian leader followed this claim with visits to Burma, Afghanistan, and India, and, to the alarm of Washington, $1.4 billion in economic aid. Nor was the incoming Kennedy administration to be spared this effort. A Soviet announcement made on 6 December 1960 and endorsed by eighty-one Communist Parties across the world advocated the selective use of violence where necessary to bring about the condition for "peaceful" revolution.[5]

The instability caused by the collapse of colonial empires also heralded a new age of upheaval and guerrilla war. The early 1960s marked the arrival of revolutionary movements openly challenging the authority of the West. By 1960, all the former colonies of French West Africa and French Equatorial Africa were independent. Seventeen African nations emerged from the chaos that followed Europe's scramble out of the continent between 1960 and 1961 alone.[6] In Southeast Asia, North Vietnam embarked upon the completion of its own revolution in the south. Tumult in Laos soon followed.[7]

Events demanded an American response. A Department of the Army report intoned in June 1961,

> Unless the United States and the remaining free nations take prompt, decisive actions, the situation will continue to deteriorate. . . . Communism forges ahead partly because the Soviet Union, exploiting its revolutionary heritage, identifies itself with the impatient desires of many less developed countries for rapid social change.[8]

This sense of crisis and inadequacy was not lost on the country's new president. As the Democratic candidate, Kennedy had pressed for a "strategy of action," in which American national security interests would be supported by a broad array of usable military options. In a "Special Defense Message" issued to all branches of the U.S. military in March 1961, Kennedy demanded a rapid reorientation of defense policy toward conventional warfare. Specifically, he wanted the Defense Department to reevaluate American capabilities to deploy mobile forces for limited war, explore means to increase nonnuclear firepower, and expand special forces designed to counter the growing guerrilla threat.[9] Most important was Kennedy's recognition that the United States needed to regain the policy initiative in the Cold War. Simply reacting to multiplying crisis situations was an option the country could no longer afford.[10]

The largest postwar buildup of conventional forces since the Korean War followed in the wake of this resolve. Regular ground forces rose from 875,000 to over 1 million during Kennedy's first year in office.[11] Subsequent defense spending also increased, jumping from $45.3 billion in 1960 to $52.2 billion in 1963.[12] Specific funding was allocated to counterinsurgency in particular. In February 1961, NSAM 2 directed $100 million toward "paramilitary and sub-limited or unconventional wars."[13]

As this new era developed, military advisory groups assumed a critical role in "low intensity, ambiguous conflict situations."[14] NSAM 131, issued in March 1961, began a series of multiagency training programs to study the history of rebellion and the development of viable measures to prevent it.[15] For its own part, the Army forwarded a recommendation to create "Free World Liaison and Assistance Groups," comprised of administrative, logistical, and combat personnel and sent abroad to provide both security training and "civic action" programs to host countries.[16] Subsequently, the administration would request funding for forty-one special organizations dedicated to circumventing the insurgent threat.[17]

All these initiatives operated under the general assumption that local revolutions were caused by external prodding, specifically from the Soviet Union.[18] To a large extent this type of attribution was a carryover from an earlier, World War II–era model in which the United States itself supported local partisans in their struggle against the Axis powers. Many of Kennedy's key advisors, in fact, had practiced this very type of war as young officers in Europe and Asia. Roger Hilsman, who occupied a post in the State Department's Bureau of Intelligence and Research in 1961, had led guerrilla forces behind Japanese lines in Burma and rescued his own father from captivity.[19] Secretary of Labor Arthur Goldberg had served with guerrilla units as an OSS operative in Europe.[20] Within this group, the basic concept that rebels served as proxies of a greater power became an article of faith in American counterinsurgency policy in the 1960s.[21]

The early stumbles experienced by the American counterinsurgency effort reflected the dangers of this assumption. Perhaps the best example was the exile invasion against Cuba. For many American policy makers, Castro's Cuba was a simple extension of Moscow. Ruling as a dictator over an oppressed and restive populace, Washington saw the Cuban leader as the thin tip of a Soviet wedge forcing itself into Latin America. To meet this perceived threat, American leaders attempted to marshal their own proxy forces against Communist Cuba. Their intent was to use this proxy force as a trigger for a large-scale, anti-Castro uprising.[22] The resulting Bay of Pigs invasion proved to be a debacle in terms of both planning and execution. But what left the United States publicly stymied was the fundamental mistake in the assumption that an exile invasion would trigger a popular revolution within Cuba against foreign domination.[23] The only relevant foreign power turned out to be America itself.

The Bay of Pigs disaster was what McGeorge Bundy called "a brick through the window," a minor setback but a wake-up call for American efforts to contain communism in the Western Hemisphere.[24] It served to reinforce Kennedy's desire to create a distinct and more efficient program to address low-intensity warfare. The creation of the Special Group (Counterinsurgency; CI) under the National Security Council in January 1962 represented an attempt to do just that. In part, it was designed to administratively recapture unconventional warfare policy from the discredited elements of the intelligence community. Representing a broad-based coalition of agencies, including the Justice Department and the Agency for International Development, and chaired by Maxwell Taylor, the Special Group devoted its energies to two basic tasks:

a. To insure proper recognition throughout the U.S. Government that subversive insurgency ("wars of liberation") is a major form of politico-military conflict equal in importance to conventional warfare.
b. To insure that such recognition is reflected in the organization, training, equipment, and doctrine of the U.S. Armed Forces and other U.S. agencies abroad and in the political, economic, intelligence, military aid and information programs conducted abroad by State, Defense, AID, USIA, and CIA.[25]

The Special Group (CI) represented an important shift in emphasis from covert to overt counterinsurgency. This was partially the result of simple practicality. According to Charles Ameringer, "The Bay of Pigs demonstrated that there was an inverse relationship between the requirements of military victory and the need to preserve plausible denial."[26] After 1962, the emerging preference for U.S. policy makers was that Americans become directly involved in the internal security planning and training of Third World nations. In subsequent meetings held after its formation, the Special Group would offer a host of recommendations in support of assistance for riot-control instruction, police training, and civil engineering projects.[27]

This decision had not come without a fight. In *The Best and the Brightest*, David Halberstam observed that one of the most often-heard words in government circles in 1961 was "pragmatism." Many of those who worked within the administration were self-described "ultrarealists," who sincerely believed

that this attitude also made one less vulnerable to attacks from the right about softness on Communism did not hurt; it dealt at once with totalitarians abroad and wild men at home. Force was justified by what the Communists did; the times justified the acts which decent men did not seek, but which historic responsibilities made necessary.[28]

But it was a losing argument amidst the growing sentiment that nation building could not be solely left to warriors. NSC staffer Robert Komer noted in a September 1961 memo,

What we are really driving at is that internal security measures, counter-guerrilla operations, and a broad range of civic actions essentially deal with manifestations of a central problem encountered in many of the underdeveloped countries. This problem involves the critical area where internal political, economic and social tensions interact with external manipulation and/or local initiatives for irregular forms of armed violence or civic disturbance. The resulting disorder can take different forms, varying considerably from one country to the next. But in all cases it has deep roots in civil turmoil which is *not originally* of a military nature.[29]

As the administration moved ever closer to the Punta del Este conference and, later, began a legislative campaign to support the commitments made in Uruguay, military assistance developed as one of the many options envisaged by the United States to treat the problem of revolution, not an end unto itself.

The immediate obstacles to an effective U.S. military assistance program in 1961–1962 appeared to be primarily of American making. One issue that concerned policy makers in particular was the problem of timeliness as it applied to the procurement of weapons and equipment. The waiting period for internal security equipment, for example, ranged from six to twenty months.[30] The causes of these delays ranged from simple shortages to conflicts over the priority granted to other crisis areas such as Laos and South Vietnam. Administration officials worried that, while recipient governments awaited assistance, events beyond the control of the American defense bureaucracy would overcome even the best planned security program.

A second, related concern centered on the growing number of legislative restrictions being placed on American foreign assistance. In a memorandum to the president in early 1961, titled "A Plea for Flexibility," McGeorge Bundy moved for basic changes in the appropriations process:

It is just too inflexible for the fast-moving cold war environment in which we are caught up. You have already been confronted with emergency fund requests on Laos, Cuba, and the Congo—with more yet to come. And many other crises of one sort or another are bubbling away on the back burner; Vietnam, Berlin, Iran, Indonesia, or Angola are only the obvious contenders.[31]

Bundy recommended that Kennedy attempt to win approval of a $500 to $750 million contingency fund that could be transferred between major security programs.[32] In a 1961 special message to Congress, Kennedy compared the "uneven and undependable short-term financing" that weakened American aid to the long-range commitments allowed in Soviet programs that were successfully advancing global communism.[33] He asked instead for Congress to set aside the normal annual approval process in favor of multiyear appropriations.[34]

Congress was also particularly resistant to the idea that the United States provide arms to support Latin American dictatorships, regardless of their loyalty to Washington or its anti-Communist policies. The so-called Morse Amendment to the Foreign Assistance Act of 1962 required that the president make an official determination that the furnishing of "defense articles" for internal security to Latin American countries was in the national interest. In practice, it was, in the words of White House Special Council Richard Goodwin, "virtually impossible to process determinations expeditiously through the three legal offices concerned (Defense, AID, State) and through the numerous other concerned offices in the bureaucracy."[35] Congressional resistance to additional credit sales of military equipment and defense grants would dog the Kennedy administration throughout its term.

After 1961, it appeared that the United States had regained its focus on the broad array of threats to American national interests. Under the stewardship of Kennedy, Secretary of Defense Robert McNamara, McGeorge Bundy, and a host of other policy makers, the days of defense based upon the Sino–Soviet monolith and "massive retaliation," what Walt W. Rostow derisively called the "Old Look," appeared to be over.[36] In its place was a sense that the burgeoning array of threats required greater flexibility. Developing the actual means toward this end was less clear, however. In the aftermath of the Bay of Pigs, officials grappled with the problem of recreating the decision-making structure that controlled counterinsurgency doctrine, with assigning priorities to types of aid, and with basic terminology. In March 1962, nearly a year after the Bay of Pigs, the Special Group (CI) was soliciting interagency opinions on "defining various terms relating to counter-insurgency, and assuring that understanding of them is uniform throughout the government."[37] Cultivating a consensus on proper approaches to military aid or the countries to which it would apply proved to be even more problematic.

THE THREAT TO CENTRAL AMERICAN SECURITY

In the early 1960s, events in Latin America represented both the threat of low-intensity war and its challenge to nascent U.S. security policy. There was no question of the region's importance as a source of trade, for strategic resources, or as a ward of American influence for more than a century.[38] The threat to these interests was equally apparent. A January 1962 intelligence estimate noted the vulnerability of the Caribbean to Soviet ICBMs and long-range bombers and the possibility that additional Soviet bases would be constructed in Cuba.[39] On the whole, however, the possibility of overt aggression appeared remote. "Soviet leaders," the report stated, "for the present at least, appear to prefer not to make their presence too obvious or apparent, lest they discourage rather than encourage the spread of communism to other Latin American countries."[40]

Open Soviet influence in Latin America was marginal at the time of the Cuban revolution. Moscow maintained official relations only with Mexico, Argentina, and Uruguay. In 1960, the Allessandri government in Chile dispatched a trade and industrial delegation to Moscow. Brazil reestablished formal relations with the USSR in 1961.[41] What appeared more probable was the use of Cuba as a proxy to advance Soviet influence in the region. Cuba, according to the American intelligence estimate, could serve as "a symbol of spontaneous popular revolution and as a base for subversive operations."[42] In fact, this was an expressed Cuban intent. Ernesto "Che" Guevara explained that the revolution against Batista "showed plainly the capacity of the people to free themselves by means of guerrilla warfare from the government that oppresses them." According to this logic, guerrilla movements could flourish within the unequal political, social, and economic conditions that characterized most of Latin America in the early 1960s. More important, Guevara suggested, "It was not necessary to wait until all conditions for making revolution exist; the insurrection can create them." Rebels could therefore promote insurrection by embracing the role of "social reformer," particularly in the capacity of "agrarian revolutionary."[43]

Fidel Castro's inflammatory rhetoric provided an important counterpoint to Guevara. During the spring of 1960, as U.S.–Cuban relations began their marked descent, he declared before a mass rally, "Cuba will never become cowardly, Cuba will not step back, the Revolution will not be detained. . . . The Revolution will march ahead victoriously! . . . We shall continue to make our fatherland an example that will make the Andes mountain range into the Sierra Maestre of all America."[44] These statements enjoyed considerable traction in U.S. circles because they accompanied the general recognition that Latin America was vulnerable either if it stood still or attempted reform. The former maintained a continuation of inequality, while the latter potentially offered the prospect of considerable upheaval as reforming nations negotiated the various stages of socioeconomic and political development.[45]

Of secondary U.S. concern was the growing preference among Latin American nations to pursue security policies, particularly regarding the procurement of weapons, without consultation with Washington. Nicaragua, for example, reportedly purchased 50,000 rifles from West Germany in 1961.[46] British efforts to increase jet aircraft sales to Latin American customers caused even greater alarm.[47] More ominous were indications that Latin Americans were willing to seek out Czechoslovakian sources for more modern weapons systems.[48] Without American control, these acquisitions held the possibility of a regional arms race. In addition, U.S. officials understood that the foreign logistical support, technicians, and military missions that would inevitably support the more complex modern weapons would also erode American leverage over the military-dominated governments of the hemisphere.

Against this perceived assault on stability and U.S. influence, American military aid was intended to complement the Alliance for Progress by providing a necessary degree of stability for economic and political assistance. Security against subversion was an absolute requirement for the alliance's success. One of the administration's first looks at the question, NSAM 2, recommended that American assistance place "more emphasis on the development of counter-guerrilla forces."[49] Kennedy concurred, suggesting the creation of a "Caribbean Security Force" to help other American states preserve their freedom against "Castro-communism."[50] It was important that the United States consider "organizations whose missions are in the counter-subversion, guerrilla and counter-guerrilla area."[51]

For their own part, the Joint Chiefs of Staff saw a more proactive role for the military as an agent of social and economic change. In this context, they saw local militaries performing a civic action role, providing men and materiel to such projects as the construction of schools and public buildings.[52] NSAM 119 recommended a further exploration of military programs that supported transportation, communications, health, and sanitation. In this manner, client nations could make civic action "an indispensable means of strengthening their society's economic base and establishing a link between [the] army and populace."[53] Regarding the manner in which this would be accomplished, the Joint Chiefs of Staff recommend in late 1961 that Latin American governments,

should be made to understand the importance of the educational phase in particular, and persuaded to accept it and fill all available quotas in US schools. Latin Americans must also discard the philosophy that a corps of US trained country personnel are dangerous to the indigenous governments because of the radical changes they could impose as a result of their exposure to the US and the US way of life.[54]

The upper echelons of the State Department essentially endorsed this assessment. In an April 1961 letter to Dean Rusk, Deputy Assistant Secretary of State for Inter-American Affairs Wymberley De R. Coerr noted that the basic assumptions upon which the United States formed its policies in Latin America had changed. Many Latin American nations were making the transition from right-wing dictatorship to constitutional government. The overall situation in the hemisphere was fluid and open to manipulation by Communist-inspired insurgents, especially those supported by Cuba. It was important that the United States preserve democratic government and its own influence by supporting this transition. In this respect, Coerr believed that military aid was a means to "maintain the United States as the predominant foreign military interest."[55] In a letter to the Agency for International Development in late 1961, Assistant Secretary of State Robert F. Woodward plainly stated,

While we recognize that the Latin American countries can ill-afford an expanded program of military purchases and that we should take an ardent position against excessive arms purchases, we must not lose sight of the fact that our contemporary military policy in Latin America is primarily for political ends, and that our key concern is to keep the military friendly, cooperative, and aligned with U.S. politico-military objectives on one hand while we are implementing the Alliance for Progress economic programs on the other.[56]

In order to explore the practical application of these discussions, Kennedy ordered the formation of the Internal Security Assessment and Programming Team, or the Washington Assessment Team, in April 1961. Comprised of a membership drawn from the Departments of State and Defense as well as the International Cooperation Administration, its mission was to travel to Latin America and interview individual U.S. "country teams" regarding the nature of their internal security threats and potential solutions.[57] The Washington Assessment Team that traveled to Nicaragua met with the embassy and related staff between 27 April and 12 May 1961 and discussed topics ranging from transportation and communication to local leadership and intelligence-collection techniques.[58] The team also determined whether conventional units created under the auspices of earlier military assistance were "no longer necessary for other valid defense missions."[59]

A consensus was less clear when the time came to implement subsequent Washington Assessment Team recommendations at the country level. The State Department urged prompt action, arguing that bilateral security agreements could precede or be made simultaneously with offers of U.S. aid. Officials noted that unilateral American intervention was necessary in instances where the Organization of American States would fail to act or act too slowly.[60] However, State tempered this endorsement with the recommendation that internal security assistance follow a "careful evaluation at the country level."[61]

American diplomats backtracked further on the issue of providing weapons to local armies, recognizing that aid for internal security had been provided "only in exceptional cases" in the past and constituted a considerable risk to stability if not handled with care. State Department officials wanted countries to demonstrate a "critical requirement" for such assistance.[62] Edward A. Jamison, the director of the

Office of Inter-American Regional Political Affairs, also added the caveat that the United States carefully distinguish between subversives and bona fide internal opposition movements before embarking upon any new programs.[63]

The U.S. Army Caribbean Command was equally circumspect regarding the issue of additional arms to Central American security forces. In a cable distributed to advisory groups throughout the region, it noted, "CINCARIB does not normally subscribe to establishment of arming of police forces of para-military forces for internal security purposes in those LA countries where armed forces are either assigned this function as its primary responsibility or have historically exercised the nations' police powers." This was, in the opinion of the command a "delicate matter that should be carefully considered," and, further, that "such actions could be inimical to the policy which stipulates that US representatives could encourage a reduction of excessive military forces and expenses in Latin America. It is also important to note that the neutralization of the basically conservative armed forces is a prerequisite to Communist takeover."[64]

Despite these reservations, the United States moved forward with military aid for Central American security. In 1961, the total cost of Latin American assistance was a relatively modest $49 million, with $10.1 million allocated for training, $14.9 million for force maintenance, $18 million for "force improvement," and $5.9 million for packing and shipping.[65] The following year, the Defense Department recommended that military aid increase to $112.5 million during FY1962, to include $57.5 million in grants, $20 million for civic action support, and $35 million in credit sales.[66]

As additional defense support worked its way into the region, the tempo of activity increased. During "Operation Solidarity," held in the Panama Canal Zone in March 1961, the uniformed chiefs of various Latin American militaries were treated to a series of weapons demonstrations by the U.S. military and given the opportunity to discuss the Cuban threat. Caribbean Command noted that the assembled officers were "pleased but not overly enthusiastic" with the demonstrations.[67] In August, the first special-forces course for Latin American students began in the Canal Zone. Three additional classes were planned for 1962, with four scheduled for 1963.[68]

This activity was coupled with U.S. efforts to build a permanent regional defense organization in Central America. Initial meetings on the topic were held in Managua in October 1961 to discuss bylaws under which a "defense council" of Central American countries would be established.[69] In the meantime, neighboring countries began sponsorship of a series of joint military training exercises. In September 1962, for example, sixty Nicaraguan *Guardia Nacional* troops from the Somoza Battalion departed for "Operation Fraternidad" maneuvers with the Honduran military.[70] CINCARIB also made plans for the first joint U.S.–Central American military exercises in 1963.[71]

As these efforts unfolded, additional meetings on a Central America defense council were held in Managua between 3 and 4 April 1963. Delegates discussed issues such as travel controls, additional banking regulation to prevent funding for subversive organizations, arms control, propaganda, coastal surveillance, and internal security measures.[72] These meetings culminated in the creation of the Central American Defense Council the following year. Member nations included El Salvador, Nicaragua,

Honduras, and Guatemala. All agreed to share intelligence information and conduct joint maneuvers dedicated to prevent the spread of Castroism in the region.[73]

CONDECA proved to be a problematic construct. According to Morris Morley, Nicaraguan *Guardia* chief Anastasio Somoza Debayle considered the council a simple vehicle for exerting his own influence over the isthmus, an opinion not unique to Managua.[74] While some joint maneuvers were conducted under U.S. auspices in 1963, cooperation diminished soon afterward.

This lack of a consensus was similarly reflected in the American policy community. Counterinsurgency had envisioned a complicated combination of agencies orchestrating a series of complementary projects in a coordinated fashion. This proved difficult in both conceptual and practical terms. In a report issued to the president in March 1963, General Lucius D. Clay noted that American foreign aid programs had become "too diffuse" and tried to do "too much in too many countries." The Clay Committee recommended greater prioritization and, in the case of Latin America, "a higher standard of self-help" than had been required in the past.[75] That same year, State Department official Thomas W. Davis complained to Robert Kennedy that the Special Group (CI) was simply not up to the job of coordinating policy at the national level. He recommended that it either expand its purview and authority or be disbanded and replaced by the State Department.[76] From the National Security Council, Michael V. Forrestal argued that the Special Group "tended to reach decisions without adequate preparation in the Departments concerned and without effective follow-up of the decisions once they are made."[77]

The evolution of police assistance to Latin America offers a specific case in point. Generally, policy makers could agree that local police agencies would be critical in the successful application of any counterinsurgency program. AID Administrator David Bell described police forces as the "first line of defense in maintaining local order."[78] What worried Americans, however, was the basic fact that police functions in Latin America were traditionally the purview of the military. In a January 1961 memorandum issued to key military leaders, Army chief of staff General George H. Decker warned that while U.S. aid could improve ties with client nations in Latin America, it must remain wary of the "oligarchy problem" as the region experienced disruptions born of social, economic, and political reform.[79]

In an effort to promote police responsibilities within the civilian sphere, Kennedy formally placed police assistance under the Agency for International Development's new Office of Public Safety in 1962. NSAM 206, "Military Assistance for Internal Security in Latin America," noted specifically, "In the complex and rapidly shifting circumstances in Latin America, it is essential that our military aid program be a carefully-tailored and constantly updated part of our overall strategy aimed at development and security in the hemisphere."[80] Specifically, the OPS was charged with the mission of providing "centralized professional and technical planning guidance to the country teams, police missions and State and AID regional bureaus."[81] The Office of Public Safety would later serve as a conduit for training missions from American universities, police departments, and the Federal Bureau of Investigation, and supervise the creation of the Inter-American Police Academy at Ft. Davis in

Panama.[82] However, NSC staffer Robert Komer expressed doubts that AID was up to the task of police assistance, not because it lacked the expertise, but because

the police program has never found a congenial home in ICA [International Cooperation Administration] or AID, and is now practically buried on the sub-regional level. Until it is given sufficient status and room to operate, it will remain at a severe competitive disadvantage vis-a-vis AID's primary activities.[83]

On the face of it, Komer's statement was true. The Office of Public Safety was only one of the many programs competing for attention within AID during the Kennedy administration. More important, however, was the basic reality that while administrators had isolated police functions within the American foreign assistance bureaucracy, Latin Americans had not. Local military institutions continued to play a critical role in internal security, as would their American military advisors.

This lack of clarity in American assistance policy offered ample opportunities to both local country teams and their host nations. To the former, doctrine granted them the responsibility of devising individual programs to meet the particular security requirements of each nation. For individual Latin American governments, Washington emphasized "self-help" and their responsibilty for reform and stability over the long term. In neither case was the final, ultimate means or ends of achieving internal security clear.

THE *FOCO* IN NICARAGUA

On 15 August 1963, a radio station identifying itself as "La Havana" broadcast a call for an end to the "Somozato" in Nicaragua. The speaker was identified as Blanca Segovia Sandino, daughter of what she described as "the general of free men."[84] It was but one small incident in a history of long-standing antagonism between the Somoza regime, Nicaraguan exiles, and Castro's Cuba.

Nicaraguan claims of Cuban interference in the nation's internal affairs had surfaced as early as 1960, when Managua alleged that the Cuban ambassador to El Salvador, Pino Machado, was channeling $50,000 to Nicaraguan dissident Indalecio Pastora. According to the American embassy, Pastora's forces in Honduras were preparing to invade Nicaragua in June 1960. They were reportedly augmented by Nicaraguan Communists from Venezuela and "independent liberal elements" in Esteli, Nicaragua.[85] U.S. officials in Caracas speculated that the Nicaraguan exile community in Venezuela was "heavily infiltrated, if not controlled, by Communists."[86] In Tegucigalpa, American diplomats reported funding of Frente Revolucionario Sandino by American Communists via the Mexican Sindicato El Aguila. They noted as well that twenty-six members of the FRS had traveled to Cuba for political training.[87] Meanwhile, Honduran authorities announced in October 1960 the capture and deportation of twenty-eight Cubans bound for the Nicaraguan border.[88] Observers present during a November 1960 clash between guerrillas and the Costa Rican *Guardia Civil* also noted the presence of several Cubans among the forces engaged.[89]

This activity had resulted in a limited number of attacks on the Nicaraguan frontier. On 11 November 1960, a *Guardia* detachment was raided by an undetermined number of guerrillas.[90] Armed groups were reported operating near the Bocay River on 30 July 1963. Three days later, clashes with patrols in Nueva Segovia resulted in five *Guardia* deaths.[91] Overall, the guerrilla threat against the country was minimal in the early 1960s.

Despite this, the threat of rebel invasions created an important degree of friction between Nicaragua and its neighbors. At the start of the decade, Nicaragua and Honduras had formed a "Mixed Military Commission" in an effort to cooperate against guerrilla incursions. However, as multiple claims of rebel activity in Honduras accumulated throughout the summer and fall of 1960, strains in the relationship began to appear. In September, Managua claimed that the Republican Mobilization Party— a leftist, antigovernment organization—was in Honduras preparing an invasion in coordination with Nicaraguan Communists.[92] Luis Somoza used this as an opportunity to openly question Honduras's dedication to the counterguerrilla effort, threatening to withdraw from the commission and recall its ambassador from Tegucigalpa.[93] Tensions also rose to the south when a Costa Rican officer, Major Jesus Salazar, was captured by rebels on 9 November 1960 near El Amo in the northwestern part of the country. Two days later, when the Costa Rican *Guardia Civil* clashed with thirty-five to forty rebels, its commander, Colonel Alfonso Monge, was mortally wounded by a burst of machine-gun fire.[94]

The Somozas were perfectly willing to level claims that the domestic opposition was intimately linked with these plots. Luis Somoza specifically blamed the Conservative Party, more specifically its youth affiliate, the *Juventud Conservador Revolucionaria* and Pedro Chamorro's *La Prensa* for their "Castro–Communist" links in subverting the government.[95] In reality, beyond the government's claims, it was difficult at best for outside observers to determine the exact extent of dissident activity or its Communist composition.[96]

One emerging organization that did fit this model was the Frente Sandinista de Liberacion Nacional. The FSLN explicitly rejected either cooperation with the regime or a military coup that would simply substitute one *caudillo* for another. Instead, *Sandinista* leaders proposed a course of action that drew selectively from Nicaragua's past and contemporary regional events. In the main, the historical tenants of the FSLN were centered firmly around Augusto César Sandino and his guerrilla war of the late 1920s. According to historian Andrew Kimmens, Sandino became the Joan of Arc of Nicaragua.[97] Through the work of Ernesto Cardenal, Pedro Joachim Chamorro, and especially Carlos Fonseca Amador, this interpretation continued into the 1950s and early 1960s, depicting the slain rebel leader variously as a symbol of nationalism, anti-imperialism, and opposition to the *Somocista* state. Fonseca in particular took great pains to portray Sandino as a nationalist fighting a popular war against American imperialists and their adherents in Managua.[98]

Fidel Castro's war against the Batista regime provided the link between historical interpretation and practical application. Che Guevara's concept of the guerrilla *foco* excited FSLN leaders in particular. By emphasizing a gradualist, rural-based, popular movement, the Cuban *foco* illustrated a contemporary military strategy with antecedents in the low-intensity war waged by Sandino in the 1920s and 1930s. FSLN leaders like Fonseca quickly adapted the *foco* as a means to mobilize Nicaragua's rural population, with the expectation that they could reproduce Castro's victory.[99]

It is important to note that the FSLN was not alone in this interpretation. Many young Nicaraguan opposition leaders, men like Hernan Silva Argüello, Leonte Herdocia, Enrique Lacayo Farfan, Pedro Joachim Chamorro, and Adan Selva, also saw the banner of revolution passing into their hands during the late 1950s.[100] Many fled to Tegucigalpa, San Salvador, and San Francisco and began the arduous process of collecting money, men, and weapons. Some made contact with Cubans eager to spread *focos* throughout the Caribbean. The Nicaraguan Republican Mobilization Party in particular maintained close contact with Havana, utilizing links maintained through the Betancourt regime in Venezuela.[101] In the end, the cumulative effect of these movements, whether Communist or non-Communist, was to place a growing number of organized and determined political dissidents in proximity to a correspondingly increasing amount of small arms, and provide them with a proven insurgent strategy. The combination of these three factors enhanced already substantial domestic problems for the Somoza Debayle regime.

To the American country team in Managua, this complex series of rebel movements was captured under the label "internal security threats."[102] Specifically, threats to Nicaragua were considered in the following order of likelihood: (1) demonstrations and/or mob violence, (2) terrorism or sabotage, (3) border incursions, (4) clandestine shipment of arms into the country, (5) guerrilla warfare, and (6) internal revolution.[103] On 11 May 1961, a joint State–Defense–ICA report noted that Nicaragua's primary vulnerability was to internal subversion:

Heretofore the various dissident groups have justified the use of violence with charges of political and economic dictatorship by the Somoza family involving denial of democratic rights and military oppression. Since Castro's accession to power in Cuba all these groups in varying degrees have also adopted Communist inspired grievances such as claims of GON's subservience to U.S. imperialism in exchange for U.S. support, to the detriment of the people's aspirations.[104]

The report admitted the possibility that the various threats could occur in combination, posing a "serious threat" to the country, particularly if the "hundreds" of exiles residing in Central America could stage a coordinated effort with know anti-Somoza elements. In this scenario, the possibility existed that Communists within and outside Nicaragua could form a "national liberation government" as an open alternative to the regime in Managua.[105]

To counter this threat, the Military Advisory and Assistance Group, Nicaragua, requested a mobile training team to begin counterinsurgency instruction for the *Guardia Nacional* in 1964.[106] The embassy country team believed that in the meantime the GN was up to the task of internal security. Comprised of 5,000 personnel organized into both combat units and twenty police companies, the *Guardia* appeared adequate to the task of maintaining internal order. The Nicaraguan National Security Office, for example, was able to provide efficient intelligence regarding dissident activities. The primary inadequacies identified by MAAG were in the areas of available transportation, communications, and maintenance facilities. Maintenance was a severely deficient category within the Nicaraguan military. Of the sixty-five transport and combat aircraft owned by the Fuerzas Aérea de Nicaragua, only five were usable in 1961.[107] As a stop-gap measure to meet this shortage, Nicaragua received six American TV-2 jet trainers in June.[108]

Beyond material assistance for the maintenance of Nicaraguan military capabilities, American officials also struggled with the appropriateness of political support. From his desk in the State Department's Office of Inter-American Regional Political Affairs, Edward A. Jamison recommended that bilateral assistance be kept confidential. He worried that military aid to the Nicaraguan government might be misconstrued as open support for the Somoza regime.[109] The embassy counsel, Louis F. Blanchard, warned that Anastasio Somoza might reveal negotiations over a new internal security agreement to intimidate the political opposition.[110] American military leaders disagreed with this assessment, countering that open U.S. support was necessary to encourage anti-Communist efforts against Castro. To this end, the Pentagon encouraged a visit by the U.S. Air Force's Thunderbird squadron to Nicaragua in 1962.[111]

As events transpired, it appeared that Jamison's concerns were justified. One particularly prickly issue involved the jet aircraft provided to the FAN. When the chief of the U.S. Air Force mission to Nicaragua questioned their value, Anastasio Somoza obliquely replied that "their mere presence on the airfield would be sufficient for his purposes."[112] The opposition newspaper *La Prensa* devoted a barrage of editorials to the aircraft, questioning in April 1962, for example, the purchase of "modern airplanes which the Nicaraguan people neither need nor want nor can afford."[113] The paper stated further,

On one day it is said that North American policy is one of non-intervention in our affairs, but on the next day in the United States Congress itself the Chief of the military area that exercises vigilance over us [Gen. Andrew P. O'Meara] declares that the main emphasis of his budget is shifting toward the attainment of *internal security* in our countries.[114]

The regime was nonplused. The jets' inaugural flight was made during Holy Week in 1962. Four of the newly acquired aircraft later performed a series of acrobatic maneuvers for the Armed Forces Day parade on 27 May 1962, whereupon they overflew the American embassy. A subsequent "test flight" followed over the cities of Leon, Corinto, and Granada.[115]

Nicaraguan support for the abortive exile invasion of Cuba also haunted American policy makers. The employment of Cuban exiles in Nicaragua became public knowledge when disputes with the Confederacion General de Trabajo labor union erupted over access to work in Montelimar and Puerto Somoza.[116] Managua's open support for a second invasion of Cuba also proved to be an embarrassment for Washington. In a 1963 Miami conference attended by the Somoza brothers, President René Schick, and Cuban counterrevolutionary Carlos Prio Socarras, the regime openly discussed the creation of an "anti-Castro common front" in Central America.[117]

As they cast about looking for a means to regain control of this situation, American officials latched onto the concept of civic action. The embassy believed that civic action would undercut anti-American sentiment among the "reservoir of impression-able youths" in the country.[118] It could also serve to encourage local military initia-tive, while building bridges to the local population. Moreover, forces trained to support civic action (e.g., medical or construction units) could serve multiple functions in standard military field operations, civil emergencies, or natural disasters.[119] In July 1961, MAAG began equipping one medical company within the *Guardia* for civic action duties.[120] The embassy also recommended the activation of a combat engineer company for use in "isolated areas" and the creation of an air-transportation squad-ron for military airlifts and civilian economic development.[121]

A major obstacle to the Nicaraguan civic action program was not leftist rebels, but the upcoming 1963 elections. Ambassador Aaron Brown wanted the civic action effort downplayed because he perceived a negative impact on the local politics. Brown wanted to avoid the inevitable perception that regime opponents would gain cre-dence if the United States provided assistance to the *Guardia*, an institution widely regarded as a simple extension of the Somoza family.[122] The State Department con-curred with this cautious approach. In a letter to Deputy Assistant Secretary of State for Politico-Military Affairs Jeffrey C. Kitchen, Wymberly De R. Coerr noted,

We are endeavoring, through emphasis on self-help school construction and other social de-velopment programs, to disengage the United States from the myth that we support the Somozas personally and the Guardia as an instrument of the Somozas. Judging from past experience the Somozas would exploit a civic action program as a further demonstration to the Nicaraguan people that the U.S. supports the Somozas and their personal regime.[123]

One interesting voice of dissent came in the form of Charles Maechling, a member of Kitchen's staff:

I question whether a worthwhile civic action program should be delayed on the ground that the domestic public relations of the local army or constabulary will be improved as a conse-quence. If this is to be the test elsewhere, it will frustrate all civic action programs in critical areas. There is such a thing as being too responsive to every political wind.[124]

Nicaraguan civic action proceeded regardless of these objections and took a num-ber of strange forms in its initial stages. During the late summer of 1962, the *Guardia* began an artificial-insemination program to assist the Nicaraguan cattle industry. Somoza requested that a U.S. veterinarian be assigned to MAAG, causing the em-bassy to comment,

The General appears to have missed the point that military civic action programs are sup-posed to make use of the human and material resources that the military already have avail-able. Otherwise, there is nothing to prevent the GN from commandeering for its own purposes the operation of any kind of civilian technical assistance, as in this case.[125]

Officials also thought it notable that the program was not dedicated to general public welfare. Instead, it embellished an ongoing industrial concern dominated by the Somozas. The first comprehensive steps toward a civic action program were finally taken in July 1963, five months after the presidential election.[126]

CONCLUSIONS

By the time John F. Kennedy assumed office, the Cold War dominated questions related to Latin American security. The transition of Cuba from a Communist proxy for guerrilla warfare in 1961 to the launch point for nuclear weapons only a year later offered a worst-case scenario for U.S. policy makers watching the Western Hemisphere.[127] The emphasis of the Cold War, however, created three basic misassumptions in American policy.

One pertained to the Cuban threat itself. It is true that Castro was willing to offer training and financing to Latin American rebels. Cuba provided money to leftists in British Guyana in 1960 and supported Venezuelan rural and urban dissidents that same year. Castro's involvement in the subversion of the Dominican Republic is also well known.[128] However, the wide-scale spread of Cuban revolution was severely restricted by other events outside Castro's control. In point of fact, Castro remained on the strategic defensive throughout the 1961–1963 period. The problem of internal rebellion, particularly in the Escambray Mountains, where as many as 5,000 *guerrillos* operated, plagued Havana during the early part of the decade.[129] In early 1963, the Special Group (CI) recognized that sporadic threats of terrorism in Honduras, Peru, and Venezuela, whether Cuban-supported or not, had failed to compromise any of these countries to the point where local security forces were inadequate.[130] American efforts subsequently were devoted more to fine-tuning existing counterinsurgency and civic action programs than responding to a crisis situation. The perceived threat to Latin America was relegated to the potential rather than the existing impact of Cuban actions.

A second misassumption related to the ability of American country teams to exercise leverage toward military reform in Central America. The Kennedy administration considered military assistance to be a formidable and positive means to shape the development of client military institutions. The Joint Chiefs, for example, saw in the U.S. military education system a means to transfer not only practical knowledge, but the basic ethic that guided proper civil–military relations. Unfortunately, this hope dissipated when the host nation was either unable to make expected changes or simply refused to cooperate. From his post in Managua, ambassador Aaron Brown presented U.S. options with regard to the jet fighter issue: "In the circumstances of our inability to repair or replace Nicaragua's Air Force piston planes in kind it was either a case of selling them jets, facing the prospect of their purchase elsewhere, or allowing the Air Force to disappear entirely."[131] In many cases, the regressive nature of Central American military logistics prevented material reforms in capability. In others, centuries of social tradition blocked American efforts to build apolitical military institutions. Either case presented the United States with the options of staying the course or withdrawing aid and suffering the consequences.

A third, equally pointed problem involved civic action in Central America. In principle, American-sponsored civic action programs placed local militaries close to the public domain and public concerns. They attempted to construct institutions that supported public welfare without the expectation of reciprocity. This, in essence, was an effort to reconstruct the U.S. civil–military tradition abroad, one that focused on duty and service in the place of self-aggrandizement and corruption. In Nicaragua, the *Guardia* retained this latter direction and embraced anti-Communist nationalism as its motive rather than apolitical loyalty to the civilian authority.[132] Again, Brown recognized in 1963 that this practice could create significant difficulties for the United States:

U.S. Military Assistance Plans, therefore, have recently intended to accomplish the delicate task of de-emphasizing the purely domestic political role of the armed forces as a means of encouraging the establishment of full civilian supremacy in the government without affecting the military establishment's capability to maintain internal security and without prejudicing the United States [*sic*] position as the predominant foreign military influence in the area.[133]

Brown was thus attempting to create a military subordinant to René Schick, for all intents a Somoza appointee, while reducing its involvement in politics. The United States was on the horns of a dilemma: exercising leverage through a thoroughly politicized military without poisoning the political atmosphere. In practice, American officials were willing to abandon leverage in the face of potential political reversals. Faced with this scenario, the embassy simply chose to wait:

As a matter of policy and principle, however, there is conviction that U.S. military assistance not directly related to the function of defense should, except for token programs, quietly be deferred here until credible indications are apparent that such assistance will not be employed for political purposes. Civic action programs are for the present deemed to come within this category.[134]

In Nicaragua, the primary obstacle to American military assistance and all its concurrent attempts at influence was the fundamental success of the *Guardia* in accomplishing its mission without U.S. assistance. The demonstrations and rebel raids that accompanied the 1962–1963 political season were easily handled by Nicaraguan military forces. U.S. embassy officials attributed this to potency of the GN and internal divisions within the opposition, whose idealistic and youthful membership frequently split along ideological lines.[135]

As the *Guardia* proceeded with its business, American institutions struggled to maintain pace. The State Department Office of Central American and Panamanian Affairs noted in July 1961 an "absence of coordination" among the various agencies that comprised local country teams. Military maintenance in one country, for example, failed despite the fact that the U.S. Operations Mission offered training courses that would have supported it. The chief of the military mission claimed that he was totally unaware such programs even existed.[136] George O. Spencer remarked on the same problem during a review of NSAM 118 at the end of 1961: "I frankly question the capability of Country Teams and the Washington bureaucracy to bring to bear on some of the programs proposed in this paper the type of continuing review and direction that they will require if they are not to be counter-productive."[137] Maxwell Taylor observed during a May 1962 Special Group (CI) meeting that while policy makers were setting forth the current status of programs in Guatemala and Ecuador, the State

Department had not evaluated "how we are doing or whether or not the current programs are the optimum under the circumstances prevailing in each country."[138] Taylor's statement clearly was the product of an ongoing turf battle between the Special Group and the State Department. The former claimed that once an internal security situation in a country had noticeably deteriorated, its care should shift to the the Special Group. Conversely, the State Department questioned whether Taylor's group had adequate personnel to simultaneously monitor more than "one or two" countries.[139]

Central America was able to maintain adequate internal security almost despite U.S. efforts. For the most part, local military institutions fulfilled their basic function with limited American assistance and less input from Washington. U.S. policy focused instead on its perception of the Cuban bugbear, subsequent contingency planning, and interdepartmental squabbles. In the meantime, host militaries like Nicaragua's *Guardia Nacional* forged ahead with current security practices, mindful of American objectives, but largely convinced of their own efficacy.

NOTES

1. John Lewis Gaddis, *Strategies of Containment: A Critical Appraisal of Postwar American National Security Policy* (New York: Oxford University Press, 1982), 207–208.

2. Maxwell D. Taylor, *The Uncertain Trumpet* (New York: Harper and Brothers, 1959), 4, 17; A. J. Bacevich, *The Pentomic Era: The U.S. Army between Korea and Vietnam* (Washington, D.C.: National Defense University Press, 1986), 9.

3. U.S. Department of Defense, *Semiannual Report of the Secretary of Defense, 1 January–30 June 1957* (Washington, D.C.: U.S. Government Printing Office, 1957), 4; U.S. Department of Defense, *Semiannual Report of the Secretary of Defense, 1 January–30 June 1959* (Washington, D.C.: U.S. Government Printing Office, 1959), 9.

4. Adam B. Ulam, *Expansion & Coexistence: The History of Soviet Foreign Policy, 1917–67* (New York: Praeger, 1968), 566–582; Nicholas V. Riasanovsky, *A History of Russia* (New York: Oxford University Press, 1984), 558–561.

5. Memorandum, Bob Amory (Bureau of Budget) to J. Foster Collins, 19 April 1961, John F. Kennedy Library (hereafter JFK), National Security File (hereafter NSF), Meetings & Memoranda, Box 326; U.S. President's Message to Congress on the Mutual Security Program, in *The Mutual Security Program: Fiscal Year 1958, A Summary Presentation* (Washington, D.C.: U.S. Government Printing Office, 1957), 47.

6. Kevin Shillington, *History of Africa* (New York: St. Martin's Press, 1995), 374–394; Ronald Oliver and J. D. Fage, *A Short History of Africa* (New York: Penguin Books, 1995), 221; Wilfred Cartey and Martin Kilson, *The African Reader: Independent Africa* (New York: Vintage Books, 1970), 59–120.

7. George C. Herring, *America's Longest War: The United States and Vietnam, 1950–1975* (New York: McGraw-Hill, 1996), 72–79; Joseph Buttinger, *Vietnam: A Political History* (New York: Praeger, 1968), 454–459; Denis Warner, *The Last Confucian* (New York: Macmillan, 1963), 194–223.

8. U.S. Department of the Army, Office of the Chief of Staff, "A United States Military Program," 27 June 1961, JFK, NSF, Departments and Agencies, Box 265.

9. U.S. Department of Defense, Office of Public Affairs, 1 April 1961, JFK, NSF, Departments and Agencies, Box 269.

10. U.S. Department of the Army, "A United States Military Program."

11. Warren W. Hassler, *With Shield and Sword: American Military Affairs, Colonial Times to the Present* (Ames: Iowa University Press, 1982), 375–376.

12. Paul Kennedy, *The Rise and Fall of the Great Powers: Economic Change and Military Conflict from 1500 to 2000* (New York: Vintage Books, 1989), 384.

13. NSAM 2, "Development of Counter-Guerrilla Forces," 3 February 1961, National Archives and Records Administration (NARA), Records Group 59 (hereafter RG 59), General Records of the Department of State, National Security Action Memoranda Files, 1961–1968, Box 1. See also Michael McClintock, *Instruments of Statecraft: U.S. Guerrilla Warfare, Counter-Insurgency, Counter-Terrorism, 1940–1990* (New York: Pantheon Books, 1992), 163.

14. U.S. Department of the Army, "A United States Military Program."

15. NSAM 131, "Training Objectives for Counter-Insurgency," 13 March 1962, NARA, Records Group 286 (hereafter RG 286), Records of the Agency for International Development, Office of Public Safety, Latin America, Country File, Nicaragua, Box 139.

16. U.S. Department of the Army, "A United States Military Program."

17. McClintock, *Instruments of Statecraft*, 182.

18. John A. Booth and Thomas W. Walker, *Understanding Central America* (Boulder, Colo.: Westview Press, 1989), 47.

19. See Roger Hilsman, *An American Guerrilla: My War Behind Japanese Lines* (Washington, D.C.: Brassey's, 1990).

20. David Halberstam, *The Best and the Brightest* (Greenwich, Conn.: Fawcett, 1969), 90–91.

21. McClintock, *Instruments of Statecraft*, 173.

22. Lloyd S. Etheredge, *Can Governments Learn? American Foreign Policy and Central American Revolutions* (New York: Pergamon Press, 1985), 18; Tad Szulc, *Fidel: A Critical Portrait* (New York: Avon Books, 1986), 596–615; Trumbull Higgins, *The Perfect Failure: Kennedy, Eisenhower, and the CIA at the Bay of Pigs* (New York: W. W. Norton, 1987), 74, 104; John Morton Blum, *Years of Discord: American Politics and Society, 1961–1974* (New York: W. W. Norton, 1991), 37–42.

23. Charles D. Ameringer, *U.S. Foreign Intelligence: The Secret Side of American History.* (Lexington, Mass.: Lexington Books, 1990), 271–296.

24. Halberstam, *The Best and the Brightest*, 91.

25. NSAM 124, "Establishment of the Special Group (Counter-Insurgency)," 18 January 1962, JFK, NSF, Meetings and Memoranda, Box 319; Memorandum to the Members of the Special Group, "Establishment of the Special Group," 2 January 1962, JFK, NSF, Meetings and Memoranda, Box 319. See also Ameringer, *U.S. Foreign Intelligence*, 293; McClintock, *Instruments of Statecraft*, 168.

26. Ameringer, *U.S. Foreign Intelligence*, 281.

27. Memorandum for the President from Maxwell Taylor, 22 March 1962, JFK, NSF, Meetings and Memoranda, Box 319.

28. Halberstam, *The Best and the Brightest*, 55–56, 77.

29. Memorandum, Robert Komer to K. R. Hansen (Bureau of Budget), "Guerrilla Warfare Problem," 18 September 1961, JFK, NSF, Meetings and Memoranda, Box 326. Emphasis in original.

30. Memorandum, Edward A. Jamison (Director, Office of Inter-American Regional Political Affairs) to Richard N. Goodwin (Special Counsel to the President), 26 February 1962, NARA, RG 59, State Department Lot Files, 65D159, 66D131, Box 5.

31. Memorandum for the President from McGeorge Bundy, "A Plea for Flexibility," 18 March 1961, JFK, NSF, Meetings and Memoranda, Box 325.

32. Ibid.

33. Office of the White House, "Special Message on Foreign Aid," 22 March 1961, JFK, NSF, Subjects, Box 297.

34. Ibid.

35. Memorandum, Jamison to Goodwin, 26 February 1962.

36. Memorandum to the President from Walt W. Rostow, 28 February 1961, JFK, NSF, Meetings and Memoranda, Box 324.

37. Memorandum for the President from Maxwell Taylor, 22 March 1962, JFK, NSF, Meetings and Memoranda, Box 319.

38. Draft Paper Prepared in the Department of Defense, "U.S. Policy for the Security of Latin America in the Sixties," 19 May 1961, in U.S. Department of State, *Foreign Relations of the United States, 1901–1903, American Republics*, vol. 12 (hereafter *FRUS*) (Washington, D.C.: U.S. Government Printing Office, 1996), 174.

39. SNIE 80-62, U.S. Department of State, *FRUS*, 210–211.

40. Ibid.

41. Cole Blasier, *The Giant's Rival: The USSR and Latin America* (Pittsburgh: University of Pittsburgh Press, 1987), 19, 37; Szulc, *Fidel*, 563.

42. SNIE 80-62.

43. Che Guevara, *Guerrilla Warfare* (New York: Vintage Books, 1969), 1, 4–5.

44. Szulc, *Fidel*, 568, 574.

45. Max F. Millikan and Walt W. Rostow, *A Proposal: Key to an Effective Foreign Policy* (New York: Harper and Brothers, 1957), 22. See also Max F. Millikan, "Objectives for Economic Policy in a Democracy," in *Income Stabilization for a Developing Democracy*, ed. Max F. Millikan (New Haven, Conn.: Yale University Press, 1953), 13–76.

46. Cable, Embassy (Managua) to State, 8 August 1961, NARA, RG 59, State Department Decimal File, 1960–1963, 717.56/8-861, Box 1529.

47. Background Paper for Defense Department on British Sale of Arms to Latin America, 25 May 1960, NARA, RG 59, State Department Lot Files, 63D127, Box 2.

48. Memorandum from Robert F. Woodward (Assistant Secretary of State for Inter-American Affairs) to Hollis B. Cherney (Director, Program Review and Coordination Staff, AID), 17 November 1961, NARA, RG 59, State Department Lot Files, 643D310, 66D131, Box 3.

49. NSAM 2, 3 February 1961. See also Willard F. Barber and C. Neale Ronning, *Internal Security and Military Power: Counterinsurgency and Civic Action in Latin America* (Columbus: Ohio State University Press, 1966), 13–90; Douglas S. Blaufarb and George K. Tanham, *Who Will Win? A Key to the Puzzle of Revolutionary War* (New York: Crane Russak, 1989), 17–48.

50. Letter, Edward A. Jamison (Director, Office of Inter-American Regional Political Affairs) to Robert F. Woodward (Assistant Secretary of State for Inter-American Affairs), 17 July 1961, NARA, RG 59, State Department Lot Files, 643D310, 66D131, Box 3.

51. Memorandum from George S. Newman (State) to Jeffrey C. Kitchen (Deputy Assistant Secretary of State for Politico–Military Affairs), 25 July 1961, NARA, RG 59, National Security Action Memoranda Files, 1961–1968, Box 1.

52. JCSM 832-61, Memorandum for the President from the Joint Chiefs of Staff, "Military Actions for Latin America," 30 November 1961, JFK, NSF, Departments and Agencies, Box 276.

53. NSAM 119, 18 December 1961, NARA, RG 59, National Security Action Memoranda Files, 1961–1968, Box 2.

54. JCSM 832-61.

55. Memo, Wymberly De R. Coerr (Deputy Assistant Secretary of State for Inter-American Affairs) to Dean Rusk, 15 April 1961, NARA, RG 59, State Department Lot Files, 643D310, 66D131, Box 3.

56. Letter, Woodward to Cherney, 17 November 1961.

57. State–Defense–ICA Circular Message, 19 April 1961, NARA, RG 286, Records of the Agency for International Development, Office of Public Safety, Latin America, Country File, 1957–1974, Nicaragua, Box 136.

58. Memorandum, Chester Bowles to Kennedy, 29 September 1961, *FRUS*, 188–189; Cable, State to Managua, 25 April 1961, NARA, RG 286, Records of the Agency for International Development, Office of Public Safety, Latin America, Country File, 1957–1974, Nicaragua, Box 136.

59. Memo, Coerr to Rusk, 15 April 1961.

60. Memo, Charles Higdon (Office of Central American and Panamanian Affairs) to Wymberly De R. Coerr, 15 June 1961, NARA, RG 59, State Department Lot Files, 643D310, 66D131, Box 3.

61. Memo, Wymberly De R. Coerr (Deputy Assistant Secretary of State for Inter-American Affairs) to George O. Spencer (Office of Inter-American Regional Political Affairs), 29 December 1960, NARA, RG 59, State Department Lot Files, 63D127, Box 2.

62. Memo, Coerr to Rusk, 15 April 1961.

63. Letter, Jamison to Woodward, 17 July 1961.

64. Cable, CINCARIB to Chief, U.S. Army Mission Nicaragua, 15 April 1961, NARA, RG 286, Records of the Agency for International Development, Office of Public Safety, Latin America, Country File, 1957–1974, Nicaragua, Box 136.

65. Letter, John O. Bell (Deputy Coordinator for Foreign Assistance) to Roy R. Rubottom (Ambassador to Argentina), 27 May 1961, NARA, RG 59, State Department Lot Files, 63D127, Box 2.

66. Memorandum, Jamison to Goodwin, 26 February 1962.

67. Cable, USARCARIB to Department of the Army, 8 March 1961, JFK, President's Office File, 1961–1963, Box 121a.

68. Memorandum for the President from General G. H. Decker (Army Chief of Staff), 24 July 1961, JFK, NSF, Departments and Agencies, Box 269.

69. Cable, Embassy to State, 27 October 1961, NARA, RG 59, State Department Decimal Files, 1960–1963, 717.00 (W)/10-2761.

70. Cable, Embassy (Managua) to State, 7 September 1962, NARA, RG 59, State Department Decimal File, 1960–1963, 717.00(W)/9-762.

71. Letter, Jeffrey C. Kitchen (Deputy Assistant Secretary for Politico-Military Affairs) to Haydn Williams (Deputy Assistant Secretary of Defense for International Affairs), 15 January 1962, NARA, RG 59, State Department Lot Files, 65D159, 66D131, Box 5.

72. "Report of the Interdepartmental Team on Countersubversive Measures in Central America and Panama," (n.d.), NARA, RG 59, State Department Lot Files, 65D159, 66D131, Box 5.

73. John H. Coatsworth, *Central America and the United States: The Clients and the Colossus* (New York: Twayne, 1994), 106–107; Morris H. Morley, *Washington, Somoza, and the Sandinistas: State and Regime in U.S. Policy toward Nicaragua, 1969–1981* (New York: Cambridge University Press, 1994), 2–3, 6–8.

74. Morley, *Washington, Somoza, and the Sandinistas*, 38.

75. Memorandum for the President, "Clay Committee Report and the FY 64 Foreign Aid Program," 4 March 1963, JFK, NSF, Subjects, Box 297.

76. Thomas W. Davis (State) to Robert Kennedy, "Future Role of the Special Group (Counterinsurgency)," 16 January 1963, JFK, NSF, Meetings and Memoranda, Box 319.

77. Memorandum, Michael V. Forrestal (NSC) to McGeorge Bundy, 18 October 1962, JFK, NSF, Meetings and Memoranda, Box 319.

78. Memorandum for the Secretary of State from David E. Bell (Administrator, AID), 25 March 1964, NARA, NSAM Files, 1961–68, Box 4.

79. Memorandum CS 091, "Review of Latin American Policies, 18 January 1962, JFK, NSF, Departments and Agencies, Box 269.

80. NSAM 206, "Military Assistance for Internal Security in Latin America," 4 December 1962, NARA, RG 59, NSAM Files 1961–68, Box 5.

81. NSAM 177, "Police Assistance Programs," 7 August 1962, NARA, RG 59, NSAM Files, 1961–68, Box 4.

82. McClintock, *Instruments of Statecraft*, 190.

83. Memorandum for McGeorge Bundy and General [Maxwell] Taylor, 18 April 1962, JFK, NSF, Meetings and Memoranda, Box 319.

84. Foreign Broadcast Information Service (FBIS), "Daily Report: Latin America," 16 August 1963, JFK, FBIS, Box 33.

85. Cable, Embassy (Managua) to State, 25 May 1960, NARA, RG 59, State Department Decimal File, 1960–1963, 717.00/5-2460.

86. Cable, Embassy (Caracas) to State, 18 May 1961, NARA, RG 59, State Department Decimal File, 1960–1963, 717.00/5-1861; FBIS, "Daily Report: Latin America," 26 July 1963, JFK, CIA, FBIS, Box 33.

87. Embassy (Tegucigalpa) to State, 31 May 1961, NARA, RG 59, State Department Decimal File, 1960–1963, 717.00/6-861.

88. "Honduras Returns 28," *New York Times*, 22 October 1960, 5.

89. "Costa Rica Fights Nicaraguan Rebels, " *New York Times*, 13 November 1960, 1.

90. Cable, Managua to State, 22 November 1960, NARA, RG 59, State Department Decimal File, 1960–1963, 717.00/11-1160.

91. FBIS, "Daily Report: Latin America," 2 August 1963, JFK, FBIS, Box 33; FBIS, "Daily Report: Latin America," 20 August 63, JFK, FBIS, Box 33.

92. Cable, Embassy (Managua) to State, 2 September 1960, NARA, RG 59, State Department Decimal File, 1960–1963, 717.00 (W)/9-260.

93. Memorandum, Roy R. Rubottom to Richard A. Godfrey, 7 June 1960, NARA, RG 59, State Department Lot Files, 63D127, Box 2.

94. Cable, Embassy (San Jose) to State, 14 November 1960, NARA, RG 59, State Department Decimal File, 1960–1963, 717.00/11-1460; "Costa Rica Fights Nicaraguan Rebels," *New York Times*, 13 November 1960, 1.

95. Cable, Embassy (Managua) to State, 15 November 1960, NARA, RG 59, State Department Decimal File, 1960–1963, 717.00/11-1560.

96. Cable, Embassy (Managua) to State, 15 August 1962, NARA, RG 59, 1960–1963, 717.5/ 8-1562.

97. Andrew C. Kimmens, ed., *Nicaragua and the United States* (New York: H. W. Wilson, 1987), 14–15. See also Michael D. Gambone, *Eisenhower, Somoza, and the Cold War in Nicaragua, 1953–1961* (Westport, Conn.: Praeger, 1997), 213–214.

98. Steven Palmer, "Carlos Fonseca and the Construction of Sandinismo in Nicaragua," *Latin American Research Review* 23 (1988): 94–95.

99. Carlos Fonseca Amador, *Bajo la bandera del sandinismo* (Managua: Editorial Neuva Nicaragua, 1981); Sheldon B. Liss, *Radical Thought in Central America* (Boulder, Colo.: Westview Press, 1991), 159–199; Donald C. Hodges, *Intellectual Foundations of the Nicaraguan Revolution* (Austin: University of Texas Press, 1986), 161–171; Carlos Fonseca Amador, "Nicaragua: Zero Hour," in *Sandinistas Speak*, ed. Tomas Borge, Carlos Fonseca, Daniel Ortega, Humberto Ortega, and Jaime Wheelock (New York: Pathfinder Press, 1981), 23–42. See also Carlos Fonseca, "The Historic Program of the FSLN," in *Conflict in Nicaragua*, ed. Jiri Valenta and Esperanza Duran (Boston: Allen and Unwin, 1987), 321–329; Claribel Alegria and D. J. Flakoll, *Nicaragua: la revolucion sandinista: Una Cronica politica, 1855–1979* (Mexico City, D.F.: Ediciones Era, S.A., 1982), 141–175.

100. "More Nicaraguans Flee," *New York Times*, 29 March 1959, 82.

101. Paul P. Kennedy, "Nicaragua Fears Leftists Attacks," *New York Times*, 15 February 1959, 4.

102. Cable, Embassy (Managua) to State, 5 May 1961, NARA, RG 286, Records of the Agency for International Development, Office of Public Safety, Latin America, Country File, 1957–1974, Nicaragua, Box 136.

103. Ibid.

104. Cable, Embassy (Managua) to State, 11 May 1961, NARA, RG 286, Records of the Agency for International Development, Office of Public Safety, Latin America, Country File, 1957–1974, Nicaragua, Box 90.

105. Ibid.

106. Cable, Embassy (Managua) to State, 17 April 1962, NARA, RG 59, State Department Decimal File, 1960–1963, 717.5/4-1762.

107. Cable, Embassy to State, 11 May 1961.

108. Memorandum, Jacob J. Kaplan (Assistant Coordinator for Programming) to the Director of Military Assistance, Office of the Assistant Secretary of Defense, 21 June 1961, NARA, RG 59, State Department Decimal File, 1960–1963, 717.5622/2-961.

109. Memorandum, Edward A. Jamison (Director, Office of Inter-American Regional Political Affairs) to Richard N. Goodwin (Special Counsel to the President), 26 February 1962, NARA, RG 59, State Department Lot Files, 65D159, 66D131, Box 5.

110. Letter, Louis F. Blanchard to John M. McIntyre (Officer in Charge of Nicaraguan Affairs, Office of Central American and Panamanian Affairs), 28 May 1962, NARA, RG 59, State Department Lot Files, 65D159, 66D131, Box 5.

111. U.S. Air Force Attache (Guatemala City) to State, 12 January 1962, NARA, RG 59, State Department Decimal File, 1960–1963, 720.5811/1-1/62.

112. Letter, Aaron Brown to John M. McIntyre (Officer in Charge of Nicaraguan Affairs), 29 June 1962, NARA, RG 59, State Department Decimal File, 1960–1963, 717.5622/6-2962.

113. Cable, Embassy (Managua) to State, 13 April 1962, NARA, RG 59, State Department Decimal File, 1960–1963, 717.00(W)/4-1362.

114. Ibid. Emphasis in original.

115. Letter, Brown to McIntyre, 29 June 1962.

116. FBIS, "Daily Report: Latin America," 23 August 1963, JFK, FBIS, Box 33.

117. FBIS, "Daily Report: Latin America," 7 August 1963, JFK, FBIS, Box 33.

118. Cable, Embassy to State, 11 May 1961.

119. NSAM 119.

120. Cable, Embassy (Managua) to State, 25 July 1961, NARA, RG 59, State Department Decimal File, 1960–1963, 717.5-MSP/7-2561.

121. Cable, Embassy (Managua) to State, 21 August 1962, NARA, RG 286, Records of the Agency for International Development, Office of Public Safety, Latin America, Country File, 1957–1974, Nicaragua, Box 90.

122. Cable, Embassy (Managua) to State, 19 August 1961, NARA, RG 59, State Department Decimal File, 1960–1963, 717.5-MSP/8-2161.

123. Letter, Wymberly De R. Coerr to Jeffrey C. Kitchen (Deputy Assistant Secretary of State for Politico–Military Affairs), 5 September 1961, NARA, RG 59, State Department Decimal File, 1960–1963, 717.5-MSP/9-561.

124. Memorandum, Charles Maechling to Jeffrey C. Kitchen, 23 August 1961, NARA, RG 59, State Department Decimal File, 1960–1963, 717.5-MSP/9-561.

125. Cable, Embassy (Managua) to State, 31 August 1962, NARA, RG 59, State Department Decimal File, 1960–1963, 717.00(W)/8-3162.

126. FBIS, "Daily Report: Latin America," 26 July 1963, JFK, FBIS, Box 33.

127. Charles H. Savage, Jr., "After Castro," *America*, 24 November 1962, 1129–1130.

128. Szulc, *Fidel*, 549–550, 599.

129. Ibid., 584–586.

130. Memorandum for the Record, Minutes of the Meeting of the Special Group (CI), 5 January 1963; Memorandum for the Record, Minutes of the Meeting of the Special Group (CI), 19 December 1963, NARA, RG 286, Records of the Agency for International Development, Office of Public Safety, Latin America, Country File, 1957–1974, Nicaragua, Box 137.

131. Letter, Brown to McIntyre, 29 June 1962.

132. See Steven C. Ropp, "Goal Orientation of Nicaraguan Cadets: Some Applications for the Problems of Structural/Behavioral Projection in Researching the Latin American Military," *Journal of Comparative Administration* 4 (May 1972): 107–116.

133. Letter, Louis F. Blanchard (Charge d'Affaires, Nicaragua) to V. Lansing Collins, 10 June 1963, NARA, RG 59, State Department Lot Files, 66D131, Box 6.

134. Ibid.

135. Cable, Embassy (San Jose) to State, 4 April 1960, NARA, RG 59, State Department Decimal File, 1960–1963, 717.00/4-460.

136. Memorandum, Charles Higdon (Office of Central American and Panamanian Affairs) to Wymberley De R. Coerr, 6 July 1961, NARA, RG 59, State Department Lot Files, 643D310, 66D131, Box 3.

137. Letter, George O. Spencer (Office of Inter-American Security and Military Assistance) to Milton Barrall (Deputy Assistant Secretary for Inter-American Affairs), 16 December 1961, NARA, RG 59, State Department Lot Files, 65D159, 66D131, Box 5.

138. Memorandum for the Record, Minutes of Meeting of Special Group (CI), 10 May 1962, RG 286, Records of the Agency for International Development, Office of Public Safety, Latin America, Country File, 1957–1974, Nicaragua, Box 137.

139. Memorandum, George O. Spencer (Office of Inter-American Regional Political Affairs) to Edwin M. Martin (Assistant Secretary of State for Inter-American Affairs), 22 June 1962, NARA, RG 59, State Department Lot Files, 1960–1963, 65D159, 66D131, Box 5.

CHAPTER 3

The Economic Revolution in Central America

Castro is not the fundamental problem. What is required is an attack on the conditions which produced him. If he is eliminated and these conditions are left unchanged, new Castros will arise all over the continent.

Arturo Frondizi, 1961

In the eyes of the American diplomatic community, effective economic development was the foundation of stability. Growth could sustain both social stability and military spending necessary to contain communism. Drawing from this perspective, U.S. policy makers attempted to craft a broad array of programs that would translate million of dollars of aid into broad-based development. Central America appeared well prepared to embrace this support at the start of the 1960s. During the late 1950s, the five nations had initiated their own programs to collectively organize the regional economy into a more diversified and productive unit. Nicaragua also seemed prepared to address the new emphasis on well-planned socioeconomic reforms. The Somoza government had invited a World Bank mission to survey its first national development plan in 1954. By 1961, faced with declining revenues from its coffee exports, Managua appeared even more willing to adopt progressive changes into its economy.

THE DEVELOPMENT DILEMMA

At the start of the 1960s, the basic structure of the global economy was changing in ways that alarmed many Americans. Western Europe and Japan had begun their respective postwar economic "miracles" and were mounting a significant challenge to U.S. economic dominance of the world marketplace. For the first time since World War II, the American share of trade abroad began to deteriorate. Clear evidence of this trend was available in the United States's own backyard. Latin America was a instrumental factor in the reconstruction of U.S. competitors. The postwar Japanese textile industry, for example, imported significant quantities of raw cotton produced by new Central American plantations. Foreign exports to the Western Hemisphere also grew. Many Latin American nations, attracted by lower prices and more flexible commercial policies offered by Europe and Asia, imported an increasing volume of steel, autos, machine tools, electronics, and other products from non-American sources. Between 1958 and 1963, U.S. exports to the nineteen nations of the hemisphere declined from $3.5 to $3.1 billion.[1]

As the United States grappled with these economic challenges abroad, its problems at home were compounded by a recession in the late 1950s. The Eisenhower administration had, as part of its fiscally conservative mantra, maintained low inflation rates and balanced budgets throughout its tenure. However, these achievements had come at the cost of uneven economic growth and rising joblessness as the decade progressed.[2] During the latter years of the Eisenhower era, the postwar economy stumbled into its third recession since the Korean War. By 1958, unemployment stood at a troubling 6.8 percent, accompanied by a $4-billion balance-of-payments deficit.[3] That same year, American gold reserves declined by more than $2 billion, the largest loss in a single year to that point.[4]

One of the first tasks of the Kennedy administration was to find redress for this stagnation, as it applied both to the American economy and the conceptual basis of American policy. As John Morton Blum has commented,

Yet there was also in 1960 a need for a more transcendent cast, for a national purpose that would evoke support for domestic reform without intensifying dormant antagonisms among different classes and ethnic groups. It had, too, to infuse international policies that would protect the national interest without mobilizing chauvinistic hostility to the Soviet Union.[5]

As a group, Kennedy's advisors invoked the need for substantial theoretical departures to solve the problems of the present day. In his seminal work, *The Affluent Society*, John Kenneth Galbraith argued the need for a "New Class" of managerial talent rooted in the hard realities of rationalism and social science rather than the weary fiscal dogma of the previous administration.[6] Walter Heller, his counterpart in the administration and head of the president's Council of Economic Advisors, carried this belief into the policy-making apparatus of the administration: "Our statistical net is now spread wider and brings in its catch faster. Forecasting has the benefit of not only more refined, computer-assisted methods but of improved surveys of consumer and investment intentions."[7] Armed with these new tools, American officials pursued prosperity supported by the belief that the economy was quantifiable and, therefore, subject to efforts to fine tune and control its progress. As a group, Kennedy's economic advisors embarked on a general movement away from the strict emphasis on balancing the budget to a much looser interpretation of federal spending, one that contemplated, for example, "countercyclical" federal deficits to cure the ills of recession.[8] The following is a list of overall U.S. balance of payments from 1960 to 1967, in billions of U.S. dollars:[9]

1960	−3.4
1961	−1.35
1962	−2.65
1963	−1.94
1964	−1.53
1965	−1.29
1966	0.24
1967	−3.38

The Kennedy administration approached foreign-assistance policy from the same basic perspective. More important, it had arrived at a time when the relevance of economic aid in foreign policy had reached a distinct turning point.[10] Adolf Berle, chairman of Kennedy's Task Force of Latin American Problems, argued that the growing sophistication of economics had given it at least equal relevance with traditional political concerns in conduct of international relations. Berle believed that recognition of this relationship would provide U.S. policy makers with a tool that would transcend the traditional Cold War model.[11] Such a strategy focused on building countries into "cooperative economic units" that would displace outdated nineteenth-century empires with cooperative economic blocs. It suggested an attempt to duplicate the recent success of the European Economic Community (1958) on a regional scale in other portions of the world. Berle concluded, "Diplomacy may not be new. But the approach to economic problems has almost completely changed. In almost exact opposition to the Marxist thesis, economics must be in a measure altruist if it is not to be regressive and unproductive. This is the modern diplomacy of peace!"[12]

One opportunity to apply these theories was very close to home. According to Kennedy advisor Arthur Schlesinger, the United States faced a crisis in Latin America:

All across Latin America the ancient oligarchies—landholders, Church, and Army—are losing their grip. There is a groundswell of inarticulate mass dissatisfaction on the part of the peons, Indians, miners, plantation workers, factory hands, classes held down past all endurance and now approaching a state of revolt.[13]

Schlesinger, who served as the administration's touchstone for Latin America in much the same manner Milton Eisenhower had for its predecessor, saw socioeconomic upheaval in Latin America after World War II. In *A Thousand Days*, he ridiculed American policy makers for their postwar neglect, noting the fact that Yugoslavia had received more aid between 1945 and 1960 than all of Latin America combined.[14] Schlesinger noted that public monies were essential in places that the private sector would not explore and remarked, with more than a little disdain regarding contemporary fiscal conservativism, "In preaching fiscal orthodoxy to developing nations, we were somewhat in the position of the prostitute who, having retired on her earnings, believes that that public virtue requires the closing down of the red-light district."[15]

Economic planning for the Alliance for Progress followed with the intent to create a framework for growth. As early as July 1961, Undersecretary of State Chester Bowles articulated that the three basic goals of the *Alianza* would be to (1) provide resources for growth, (2) bring about basic reforms in the distribution of wealth, and (3) promote the welfare of rural populations.[16] What remained for policy makers was to create the programmatic means necessary to meet these objectives. George Ball would explain,

The only way, I repeat, the *only* way, in which the developing countries can achieve the economic growth they desire is by expanding the capital resources upon which they draw. If a country is to be able to achieve self-sustaining growth within a reasonable future, it will have to pursue realistic policies *to acquire the capital it needs.*[17]

In practice, these "realistic policies" boiled down to a complex hybrid of U.S. assistance and Latin American reforms. In order to produce the degree of modernization sought by the alliance, host governments and American policy makers alike contemplated the concurrent development of capital investment, financial and technical assistance, and a thorough reform of existing economic institutions.

The effort began in earnest at the Punta del Este meeting in August 1961. Accompanying American calls for substantive political reforms, agenda item number one addressed the need for "planning for economic and social development" throughout the hemisphere. Specifically, U.S. representatives to the conference wanted their counterparts "to initiate action to establish adequate planning machinery in each country to formulate national plans."[18] The end point of these plans was "to achieve balanced diversification in national economic structures" and "to accelerate the process of rational industrialization."[19] American delegates offered their complete cooperation toward this goal.

Assistance would obviously come at a cost and with a caveat. In order to receive the billions in U.S. aid and private investment that Latin America sought, host governments would have to restructure their national economies and, more important, surrender a degree of sovereignty to the scrutiny of U.S. advisors charged with monitoring assistance programs. The final resolution signed by twenty nations pledged to address planning that covered the gamut of development issues, from illiteracy programs to tax reform and regional integration.[20]

The following are the U.S. aid commitments after Punta del Este:[21]

U.S. Public Funds

$400 million	Eximbank
$250 million	Contributions to social development
$150 million	Food for Peace program
$75 million	Technical assistance
$75 million	Development Loan Fund

Private Funds

$300 million	U.S. private investment
$300 million	International lending agencies
$300 million	European and Japanese investment

Washington followed this emphasis on planning with a concrete commitment of financial assistance. In a speech delivered on 11 September 1961, Douglas Dillon clarified his position on U.S. commitments to the alliance and promised an aid package that included $950 million in public funds and more than $900 million in new private investment (Table 3.1). The amount was unprecedented, triple the amount of U.S. funds granted in 1960 and more than double the annual average between 1950 and 1960.[22]

American officials also attempted to assuage Latin American concerns about sovereignty by sponsoring the creation of a panel of nine international experts, the so-

Table 3.1
U.S. Assistance to Latin America, 1960–1963 (US$ millions)

	1960	1961	1962	1963
AID/ICA	104.8	256.3	474.8	555.9
Exim	113.4	575.8	253.9	91.2
Food for Peace	75.7	147.7	134.5	185.5
IDB	N/A	N/A	224.4	124.8
Other	86.5	1.9	120.0	15.2
Total	380.4	981.7	1,207.6	972.6

Source: AID, *U.S. Assistance to Latin America: Obligations and Loan Authorizations, FY1949–FY1963* (Washington, D.C.: AID, 1963), JFK, Teodoro Moscoso Papers, Box 2.

called wise men, appointed by the Organization of American States in December to assist countries that voluntarily requested help in the formation of national development plans. Comprised of seven Latin Americans who had served at the ministerial planning level, the group included only one American, Harvey Perloff, a professor of economic planning at the University of Chicago. Raul Prebisch, the first director of the Economic Commission for Latin America, served as the board's coordinator.[23]

Economic assistance to Nicaragua essentially followed the same emphasis on national planning and diversified development, while establishing the important linkages between growth and stability. American policy makers in Managua made no attempt to separate political and economic affairs, recognizing that the primary actors from most parties contesting the 1963 presidential election were also the economic elite of the country. The embassy acknowledged as well that any economic downturn, particularly if it produced significant increases in unemployment, could seriously disrupt any hope of democratization in Nicaragua.[24]

Throughout the 1961–1963 period, the U.S. country team in Nicaragua sought out measures to demonstrate the need for a good-faith effort on both sides. Officials were pragmatic about both the pace and depth of reform. Basic American expectations were well articulated in a 1961 U.S. Operations Mission cable to the State Department:

Primary US objectives are continued progress toward democratization and coincidental improvement economic/social conditions of underprivileged masses. Alliance for Progress criteria (land and fiscal reform, long-range planning, democratization) pertain here and must be met before we cooperate in 10-year program. For next 1 or 2 years however we can best shove Nicaragua toward desired goals by modest measured program with occasional approvals projects having self-help aspects and within putative long-range program, while we reshape aid program to new concepts and observe progress Nicaraguans are making toward criteria.[25]

Between 1961 and 1963, Nicaragua received $36.1 million in civilian and military assistance from the United States. Drawn primarily from the Agency for International Development and the Social Progress Trust Fund, American assistance focused particularly on infrastructure projects such as road construction, rural electrification, and public housing (see Tables 3.2 and 3.3).[26]

Two major obstacles blocked an effective American assistance program in both Central America and Nicaragua. In part, the problem was the product of local shortfalls in planning, the often lengthy process of passing reform programs by Central

Table 3.2
U.S. Assistance to Nicaragua, 1961–1963 (US$ millions)

	1961-62	1962-63
AID	3.6	2.6
Social Progress Trust Fund	7.7	0.8
Exim Bank	N/A	0.4
Food for Peace	0.7	0.7
Total	12.0	4.5

Source: AID, *U.S. Assistance to Latin America: Obligations and Loan Authorizations, FY1949–FY1963* (Washington, D.C.: AID, 1963), JFK, Teodoro Moscoso Papers, Box 2.

Table 3.3
Project Loans to Nicaragua, 1960–1962 (US$ millions)

Source	Purpose	Authorized	Amount	Undisbursed	Disbursed
DLF/AID	Hydroelectric Power	1960	2.5	1.9	0.6
	Highway Construction	1961	4.3	4.0	0.3
IBRD	Electric Power Development	1960	12.5	11.0	1.5
IBD	Industrial Development	1961	2.0	1.7	0.3
SPTF	Housing	1962	5.2	5.2	0.0
	Rural Credit	1962	2.5	2.5	0.0
			29.0	26.3	2.7

Source: Memorandum, "The Loan Pattern in Central America," 15 December 1962, NARA, RG 59, State Department Lot Files, 66D131, Box 8.

American legislatures, the absence of technical expertise, and delays in submitting bids to contractors.[27] Combined, these impediments prevented the timely distribution of aid to much of the region. The end result alarmed U.S. officials. Between 1958 and 1962, for example, 80 percent of the Developmental Loan Fund–AID loans made to Central America were undisbursed. The same could be said of 76 percent of IBRD loans between 1959 and 1962 and 96 percent of Social Progress Trust Fund grants between 1961 and 1962. For its own part, 93 percent of Nicaraguan grants and loans remained undisbursed in 1962.[28]

American bureaucracy also bedeviled embassies throughout Central America. Difficulties over the interpretation and implementation of aid programs constantly produced delays in the American assistance community. In Managua, Aaron Brown complained loudly and consistently about the amount of data required by the Agency for International Development in order to approve new development projects.[29] He worried as well that these delays would damage not only the aid program, but Central American perceptions of the U.S. commitment to the Alliance for Progress. In a letter to Lansing Collins at the Office of Central American and Panamanian Affairs, Brown commented on obstacles to aid for Nicaraguan education:

We cannot avoid the suspicion that a request at this late date for additional information of such enormously demanding scope, and largely of such questionable relevance to a serious consideration of the loan application, can only have been concocted with the deliberate intent of delaying indefinitely any real action on this loan, or even of burying it once and for all under the weight of a hostile bureaucracy.

For a number of easily imaginable reasons, I find this all both discouraging and annoying. One of the reasons is that this is a typical case where the U.S. Government, theoretically trying to do good, succeeds only in spreading the impression that it is hopelessly permeated with unsympathetic and bumbling bureaucrats. Bringing it closer to home is of course the fact that, rightly or wrongly, this bad impression comes to include those of us here who think we don't deserve it.[30]

On the whole, the Alliance for Progress contained many of the features that represented the best and the worst of Kennedy-era foreign policy. Its objectives were clearly sweeping, encompassing the contemporary wisdom that the United States could solve the systemic dilemma of socioeconomic development. Concurrently, it also swept up in its rhetoric the impatience and hope of many Latin Americans themselves. Expectations rose with each speech devoted to the *Alianza*, the Punta del Este meeting, and, finally, the billions in new aid committed by the end of 1961.

Programs failed to keep pace with these expectations. As the alliance progressed, it became increasingly apparent that neither Washington nor local governments were prepared to properly guide the deluge of new programs that flowed toward Central America. In a report issued to the Organization of American States in June 1963, former Brazilian president Juscelino Kubitschek protested,

In lieu of a vital dialogue of the Americas, a sort of discouraging monologue has been going on. What I had opportunity to observe about the implementation of the Alliance for Progress is that its administrators have remained entangled in the same traditional difficulties that hitherto obstructed the kind of broad and thorough-going collaboration that would be capable of advancing hand in hand with the people of Latin America on the way to prosperity.[31]

The "shrill bleats" of Kubitschek were generally dismissed by American officials, although the administration concurred with requests to "multilateralize" the alliance and agreed to the creation of an Inter-American Development Committee under the Inter-American Development Bank in 1963.[32] Nevertheless, Kubitschek's observations regarding the growing gap between rhetoric and outcome gained increasing traction among many of his contemporaries. As the decade progressed, the collective efforts promoted by the alliance would be accompanied by additional labors within the Central American community to spark its own regional development.

THE INTEGRATION OF CENTRAL AMERICA

During the postwar period, Central American integration was prompted by the declining utility of traditional commerce and the inherent limits of nontraditional alternatives. In the early 1950s, coffee exports—a regional mainstay—were spurred on by the general increase in global prices created by the Korean War. However, after 1957, overproduction led to a collapse of prices. From a peak of 80 cents per pound in 1954–1955, prices declined to 44 cents per pound in 1960.[33] Improvements in yields and attempts to impose export quotas in 1958 and 1959 only temporarily arrested the drop in earnings. Likewise, the banana industry found itself handicapped by increasing incidences of disease and the stagnant foreign market throughout the 1950s. Central American earnings from bananas declined from $85.5 million in 1954 to $65.8 million in 1960.[34]

In order to compensate, Central American countries individually pursued other nontraditional industries and export crops. Sugar, cotton, and cattle soon accompanied traditional export commodities. They found ready markets abroad. Japan's nascent textile industry and a growing number of American fast-food companies became major consumers of the region's new products.[35] However, as helpful to local economies as these new initiatives were, they were no less tied to global market fluctuations or even more problematic limits on arable land.[36]

To expand existing opportunities, Central America joined in a general regional movement toward economic cooperation in the 1950s. Initially, development focused on what Enrique Delgado has described as the "principle of reciprocity," in which integration, and the trade that resulted, would be achieved on the basis of both reciprocal interests and shared risk.[37] This cooperation led to the formation of the Organizacion de Estados Centroamericanos in 1951. Between 1951 and 1956, ODECA served primarily as a vehicle for the negotiation of bilateral treaties between the five Central American nations. In 1951, for example, Nicaragua and El Salvador signed a series of agreements establishing a free-trade zone between their countries. By mid-decade, all five countries had signed at least one agreement that governed free trade for a limited range of products. Subsequent gains in intraregional imports were impressive, rising from $8.6 million in 1950 to $13.7 million six years later.[38]

Attempts to expand the benefits of reciprocal cooperation did not end with ODECA. Adhering to the basic principles governing economies of scale, Latin Americans successfully lobbied the United Nations for the creation of a regional organization dedicated to trade and development. In 1950, the Economic Commission for Latin America was created. ECLA officials, such as Raul Prebisch, argued that unilateral capital investment programs were pitifully inadequate to the task of sustained national or regional growth. Revenue collection required greater integration, with stricter enforcement of tariffs and income taxes. Regional and national banking systems were needed to support capital investment over the long term. New funding could break cycles of low domestic capital availability caused by poor savings rates and increasing import costs.[39] Latin Americans were, in other words, contemplating an economic scheme that moved quite beyond the Millikan–Rostow model, one that pursued national development within the context of regional integration.[40]

Regional integration would become both the keystone of and the holy grail for Latin American efforts to create economies of scale. In 1955, ECLA considered the prospect of coordinating existing regional economic concerns with the development of a variety of new enterprises.[41] Studies of the Central American economy conducted by the commission, some in cooperation with the United Nation's Technical Assistance Council, examined the viability of cattle and cotton, the manufacture of fats and oils, as well as statistical coordination among the five nations and a variety of regional infrastructure projects. ECLA also generally agreed with the host nations that there was a need for greater long-range regional planning.[42]

The Central American integration effort subsequently shifted its focus to three basic objectives. First, it attempted to diversify production to reduce dependence on a narrow range of export agriculture products. Second, it pursued the integration of the Central American market to create economies of scale and encourage a degree of cost effectiveness. Last, it planned to modernize industry and manufacturing in order to better exploit natural resources and train a labor force that could both produce local products and earn income that would allow the population to actively participate in a regional economy.[43]

The Central American Common Market was the final culmination of these plans and a recognition that bilateral trade could not sustain regional development. In June 1958 and September 1959, all five isthmian nations signed both the Agreement on the Regime for Central American Economic Integration and the Multilateral Treaty on Free Trade and the Integration Industries Convention. The Multilateral Treaty included 239 groups of Central American products in a regional free-trade area and planned to expand the protocol to include all products of local origin over the next decade. The IIC planned to organize a carefully balanced regime of Central American enterprises that would receive "integration industries" status and concurrent co-ordination of production, pricing, and expansion.[44] One year later, a Tariff Equalization Convention was approved, with the provision for a common regional tariff policy within five years.[45] Bickering between individuals governments, particularly Honduras and Costa Rica, delayed final ratification of the industries convention and the Multilateral Treaty well into the summer of 1959.

As Victor Bulmer-Thomas has noted, it is unlikely that regional integration would have proceeded further without American intervention.[46] By the time the Eisenhower administration began its second term, Washington was eyeing regional development efforts with a growing sense that U.S. policy had lost the initiative in Latin America. A number of events informed this perception. In 1958, Brazilian president Juscelino Kubitschek put a new twist on the concept of self-help that Americans had promoted throughout the decade and, in doing so, became a standard bearer for Latin American development. In late May 1958, with American officials still backpedaling furiously over the furor that surrounded Vice President Nixon's visit to Caracas, Kubitschek wrote to Eisenhower concerning the need for a "Pan American policy."[47] In his appeal, the Brazilian president forged an explicit link between economic underdevelopment and regional unrest, demanding support for a program to combat the "extreme pauperism" at the heart communism's growing appeal in Latin America.[48] In one fell swoop, Kubitschek managed to do what Eduardo Crawley describes as "playing the American card," rather deftly capturing the United States within its own Cold War rhetoric, while at the same time linking the anti-Communist crusade with regional development.[49] Castro's victory in January 1959 served only to provide even more impetus to Kubitschek's demands. In August 1958, U.S. representatives to the Organization of American States announced support for a regional development bank that would later grow into the Inter-American Development Bank.[50]

Central America was also captured within the trajectory of this new American policy. In late 1959, U.S. officials signaled that they would support the principle of unrestricted regional free trade and offered additional U.S. assistance toward local economic-development projects. However, not all Central American nations were convinced that this American involvement was a reason for optimism, particularly when Washington demanded that the proposed CACM remove tariff protections for local economies. Only three republics, Guatemala, Honduras, and El Salvador, agreed to U.S. conditions as part of the Tripartite Treaty in February 1960. Faced with the prospect of missing out on an American aid bonanza, Nicaragua followed suit, signing the General Treaty on Central American Economic Integration with its three northern neighbors in December. Taken as a whole, the General Treaty provided the legal basis for the Central American Common Market. Only Costa Rica steadfastly refused to join in the new agreement.

Overall, the various integration treaties had a significant impact on the regional economy. Total exports rose from $452 million in 1961 to $503.2 million in 1962. Central American imports as a portion of regional trade increased from 4.2 percent in 1958 to 7.5 percent in 1961. The Central American market for regional exports also increased from 4.7 percent to 8.2 percent during this same period. The goods and services most affected were foodstuffs, raw materials, chemical products, and light manufactures. Among CACM nations, Nicaragua and El Salvador registered the most impressive gains, seeing their gross domestic products grow by an annual rate of 6.4 and 6.6 percent, respectively, between 1959 and 1964 (see Table 3.4).[51]

However, the General Treaty also came with a hefty price tag. Most obvious was the abandonment of local tariff protections in favor of a free-trade zone throughout the region. Rather than cultivate a Central American trade regime and enjoy the benefits of at least regional economies of scale, the area was forced to incorporate foreign products into its import–export structure without restriction. Trade imbalances inevitably followed with countries outside the region. Without the necessary

Table 3.4
Central American Balance of Trade, 1960–1963 (US$ millions)

	1960	1961	1962	1963
Costa Rica				
Exports	86	84	93	95
Imports	110	107	113	124
	-24	-23	-20	-29
El Salvador				
Exports	117	119	136	154
Imports	122	112	125	152
	-5	+7	+11	+2
Guatemala				
Exports	117	113	114	153
Imports	138	134	133	166
	-21	-21	-19	-13
Honduras				
Exports	64	73	81	82
Imports	72	72	80	95
	-8	+1	+1	-13
Nicaragua				
Exports	56	61	83	100
Imports	72	74	98	111
	-16	-13	-15	-11
Total				
Exports	440	450	507	584
Imports	514	499	549	648
	-74	-49	-42	-64

Source: Norris B. Lyle and Richard A Calman, *Statistical Abstract of Latin America: 1965* (Berkeley and Los Angeles: University of California Press, 1966), 138–139.

means to provide balanced development, internal trade deficits would also plague the CACM throughout the 1960s. Lacking the coordination provided for in the moribund Integration Industries Convention, individual Central American nations forged ahead with development projects without adequate consideration of their impact. Honduras would protest repeatedly, for example, that its balance of payments lagged behind other CACM members because it possessed the most primitive regional economy.[52]

Central American economic integration reached its fruition as the Kennedy administration prepared new billions in aid for the Western Hemisphere. The Common Market, as it was established, enjoyed access to American assistance, but failed to provide an adequate conceptual framework for the balanced regional development that member nations sought. Part of this difficulty was the product of the absence of any resolution regarding the meaning or practice of "reciprocal" development. Central American nations could agree on the general principles of cooperation, but differed markedly on specific issues as they related to "integration" industries, tariffs, and financing. Unfortunately, before any of these concerns were resolved, the United States embraced the concept of regional development, altered it to incorporate the free market as its guiding light, and moved forward to address the larger needs of the hemisphere. Littering the path behind an increasingly expansive American policy would be an array of untreated systemic economic difficulties, political rivalries, and general interregional friction. These unanswered questions would bedevil the Kennedy administration and its largess as Central American development struggled into the 1960s.[53]

RETRENCHMENT IN NICARAGUA

Nicaragua began the 1960s in need of an economic spark. The remarkable growth that characterized much of the 1950s, from new gains in cotton, copper, and cattle, to the beginnings of a manufacturing sector, appeared to be at an end as the new decade started. There was a recession in 1959, one that saw the gross national product shrink by 3 percent, the first time since 1950.[54] In 1961–1962, the nation's budget declined by nearly 10 percent, forcing Managua to curtail spending for municipal services and construction. That same year, the government contribution to Nicaragua's limited social security program was terminated.[55]

As was the case with most of the isthmus, Nicaraguan decline was the product of the demise of traditional exports as a source of national revenue. Although Managua had devoted considerable time and energy to diversification during the 1950s, it fundamentally failed to solve the country's basic dependency on a single export crop: coffee. The collapse of coffee prices after 1955 from approximately 80 cents per pound to less than 40 cents per pound in 1963 was primarily responsible for triggering Nicaragua's economic dilemma.[56] Coffee revenues followed suit, dropping in value continuously from 1957 onward, from $28.5 million that year to $13.8 million in 1959.[57]

As the economy staggered, Nicaraguan population growth rocketed ahead. According to the U.S. embassy, the annual rate of increase was estimated at 3.4 percent, a disturbing trend that exacerbated already considerable problems of housing, health care, and employment.[58] In 1960, Nicaragua's housing deficit stood at 158,000 units and was increasing at an estimated rate of 10,700 units each year.[59]

Compounding this formidable array of challenges was the absence of a national development plan. A decade earlier, Nicaragua had shown considerable initiative when it had formed, with the assistance of the World Bank, a comprehensive program to develop and diversify its economy.[60] Progress toward national integration, modernization of the infrastructure, and economic diversification had followed in the wake of the coffee and cotton boom of the mid-1950s, but was cut short by the assassination of Anastasio Somoza Garcia in 1956. From that point onward, the regime was forced to consider its own survival before administrative coherence.[61] Even after the imminent danger of a coup had passed from the scene, observers in Managua expressed doubt that Somoza Garcia's sons had the capacity to carry on with the work of the old regime. Luis Somoza maintained his father's predilection toward centralizing coordination and decision making around his own office. In too many cases, the American embassy worried that public policy extended only as far as his own limited perspective.[62]

Some poor decisions were the result of this inattention. Despite Nicaragua's relative gains in productivity, Managua paid little heed to the country's balance-of-payments deficits and did not accumulate foreign exchange to offset its increasing import purchases during the 1950s. One solution to the problem of the emerging trade imbalance was a sharp increase in the 1958 tariff schedule, which raised duties on certain items as high as 80 percent, but severely cut trade in durable goods as well as capital equipment imports.[63] However, as revenues dropped sharply, government expenditures continued their progressive increase into the 1960s, peaking in 1959–1960 at $39.2 million. A budget deficit of $4.1 million subsequently accompanied a $16-million trade deficit in 1960. Between 1960 and 1962, Nicaraguan public debt approximately doubled, from 152 million cordobas to 307 million cordobas.[64] The fiscal cushion available to the Somozas at the start of the Alliance for Progress era was very thin indeed.

One of Managua's first answers to this challenge was to embrace a primary recommendation made by the Kennedy administration at Punta del Este when it urged attendees to pursue national economic planning. In fact, Nicaragua's own national planning agency, the Instituto de Fomento Nacional, had begun preparation of a ten-year development plan as early as 1960. Focusing on industrial development and agricultural diversification, INFONAC projected a need for $10.7 million in new investment for the 1961–1962 period and requested technical assistance from ECLA, the Inter-American Development Bank, and the Organization of American States to carry out research and program development.[65] The regime followed these recommendations by hiring consultants from Stanford University to prepare feasibility studies for twenty selected industries and a five-year plan for agricultural and industrial development. A National Institute for Foreign and Domestic Trade was organized in October 1960 to maintain domestic agricultural price stability and act as an intermediary for industrial raw materials imports.[66] Much to the consternation of the U.S. Operation Mission, the Somoza government also retained Henri Favre, a French industrial advisor, and brokered the installation of the French Industrial Productivity Center across the street from the USOM's own office building.[67]

INFONAC's own efforts were bolstered by the creation of the National Planning Office by presidential decree no. 52 on 31 January 1962. The office was given the mission of overall economic-development coordination at the national and regional levels, specifically in agriculture, manufacturing, and industry.[68] Reporting directly to Luis Somoza, it was also charged with initiating administrative reform, improving tax administration, and the preparation of the national budget. In its first year of operations, the National Planning Office supervised the farm credit operations of the National Bank, land acquisitions made by the Nicaraguan Housing Institute, and a series of population, agricultural-livestock, and housing censuses.[69]

Efforts to foster coherence within Nicaragua's financial system also followed in the midst of this planning. A new, independent Central Bank was created on 1 January 1961.[70] On 1 February 1962, a presidential decree established the National Bank as the primary agent for long-term public lending, emphasizing agricultural and industrial credit operations.[71] This decision was particularly important because high interest rates in 1961–1962—first mortgage rates were as high as 18 to 24 percent and unsecured loans to the poor ran as high as 200 percent—were drawing local capital away from potentially successful industrial and manufacturing enterprises.[72]

A number of substantive reforms followed the planning process. In January 1962, the Chamber of Deputies passed a series of bills levying additional taxes on soft drinks, cigarettes, and entertainment.[73] That same month, it approved a 3-percent income tax and a progressive capital-gains tax that increased collections on transfers of real estate from 0.5 to 3 percent. Additional reforms allowed the National Bank of Nicaragua a more active role in collection. American officials estimated that these steps would increase annual government revenues by $1.4 million.[74]

Public works spending, efforts at land reform, and amendments to labor policy were also added to the Nicaraguan policy inventory. The departments of Development, Public Works, and Education received budget increases totaling $13.3 million for 1962–1963; the only other increase registered was by the *Guardia Nacional*.[75] A rural land credit system, started in 1956, was expanded after 1960 with a $2-million loan from the Inter-American Development Bank. The IADB projected an investment of $28.6 million to Nicaraguan agriculture between 1961 and 1969.[76] In addition, the Somozas took special pains to cultivate the organized labor movement, continuing their father's practice of dividing labor without granting explicit endorsement to any one union. A new national labor planning committee, formed in 1960, allowed the pro-Somoza Confederacion Nacional de Trabajadores greater access to Nicaraguan media outlets in order to counter the virulent editorials emanating from opposition organs, such as Pedro Joachim Chamorro's *La Prensa*. CNT columns later began appearing in the progovernment *Novedades*, as well as *La Hora*.[77] Conversely, during a strike against two major construction firms in the Nicaraguan capital, the Managua Labor Conciliation and Arbitration Board intervened in favor of the leftist Sindicato de Carpinteros, Albañiles, Armadores y Similares de Managua, and asked owners to consider demands for a new collective contract.[78] In the midst of a June 1960 construction strike, Luis Somoza himself actually fed workers before granting them a 50-percent pay increase.[79]

This approach was designed to do more than provide a counterbalance to local union activity. There was ample evidence as early as 1961 that Communists had made substantial inroads in Nicaraguan organized labor. CGT Secretary General Andrés Ruiz Escorcia was openly pro-Communist in his public speeches. The Managua Worker's Federation and its principle components were also led by militant communists. The U.S. embassy remarked in September 1962,

There are signs that communism is gaining ground among the masses, although it is practically impossible to measure how much or how fast. In the FTM, the communists are now bold enough to show their faces as such. The Somozas remain confident that they can use communist leaders in the labor movement for their own purposes, but this use is a game at which two can play, and the communists are notoriously good at playing it themselves.[80]

The Somozas countered this anxiety by emphasizing the general disorganization of labor unions and the paucity of qualified leadership, characterizing the latter, in the embassy's words, as possessors of "venal morality, a gift of gab and some intuitive political skill."[81] The Somozas themselves had gone so far as to tolerate both Communists and non-Communists in minor government positions. Labor policy was, in this context, an easy means to contain local troublemakers and, more important, keep pace with American anti-communism.

Nicaraguan participation in the Central American Common Market was much less successful than its effort to reform the national economy. A working group on Central American integration that met in Managua in December 1961 rejected the 1960 General Treaty of Central American Integration Industries' provision for free-market competition. Led by Nicaraguan and Guatemalan representatives, the meeting endorsed a return to specific industrial monopolies, a determination that hearkened back to the original proposals made by ECLA in 1955. Based upon the consensus reached at the meeting, a tire monopoly was tentatively assigned to Guatemala, while Nicaragua received authorization for a caustic soda plant.[82]

Despite this minor departure, signs of growth almost immediately followed the final signing of the General Treaty. Once Nicaragua had signed, local business began to prepare to take advantage of opportunities offered by the decision. The textile industry added new equipment to improve quality and competitiveness within the regional marketplace. Manufacturers throughout the country purchased equipment for metal work, plastics, building materials, and shoemaking from U.S. and European suppliers.[83] Some Central American businesses considered relocation to Managua to take advantage of a new market. Amidst this growing sense of confidence, the U.S. Embassy commented, "The business community, as a whole, and at least at the moment, is in a state of optimism it has not known since the salad days of the 1957 boom."[84] Hard evidence supported this optimism. The value of trade conducted within Central America increased from $32.7 million in 1960 to $72.1 million in 1963.[85]

Acquiring capital for these new enterprises continued to be a distinct problem, however. It was clear in 1960 that INFONAC could not bolster manufacturing, industry, or agriculture without additional infusions of capital.[86] Beyond the revenue generated by traditional exports, a ready source of capital for all Central American nations, Nicaragua sought out and received third-party financial support from multilateral lending agencies. Between 1961 and 1963, the country received $7.2 million from the International Bank for Reconstruction and Development, the Inter-American Development Bank, the International Development Association, and United Nations sources (i.e., UNICEF, UNTA, UNEPTA).[87] For the most part, this assistance, like its American counterpart, focused on road construction, electrification, and other infrastructure projects.

Private investment followed to support specific economic enterprises. By far, food processing attracted the most foreign interest. In 1962, the value of Nicaraguan food processing alone stood in excess of $78 million, nearly half of all its manufacturing.[88] Diversification in this sector took advantage of new enterprises (e.g., milk processing from the cattle industry) and growth in local and regional consumption (e.g., beer, matches, insecticides, naval stores).[89] Joint partnerships, such as Cafe Soluble (U.S.–Nicaraguan), GEMINA (Canadian–Nicaraguan), and Nestlé (U.S.–Central American), all jumped on the bandwagon.[90] Private monies were not limited to light industry. Royal Dutch Shell, for example, actively planned to open a second oil refinery in

Nicaragua in 1960, whereas Esso Standard Oil committed $8 million for the construction of a refinery in Managua to process Venezuelan crude oil. Edmundo Tefel, in a partnership with Westinghouse, also planned the construction of a plant that produced refrigerators and air conditioners.[91] Overall, direct foreign investment in Nicaragua tripled between 1960 and 1962, from $800,000 to $2.4 million.[92]

This upsurge in investment was an important indication of the growing role of foreign investment in Nicaragua's economic recovery. Continuing a trend begun in the 1950s, the country continued and expanded its lucrative trade with non–U.S. sources (see Table 3.5).[93] The American embassy noted with some concern in 1960 that "the fact remains that price competition from Europe and Japan continues and U.S. exports to Nicaragua can be expected to decline through the coming decade, possibly with increased intensity."[94] The Dutch Antilles and Venezuela became the primary sources of fuel oil, while Sweden supplied an increasing amount of paper imports.[95] The market changed as well for Nicaraguan exports. Japanese textile manufacturers, for example, absorbed the bulk of Nicaraguan cotton harvests. Peru became a key consumer of Nicaraguan beef.[96] The growth of trade with West Germany and Japan was particularly notable. By 1963, these two countries accounted for one-third of Nicaraguan exports, approximately equal to the United States (see Table 3.6).[97]

Overall, available capital increased from $8.9 million in 1960 to $23.4 million in 1963.[98] With this broad spectrum of sources available, INFONAC was able to ad-

Table 3.5
Sources of Nicaraguan Imports, 1960–1964 (US$ millions)

	1960	1961	1962	1963	1964
U.S.	37.7	36.3	49.4	53.7	64.2
W. Germany	5.5	6.1	7.0	8.1	10.7
Great Britain	3.0	3.2	4.1	5.9	5.3
Netherlands	1.1	1.9	2.3	2.6	4.2
Japan	4.6	4.4	5.7	6.4	8.3
China	.386	n.a.	n.a.	n.a.	n.a
Central America	4.7	4.2	5.3	7.3	14.8
South America	1.8	1.8	1.8	4.3	8.9

Sources: United Nations, Department of Economic and Social Affairs, *Yearbook of International Trade Statistics, 1964* (New York: United Nations, 1966), 553; James W. Wilkie, ed., *Statistical Abstract of Latin America, 1965* (University of California at Los Angeles: Latin American Center, 1966), 144–149; Republica de Nicaragua, Recaudador General de Aduanas, *Memoria de la Recaudacion General de Aduanas por el Periodo del 1 de Enero al 31 de Diciembre de 1961* (Managua: Gobierno de Nicaragua, 1962), 35–38.

Table 3.6
Destination of Nicaraguan Exports, 1960–1964 (US$ millions)

	1960	1961	1962	1963	1964
United States	26.8	30.8	31.9	39.0	34.5
W. Germany	8.8	8.1	12.7	12.2	24.2
Great Britain	2.6	2.0	3.4	3.0	6.1
Netherlands	3.2	2.9	4.0	4.1	5.5
Japan	8.6	13.2	17.9	22.9	28.6
India	0.3	n.a.	n.a.	n.a.	6.0
Central America	2.6	1.8	3.5	4.7	7.2
South America	1.2	1.2	1.2	0.4	0.4

Sources: United Nations, Department of Economic and Social Affairs, *Yearbook of International Trade Statistics, 1964* (New York: United Nations, 1966), 553; James W. Wilkie, ed., *Statistical Abstract of Latin America, 1965* (University of California at Los Angeles: Latin American Center, 1966), 144–149; Republica de Nicaragua, Recaudador General de Aduanas, *Memoria de la Recaudacion General de Aduanas por el Periodo del 1 de Enero al 31 de Diciembre de 1961* (Managua: Gobierno de Nicaragua, 1962), 35–38.

dress both manufacturing and infrastructure projects. Managua also enjoyed increasingly diverse sources of capital, a development that allowed the government greater discrimination in awarding contracts. Non-American companies soon began to compete with their U.S. counterparts in Alianza projects. The French firm Société des Grands Travaux de Marseilles, for example, was awarded the Tuma river electrification project in 1961.[99]

Thus bolstered, nontraditional products significantly rebounded during the Kennedy era. The value of cotton reached $31.3 million in 1962, surpassing its previous peak year of $31 million in 1955. Between 1957 and 1962, sugar exports more than quadrupled in value, from $1 to $4.5 million. The value of meat exports doubled between 1959 and 1961, from $1.8 to $4 million, the result of improved breeding techniques and better meat processing and storage facilities.[100]

The Nicaraguan mineral industry also made impressive gains. Copper production in 1960 was five times that of the previous year. The 10.7 million pounds of copper processed from mining efforts gained almost $3 million in revenue.[101] In order to build upon the copper boom, the Atlantic Coast Mineral Development Commission moved forward with mineral surveys started in the mid-1950s by INFONAC, and reported in late 1961 the discovery of extensive iron-ore deposits in northeastern Nicaragua. The survey also found substantial deposits of tungsten, lead, and zinc.[102]

The success of the mining and food processing sectors reflected the growing importance of manufacturing in the Nicaraguan economy. By 1963, it accounted for nearly one-fifth of total national production and served as an important contributor to economic recovery. Construction (10.2%), power (12.2%), and industry (10.0%) all led with the highest annual growth rates from 1960 to 1963. Among all Latin American nations, Nicaraguan industry and basic services marked the highest annual expansion in the hemisphere.[103] New products led this trend, comprising 39.4 percent of total production by value in 1960 and 60 percent by 1963. All told, the value of exports surged from $62.1 million in 1960 to $105.6 million three years later.[104]

Some significant internal problems lingered despite these successes. Of particular concern was the changing structure of the Nicaraguan labor force in the early 1960s. According to the United Nations, improvements in agriculture and manufacturing had not translated into greater employment opportunities for the average citizen. Improved productivity actually had an inverse effect on total employment. The number of workers in agriculture and manufacturing began to markedly decline at the start of the decade, a trend that would continue throughout the 1960s.[105] Other socioeconomic indicators were equally worrisome. According to the Social Progress Trust Fund, in 1963, less than one-third of Nicaragua's urban population had access to potable water and only 16 percent had sewerage service. Conditions in the rural areas of the country were considerably worse. At the end of 1961, officials of the Inter-American Development Bank estimated that 2,300 new classroom were required to instruct the two-thirds of the population that remained illiterate.[106]

Most leaders concerned with Central American and Nicaraguan development were confident that the future held solutions to these problems. The continuing progress of regional integration and internal national development had produced significant gains in productivity and managed to diversify production itself. Nicaragua's own success at expanding the manufacturing sector and nontraditional agriculture served as an example for its partners in the Central American Common Market. The task that remained for policy makers was to refine equitable development—both internal and regional—and construct an acceptable mechanism to foster balanced development within the isthmus. These tasks, while conceptually simple, would bedevil the United States, the CACM, and the Somoza regime in coming years.

CONCLUSIONS

The strident calls for broad socioeconomic development, first heard in the summer of 1961, were considerably muted by the time the Kennedy administration neared its end. In part, the basic redistributive concepts endorsed during the Punta del Este conference were largely superseded by a drive for immediate economic efficiency and productivity. Economic prosperity clearly offered considerable benefits to the United States. The promotion of growth in a traditional area of American economic dominance was a tempting prospect for officials interested in addressing the U.S. trade deficit and arresting non-American economic penetration of the hemisphere. From a very early point, the Alliance for Progress became a vehicle to forestall American hegemonic decline, both in Latin America and on a larger global scale.[107]

In Central America, the principle of free-market competition set the initial standard for regional integration. Advocates of the common market in the 1950s had attempted to construct regimes dedicated to the principle of balanced regional development, but had found their efforts overcome by economic nationalism. The individual Central American nations desired foremost their own self-sufficiency within the larger common market. Sacrificing the opportunity to diversify internal national economies to the various integration programs was unacceptable, particularly after primary commodity prices began their decline in the mid-1950s. American sponsorship of the common market, predicated on the principle of open markets, only reinforced this trend. From the very start, the free market would provide the Central American economy with both its strongest engine and its most difficult point of contention.

In another important sense, the American emphasis on equitable social development foundered on the reality of local economic oligarchies. A contemporary contributor to the Alliance for Progress, Raymond Mikesell remarked that the "vast majority of the leaders of the articulated electorate" embraced the principles of Punta del Este. Unfortunately, their inclusion in policies that incorporated the echelons of society below the traditional economic and political elites of Latin America proved problematic.[108] As many U.S. policy makers recognized, political and economic elites were inseparable in Latin America. Embassy officials in Managua noted, for example, that Juan José Morales, president of the Nicaraguan Chamber of Deputies, was also one of the largest single landowners in Boaco Department, northeast of Managua. It was commonplace to find senior *Guardia* officers among the stockholders of many Nicaraguan companies.[109] The embassy stated in 1961 that "the traditional dependence upon the Government for the initiative in economic activity has permitted little or no local municipal spirit of community investment or cooperation to develop." It recommended that the economy decentralize so that "a spirit of social responsibility, developed through community activity, would help to serve as a foundation for social justice as well as private investment and the return of capital previously invested abroad."[110] However, the evidence suggests that the ruling class was more interested in decentralizing its investments than the country's distribution of wealth.[111]

The Somoza family itself illustrates the nature of this preference and the resulting obstruction of the spirit of Punta del Este. According to American estimates, the Somoza family possessions totaled $20.8 million in 1960. Family investments in agriculture and cattle were valued at $6.7 million. An additional $7.8 million was invested in air and sea transport, as well as numerous port facilities on the Pacific coast.[112] In the official government documents concerning post–Punta del Este development, it was apparent that the Somozas were willing to pay lip service to equitable development, but little else. The National Planning Office, for example, recognized the need for balanced economic, social, and political growth in a 1963 report to Luis Somoza, but repeatedly added the caveat that effective change could only be coupled with the unlikely prospect of complementary cooperation with Nicaragua's external trading partners.[113] The regime's tolerance of internal dissent within the Liberal Party indicated a willingness to sacrifice a degree of political power to pluralism. However, neither the Somozas nor their peers were willing to sacrifice the economic power they possessed in Nicaragua. The final failure of tax reform in 1962 was perhaps the best illustration of this basic reality. Tax reform was passed, after repeated delays, in June 1962, only to be suspended a month later by the Nicaraguan Congress, foundering on increasing protests by the National Association of Lawyers, local business, and agricultural interests. While the impact of the Somoza family's interests was self-evident, it was also apparent that they had no desire to resist strong bipartisan resistance to the new law.[114]

At key moments, policy encouraging economic development sometimes stumbled across the path of Nicaraguan sovereignty. The need to encourage internal reform and identify progress with the *Alianza* often contrasted sharply with Nicaragua's domestic political minefield and the regime's desire to place its interests over those of the United States. The Somoza brothers understood, as their father had before them, that it was comparatively easy to trap the United States in its own lofty rhetoric. One such skirmish appeared over a funding request for new Nicaraguan hospitals, a project that clearly addressed the quality-of-life problems raised at Punta del Este. In a June 1962 meeting between Luis Somoza and the American country team, the president raised the issue of funding for two hospitals near Managua. Neither the ambassador nor AID officials present made any commitments to the idea at the time. However, shortly thereafter a $1-million U.S. loan for the project was announced in *Novedades*. The embassy was able to deflect further inquiries by showing "polite interest" regarding the funding controversy.[115] However, the very audacity behind it became a disturbing benchmark for the alliance in Nicaragua.

In many instances, Managua was also perfectly willing to simply not participate in alliance programs if they did not conform with local priorities. In February 1962, the U.S.–Nicaraguan firm Gemina, S.A. protested the qualifications placed by the Inter-American Development Bank on a loan for a wheat and corn mill in Chinandega. The loan was offered on the special condition that the company limit its profits so that other mills could enjoy a degree of equitable competition. The condition was emblematic of American support for the principle of national and regional balanced development. The Nicaraguan Ministry of Economy disagreed, claiming that this policy could not "be accepted by any country which is struggling to industrialize because it intervenes unlawfully in the development of free enterprise," and successfully lobbied on behalf of Gemina when it refused the IADB loan and successfully sought out private British capital for its new mill.[116]

In the final analysis, American economic-development policy was superseded by a set of contradictory priorities. From the very start of the Central American Common Market, the United States had pressed its membership to endorse the free-market standard and, important, the idea that local initiative was key to future economic progress. A State Department circular from June 1961 placed a premium on "maximum self-help efforts by aid-receiving countries as prerequisites for US assistance."[117]

This was, as it turned out, a dangerous commitment to make, one that opened the door to local initiatives, local priorities, and local obstruction in equal measure. The Treasury Department commented in January 1962 that "well-founded" national development plans were not being formulated in Central America, "nor is it likely that any substantial number of plans will be available for some time."[118] Central American policies instead pursued economic dynamism, the product of free market capitalism, and the likely possibility that American economies of scale would serve as the primary engine of development.

NOTES

1. U.S. Department of Commerce, Bureau of International Commerce, *Market Indicators for Latin American Republics*, OBR 65-41 (Washington, D.C.: U.S. Government Printing Office, 1965), 15; Harry Gemmill, "How to Lose Sales: Gringo Grip on Latin Markets Is Loosened by Pushing Up Prices," *Wall Street Journal*, 29 May 1959, 1; "Eighteen Examples of Growing Worry for U.S. Business," *U.S. News*, 27 June 1960, 62–63; Harold T. Kennedy, "The Flood of Imports—How Serious Is It," *American Import–Export Bulletin* 53 (1963): 603–604.

2. John Morton Blum, *Years of Discord: American Politics and Society, 1961–1974* (New York: W. W. Norton, 1991), 6–15.

3. Walt W. Rostow, *Eisenhower, Kennedy, and Foreign Aid* (Austin: University of Texas Press, 1985), 125; U.S. Department of Commerce, Bureau of International Commerce, *United States Trade with Major World Areas, January–December, 1963*, OBR 64-48 (Washington, D.C.: U.S. Government Printing Office, 1964), 1.

4. Burton I. Kaufman, *Trade and Aid: Eisenhower's Foreign Economic Policy, 1953–1961* (Baltimore: Johns Hopkins University Press, 1982), 177; Diane B. Kunz, *Guns and Butter: America's Cold War Economic Diplomacy* (New York: The Free Press, 1997), 114–115.

5. Blum, *Years of Discord*, 11.

6. John Kenneth Galbraith, *The Affluent Society* (Boston: Houghton Mifflin, 1958), 334–348.

7. James T. Patterson, *Grand Expectations: The United States, 1945–1974* (New York: Oxford University Press, 1996), 464.

8. James Tobin, "Defense, Dollars, and Doctrines," *The Yale Review* 47 (1958): 326–334.

9. Kunz, *Guns and Butter*, 114.

10. John Lewis Gaddis, *Strategies of Containment: A Critical Appraisal of Postwar American National Security Policy* (New York: Oxford University Press, 1982), 223–225.

11. Adolf A. Berle, "Economics and the New Diplomacy," in *The Dimensions of Diplomacy*, ed. Edgar A. J. Johnson (Baltimore: Johns Hopkins University Press, 1964), 90.

12. Ibid., 115.

13. Arthur M. Schlesinger, Jr., "Good Fences Make Good Neighbors," *Fortune*, August 1946, 131–135, 161–171.

14. Arthur M. Schlesinger, Jr., *A Thousand Days: John F. Kennedy in the White House* (Boston: Houghton Mifflin, 1965), 172.

15. Ibid., 175.

16. Memorandum, Bowles (Undersecretary of State) to Dean Rusk (Secretary of State), 25 July 1961, U.S. Department of State, *Foreign Relations of the United States, 1961–63, American Republics*, vol. 12 (hereafter *FRUS*) (Washington, D.C.: U.S. Government Printing Office, 1996), 44.

17. George W. Ball, speech at the seventeenth annual meeting of the IBRD, 18 September 1962, John Fitzgerald Kennedy Library (hereafter JFK), Jack N. Behrman Papers, Box 1. Emphasis in original.

18. Scope Paper, United States Delegation to the Special Meeting of the Inter-American Economic and Social Council, Punta del Este, Uruguay, 6 July 1961, JFK, U.S. Department of the Treasury, Office of International Affairs, Box 11.

19. U.S. Agency for International Development, Bureau for Latin America, *The Charter of Punta del Este* (Washington, D.C.: U.S. Government Printing Office, 1961), 6.

20. Ibid., 1–4.

21. Memorandum, Edwin C. Randall to Ray Vernon, 20 January 1964, JFK, U.S. Department of the Treasury, Office of International Affairs, Box 11.

22. Memorandum, Dillon (Secretary of the Treasury) to President Kennedy, 1 August 1961, in *FRUS*, 47.

23. OAS Press Release, 8 December 1961, JFK, U.S. Department of the Treasury, Office of International Affairs, Box 13; Memorandum, Edwin C. Randall (Treasury) to John M. Leddy (Assistant Secretary), 29 March 1962, JFK, U.S. Department of the Treasury, Office of International Affairs, Box 13. The other "wise men" included Hernando Agudelo Villa (Colombia), Ernesto Malaccorto (Argentina), Manuel Noriega Morales (Guatemala), Felipes Pazos (Cuban exile), Gonzalo Robles (Mexico), Paul Rosenstein-Rodan (U.K.), Raul Saez (Chile), and Ary Torres (Brazil).

24. Cable, Embassy (Managua) to State, 8 March 1962, National Archives and Records Administration (hereafter NARA), Records Group 59 (hereafter RG 59), State Department Decimal File, 817.00/3-862.

25. Cable, Embassy (Managua) to State, 22 November 1961, NARA, Records Group 286 (hereafter RG 286), Records of the Agency for International Development, Office of Public Safety, Latin America, Country File, Nicaragua, Box 90.

26. U.S. Agency for International Development, Statistics and Reports Division, *U.S. Overseas Loans and Grants and Assistance from International Organizations: Obligations and Loan Authorizations, July 1, 1945–June 30, 1966* (Washington, D.C.: U.S. Government Printing Office, 1967), 45; Naciones Unidas, *Informe Sobre Los Planes Nacionales de Desarrollo y el Proceso de Integracion Economica de Centroamerica: Informe Presentado por el Comite Ad Hoc a los Gobiernos de las Republicas Centroamericanas* (Washington, D.C.: Comite de los Alianza para el Progreso, 1966), 104.

27. Memorandum, Edwin Martin (Assistant Secretary of State for Inter-American Affairs) to William V. Turnage (Director, Office of Inter-American Regional Economic Affairs), 21 December 1963, NARA, RG 59, State Department Lot Files, 66D131, Box 8.

28. Memorandum, "The Loan Pattern in Central America," 15 December 1962, NARA, RG 59, State Department Lot Files, 66D131, Box 8.

29. Letter, Aaron S. Brown to Lansing Collins, 13 September 1963, NARA, RG 59, State Department Lot Files, 66D131, Box 6.

30. Ibid.

31. Juscelino Kubitschek, *Report on the Alliance for Progress*, 15 June 1963, JFK, Teodoro Moscoso Papers, Box 2.

32. Memorandum, "Lleras and Kubitschek Reports on the Alliance for Progress," 3 July 1963, JFK, U.S. Department of the Treasury, Office of International Affairs, Box 14.

33. U.S. Agency for International Development, Bureau for Program and Policy Coordination, Office of Statistics and Reports. *A.I.D. Economic Data Book: Latin America.* (Washington, D.C.: U.S. Government Publication Office, 1971), 32; Jeffrey B. Nugent, *Economic Integration in Central America: Empirical Investigations* (Baltimore: Johns Hopkins University Press, 1974), 12–15.

34. Norris B. Lyle and Richard A Calman, *Statistical Abstract of Latin America: 1965* (Berkeley and Los Angeles: University of California Press, 1966), 73, 76, 96, 104; Victor Bulmer-Thomas, *The Political Economy of Central America since 1920* (New York: Cambridge University Press, 1987), 105–106, 152–153, 155; John F. McCamant, *Development and Assistance in Central America* (New York: Praeger, 1969), 14–15.

35. Committee on Latin American Studies, *Statistical Abstract of Latin America for 1956* (Berkeley and Los Angeles: University of California Press, 1957), 23–26; *Statistical Abstract of Latin America for 1957* (Berkeley and Los Angeles: University of California Press, 1959), 38–41; Center of Latin American Studies, *Statistical Abstract of Latin America: 1960* (Berkeley and Los Angeles: University of California Press, 1960), 38–43; *Statistical Abstract of Latin America: 1961* (Los Ange-

les: Center of Latin American Studies, 1961), 42–47; *Statistical Abstract of Latin America: 1963* (Los Angeles: Center of Latin American Studies, 1963), 94–99; Republica de Nicaragua, Direccion General de Estadistica y Censos, *Resumen Estadistico, 1950–1960* (Managua: Govierno de Nicaragua, 1961), 94.

36. Bulmer-Thomas, *Political Economy of Central America*, 156–159.

37. Enrique Delgado, "Institutional Evolution of the Central American Common Market and the Principle of Balanced Development," in *Economic Integration in Central America*, ed. William R. Cline and Enrique Delgado (Washington, D.C.: The Brookings Institution, 1978), 18, 23–25.

38. Bulmer-Thomas, *Political Economy of Central America*, 171–174.

39. United Nations, Economic Commission for Latin America, *The Economic Development of Latin America and Its Principle Problems* (New York: United Nations Publications, 1950), 37; Michael D. Gambone, *Eisenhower, Somoza, and the Cold War in Nicaragua* (Westport, Conn.: Praeger, 1997), 48–49.

40. Max F. Millikan and Walt W. Rostow, *A Proposal: Key to an Effective Foreign Policy* (New York: Harper and Brothers, 1957).

41. Delgado, "Institutional Evolution of the Central American Common Market," 24.

42. Alberto Fuentes Mohr, *La creacion de un mercado comun: Apuntes historicos sobre la experiencia de Centroamérica* (Buenos Aires: Instituto para la integracion de America Latina, 1973), 122–147.

43. Delgado, "Institutional Evolution of the Central American Common Market," 21. See also David E. Ramsett, *Regional Industrial Development in Central America: A Case Study of the Integration Industries Scheme* (New York: Praeger, 1969), 6–8.

44. William R. Cline and Alan I. Rapoport, "Industrial Comparative Advantage in the Central American Common Market," in *Economic Integration in Central America*, ed. William R. Cline and Enrique Delgado (Washington, D.C.: The Brookings Institution, 1978), 267–275; Joseph S. Nye, "Central American Regional Integration," *International Conciliation* 572 (March 1967): 10–13, 26–29.

45. United Nations, Economic Commission for Latin America, *Annual Report, 24 May 1959–29 May 1960* (New York: United Nations, 1961), 21; Committee on Economic Development, *Economic Development of Central America* (New York: CED Publications, 1964), 116–120, Bulmer-Thomas, *Political Economy of Central America*, 173–174.

46. Bulmer-Thomas, *Political Economy of Central America*, 173.

47. Memorandum, Elmer B. Staats to James S. Lay, "Updating Memo on Latin American Report (NSC 5613/1)," 18 June 1958, Dwight D. Eisenhower Library (hereafter DDE), White House, Office of the Special Assistant for National Security Affairs, NSC Series, Policy Papers Subseries, Box 18.

48. Letter, Kubitschek to Eisenhower, 22 August 1958, DDE, Ann Whitman File, International Series, Box 4.

49. Eduardo Crawley, *Nicaragua in Perspective* (New York: St. Martin's Press, 1979), 123–133.

50. R. Peter DeWitt, *The Inter-American Development Bank and Political Influence* (New York: Praeger, 1977), 10.

51. Committee on Economic Development, *Economic Development of Central America*, 64–65, 107–108; United Nations, Economic Commission for Latin America, *Economic Survey of Latin America, 1970* (New York: United Nations, 1972), 34; Donald H. McClelland, *The Central American Common Market: Economic Policies, Economic Growth, and Choices for the Future* (New York: Praeger, 1972), 49–53; William R. Cline, "Benefits and Costs of Economic Integration in Central America," in *Economic Integration in Central America*, ed. William R. Cline and Enrique Delgado (Washington, D.C.: The Brookings Institution, 1978), 59–124.

52. Delgado, "Institutional Evolution of the Central American Common Market," 40.

53. Bulmer-Thomas, *Political Economy of Central America*, 175–180.

54. Cable, Embassy (Managua) to State, 5 July 1960, NARA, RG 59, State Department Decimal File, 817.00/7-560.

55. Cable, Embassy (Managua) to State, 5 June 1961, NARA, RG 59, State Department Decimal File, 817.10/6-561.

56. Naciones Unidas, *Informe Sobre Los Planes Nacionales*, 70.

57. Republica de Nicaragua, Direccion General de Estadistica y Censos, *Boletin de Estadistica, 1964*, no. 10 (Managua, 1964), 196.

58. Cable, Embassy (Managua) to State, 5 July 1960; Country Briefing Paper: Nicaragua, 19 July 1961, JFK, U.S. Department of the Treasury, Office of International Affairs, Box 11.

59. Inter-American Development Bank, Social Progress Trust Fund, *Second Annual Report, 1962* (Washington, D.C.: IADB, 1962), 339.

60. International Bank for Reconstruction and Development (IBRD), *The Economic Development of Nicaragua* (Baltimore: Johns Hopkins University Press, 1954).

61. Cable, Embassy (Managua) to State, 17 April 1961 NARA, RG 59, State Department Decimal File, 817.00/4-1761; U.S. Treasury, "Economic Development in Latin America," 13 July 1961, JFK, U.S. Department of the Treasury, Office of International Affairs, Box 11.

62. Cable, Embassy (Managua) to State, 28 April 1961, NARA, RG 59, State Department Decimal File, 717.5-MSP/4-2861.

63. Cable, Embassy (Managua) to State, 5 July 1960.

64. Naciones Unidas, Comision Economica para America Latina, *Analisis y Proyecciones del Desarrollo Economico: IX El Desarrollo Economico de Nicaragua* (New York: Naciones Unidas, 1966), 66; IADB, *Second Annual Report*, 338–339.

65. IADB, Social Progress Trust Fund, *First Annual Report, 1961* (Washington, D.C.: IADB, 1961), 160.

66. Ibid., 163.

67. Cable, Embassy (Managua) to State, 13 March 1961, NARA, RG 59, State Department Decimal Files, 817.19/3-1361; Cable, Embassy (Managua) to State, 10 March 1961, NARA, RG 59, State Department Decimal File, 817.05151/3-7061TS.

68. IADB, *Second Annual Report*, 340–341.

69. U.S. Department of Commerce, Bureau of International Commerce, Overseas Business Reports, *Investment in Nicaragua*, OBR-62-14 (Washington, D.C.: U.S. Government Printing Office, 1962), 3; McCamant, *Development and Assistance in Central America*, 61; IADB, *Second Annual Report*, 341.

70. IADB, *First Annual Report*, 163.

71. Cable, Embassy (Managua) to State, 25 January 1962, NARA, RG 59, State Department Decimal File, 817.00/1-2562.

72. Cable, Embassy (Managua) to State, 18 July 1961, NARA, RG 59, State Department Decimal File, 817.10/7-1861.

73. Cable, Embassy (Managua) to State, 25 January 1962; IADB, Social Progress Trust Fund, *Third Annual Report, 1963* (Washington, D.C.: IADB, 1963), 310.

74. U.S. Department of Commerce, *Investment in Nicaragua*, 3; IADB, *First Annual Report, 1961*, 161–162.

75. Cable, Embassy (Managua) to State, 18 July 1962, NARA, RG 59, State Department Decimal File, 817.10/7-1862.

76. IADB, *First Annual Report, 1961*, 164.

77. Cable, Embassy (Managua) to State, 12 February 1960, NARA, RG 59, State Department Decimal File, 817.062/2-1260.

78. Cable, Embassy (Managua) to State, 25 January 1962.

79. Cable, Embassy (Managua) to State, 19 July 1960, NARA, RG 59, State Department Decimal File, 817.062/7-1960.

80. Cable, Embassy (Managua) to State, 25 September 1962, NARA, RG 59, State Department Decimal File, 817.062/9-2562.

81. Ibid.

82. Cable, Embassy (Managua) to State, 25 January 1962.

83. Cable, Embassy (Managua) to State, 30 August 1961, NARA, RG 59, State Department Decimal File, 817.3976/8-3061.

84. Cable, Embassy (Managua) to State, 19 May 1961, NARA, RG 59, State Department Decimal Files, 817.19/5-1961; Cable, Embassy (Managua) to State, 2 February 1962, NARA, RG 59, State Department Decimal File, 817.332/2-262.

85. McCamant, *Development and Assistance in Central America*, 256.

86. Cable, Embassy (Managua) to State, 5 July 1960.

87. U.S. Agency for International Development, *U.S. Overseas Loans and Grants*, 159; IBRD, *The World Bank and the IDA in the Americas* (Washington, D.C.: IBRD, 1962), 71–72.

88. "Nicaragua at the Heart of the Central American Common Market," *Industrial Development*, February 1964, 30.

89. Cable, Embassy (Managua) to State, 17 April 1961; Cable, Embassy (Managua) to State, 23 March 1961, RG 59, State Department Decimal File, 817.19/3-2361.

90. Cable, Embassy (Managua) to State, 7 September 1960, NARA, RG 59, State Department Decimal File, 817.2553/9-760; "Nicaragua at the Heart of the Central American Common Market," 29–30.

91. U.S. Department of Commerce, Bureau of International Commerce, *Investment in Nicaragua*, OBR-62-14 (Washington, D.C.: U.S. Government Printing Office, 1962), 3–4, 6; *Basic Data on the Economy of Nicaragua*, OBR-65-42 (Washington, D.C.: U.S. Government Printing Office, 1965), 10–11; "Nicaragua at the Heart of the Central American Common Market," 28–31.

92. Ramsett, *Regional Industrial Development in Central America*, 31.

93. Gambone, *Eisenhower, Somoza, and the Cold War in Nicaragua*, 64–65.

94. Cable, Embassy (Managua) to State, 5 July 1960.

95. Cable, Embassy (Managua) to State, 30 April 1962, NARA, RG 59, State Department Decimal File, 817.392/4-3062; Cable, Embassy (Managua) to State, 28 August 1961, NARA, RG 59, State Department Decimal File, 817.3932/8-2861.

96. Cable, Embassy (Managua) to State, 17 April 1961.

97. Naciones Unidas, *Analisis y Proyecciones del Desarrollo Economico*, 19.

98. Ibid., 40.

99. Cable, Embassy (Managua) to State, 10 March 1961.

100. Naciones Unidas, *Informe Sobre Los Planes Nacionales de Desarrollo*, 111, 113–114.

101. Cable, Embassy (Managua) to State, 8 March 1961, NARA, RG 59, State Department Decimal File, 817.25/3-861; Cable, Embassy (Managua) to State, 17 April 1961. The U.S. embassy attributed a loss of $14 million in exchange earnings to the poor 1959–1960 cotton crop. See U.S. Department of Commerce, Business and Defense Services Administration, *Copper Quarterly Industry Report* 5 (Spring–Summer 1960).

102. Cable, Embassy (Managua) to State, 27 September 1961, NARA, RG 59, State Department Decimal File, 817.25/9-2761.

103. Republica de Nicaragua, *Estadisticas del Desarollo Economico de Nicaragua, 1960–1967, Programacion Global* (Managua: Consejo Nacional de Economia, Oficina de Planificacion, 1968), Cuadro no. 1–3; Comision Economica para America Latina, *El Desarrollo Economico de Nicaragua*, 83; Economic Commission for Latin America, *Economic Survey of Latin America, 1970*, 38–41.

104. Comision Economica para America Latina, *El Desarrollo Economico de Nicaragua*, 11.

105. Economic Commission for Latin America, *Economic Survey of Latin America, 1970*, 45.

106. IADB, *Third Annual Report, 1963*, 310–311.

107. Schlesinger, *A Thousand Days*, 788–790.

108. Letter, Raymond F. Mikesell to Senator Wayne Morse, 15 May 1962, JFK, Jack N. Behrman Papers, Box 1.

109. Cable, Embassy (Managua) to State, 21 June 1960, NARA, RG 59, State Department Decimal File, 817.00/6-2160 HBS; Cable, Embassy (Managua) to State, 1 February 1961, NARA, RG 59, State Department Decimal File, 817.06/2-161.

110. Cable, Embassy (Managua) to State, 17 April 1961.

111. See also Morris H. Morley, *Washington, Somoza, and the Sandinistas: State and Regime in U.S. Policy toward Nicaragua, 1969–1981* (New York: Cambridge University Press, 1994), 40.

112. Cable, Embassy (Managua) to State, 20 May 1960, NARA, RG 59, State Department Decimal File, 717.11/5-2060.

113. Republica de Nicaragua, Oficina de Planificacion, Consejo Nacional de Economica, *Informe Parcial al Señor Presidente de la Republica* (Managua: Gobierno de Nicaragua, 1963), 4.

114. Cable, Embassy (Managua) to State, 24 July 1962, NARA, RG 59, 817.11/7-2462.

115. Cable, Embassy (Managua) to State, 22 June 1962, NARA, RG 59, State Department Decimal File, 811.0017/6-2262.

116. Cable, Embassy (Managua) to State, 23 February 1962, NARA, RG 59, State Department Decimal File, 817.313/2-2362.

117. U.S. Department of State, "State Department Circular to All Diplomatic Posts," CG-1065, 23 June 1961, JFK, NSF, Subjects, Box 297.

118. Letter, Stanley D. Doremus (Executive Secretary) to Members of the Alliance for Progress Committee, 9 January 1962, JFK, U.S. Department of the Treasury, Office of International Affairs, Box 13.

PART II

THE REVOLUTION CONTAINED, 1963–1968

CHAPTER 4

Revolution and Lyndon Johnson

Nicaragua is getting back to being
(or may be for the first time)
a free country
without affronts and without stains

Rigoberto López Pérez

John F. Kennedy's assassination abruptly interrupted American support for the Alliance for Progress. Kennedy was viewed, particularly by Latin Americans, as the godfather and mentor of the alliance. Lyndon Johnson did not inspire similar confidence. Widely known as a domestic political maven, Johnson's record regarding Latin America was noticeably lacking in substance after decades of public service. Beset by priorities established by the Great Society and the emerging conflict in Vietnam, the White House appeared unprepared to offer either new initiatives or a new impetus to American policy in the hemisphere. In the meantime, Central American stability suffered, brutally preserved by a host of military-dominated governments and challenged by a growing array of armed revolutionaries fighting pitched battles in the countryside. In the arena of open political discourse, new voices also added their ideas, particularly those movements dedicated to the abandonment of traditional arrangements of power. Offering a "third position" or tercerismo that departed from Liberal–Conservative politics and the Cold War, they sought to transform social, economic, and political reform. At mid-decade, Nicaragua faced its own period of transition. The year 1967 saw another presidential election, one that marked the final foray of Anastasio Somoza Debayle into Nicaraguan politics. Opposing him was a young generation of leaders, tempered by defeat in 1963 and distracted by internal squabbling, but hopeful that they could forge their own departure from the old system of leadership. Their challenge was to overcome the formidable political ambition of the last Somoza.

RESHAPING THE KENNEDY LEGACY

In his 1990 memoir, Dean Rusk offered an important insight into Lyndon Johnson's relationship with U.S. policy in Latin America. When the new president asked for a progress report on the Alliance for Progress, the Secretary of State replied with generalities and addressed the principles that guided the U.S. programs in Latin America. According to Rusk, Johnson exploded, "I don't mean that! I mean, what are we doing? What are we actually doing? What's going on down there in Latin America?"[1]

The moment was emblematic of both Lyndon Johnson's sketchy understanding of events in the hemisphere and his marked impatience with the policy makers left over from his predecessor's administration.

One important factor accounted for this frustration. Unlike John F. Kennedy, Johnson lacked a predecessor whose policies he could use as a point of departure. When he came to office in 1961, Kennedy could, at least in his rhetoric, contrast the dynamism of his administration and its commitment to the underdeveloped world with the intransigence and stagnation of the Eisenhower years. Johnson lacked that opportunity in 1963 and instead found his own administration's identity in Latin America captured by the Kennedy mystique and the rapidly growing nostalgia that surrounded the fallen president.

Consequently, Johnson consistently paid homage to the Kennedy years and the actions of "a brilliant new President of the United States" whose "unmatched vision" had created the Alliance for Progress.[2] Throughout his presidency, Johnson indulged his audiences with lofty rhetoric that enshrined the past. At a ceremony celebrating the fourth anniversary of the alliance, he lauded,

The goals towering, almost beyond achievement. The hopes were soaring, almost beyond fulfillment. The tasks were immense, almost beyond capacity. But entire nations are not stirred to action by timid words or narrow visions. The faith and will of millions do not take fire brands that are muffled in reluctance and fear. And if the reality of progress was to be slow, the radiance of ultimate achievement must be bright enough to compel the efforts and sacrifice of generations.[3]

In the year prior to his own election, Johnson dedicated himself to making the program "his living memorial" to the Kennedy legacy.[4]

He did so amidst a growing critique of the Alliance for Progress. In part, concerns were the product of Johnson's lack of a foreign policy record, particularly with respect to the Western Hemisphere. Congressional liaison officer Sherwin J. Markman noted upon his return from a tour of South America in 1965,

Latin Americans appear to have an extremely romanticized memory of President Kennedy which, in practical terms, results in negative to neutral feelings toward President Johnson. They neither understand him nor have sufficient awareness of his deep commitments against ignorance and want. Sadly, this lack would appear to apply to a good many U.S. field personnel. In Peru, for instance, neither the U.S. nor Peruvian educational leaders were aware of the President's Smithsonian speech on education. I think it imperative that this problem be attacked, and at once.[5]

Much to his chagrin, Johnson was also taken to task by Latin Americans regarding shortfalls in both the conceptual foundation of the *Alianza* and its ongoing support of regimes (e.g., the Somozas in Nicaragua) that many considered to be antithetical to the purposes of Punta del Este. The *Jorno do Brasil*, for example, criticized the Alliance for Progress for lacking "a defined philosophy, and without objectives clearly outlined."[6] Author Sacha Vollman pointed out that although a great deal of economic growth had followed American assistance, much progress had also been made toward "false democracy" by "pseudo revolutionaries."[7] Historian Albert O. Hirschman observed in 1963 that efforts to compensate for these problems had produced a pattern of chronic "reformmongering" that was ruining American foreign-policy efforts and contributing to regional resentment. In order to become more effective, Hirschman advised that the United States recognize a Latin American "style" of progress, a sentiment echoed repeatedly by former Brazilian president Juscelino Kubitschek.[8]

Added to this chorus were the usual Congressional voices that upbraided any increase in American commitments abroad. One of the most vocal administration critics was Louisiana Congressman Otto Passman, a Democrat who had claimed even before passage of the Alliance for Progress that "we are rapidly approaching the time when it is quite possible we shall not have any more money to spend."[9] Subsequent legislators returned to this theme in the early alliance years. A 1962 report commissioned by the office of Senator Wayne Morse lauded efforts by the "articulate electorate" to promote social and political reforms, but expressed concerns regarding the ability of Latin American countries to cope with inflation, attract foreign investment, or diversify current agricultural and industrial production. It noted that "few, if any, of the Latin America countries, has the broadly based rate of economic growth and individual well-being equivalent to the two and a half per cent per capita growth goal of the Punta del Este Charter."[10] The question left open by the Morse report was the final cost this lack of progress would entail for the United States.

Caught in the path of these questions, Johnson sought most of all the opportunity to answer critics and make his own imprint on Latin America. It would be a distinct departure from the past. As vice president, Johnson had opposed the Bay of Pigs operation, but had kept his reservations out of the public domain, instead choosing to discuss the matter alone with Kennedy.[11] Privately, Johnson was also highly critical of Kennedy's Alliance for Progress, describing it as a "thoroughgoing mess" that placed far too much credence in the United States's ability to foster democracy in Latin America. Johnson believed that Kennedy advisors, enamored of political-development theory, failed to understand the particularities of Latin American culture.[12] To those who would listen, Johnson would embellish his own past contacts with Mexican Americans in central Texas as well as his understanding of their unique needs and desires. In fact, as Doris Kearns points out, Johnson had rarely interacted with Latin American culture during his lifetime. His one great moment, something that Johnson cited throughout his life, was service as principal of a predominantly Mexican American elementary school in Cotulla, Texas, for nine months.[13]

In order to articulate his own distinct program for the hemisphere, Johnson focused specifically on the human costs of underdevelopment and borrowed heavily from themes that would dominate his domestic presidency. In a May 1964 speech to Latin American ambassadors, he announced "an all-out war on poverty" in their countries. Adopting a rhetorical device that he had used throughout his political career, Johnson produced laundry lists of American achievements under his leadership. He made sure to tell audiences that the U.S. contribution to Latin America since Kennedy's death included $430 million in additional aid. These projects had produced 52,000 homes, 7,000 classrooms, 10,000 teachers, 25,000 loans to farmers, and 300 water systems that benefited 10 million people.[14] Development, from

Johnson's perspective, would arrive in the wake of basic improvements in economy, not from the problematic path of political reform.

Pursuing this form of progress, Johnson stressed the importance of the private sector in development and, importantly, the need for local initiative in developing specific programs. The former emphasis was based upon his faith in free enterprise as the only sustainable means to answer the systemic problems of poverty. Perhaps more important, Johnson's stress on private investment was also a politician's recognition of growing public impatience with the cost of foreign assistance and its potential distractions from the Great Society. In his autobiography, *The Vantage Point*, Johnson noted,

After twenty years of sacrifice, generosity, and often lonely responsibility, the American people felt that other nations should do more for themselves. What worried me most was that we might be tempted to pull away from the world too quickly, before solid foundations could be built to support the desire of other nations for self-reliance.[15]

The latter point, that which addressed the importance of self-help, was equally significant to Johnson's worldview. Like Eisenhower before him, the president wanted a specific point of departure built into the structure of American assistance programs, one that identified where U.S. effort diminished and local responsibility started. Johnson ideally wanted a structure that was "somewhere between a world community and a system based on narrow nationalism," and endorsed the principle of "interdependence" rather than American paternalism. In practice, he supported the creation of a Latin American common market as the ideal vehicle for nations to cooperate and collectively assert regional priorities.[16]

Conversely, Johnson's Latin America policy would also suffer for the same reasons that would later plague the Great Society. The urgency and concurrent lack of focus that characterized U.S. efforts in Latin America reflected Johnson's sense that there was a distinct time limit on what he could accomplish in the foreign-policy realm. His comment to Doris Kearns "that the '64 election had given me a loophole rather than a mandate and that I had to move quickly before my support disappeared" captured Johnson's extraordinary sensitivity to criticism of his policies if they bogged down at an early point.[17] According to Dean Rusk, a pass phrase of the Johnson presidency became "Get on with it."[18]

Johnson's lack of focus on the particulars of policy would also significantly shape U.S. efforts in Latin America. In the frenzy of activity that captured the country's attention during 1964–1965, the pursuit of action at the expense of coherence became a defining feature of the Johnson White House. As president, Johnson retained his senatorial bent, pursuing legislative strategies that would garner support for foreign assistance and concurrent credit for their success. His relationships with political advisors such as Bill Moyers, Jack Valenti, and Walter Jenkins, according to Waldo Heinrichs, would subsequently remain much closer than those with his own cabinet.[19]

The problems of bureaucratic implementation were delegated to established experts, individuals like Walt Rostow, McGeorge Bundy, and Dean Rusk, men with whom Johnson had established general points of agreement regarding American policy, if not its specific details. The president maintained consistent contact with this group, as evidenced in his routine Tuesday luncheons with what amounted to a rump National Security Council. Sure of their support regarding national objectives, Johnson was prepared to grant his key advisors considerable latitude in the policy process.[20]

Lyndon Johnson's choice of Thomas C. Mann to lead U.S. Latin American policy was consistent with this pattern of policy making. Mann's appointment, made with great fanfare in December 1963, was Johnson's first major departure from the Kennedy legacy.[21] As Assistant Secretary of State for Inter-American Affairs and Special Assistant to the President for Latin American Affairs, Mann wielded formidable power because he concurred with Johnson on virtually every matter of Latin American policy. A fellow Texan and bilingual foreign-service officer with experience in Guatemala, Uruguay, El Salvador, and Mexico, Mann desired most of all to bring order to the amorphous ideas and often chaotic bureaucracy of the Kennedy-era *Alianza*. When asked to describe himself in a January 1964 interview, Mann declared, "I am a pragmatist, not a dogmatist and I am certainly not a miracle worker."[22]

Mann saw in the Kennedy-era Alliance for Progress a program that had generated unrealistic hopes for development without creating an adequate means to achieve them. Speaking on the deluge of plans made in 1961, he criticized the fact that "too much was promised for too short a time. Judgments were made by United States officials about conditions in Latin America were often inaccurate. The U.S. underestimated the resistance of Latin Americans to speeches by North Americans calling for sudden, sweeping reforms."[23] In this context, American policy provoked resentment over unachievable goals and, more important to Mann's perspective, made the United States vulnerable to "blackmail" from countries who complained that Castro would follow in the wake of any aid cutbacks.[24]

It was equally wrong, according to Mann, to subscribe to the idea that Latin America represented a uniform bloc of nations or that U.S. policy was applicable to the region in a uniform manner. In a speech made at Notre Dame in June 1964, he cited a failed history of unilateral intervention in the twentieth century:

Our interventions were, in the Latin American point of view, patronizing in the extreme. By making the United States the sole judge of Latin America's political morality, they were degrading to proud peoples who believed that, in their own wars of independence, they had earned the right to manage their own affairs—to be masters in their own houses. They produced schismatic tendencies in the inter-American family and brought our relations with Latin America to an all-time low.[25]

The United States needed to recognize individual sovereignty and "national dignity" before it could proceed with collective action.[26] "Our job," according to Mann, "is to convince the Latin Americans that their interests lie parallel to ours—not because of sentiment, but in their own self-interest. Democracy is a tie in these cases, economics is a tie, and Christianity is another tie. The total of these is where our interests lies, and when these ties are strong enough, no Marxist can separate us."[27]

From his perspective, the best means to achieve this goal would be to rely upon the dynamism of free enterprise. To do so would allow the United States to cultivate Latin American self-interest as the engine of progress rather than promote reforms imposed from the outside. As ambassador to Mexico, Mann had brokered a $20-million assistance program that provided agricultural loans for small farmers through the country's Central Bank. The bank itself acted as a funnel for loans to smaller private banks, which in turn disbursed money for fertilizer, equipment purchases, and infrastructure projects. Mann's idea was to encourage the small farmer to improve his operations through local bank credit and, in the meantime, encourage the Mexican government to transfer land titles to private owners who could productively implement land reform.[28] Self-help could therefore serve as both a means of economic growth and some degree of social reform. In his own words, "You have to make a pie before you can proceed to divide it fairly."[29] As 1964 progressed, Mann was optimistic in official correspondence to the president, highlighting an "atmosphere of increasing confidence" that was encouraging an increasingly "vigorous role" among private investors.[30]

Critics of "Mann Doctrine" pointed out at the time that his focus on free enterprise sidestepped the need for an American commitment to democracy and ultimately encouraged the proliferation of reactionary military regimes in the hemisphere. One editorial writer in 1964 described Mann's new primacy in the policy-making community as a stark contrast between "the old New Frontiersman of the Kennedy Administration and the new Old Frontiersman of the Johnson Administration."[31] Clearly, Mann relied upon the principle of noninterference in the pursuit of U.S. policy in Latin America. In his Notre Dame speech, he cited Resolution 35 of the Ninth Inter-American Conference of American States: "That the establishment or maintenance of diplomatic relations with a government does not imply any judgment upon the domestic policy of that government."[32]

What is equally clear, however, is the basic fact that Mann Doctrine was the product of Congressional pressure, public concerns, and Johnson's own directives to redefine American policy in terms that were concrete and achievable. When asked to explain his basic approach to Latin American affairs in a 1968 interview, Mann stated,

I suppose the words realist and pragmatist and that sort of thing stem from perhaps a difference of opinion on whether we should, in effect, espouse revolution without defining what kind of revolution we're talking about. I think in the Latin American mind, one who talks about revolution is understood to be saying that he favors violence in the streets and disorders. I thought we should favor orderly evolution and be careful of what we said and orient our program so that would be made clear. If there was a difference, perhaps that was it.[33]

The phrase "orderly evolution" became a keystone of Mann's approach to Latin America. An orderly evolution of policy could produce clear endpoints in Latin America, ones that would circumvent the increasing number of restrictions placed by Congress on alliance aid. In approving *Alianza* loans, for example, Congress mandated thirty-three separate tests (e.g., their impact of free enterprise in the recipient nation, adverse effects on the U.S. economy, etc.) before it would grant final funding approval.[34] An orderly process of evolution could also assuage public concerns regarding open-ended U.S. commitments abroad, an important element in 1964 as crises in Panama and Vietnam bookended an election year. Last, by maintaining his role as pragmatist, Mann could produce for his president a measure of success that had eluded Kennedy's New Frontiersmen.

The first perceived obstacle to this progress was communism. From Mann's perspective, communism was less a direct threat to Latin America than the primary beneficiary of failed U.S. policies. An American intelligence report noted in 1965 that an even dozen Latin American countries were threatened by instability. The causes of internal troubles ran the gamut from "severe economic and financial difficulties, ineffective governments, a distaste for the old order of Latin America (military–church–wealthy oligarchy domination), and active subversive elements which, in most cases, are supported by Castro and the Soviet bloc."[35] However, a 1964 report by the State Department Bureau of Intelligence and Research regarded the chances of a Communist takeover as "slim," citing failures in the 1963 Venezuelan and 1964 Chilean elections.[36] Scholars have since described Moscow's unwillingness to confront Washington as simple "geographic fatalism."[37] The State Department noted at the time that no single unifying Communist platform coordinated dissident activities in Latin America. Moscow, for example, appeared to cultivate legal opposition within the old "popular front" context. China, in contrast, appeared more willing to support violent factions within Latin American Communist organizations, but did so more to win influence from Russian-oriented groups. Cuba stood alone in its advocacy of popular rebellion.[38]

What concerned American officials most were the inroads Communist nations were making outside the areas of traditional revolutionary activity. Many Latin American nations desperate for economic development sought out new markets for their export agriculture. Countries experiencing currency convertibility problems also looked to the Eastern Bloc for easier terms of trade. Among South American nations, Brazil developed the most open ties. By 1964, trade with Communist nations accounted for 6 percent of its total commerce.[39] Regionally, economic relations with Communist nations expanded at an alarming rate in American eyes. Between 1960 and 1964, the number of Soviet trade missions in Latin America increased from nine in 1960 to twenty-three.[40] When Lyndon Johnson became president, Argentina, Brazil, Uruguay, and Mexico all actively traded with the Soviet Union. In 1964, Chile reestablished diplomatic relations with Moscow, and signed agreements for trade and technical training three years later.[41]

The American anti-Communist policies that followed under the alliance were subsequently often based upon the perception of a threat and, importantly, its interpretation in the domestic U.S. political realm.[42] American policy was constructed to meet potentialities, worst-case scenarios involving both armed rebellion and nonviolent encroachment upon a U.S. sphere of diplomatic and economic interests. Washington recognized, for example, that China and Cuba were more likely to aggressively support armed revolution and possessed hard evidence of this fact. The existence of small groups of armed resistance scattered over the hemisphere thus pointed not to the paucity of revolution, but the possibility of another Cuba. While Americans could rationally accept the fact that Castro's influence was significantly limited, he remained, as one journalist commented in 1962, "a bogey man who could be serviceable in frightening us into action."[43] Similarly, although Soviet trade was severely hamstrung by both its focus on industrial products and nontransferability of the ruble, American leaders remained concerned that it would upset the delicate plans created for the Alliance for Progress. As a consequence, the United States frequently found itself responding to the perception of a threat rather than its actual reality.

The evolution of Mann Doctrine in 1964 and 1965 was a reflection of this search for hard realities amidst perceived threats. Its first test was in Panama. On 9 January 1964, violence engulfed the country when American students refused to allow a Panamanian flag to be flown in the Canal Zone, abrogating a standing agreement that had been reached under the Kennedy administration. Fighting between civilians followed and lasted for three days, killing twenty-four Panamanians and three Americans.[44] The crisis added to existing friction created by an earlier series of riots within the Canal Zone in 1959 and subsequent Panamanian frustrations over negotiations to reconsider U.S. sovereignty in the country.[45] Panamanian president Roberto Chiari used the violence to officially break relations with the United States and demand a negotiation of the 1903 treaty governing the canal.

Dispatched to the region in his capacity as special advisor to the president, Mann later described a crisis stage managed by the Panamanian government as "theater."[46] During the course of discussions, Johnson made clear his refusal to negotiate with Chiari on the basis of coercion. The president essentially agreed with a comment made by Senate Republican Minority Leader Everett Dirkson, who flatly stated, "We are in the amazing position of having a country with one-third the population of Chicago kick us around. If we crumble in Panama, the reverberations of our actions will be felt around the world."[47]

As it unfolded, U.S. policy in the Panama crisis was dictated more by the perceived costs of weakness rather than any actual threat to Panamanian stability. The American public was generally supportive of a hard line against the Chiari government. Polls taken at the time indicated only 9 percent of Americans wanted the crisis resolved with concessions.[48] Yet Johnson remained wary of military action so close to the aftermath of the coup against Diem in South Vietnam and the internal chaos it had produced. To strike a balance between the public domain and American foreign policy, Johnson undertook two tasks. The first was based upon a near unanimous consensus within the administration that the Chiari government alone could handle the problem of domestic instability. Rioting ended almost immediately after the president refused to negotiate a new canal treaty until order was restored. Any questions regarding Communist manipulation of the situation vanished literally overnight, along with public scrutiny of the crisis. In the meantime, Johnson allowed substantive negotiations over the status of the canal zone to bog down. It was not until November 1964 that the Department of State had prepared a draft agreement that proposed abrogation of existing treaties and provided for new negotiations recognizing Panamanian sovereignty over the canal.[49] However, as diplomats on both sides explored a new treaty, Johnson undercut the Panamanian position by initiating discussions with Nicaragua in December 1964 regarding the creation of a second, sea-level transithsmian canal. Over the next two and a half years, the United States adopted the position that a new agreement governing the canal zone could not be resolved until this new project was completed. While few Nicaraguans took the plan seriously, the message to Chiari was clear.[50] Final draft treaties on the status of the canal zone were not completed until 1967. They recognized Panama's right to exercise sovereignty over the canal, created a new means to conduct canal operations, and established provisions for the sea-level canal. Negotiations were suspended when the Panamanian National Assembly and both candidates in the pending national elections condemned the treaties, specifically the membership structure of a proposed Canal Commission and provisions for long-term American base rights.[51] The canal treaties would remain moribund for an additional decade.

The Dominican intervention offered another example of the dichotomy between perception and substance, albeit on a much more dramatic scale. In the early 1960s, the Dominican Republic lived in the vacuum created by Rafael Trujillo's assassination and the collapse of his thirty-one-year dictatorship. Initially, Trujillo was replaced by Juan Bosch, a left-of center founder of the opposition Partido Revolucionario Dominicano and former exile who rose from obscurity to become president in December 1962. Bosch managed to hold onto the office for seven months before the Dominican military overthrew him and installed a junta to lead the country.[52]

Bosch's eventual replacement, Donald Reid Cabral, received the open support of the Johnson administration and the mentorship of Thomas Mann. In the context of Mann Doctrine, Reid Cabral's pro-American and pro-business stance were adequate to the basic litmus test for U.S. aid. Moreover, in the absence of a leftist threat to the country, the United States was also perfectly willing to recognize the principle of self-determination and OAS guidelines regarding sovereignty. Under Mann, the country would receive $100 million in loans and assistance.[53]

However, under Reid Cabral, rampant corruption reminiscent of the Trujillo era returned to the Dominican Republic. Both civilian and military *golpistas* engaged in what Piero Gleijeses has described as "an open struggle for the spoils" of their victory over Bosch.[54] Military "canteens" reopened and served senior military officers as duty-free conduits for imports that were later resold on the Dominican black market. In a memorandum to the Departments of State and Defense, McGeorge Bundy openly worried that the United States should prompt "a better distribution of national budget expenditures as between social and economic programs on the one hand and military programs on the other."[55]

Nepotism and bribery also dominated the civilian government, filling offices to bursting with indolent relations of prominent families. As the country staggered onward, formerly optimistic predictions of economic growth diminished. Sugar exports, the mainstay of the Dominican economy, dropped by $2.3 million in 1964. American Peace Corps volunteers reported drought conditions and water shortages that many Dominicans blamed on the Reid Cabral government.[56] While the countryside remained relatively quiet in the midst of this growing turmoil, cities witnessed a series of strikes and demonstrations. In April 1965, ambassador W. Tapley Bennett Jr. rather cryptically cabled his superiors at the State Department that "little foxes some of them red are chewing on the grapes. It is impossible to guarantee a good harvest in view of many unfavorable aspects of local scene. It is however fair to say that a diminution of our effort or a failure to act will result in bitter wine."[57]

Later that same month, a constitutionalist countercoup broke upon this deteriorating situation. At first, American embassy officials on the scene interpreted the action as an effort by lower-ranking military officers to overturn the existing spoils system. As the fighting continued, however, it became increasingly apparent that the rebellion might reinstall Juan Bosch as president. U.S. intelligence reports began to identify the existence of left-wing groups whose purpose was the advancement of a "Castro-type government."[58] An intelligence memorandum written in May flatly stated,

The most dangerous situations exist in countries where the immediate or early result of the overthrow of the government would be the clear threat of substantial Communist gains. In general, this would be so because of the existence of strong Communist or radical extremist forces, the lack of strong democratic institutions, and the lack of either a moderating middle class or a reliable military establishment. In other words, as in the case of the Dominican Republic, there would be little in the social fabric of the society to prevent the Communists from moving quickly to gain influence. In these situations there is also a threat of bloody civil war.[59]

The impending threat to the Dominican Republic was thus based not upon the strength of internal Communist forces, but upon the paucity of stability that U.S. policy had tolerated and, in a very real sense, produced.

In late April and early May 1965, the administration struggled to find a justification for intervention in the Dominican crisis. Initially, Johnson claimed the need for American action "in order to protect American lives [and] nationals of other countries."[60] At the time, according to Robert Dallek, Johnson would engage in the type of hyperbole that typified much his presidency, claiming before listeners that thousands had already been killed in the crisis, many of whom were the victims of horrible atrocities. Later, he expressed concerns that a leftist government in the Dominican Republic would open the door for Communist influence. In conversations with Congressional leaders, the president supported the dispatch of Marines to head off an imminent takeover.[61] Before an American television audience, Johnson declared that "people trained outside the Dominican Republic" were attempting to gain control of the country.[62]

In reality, neither the president nor his key advisors had a clear or accurate understanding of Communist infiltration within the rebellion, Bosch's degree of influence over its conduct, or the danger to American citizens in the Dominican Republic. At the time the crisis broke, Ambassador Bennett was in Georgia on personal leave. Perhaps more important, eleven key members of the U.S. military mission were in Panama attending a conference.[63] For days, officials in Washington received fragmentary information at best. Policy was cast, by default, into the arena of U.S. public opinion and world criticism.

American intervention in the Dominican crisis quickly succeeded in restoring stability. Elections held in 1966 under the auspices of the Organization of American States resulted in Bosch's defeat at the hands of Joachin Belaguer. While the United States at the time complimented the peaceful transition of power into civilian hands, many Dominicans saw his electoral defeat as a simple collective recognition of the foreign and domestic forces arrayed against Bosch and constitutional government.[64]

This skepticism pointed to deeper regional concerns over America's handling of the Dominican crisis, ones that lurked very near the surface of U.S.–Latin American relations. The deployment of American soldiers and marines was the first to the region since 1927, a fact that produced a wave of protests from governments all over the hemisphere. Chile openly condemned the action, while Venezuela demanded a withdrawal of all American troops from the Dominican Republic. When Ellsworth Bunker, U.S. ambassador to the Organization of American States, proposed the formation of an Inter-American Peace Force in the aftermath of the U.S. deployment, Mexico, Uruguay, Chile, Ecuador, and Peru voted against it. A statement made by one Latin American diplomat to *Newsweek* summed up the frustrations of many: "Let's face it. The U.S. dominates this continent economically, militarily, and politically—and the main goal of your foreign policy is to keep it that way."[65]

Nearly a year after the Dominican crisis, a White House memorandum by William G. Bowdler, titled "Latin America: Year-End Round-Up," offered a much different interpretation:

On the whole, 1965 was a good year for Latin America and the United States. Only the Dominican crisis deflected us from our general line of pressing forward on economic and social progress and strengthening democratic institutions. But even this crisis was not without its positive aspects, particularly with respect to the greater awareness of the need for strengthened collective security arrangements and the organization of an Inter-American Peace Force.[66]

The creation of the peacekeeping force in 1965 represented a significant break with precedent and was, in the end, an outcome that American diplomats had sought in the twenty years following the Rio Pact.[67] Yet the degree of damage to the Alliance for Progress did not completely escape officials in Washington. At the conclusion of Johnson's term, Assistant Secretary of State for Inter-American Affairs Covey T. Oliver produced a memorandum that generally complemented the United States for its support of democracy in Latin America. He noted that there had been no unconstitutional changes in government for most of 1966 and all of 1967. On the face of it, the hemisphere was stable. However, Oliver commented,

At the same time, many Latin American countries have not really enlisted the full cooperation, borne of conviction, of those who fear integration, and those who must share economic and political power. The still unanswered question of the Alliance is whether those who have power and resources are willing to accept institutional reforms that will result in more equitable sharing.[68]

In the final analysis, this situation existed because neither "Johnson Doctrine" nor the policies produced by Thomas Mann represented a coherent blueprint for U.S. action in Latin America. Contemporary commentators remarked on the "impulsive" nature of a foreign policy that was often the product of "an improvised grab bag of scissors-and-paste decisions."[69] James Reston complained in an editorial for the *New York Times* of "an air of commotion around the White House."[70] Modern scholars have accepted this lack of focus as an article of faith. Joseph Tulchin has characterized a U.S. policy driven by "spasmodic reactions to crises in the Caribbean Basin" and "an over-powering fear that instability would lead to 'another Cuba' in the hemisphere."[71] As was the case with the Kennedy administration, anti-Communism maintained the trajectory of American efforts in Latin America. However, whereas Kennedy accepted at least the principle of political reform as a precursor for progress, his successor sacrificed it for the sake of security policies that would cultivate advocates of free trade and anti-Communism.

REVOLUTION AND COUNTERREVOLUTION
IN CENTRAL AMERICA

By the mid-1960s, political tumult prompted by the Cuban revolution, *Alianza* reforms, economic growth pains, and an array of factors continued to roil through Central America. In many cases, the political discourse devolved into armed rebellion by dissidents outside the existing power structure. In others, revolution appeared in the *golpes* that captured power from within governments. At mid-decade, the guerrilla war in Guatemala raged on, exacting a terrible toll on the rural inhabitants of the Zacapa and Izabal provinces in the northeastern portion of the country.[72] Guerrilla bands occupied border sanctuaries in both Honduras and Costa Rica, repeatedly striking minor targets all along the Nicaraguan border. Reactionary regimes also placed the political opposition in many nations under siege. In El Salvador, Colonel Julio Rivera constructed, with U.S. assistance, the Salvadoran National Security Agency, an extensive domestic intelligence service designed to root out and eliminate leftist opponents. In Honduras, a military coup against Ramon Villeda Morales resulted briefly in a U.S. aid cutoff. Assistance resumed after the Honduran military reestablished the democratic form of government and allowed a hand-picked congress to appoint Colonel Osvaldo Lopez Arellano as president.[73]

In other instances, however, the Latin American political debate coalesced around more permanent, peaceful challenges to the status quo. One excellent example of this trend was the growth of the Christian Democratic movement. By the mid-1960s, Christian Democratic parties had grown to become influential forces in Chile, Venezuela, Peru, and El Salvador. Christian Democrats were part of the Peruvian coalition that helped Fernando Belaunde to the presidency in 1963. Eduardo Frei's September 1964 victory in Chile was notable because of his affiliation with Christian Democrats.

A significant appeal of Christian Democracy was its focus on ideology rather than the *personalismo* that dominated much of Latin American politics. More specifically, Christian Democrats' advocacy of a "third position" or *tercerismo* benefited from its embrace of social reform as well as the broad populism of anti-Communism and anti-Americanism.[74] For a young class of educated, upwardly mobile Latin Americans, the product in many respects of the region's improving economy and the *Alianza*, Christian Democracy offered a credible means of political participation and social reform. A worrisome trend for American leaders was the demonstrated intent of many Christian Democratic parties to pursue political alliances with the Latin American left, particularly with organized labor. U.S. observers believed that political alliances of convenience might allow leftist radicals and Communists to infiltrate the movement from within and manipulate the concept of *tercerismo* for less noble purposes.[75]

For the most part, the Christian Democratic movement was small and localized in Central America. An official party was not founded until 1963 in Costa Rica and saw its appeal limited by the progressive policies of the Francisco José Orlich

Bolmarcich.[76] In Guatemala, the movement was tiny, but highly active and opposed by Enrique Peralta Azurdia's military regime. In El Salvador, Christian Democrats were the only legal opposition to the military governments that dominated politics in the 1960s, controlling a third of the national legislature at mid-decade.[77]

In Nicaragua, the Christian Democratic concept jelled only in the late 1950s and served to influence a rising generation of young politicians who eventually joined the Conservative Party's opposition to the Somoza regime. As a distinct political entity, it was not until 1965 that the Nicaraguan Social Christian Party held its first national convention. The party platform endorsed principles familiar to the larger movement: "integrating in the commonwealth marginal sectors of the population," and the "reconstruction of the National Unity of Central America," as well as "just and friendly relations in the Inter-American system" and "international social justice."[78] Initially, the party refused to join in an alliance with the Nicaraguan left, particularly the Republican Mobilization Party, an organization targeted by the Schick government for its Communist pretensions.[79]

Outside the realm of traditional party politics, Christian Democracy affected the Central American political discourse on two additional important levels. Christian Democrats understood that their political traction in most Central American countries was severely limited by the explicit power of established elites. Instead of confronting these interests head on, Christian Democrats focused on proselytizing at the grassroots level. Through the vehicle of the "Christian base community," advocates could challenge the fundamental assumptions of the sociopolitical order in language understandable to the average *campesino*.[80] Gustavo Gutierrez questioned, for example, the "contradiction" that existed between the egalitarian virtues stressed by democracy and the Darwinian competition of the unregulated marketplace.[81] As part of his work with the community of Solentiname, Ernesto Cardenal used New Testament passages from the gospel according to Matthew to lead discussions that addressed power, oppression, and justice.[82]

On a much broader, academic level, Christian Democracy dovetailed with a growing intellectual critique of capitalism and its role in Latin America. The post–1945 period was filled with a vehement, often vitriolic discourse regarding the proper role of private enterprise and the negative impact of U.S. investment in Latin America. Latin Americans made the case that the world capitalist system existed because of asymmetrical structures of wealth. Contrary to the arguments made by Millikan and Rostow, officials such as Raul Prebisch asserted that that the extension of orthodox Western liberal economic models had damaged rather than helped the developing economies of the hemisphere.[83] After the United States began to actually implement the suggestions of Millikan, Rostow, and other structural modernization theorists as part of the Alliance for Progress, the running critique gained a new lease on life. As Robert Packenham has pointed out, the "dependency" school that emerged during the mid-1960s in the work of Albert O. Hirschman and, later, in the scholarship of Andre Gunder Frank, Fernando Henrique Cardoso, and Enzo Faletto, attacked the basic structures introduced by modernization, pointing out, for example, the fallacy that the comparative advantage produced by industrialization could create positive derivative benefits for host nations. As the 1960s progressed, so too did this chorus of critics.[84]

Americans stationed in Central America were somewhat at sea when confronting the multiple levels of this debate. Rather than attempt to engage Latin Americans in substantive discussion at any point, U.S. officials sidestepped the issues presented by fixing their attention on the idea of neutrality in local politics. Throughout the documents that addressed U.S. policy at the operational or embassy level, Americans repeated the refrain that the United States should defer from interference in any one part of domestic Central American politics.

In place of dialogue, Americans stressed, as they had since the Eisenhower administration, the merits of self-help in both political and economic policy. A 1965 statement by the U.S. embassy in Managua reflected this emphasis:

The basic goals of a few years ago of attempting to ease violent political antipathies and of starting the country on the path of sound social and economic development appear largely to have been accomplished. While these developments have been consistent with U.S. policy objectives, the most important factor in their achievement has undoubtably been the efforts of the Nicaraguans themselves, who have in self-interest pursued moderate and constructive courses of action in an effort to capitalize upon the economic prosperity which the country has recently been enjoying.[85]

Both the U.S. Agency for International Development office and the rest of the country team in Managua made further references in 1966 to the link between entrepreneurial spirit and political liberalization. They believed that the "ever-increasing numbers of young entrepreneurs" had become a "force for democracy and against limited dictatorial or autocratic domination." This trend, the product of American loans to the small businessman and farmer, had strengthened "individual initiative and self-respect" and promoted "the will and confidence to act individually and collectively for constructive ends."[86] The problem of economic growth and democratic development could therefore be accomplished without explicit American involvement.

For Central Americans, the argument for the reforming virtue of entrepreneurship too often fell on deaf ears, deflected as it was by the animosity of embittered political opponents, but, more important, by the growing realization that free-market principles worked against their past traditions, present status, and future prospects. Some, like Marco Antonio Yon Sosa in Guatemala or Carlos Fonseca Amador in Nicaragua, were clearly willing to abandon any peaceful recourse in favor of the Cuban model of armed revolution. These individuals were in the minority, however. The remainder of the dissident political leadership of Central America struggled within the realm of overt politics against the entrenched, vested interests of the old elite. The mid-1960s would become a period, described by Edelberto Torres-Rivas, in which a new bourgeoisie, motivated by their changing socioeconomic status, sought out a means to find their political voice.[87]

THE SCHICK INTERIM

Nicaraguan politics in the period after the 1963 elections were dominated by preparations for the next presidential campaign. Although the Nicaraguan constitution prescribed campaigning until one year prior to the actual balloting, most parties began their maneuvering soon after René Schick was inaugurated.[88] Foremost among these aspirants was Anastasio "Tachito" Somoza Debayle. Commenting on the political climate in the country, the U.S. embassy noted,

The principle cloud upon the horizon appears to be the forthcoming presidential election of 1967 and the ill-disguised ambition of General Anastasio Somoza Debayle to be Nicaragua's next president. If the General does not run, political tension will undoubtably again increase and the possibility of violence exists.[89]

Ambassador Aaron Brown was particularly dismissive of the youngest Somoza, describing him after one encounter as "a small boy in a soldier suit."[90] Brown was aware that Somoza was engaged in an almost a constant effort to publicly interpret American actions as support and align the United States with his political future. The ambassador was also cognizant of Somoza's attempts to manipulate American policy makers. In a policy assessment conducted at the conclusion of 1965, he flatly stated,

He [Somoza] is not above attempting a crude policy of divide and conquer, seeking to set one agency of the U.S. Government against the other, casting himself in the role of the bluff but good hearted soldier deliberately misunderstood and misguided by U.S. civilian officials who either unwittingly encourage, or worse are sympathetic to, his "leftist" opponents. In this simple minded context, even such an avowed anti-communist as Pedro Joachim Chamorro, editor of opposition *La Prensa*, becomes a Bolshevik.[91]

American intelligence analysts speculated that Somoza believed he had essentially been promised the presidency by his family so that he could continue its line of succession. Despite warnings from his own Liberal party, Somoza began campaigning almost immediately after Schick's inauguration in May 1963.[92] Cautioned that these affairs violated electoral law, he suspended his efforts briefly in September, only to resume a series of highly orchestrated outpourings of public support for his leadership. In May 1964, thousands "celebrated" his promotion to General de Division of the *Guardia Nacional.*[93] Somoza would continue what an American observer called "seemingly endless *homenajes* to 'celebrate his promotion,'" and, in the months that followed, celebrations that included his birthday, his wedding anniversary, and a Boy Scout jamboree. The general made a point to travel to carefully placed *Guardia* civic action projects to receive his due credit, while delivering speeches that embellished the work of his soldiers and asked for their vigilance against extremism from the left.[94]

In the wake of this juggernaut, Schick struggled to establish his own political identity. Stung by accusations regarding the fraudulent origin of his administration, the new president dedicated himself to discussions with the Conservative opposition regarding electoral reform before the 1967 election. Schick symbolically reached out to Conservatives by announcing an eight-day state of official mourning upon the death of ex-president Adolfo Diaz. He also attempted to draw Liberals from the Partido Liberal Independiente back into his government by offering them administrative appointments. PLI member Jorge Ramirez Acevedo was named to the important post of Minister of Development in 1964. This action succeeded to a degree and prompted other younger PLI members to endorse the idea of rejoining the administration, arguing that they could reform it from within.[95] Overall, the president's actions were described by the American embassy as "a major improvement over the situation in which Nicaragua found itself only a decade ago."[96]

Schick surprisingly demonstrated a willingness to flex a degree of administrative muscle by opening a military investigation against *Guardia* Colonel Juan Angel Lopez for corruption.[97] The action was a reflection of the substantial degree of friction between Schick and his National Guard commander. In a discussion with Ambassador Brown, Schick mentioned that he was "deeply troubled" by Somoza's premature campaign. Privately, he had suggested, along with Luis Somoza, that Anastasio reduce or eliminate his political efforts in order to lessen growing tensions within the country.[98] Publicly, Schick often contrasted his own modest behavior with that of Tachito. Before a press conference in December 1964, he stated that the general, with his obvious popularity, had no need to engage in political propaganda.[99]

Schick was also careful to never challenge the basic assumptions of American policy at any point. His comments after Thomas Mann's 1964 speech on Latin America were blandly summarized by, "Its concepts merit the sympathy and applause of my Government."[100] His support was reciprocated by a visit from Mann in 1965 in which the American reiterated support for Nicaraguan sovereignty. Mann also engaged in token discussions of renegotiating the 1914 Bryan–Chamorro Treaty and the construction of a second canal in Nicaragua and Costa Rica.[101]

Schick's careful approach to his duties and Somoza's concurrent aggressiveness were products of a political climate notable for the degree of disarray within the Nicaraguan opposition. The Liberal Independent Party badly split over the issue of cooperation with the Schick administration. In May 1964, the PLI general secretary told those who chose to join the government that they did so on their own. Later, the party's Board of Discipline went so far as to expel a number of its members for joining the administration.[102]

Generally, the Nicaraguan left was riven with debates over the proper course of action against the new regime in Managua. The membership of openly Marxist parties argued vociferously over whether they should maintain a hard line against Schick or embrace a "popular front" approach that allowed for a coalition movement with other members of the opposition. Alvaro Ramirez Gonzalez resigned as secretary general of the Movilizacion Republicana in May 1964 because party moderates refused to align themselves more closely with overt Communist organizations such as the Partido Socialista Nicaragüense and the Sandinistas.[103] The moderate course produced fairly dubious results. May Day demonstrations in 1964 produced a small procession of perhaps 1,500 people, drawn mostly from leftist unions. Only a tiny number, thirty-five to fifty according to embassy observers, came from moderate groups such as the Social Christian Autonomous Trade Union Movement of Nicaragua.[104]

To a large extent, this turmoil was also produced by leadership disputes within the opposition. Conservative Party leader Fernando Agüero Rocha continued to be a lightning rod for interparty squabbles within the largest anti-Somoza bloc. Many loyal party members had been dismayed by Agüero's personal conduct during the 1963 elections. They were incensed, according to Thomas Walker, "by Agüero's hollow demagoguery and comic revolution."[105] In February 1963, in the aftermath of the election, Reinaldo Téfel, who had helped Agüero gain control of the party in 1960, published an article condemning the PCT leadership for "its absolute lack of imagination" during the campaign. Two months later, Téfel and the entire steering committee of the PCT resigned and joined the Social Christian Party.[106] What preserved Agüero's leadership, according to American officials, was his continued popular appeal, a *conquistando la masa*, that had occurred in 1960 and carried forward after Schick's election.[107] In its aftermath, Agüero's efforts to consolidate the local PCT party structure around his own personal leadership alienated many of the older Conservative faithful and drew criticism for his "dictatorial, tactless, and selfish" methods.[108] The American embassy characterized his belief that the increasingly divisive political atmosphere would eventually mandate direct OAS or American intervention as a "dreamworld."[109] As the unofficial campaign for the 1967 presidential election progressed, Agüero was openly challenged by Pedro Joachim Chamorro, who attempted to form a unified opposition that included elements of the PCT, the PLI, and the Partido Liberal Nacional led by Julio Quintana, a Somoza rival and presidential aspirant.[110]

Until its final, bloody end, the campaign leading to the 1967 election was notable for its lack of drama. A review of the individual platforms from the primary parties revealed very few substantive differences. Most endorsed private property, the protection of life, and the principle of due process under the law.[111] Agüero's speeches focused more on the particulars of economic development and reform than on a basic statement of objectives that would set his party apart from his Liberal rival, Anastasio Somoza.[112] Somoza's own acceptance speech at his party's national convention in July 1966 was a dry discourse on the technical aspects of the *Alianza* and his proposals to reform Nicaraguan programs currently in progress.[113]

The sparks that did fly related primarily to personalities. Agüero took a hard line against the PLN and Somoza, claiming that an election free of fraud was impossible. He lost few opportunities to denounce either the Somoza "dynasty" or its corrupt membership.[114] For his own part, Somoza labeled Conservatives as radical proponents of armed revolution. The seizure of weapons and ammunition from the home of prominent PCT official Julio Cardenal in January 1965 appeared to provide at least some evidence that a repeat of Agüero's 1963 threat of a violent rebellion was possible.[115]

As the election campaign developed, Somoza attempted to sidetrack the opposition with a political deal. Borrowing a page from his father's book, regime officials met with Agüero in early 1965 to discuss the prospect of adopting a "National Plan" in which the Liberal and Conservative parties would alternate control of the government.[116] Somoza, according to the proposal, would receive the presidency first.

In an effort to discuss more legitimate ideas and encourage engagement with the opposition, Schick also met with the PCT to discuss changes in the national electoral law. Conservatives demanded inclusion in the national electoral tribunal, a distribution of seats in the Chamber of Deputies according to voter turnout instead of the normal one-third granted to the runner-up as dictated by law, and direct elections for municipal authorities.[117] Although few contemporary observers gave Agüero a realistic chance of achieving any of his party's demands, they took some solace in the fact that he was talking instead of denouncing the political process.

For its own part, the embassy publicly embraced only the "continuation of an orderly political transition from personal authoritarian rule to representative civil government now under way."[118] Overall, American officials endorsed a hands-off approach regarding any political party. Ambassador Brown counseled the State Department in Washington that the United States should "avoid identification with *any* candidate in this political jungle."[119] Once the election process ground forward, however, he would find this stance increasingly tenuous.

As the campaign moved forward into 1966, Nicaraguan Conservatives surprised many by conducting a credible grassroots campaign that spent significant time in both the western urban enclaves and the countryside. Speaking to mass rallies of farmers and local townspeople in Granada, Chinandega, Matagalpa, and Managua, Agüero hammered away against the exclusivity and corruption of the Somoza regime and stressed the need for an "eclectic conglomeration" to form an alliance for liberty and justice.[120] In addition, the PCT convention in May was a calm contrast to the interparty squabbling that had characterized the 1962 campaign. One of the more important decisions was to join a more general opposition union. Excepting parties espousing "exotic foreign doctrines" such as communism, the motion was approved unanimously by delegates of the party.[121]

These efforts culminated in the creation of the Union Nacional Opositora, a grouping of the PCT, the Independent Liberal Party, and the Social Christians.[122] Although initially reluctant to share political power, the sense that he might enjoy broad support at the head of a coalition was reinforced by a mass rally that welcomed Agüero when he returned to Nicaragua from a visit to the United States in October 1966. The event stunned both Liberals and Conservatives. Reliable estimates of the mob that greeted him in Managua ranged from 50,000 to 100,000. Campesinos dominated the crowd, but observers noted substantial PLI, Republican Mobilization Party, and Social Christian representation. Suddenly, it appeared that the anti-Somoza opposition had polarized around the Conservatives.[123]

The event clearly placed the regime on the defensive. Long-time rival and Minister of Government Julio Quintana was openly critical of Somoza. Quintana predicted electoral fraud if Somoza managed to win in 1967 and painted an election-day scenario that would likely see violent disorders.[124]

Despite Quintana's pessimism regarding the regime's future, the united opposition proved unable to sustain itself. Problems emerged almost immediately over the composition of a joint UNO platform. In fact, amidst the euphoria of the October rally, little thought had been given to a common opposition objectives. When Agüero returned from the United States, the PCT had yet to publish its own party platform. This problem was compounded by Agüero's half-hearted efforts to reconcile differences with coalition Liberals. As the prospects of an election coalition began to diminish, he again sought out U.S. intervention to prevent a presidential ballot in 1967. Agüero dragged out arguments familiar from years past, claiming violence directed against regime opponents and, more plausibly, the possibility of fraud in the voter registration drives that occupied the month of November. Moreover, he requested intervention by the OAS Commission on Human Rights to observe the election process.[125]

Unbeknownst to Agüero, the U.S. embassy had begun to move from its strict neutrality as early as 1965. Ambassador Brown dismissed any legitimate public support for Somoza and openly entertained the possibility that someone, perhaps Luis Somoza, would attempt to talk him out his bid for the presidency. Brown speculated, "He [Anastasio Somoza] may realize as many observers of the scene do that the time has gone by when a president can peacefully be imposed on a country in the face of widespread opposition."[126] The State Department appeared prepared to consider some manner of support for the moderate opposition.[127] At the conclusion of 1965, the embassy concurred, recommending not only neutrality toward Somoza, but support for "a responsible opposition in the next election and in the next government."[128] The problem that confronted American policy makers was finding a credible candidate aside from Agüero. A significant blow to this process was the death of René Schick in the middle of the 1966 campaign year. His replacement by Lorenzo Guerrero Gutierrez, an old member of the PLN who had served as ambassador to Mexico under the elder Somoza during World War II, offered little hope of a moderate solution. According to the embassy, Guerrero was a man of substantially less stature than Schick and was more likely to consult with the Somozas and "equate national interests with those of the [Liberal] party."[129]

All attention to the political process was soon swept away by violence. An initial indicator was a clash between civilians and the *Guardia* on 7 January 1967 outside a Managua movie theater, which resulted in a number of arrests and considerable property damage. The U.S. embassy ominously warned that although incidents of campaign violence had been few, the "superficial quiet may conceal deep seated anti-Somoza frustration."[130] Further discouraging to American officials in Managua was a call by Luis Somoza one week later for voters to eschew the secret ballot and announce their votes at the polling places. This statement was criticized roundly as further evidence of the Somozas' antidemocratic attitudes.[131]

A major confrontation was not long in coming. It began on 22 January, when a march of some 60,000 people conducted by the united opposition was interrupted by the *Guardia*. The confrontation rapidly devolved into a running gun battle throughout the Nicaraguan capital. As the situation unraveled, bands of youths attempted to set fire to the National Palace, the seat of most government ministries, with Molotov cocktails. Initial reports indicated a "general melee" between civilians and troops and the exchange of automatic-weapons fire by both sides throughout the city. According to the embassy, clashes on the first day resulted in sixteen dead and sixty-six wounded.[132]

The focal point of the riot was a standoff at Managua's Gran Hotel between regime opponents led by Fernando Agüero and the National Guard. As the dissidents attempted to negotiate their surrender, American concerns focused on the fate of twenty U.S. citizens who were also trapped in the hotel. While Walt Rostow kept the president appraised of the tense situation, the embassy intervened to negotiate the safety of those trapped within the *Guardia* cordon. All were eventually released when Agüero and his fellow Conservatives finally surrendered.

A mass crackdown followed the disturbance. Radio stations and opposition newspaper offices, *La Prensa's* the most prominent among them, were seized outright by the military. Numerous arrests also followed in the wake of the clashes. The government-controlled *Novedades* published a list of 125 of those arrested, although regime opponents speculated that the actual numbers were much higher. Rumors of torture and executions held outside Managua ran rampant. During a conversation with the American ambassador, the Auxiliary Bishop of Managua, Donaldo Chavez y Nunez reported that he had personally witnessed the brutal arrests of citizens caught up in the military dragnet that had followed the uprising.[133] In a statement released to the press a few days after the riots, Senator Robert Kennedy condemned "the ugly specter of civil war" in Nicaragua.[134]

Following the aftermath of this bloody event, Somoza managed a sweeping victory against Agüero. His National Liberal Party won 480,162 votes (74%) to 157,432 (24%) for the UNO. The Nicaraguan Conservative Party managed to receive only 14,650 (2%) ballots.[135] The final outcome of the election was met with "resigned bitterness" from the united opposition and "indifference" on the part of the general public. The American embassy commented,

The Somoza margin is simply not credible, particularly in traditionally Conservative departments, and the apparent inability of the UNO to carry even one of the 134 municipalities conveys the impression of a callous Somoza determination to leave the opposition absolutely nothing in the best "public be damned" tradition.[136]

Stability was won at a very high price. While the rule of law was maintained during the February elections, its spirit suffered in their aftermath. Anastasio Somoza Debayle became the president of Nicaragua, as his father and brother had before him. The regime continued its trajectory seemingly uninterrupted. The present appeared to mirror the past. But it was a weakened trajectory. Where Luis Somoza had at least entertained the prospect of criticism and stepped aside as president in 1963, his brother pursued the office without regard for even a glancing effort at propriety. Absent was any sense that compromise was possible. In the wake of this realization was a hardening of position, both with respect to the Nicaraguan opposition and the United States. The former would seek alternatives to the political status quo, while the latter would cling to a steadily diminishing hope that the political climate could someday change.

CONCLUSIONS

Officials left over from the Kennedy administration, men like John Cabot, would claim after their departure from government that the Alliance for Progress suffered under Lyndon Johnson. They would question his level of commitment to substantive political reform in the hemisphere.[137] They would question as well the administration's apparent fixation on the need to fight communism despite its diminishing threat to Latin America. As late as 1967, for example, the U.S. embassy in Managua received instructions to provide materials to the local media to "illustrate the true nature of Communism and its threat to free nations of the world."[138]

However, American policy was more the product of constraints than of Lyndon Johnson's particular individual faults. The historical characterization of Johnson's approach to Latin America as reactionary is essentially true.[139] Unfortunately, this falls short of the mark in the sense that it focuses solely on the external factors that were relevant to foreign policy making (i.e. Castroism, communism, etc.). To understand the real nature of decision making in the Johnson White House, it is essential to reflect upon the domestic forces that played a tug-of-war with the president's attention.

The U.S. reaction to the threat of political instability in the hemisphere had more to do with domestic American pressures and the perception of communism than its actual reality. The Panamanian crisis and the Dominican intervention are replete with examples whereupon, in the absence of substantive evidence of an imminent Communist takeover, the fear of appearing weak to domestic constituencies, particularly hawks in both parties, drove the administration forward. Conversely, domestic disinterest in providing additional funding for the alliance also drove U.S. policy. As the administration progressed, so too did growing public and Congressional restiveness regarding the cost of American foreign affairs, a problem compounded by Johnson's escalation of American military deployments to Vietnam.

Within this context, Mann Doctrine appears less a dedicated effort to build pro-American, pro-capitalist alliances in Latin America at any price than the simple recognition of severe limitations on concrete action. Contemporary comparisons of Mann Doctrine to American policy during the Eisenhower era were appropriate. Mann was tasked to provide a plan for U.S. action in Latin America that would reduce U.S. costs and produce stability. His greater reliance on Latin Americans themselves indicated not only a simple shortage of resources, but of a realistic assessment of the possibility that the United States could not readily influence actual political improvements in the hemisphere.

Moreover, it is highly unlikely that, had he been inclined, Mann possessed the time necessary to influence policy beyond his own level of leadership. Mann spent barely a year as Assistant Secretary of State for Inter-American Affairs before moving on to serve as Undersecretary of State for Economic Affairs in 1965. Accordingly, his own agenda failed to penetrate in any significant manner down through the State Department hierarchy, particularly to the embassy level. There were no major systemic policy reassessments of the hemisphere made during his term. In fact, a country analysis and strategy paper for Latin American nations was not requested by the State Department until December 1968.[140]

The changing nature of challenges to Central American stability complicated U.S. efforts to effect reform. By mid-decade, it was apparent that the region was fragmenting into an array of competing revolutionary movements. Guerrillas in Guatemala and Nicaragua continued to pursue violent opposition to the regimes then in power, failing often in their attempts to replicate Castro's previous success. Increasingly, however, armed opponents found their campaigns overlapping with vocal and articulate efforts that openly challenged the political status quo and the forces that dominated it. Exemplified by the Christian Democrat movement, but present in center–left parties across the spectrum, these activists eschewed both the internal Liberal–Conservative dichotomy and the Cold War, emphasizing instead grassroots demands for political reform and socioeconomic equity. Common to their campaigns were calls for alternations to electoral laws, land reform, additional revenues for housing, and checks against U.S. economic intrusion. Their greatest obstacle, aside from official repression, was the comparative difficulty faced in cobbling together coherent, unified coalitions to achieve reform, a process that exposed Christian Democrats to considerable criticism and U.S. scrutiny. Alfredo Hoffman, president of the small Christian Democrat labor federation in Honduras, openly maintained close ties with the Honduran Communist Party to bolster his standing in the country. Overall, the Christian Democrat tendency to tolerate if not endorse the leftist fringe would prove to be a significant handicap as the 1960s progressed.

The course of political events in Nicaragua was indicative of all of these trends. The Mann Doctrine's tolerance of local initiative in the service of American interests nicely complemented a U.S. embassy inclined to remain in the background of Nicaraguan politics. Unfortunately, the doctrine also embellished American inaction at a time when Anastasio Somoza was manhandling electoral law almost at will. By 1965, the embassy discovered it had painted itself into a corner and reacted by considering the abandonment of strict neutrality and support for a viable non-Somoza candidate. The lack of consistency that characterized U.S. policy in Nicaragua proved to be a considerable handicap at a moment when the political legitimacy of the regime was suffering the most. The embassy's inability to apply a brake to the Somoza presidential campaign would only encourage further transgressions from Managua.

Within Nicaragua itself, the leftist opposition to the regime faced an interesting paradox. When Fernando Agüero began his campaign for president, he embraced the fundamentals of reformist politics, addressing the common problems of growth and corruption. In doing so, he managed to capture the support of thousands of Nicaraguans outside of his Conservative Party. Unfortunately, Agüero was marginalized by internal divisions within the united opposition, overt regime effort to peel away support for his candidacy, and his own penchant for grandstanding. Moreover, Agüero could never disassociate himself from the armed opposition to the regime, a perception the regime fed during the campaign, and one that defined his coalition during the January 1967 riots that engulfed the capital.[141] As Anastasio Somoza prepared to enter office, his political enemies were at an impasse, forced by circumstance and their own weakness to consider new avenues to power.

NOTES

1. Dean Rusk, *As I Saw It* (New York: W. W. Norton, 1990), 403.

2. Remarks of the President at the Ceremony Commemorating the Fourth Anniversary of the Alliance for Progress, 17 August 1965, Lyndon Baines Johnson Library (hereafter LBJ), White House Central File (hereafter WHCF), Subject File, Speeches, Box 177.

3. Ibid.

4. Office of the White House Press Secretary, "Remarks of the President to the Ambassadors of the Alliance for Progress Participating Nations," 11 May 1964, LBJ, Office Files of the White House Aides, Fred Panzer, Box 472.

5. U.S. Department of State, Agency for International Development, "Impressions from Latin American Tour," 20 December 1965, LBJ, National Security File (hereafter NSF), Country File, Latin America, Box 2.

6. Office of Policy and Research, Research Service, "Detailed Media Reaction to President's Alliance for Progress Speech," 24 August 1966, LBJ, WHCF, Subject File, Speeches, Box 183.

7. Sacha Vollman, *Quien impondra la democracia?* (Mexico City: Centro de Estudios y Documentacion Sociales, A.C., 1965), i.

8. Albert O. Hirschman, *Journeys toward Progress: Studies of Economic Policy-Making in Latin America* (New York: Twentieth Century Fund, 1963), 227–230, 276–298.

9. *Congressional Record*, vol. 106, part 12, 16 June 1960, 11855 (Washington, D.C.: U.S. Government Printing Office, 1960).

10. Letter, Raymond F. Mikesell to Wayne Morse, 15 May 1962, John Fitzgerald Kennedy Library (hereafter JFK), Jack N. Behrman Papers, Box 1.

11. Interview, Dean Rusk, 2 January 1970, LBJ, Oral History Collection, 6. Interview, Lincoln Gordon, 10 July 1969, LBJ, Oral History Collection, 12.

12. Robert Dallek, *Flawed Giant: Lyndon Johnson and His Times, 1961–1973* (New York: Oxford University Press, 1998), 91; Tom Wicker, *JFK and LBJ. The Influence of Personality upon Politics* (Baltimore: Penguin, 1969), 196.

13. Doris Kearns, *Lyndon Johnson and the American Dream* (New York: Harper and Row, 1976), 64–66.

14. Office of the White House Press Secretary, "Remarks of the President to the Ambassadors of the Alliance for Progress Participating Nations," 11 May 1964.

15. Lyndon Baines Johnson, *The Vantage Point: Perspectives of the Presidency, 1963–1969* (New York: Popular Library, 1971), 347.

16. Ibid., 347–351.

17. Kearns, *Lyndon Johnson and the American Dream*, 291.

18. Rusk, *As I Saw It*, 403.

19. Waldo Heinrichs, "Lyndon Johnson: Change and Continuity," in *Lyndon Johnson Confronts the World: American Foreign Policy, 1963–1968*, ed. Warren I. Cohen and Nancy Bernkopf Tucker (New York: Cambridge University Press, 1994), 21. For a specific examination of Lyndon Johnson's leadership style within the American policy-making community, see David C. Humphrey, "NSC Meetings during the Johnson Presidency," *Diplomatic History* 18 (1994). 29 46.

20. Heinrichs, "Lyndon Johnson," 24; Kearns, *Lyndon Johnson and the American Dream*, 286–308. See also H. W. Brands, *The Wages of Globalism: Lyndon Johnson and the Limits of American Power* (New York: Oxford University Press, 1995), 3–22, Humphrey, "NSC Meetings during the Johnson Presidency," 29–46.

21. Department of State, Agency for International Development, "Memorandum for Members of the Ball Committee," 11 February 1964, LBJ, WHCF, Confidential File, Subject File, Foreign Affairs, Box 46. See also "My Mr. Latin America," *Newsweek*, 6 January 1964, 39–40.

22. "One Mann & 20 Problems," *Time*, 31 January 1964, 15–18. See also Interview, Gordon, 10 July 1969, 14.

23. "Can LBJ Help Latin America Solve Its Problems?" *U.S. News & World Report*, 30 December 1963, 32–33.

24. Ibid.

25. Commencement Address by the Honorable Thomas C. Mann, Assistant Secretary of State for Inter-American Affairs at the University of Notre Dame, "The Democratic Ideal in Our Policy toward Latin America," 7 June 1964, LBJ, NSF, Country File, Latin America, Box 2.

26. Ibid.

27. "One Mann & 20 Problems," 15.

28. "Can LBJ Help Latin America Solve Its Problems?" 33.

29. Emmet John Hughes, "A Mann for LBJ's Season," *Newsweek*, 18 May 1964, 25.

30. Thomas C. Mann, "Report to the President on the Alliance for Progress," March–May 1964, 22 April 1964, LBJ, NSF, Agency File, Box 4.

31. Hughes, "A Mann for LBJ's Season," 25.

32. Mann, "The Democratic Ideal in Our Policy toward Latin America," 7 June 1964.

33. Interview, Thomas C. Mann, 4 November 1968, LBJ, Oral History Collection, 13.

34. "My Mr. Latin America," 39.

35. Central Intelligence Agency, Office of Current Intelligence, "Instability in Latin America," 18 May 1965, LBJ, NSF, Country File, Latin America, Box 2.

36. U.S. Department of State, Director of Intelligence and Research, "An Outline Guide to Communist Activities in Latin America," 20 October 1964, LBJ, NSF, Country File, Latin America, Box 2.

37. Nicola Miller, *Soviet Relations with Latin America, 1959–1987* (New York: Cambridge University Press, 1989), 5; Joseph G. Whelan and Michael J. Dixon, *The Soviet Union in the Third World: Threat to World Peace* (New York: International Defense Publishers, 1986), 280; Carol R. Saivetz and Sylvia Woodby, *Soviet–Third World Relations* (Boulder, Colo.: Westview Press, 1985), 145; John Lewis Gaddis, *The Long Peace: Inquiries into the History of the Cold War* (New York: Oxford University Press, 1987), 239.

38. State, "An Outline Guide to Communist Activities in Latin America," 20 October 1964.

39. Ibid.

40. Ibid.

41. Cole Blasier, *The Giant's Rival: The USSR and Latin America* (Pittsburgh: University of Pittsburgh Press, 1987), 37–38, 49–52.

42. John Lewis Gaddis, *We Now Know: Rethinking Cold War History* (New York: Clarendon Press, 1997), 152–158; *The United States and the End of the Cold War: Implications, Reconsiderations, Provocations* (New York: Oxford University Press, 1992), 18–86.

43. Charles H. Savage Jr., "After Castro," *America*, 24 November 1962, 1129–1130.

44. Brands, *The Wages of Globalism*, 30–61; Walter LaFeber, *The Panama Canal: The Crisis in Historical Perspective* (New York: Oxford University Press, 1978), 132–140.

45. John H. Coatsworth, *Central America and the United States: The Clients and the Colossus* (New York: Twayne, 1994), 95–96.

46. Interview, Mann, 4 November 1968, 15–17.

47. Dallek, *Flawed Giant*, 94.

48. Ibid.

49. Joseph E. Tulchin, "The Promise of Progress: U.S. Relations with Latin America during the Administration of Lyndon B. Johnson," in *Lyndon Johnson Confronts the World: American Policy, 1963–1968*, ed. Warren I. Cohen and Nancy Bernkopf Tucker (New York: Cambridge University Press, 1994), 229–230.

50. Cable, Embassy (Managua) to State, 11 February 1965, National Archives and Records Administration (hereafter NARA), Records Group 59 (hereafter RG 59), Subject–Numeric File, 1964–66, Box 2514.

51. LaFeber, *The Panama Crisis*, 145–148.

52. Piero Gleijeses, *The Dominican Crisis: The 1965 Constitutionalist Revolt and American Intervention* (Baltimore: Johns Hopkins University Press, 1978), 39.

53. Dallek, *Flawed Giant*, 262.

54. Gleijeses, *The Dominican Crisis*, 116.

55. Memorandum from McGeorge Bundy, "Latin American Military Aid," 8 October 1964, LBJ, NSF, Country File, Latin American, Box 2.

56. "How Did It Happen?" *Newsweek*, 17 May 1965, 49.

57. Ibid.; Abraham F. Lowenthal, *The Dominican Intervention* (Cambridge: Harvard University Press, 1972), 33–62; Gleijeses, *The Dominican Crisis*, 118–119.

58. Dallek, *Flawed Giant*, 263.

59. Central Intelligence Agency, "Instability in Latin America," 18 May 1965.

60. "Power—and the Ticking of the Clock," *Newsweek*, 10 May 1965, 35.

61. Dallek, *Flawed Giant*, 263–265. See also "The Coup That Became a War," *Time*, 7 May 1965, 28.

62. Walter LaFeber, *America, Russia, and the Cold War, 1945–1984* (New York: Knopf, 1985), 243–247; "Power—and the Ticking of the Clock," 38.

63. "Foreign Policy: Drift or Design?" *Newsweek*, 17 May 1965, 49.

64. Gleijeses, *The Dominican Crisis*, 280.

65. "Dominican Crisis: Help from the OAS," *Newsweek*, 17 May 1965, 44; Ronald E. Powaski, *The Cold War: The United States and the Soviet Union, 1917–1991* (New York: Oxford University Press, 1998), 154–155.

66. Memorandum, William G. Bowdler to Robert Komer, "Moyers Briefing: The Latin American Scene," 15 March 1966, LBJ, NSF, Name File, Box 7.

67. "Foreign Policy: Drift or Design?" 27.

68. Memorandum, Covey T. Oliver (Assistant Secretary of State for Inter-American Affairs) to the President, "Report on Inter-American Affairs—1967," 20 December 1967, LBJ, NSF, Agency File, Box 5.

69. "Foreign Policy: Drift or Design?" 28.

70. Ibid.

71. Tulchin, "The Promise of Progress," 227.

72. Douglas S. Blaufarb and George K. Tanham, *Who Will Win? A Key to the Puzzle of Revolutionary War* (New York: Crane Russak, 1989), 94–98.

73. Ralph Lee Woodward, *Central America: A Nation Divided* (New York: Oxford University Press, 1985), 301–302; Coatsworth, *Central America and the United States*, 105.

74. Paul W. Drake, *Labor Movements and Dictatorships: The Southern Cone in Comparative Perspective* (Baltimore: Johns Hopkins University Press, 1996), 122; Central Intelligence Agency, Office of Current Intelligence, "Latin America Nationalism and the Chilean Third-Force Concept," 23 July 1963, LBJ, NSF, Country File, Latin America, Box 2.

75. Central Intelligence Agency, Office of Current Intelligence, "The Christian Democratic Movement in Latin America," 6 November 1964, LBJ, NSF, Country File, Latin America, Box 2. For a discussion of the relationship between organized labor and the Latin American left, see Drake, *Labor Movements and Dictatorships*, and Frederick Cooper, Florencia E. Mallon, Steve J. Stern, Allen F. Isaacman, and William Roseberry, *Confronting Historical Paradigms: Peasants, Labor, and the Capitalist World System in Africa and Latin America* (Madison: University of Wisconsin Press, 1993), 3–22, 23–83.

76. Walter LaFeber, *Inevitable Revolutions: The United States in Central America* (New York: W. W. Norton, 1984), 184–187.

77. Central Intelligence Agency, "The Christian Democratic Movement in Latin America," 6 November 1964.

78. Cable, Embassy (Managua) to State, 9 October 1965, NARA, RG 59, Subject–Numeric File, 1964–66, Box 2513.

79. Cable, Embassy (Managua) to State, 30 October 1965, NARA, RG 59, Subject–Numeric File, 1964–66, Box 2511.

80. Marta Harnecker, *Los Cristianos en la Revolucion Sandinista: Del Verticalismo a la Participacion de las Masas* (Buenos Aires: Ediciones al Frente, 1987), 9–27.

81. Curt Cadorette, *From the Heart of the People: The Theology of Gustavo Gutiérrez* (Oak Park, Ill.: Meyer Stone Books, 1988), 1–17; Deane William Ferm, *Third World Liberation Theologies* (Maryknoll, N.Y.: Orbis Books, 1986), 16–22.

82. Ernesto Cardenal, *The Gospel in Solentiname* (Maryknoll, N.Y.: Orbis Books, 1976), 254–255; Michael Dodson and Laura Nuzzi O'Shaughnessy, *Nicaragua's Other Revolution: Religious Faith and Political Struggle* (Chapel Hill: University of North Carolina Press, 1990), 119–122.

83. Michael D. Gambone, *Eisenhower, Somoza, and the Cold War in Nicaragua, 1953–1961* (Westport, Conn.: Praeger, 1997), 45–49; see also Pedro G. Beltran, "Foreign Loans and Politics in Latin America," *Foreign Affairs* 34 (1956): 297–304.

84. For a general study of this scholarship, see Robert A. Packenham, *The Dependency Movement: Scholarship and Politics in Development Studies* (Cambridge: Harvard University Press, 1992), 14–39, 190–197, 247–259. See also Albert O. Hirschman and Richard M. Bird, *Foreign Aid: A Critique and a Proposal* (Princeton, N.J.: Princeton University Press, 1968), and Fernando Henrique Cardoso and Enzo Faletto, *Dependency and Development in Latin America* (Berkeley and Los Angeles: University of California Press, 1979).

85. Cable, Embassy (Managua) to State, 28 April 1965, NARA, RG 59, Subject–Numeric File, 1964–66, Box 2512.

86. Cable, Embassy (Managua) to State, 28 December 1966, NARA, RG 59, Subject–Numeric File, 1967–69, Box 486.

87. Edelberto Torres-Rivas, *Repression and Resistance: The Struggle for Democracy in Central America* (Boulder, Colo.: Westview Press, 1989), 107–114.

88. Cable, Embassy (Managua) to State, 8 February 1965, NARA, RG 59, Subject–Numeric File, 1964–66, Box 2510.

89. Cable, Embassy (Managua) to State, 11 February 1965.

90. Cable, Embassy (Managua) to State, 11 December 1965, NARA, RG 59, Subject–Numeric File, 1964–66, Box 2513.

91. Cable, Embassy (Managua) to State, 22 December 1965, NARA, RG 59, Subject–Numeric File, 1964–66, Box 2514.

92. Central Intelligence Agency, Office of Central Reference, Biographical Register, "Anastasio Somoza Debayle," December 1964, NARA, RG 59, Subject–Numeric File, 1964–66, Box 2514.

93. Cable, U.S. Military Attache (Managua) to JCS, 25 May 1964, NARA, RG 59, Subject–Numeric File, 1964–66, Box 2512.

94. Cable, Embassy (Managua) to State, 14 November 1964, NARA, RG 59, Subject–Numeric File, 1964–66, Box 2510.

95. Cable, Embassy (Managua) to State, 1 May 1964, NARA, RG 59, Subject–Numeric File, 1964–66, Box 2510; Cable, Embassy (Managua) to State, 24 October 1964, NARA, RG 59, Subject–Numeric File, 1964–66, Box 2510.

96. Cable, Embassy (Managua) to State, 28 April 1965.

97. Cable, Embassy (Managua) to State, 16 February 1964, NARA, RG 59, Subject–Numeric File, 1964–66, Box 2512.

98. Cable, Embassy (Managua) to State, 8 February 1965.

99. Cable, Embassy (Managua) to State, 5 December 1964, NARA, RG 59, Subject–Numeric File, 1964–66, Box 2510.

100. Cable, Embassy (Managua) to State, 12 June 1964, NARA, RG 59, Subject–Numeric File, 1964–66, Box 2510.

101. Cable, Embassy (Managua) to State, 6 February 1965, NARA, RG 59, Subject–Numeric File, 1964–66, Box 2511.

102. Cable, Embassy (Managua) to State, 1 May 1964; Cable, Embassy (Managua) to State, 24 October 1964.

103. Cable, Embassy (Managua) to State, 22 May 1964, NARA, RG 59, Subject–Numeric File, 1964–66, Box 2512.

104. Cable, Embassy (Managua) to State, 20 May 1964, NARA, RG 59, Subject–Numeric File, 1964–66, Box 2514.

105. Thomas W. Walker, *The Christian Democratic Movement in Nicaragua* (Tucson: University of Arizona Press, 1970), 30.

106. Ibid.

107. Cable, Embassy (Managua) to State, 8 February 1965.

108. Henry Wells, ed., *Nicaragua Election Factbook* (Washington, D.C.: Institute for the Comparative Study of Political Systems, 1967), 20; Cable, Embassy (Managua) to State, 16 February, 1964.

109. Cable, Embassy (Managua) to State, 8 February 1965.

110. Cable, Embassy (Managua) to State, 1 May 1964.

111. Cable, Embassy (Managua) to State, 21 July 1966, NARA, RG 59, Subject–Numeric File, 1964–66, Box 2512.

112. Ibid.

113. Cable, Embassy (Managua) to State, 3 September 1966, NARA, RG 59, Subject–Numeric File, 1964–66, Box 2512.

114. Cable, Embassy (Managua) to State, 21 August 1965, NARA, RG 59, Subject–Numeric File, 1964–66, Box 2512.

115. Cable, Embassy (Managua) to State, 9 January 1965, NARA, RG 59, Subject–Numeric File, 1964–66, Box 2511.

116. Cable, Embassy (Managua) to State, 6 March 1965, NARA, RG 59, Subject–Numeric File, 1964–66, Box 2511.

117. Cable, Embassy (Managua) to State, 25 September 1965, NARA, RG 59, Subject–Numeric File, 1964–66, Box 2511; Cable, Embassy (Managua) to State, 4 December 1965, NARA, RG 59, Subject–Numeric File, 1964–66, Box 2511.

118. Cable, Embassy (Managua) to State, 11 February 1965.

119. Cable, Embassy (Managua) to State, 8 February 1965. Emphasis in original.

120. Enrique Alvarado Martinez, *El Pensamiento Politico Nicaragüense: de los ultimos años* (Managua: Editorial y Lit. Artes Graficas, 1968), 23–30.

121. Cable, Embassy (Managua) to State, 22 June 1966, NARA, RG 59, Subject–Numeric File, 1964–66, Box 2513.

122. Wells, *Nicaragua Election Factbook* 20.

123. Cable, Embassy (Managua) to State, 13 October 1966, NARA, RG 59, Subject–Numeric File, 1964–66, Box 2513.

124. Cable, Embassy (Managua) to State, 22 October 1966, NARA, RG 59, Subject–Numeric File, 1964–66, Box 2512.

125. Memorandum of Conversation, "Campaign of Nicaraguan Presidential Candidate Fernando Agüero," 2 December 1966, NARA, RG 59, Subject–Numeric File, 1964–66, Box 2513.

126. Cable, Embassy (Managua) to State, 8 February 1965.

127. Cable, State to Managua, 11 February 1965, NARA, RG 59, Subject–Numeric File, 1964–66, Box 2514.

128. Cable, Embassy (Managua) to State, 22 December 1965.

129. Cable, Embassy (Managua) to State, 4 August 1966, NARA, RG 59, Subject–Numeric File, 1964–66, Box 2513.

130. Cable, Embassy (Managua) to State, 12 January 1967, NARA, RG 59, Subject–Numeric File, 1967–69, Box 2178.

131. Cable, Embassy (Managua) to State, 14 January 1967, NARA, RG 59, Subject–Numeric File, 1967–69, Box 2177.

132. James Dunkerley, *Power in the Isthmus: A Political History of Modern Central America* (New York: Verso, 1988), 233; Memorandum, Walt W. Rostow to the President, "Nicaraguan Situation," 23 January 1967, LBJ, NSF, Country File, Nicaragua, Box 63; Cable, Embassy (Managua) to State, 22 January 1967, NARA, RG 59, Subject–Numeric File, 1967–69, Box 290.

133. Cable, Embassy (Managua) to State, 26 January 1967, NARA, RG 59, Subject–Numeric File, 1967–69, Box 2178; Cable, Embassy (Managua) to State, 26 January 1967, NARA, RG 59, Subject–Numeric File, 1967–69, Box 2179. The Church later condemned Chavez y Nunez for his statements. See John M. Kirk, *Politics and the Catholic Church in Nicaragua* (Gainesville: University Press of Florida, 1992), 36–52.

134. Cable, State to Embassy (Managua), 25 January 1967, NARA, RG 59, Subject–Numeric File, 1967–69, Box 2179.

135. Cable, Embassy (Managua) to State, 4 March 1967, NARA, RG 59, Subject–Numeric File, 1967–69, Box 2177.

136. Ibid.

137. Interview, John Cabot, 28 February 1969, LBJ, Oral History Collection, 20.

138. Cable, Embassy (Managua) to State, 9 May 1967, NARA, RG 59, Subject–Numeric File, 1967–69, Box 2111.

139. Tulchin, "The Promise of Progress," 227.

140. Cable, Embassy (Managua) to State, 2 September 1967, NARA, RG 59, Subject–Numeric File, 1967–69, Box 2177.

141. See Cable, State to All ARA Diplomatic Posts and AMCONSUL Belize, ROCAP, US Mission OAS, 17 December 1968, NARA, RG 59, Subject–Numeric File, 1967–69, Box 2111.

CHAPTER 5

Influence and Internal Security at Mid-Decade

American capitalism replaced some of the old colonial capitalisms in the countries that began their independent life. But it knows that this is transitory and that there is no real security for its financial speculations in these new territories. The octopus cannot there apply its suckers firmly. The claw of the imperial eagle is trimmed. Colonialism is dead or is dying a natural death in all these places.

Ernesto "Che" Guevara, 1961

The American military expansion initiated at the start of the 1960s continued its progression in the Johnson administration. Under Robert McNamara, the Defense Department continued a lengthy list of improvements to conventional and nuclear forces and devoted additional attention to unconventional war. New teams of American military advisors deployed to regions threatened by insurgency around the world. For these soldiers, however, simply providing training and equipment was only a small part of their mission. In order to create a true counterbalance to the guerrilla threat, American advisors had to reform local military institutions. Latin America reflected both the build-up of American assistance and the need to direct its use. By the mid-1960s an increasingly sophisticated insurgent threat had begun to emerge in the hemisphere, the product of lessons learned from the failure of the Cuban foco model and accumulated pressure from both the Soviet Union and China for Latin American revolutionaries to embrace a gradualist approach to rebellion that incorporated a greater proportion of political activity with armed resistance. Winning substantive reforms from the Latin America militaries to meet this threat proved to be an ongoing battle, one that often ran afoul of local priorities. In terms of its own internal security, Nicaragua enjoyed a relative degree of stability at mid-decade. The National Guard handily defeated civil disturbances and the embryonic guerrilla war in the countryside, forcing groups such as the Sandinistas to sharply reduce their expectations regarding revolution.

DEFENSE POLICY WITHIN THE KENNEDY TRAJECTORY

When he assumed the office of his slain predecessor, Lyndon Baines Johnson found himself overshadowed at almost every turn by the Kennedy legacy, particularly with regard to the issue of national security. Among his many promises during his first year in office, Johnson would make great efforts to pledge a continuation of the unfinished work of his president. The former Senate majority leader would eventually establish his own lengthy identity in domestic affairs through the remarkable pursuit of the Great Society. However, Johnson's military policies would largely remain the product of decisions made between 1961 and 1963.[1]

One clearly lasting influence was the previous administration's methodological approach to American strategic power. As president, Kennedy had been a strong advocate of multiple layers of nuclear and conventional capability, the so-called doctrine of flexible response, and had initiated the largest postwar outlays for the American military since the Korean War.[2] The change in spending priorities was dramatic. Overall, the American defense budget jumped from $45.2 billion in 1960 to $52.3 billion in 1962. At the conclusion of Johnson's last year in office, it stood at $80.7 billion, bolstered primarily by the war in Vietnam.[3]

The American military flourished in the wake of this largess. Billions, for example, found their way to the nuclear triad, primarily into the thousand Minuteman missiles and forty-one ballistic missile submarines pursued by Secretary of Defense Robert S. McNamara.[4] In the crisis atmosphere of the early 1960s, conventional forces grew from 2.4 million in 1960 to 2.6 million in 1965, with the largest increases registered by the Army and Marine Corps.[5]

American counterinsurgency capability also expanded in concurrence with these increases. The early 1960s were the heyday of the special forces soldier, a time when Kennedy adopted the so-called Green Berets as his own, embracing as he did so the complex doctrine of low-intensity warfare. *Newsweek* depicted the government's relationship with this new unit in the following terms:

From now on, President Kennedy told the Joint Chiefs of Staff, the Special Forces would no longer languish in the shade of the atomic missile, and they would, in fact, take on a series of new duties. The hard-muscled wielders of knife and garrote would teach their back-alley arts to fighters for freedom in the jungles of Southeast Asia, the savannas of Central Africa, wherever revolt and terror encroach.[6]

Beyond the professional attributes of their training and operational capability was the vested faith many American officials had in the ability of the special forces to conduct war in a precise manner that offered success without the risk of escalation. Perhaps more important, special forces doctrine also offered the prospect of their use as a "force multiplier." A special forces officer claimed in 1961 that a twelve-man "A" detachment could train as many as 1,500 pro-American guerrillas. "Just a few teams working behind enemy lines could direct enough sabotage and infiltration to tie up two enemy divisions."[7]

This latter concept could not have been better timed for the arrival of the Johnson administration. After 1963, under siege in Congress, U.S. aid for foreign militaries and funding for training facilities overseas had decreased considerably from $1.8 billion in 1960 to slightly over $1 billion in 1965.[8] Moreover, total military assistance, "supporting assistance" (economic aid for security purposes), and a contingency fund for security emergencies together declined from $2.9 billion in 1961 to $1.7 billion in 1965.[9] The largest proportion of this spending was absorbed by Southeast Asia, particularly Laos and South Vietnam, which received half of the total aid allocated for Asia, or approximately $400 million in 1965. For its own part, Latin America received $73 million in U.S. military assistance, more than Europe ($51 million) or Africa ($29 million).[10]

U.S. military advisors were thus tasked to fill the gap between improved capabilities at home and declining security assistance abroad. To be sure, the Johnson administration had not abandoned American commitments throughout the world. In mid-March 1965, Robert S. McNamara testified before Congress that the United States had "an indissoluble relationship between our national security and the collective security pacts with which we are associated." In his opinion, the United States needed to support a military system that was both strong and flexible:

Determination, however, must be given substance and credibility by the maintenance of armed forces trained, equipped and deployed in positions from which they can respond promptly and effectively to acts of aggression. Such forces are the tangible evidence to any potential aggressor of the actions we are prepared to take. The shadow they cast is deterrence.[11]

If anything, the Johnson administration exhibited an even greater tendency toward intervention than its predecessor. McNamara's testimony came only three days after the deployment of U.S. Marines to Danang in South Vietnam and seven weeks prior to American intervention in the Dominican Republic. Despite budgetary indications to the contrary, Washington embarked upon a policy devoted to building a security infrastructure for underdeveloped nations confronting insurgency. In most cases, such as South Vietnam and the Dominican Republic, the efforts were justified in the strategic discourse as the necessary pursuit of anti-Communism.[12]

Within this context the Johnson administration would reaffirm its support for internal security and attempt to expand military assistance during its tenure. In February 1964, as part of National Security Action Memorandum 283, it essentially endorsed previous policies relevant to security assistance and training. The president concurred with the proposal that the preparation of State, Defense, USAID, and USIA officials should include increasing attention to internal defense and counterinsurgency issues.[13] One caveat offered by the administration in April 1964 was a request for a definition of "a clear relationship between military internal security missions and police functions and a rational pattern of U.S. funding for same."[14] A Defense Department rejoinder to this question defined the American objective as "the development and maintenance of free world military forces with predominant emphasis on conventional forces in order to expand the range of free world capabilities to meet a military action with sufficient, but not excessive measures."[15] Secondarily, the Defense Department supported the goal of self-help, emphasizing the need for host nations to provide maintenance items for defense purposes. Logistical independence would permit a reduction of U.S. Military Assistance Program assistance and allow the United States to redirect aid to "investment items" (i.e., weapons systems and materiel), rather than everyday operating costs.[16]

To support these initiatives, officials within the State Department, such as Jeffrey Kitchen, called for greater coordination of military assistance efforts. Kitchen recognized that defense assistance support could rapidly lead the United States into areas not directly related to security. Civic action projects that improved local infrastructure, provided technical training, and generally undercut the sources of dissidence were complex socioeconomic enterprises that incorporated military assistance as one component of their overall effort. In order to be successful, they required precise coordination between Defense Department and Agency for International Development staff representatives present within American embassies scattered throughout the world.[17] In a larger sense, a multiagency approach to assistance also offered American officials a better opportunity to pursue the "sufficient, but not excessive measures" required of client nations by U.S. military assistance policy.

It was clear to American officials that such measures were necessary in Latin America. The prospect of Castro's diminishing influence did not mean that the Communist threat to Latin America had disappeared, nor did it mark the last gasp of those interested in spreading the *foco* throughout the hemisphere. Castro himself refused to abandon support for popular revolution despite Soviet pressure to tone down his rhetoric. The Cuban leader openly endorsed a February 1965 speech made by Che Guevara in Algiers that called for socialist nations to underwrite revolutions throughout the world. In January 1966, Castro convened the "Tricontinental Conference" in Havana to reach out to Third World revolutionaries. He would later sponsor the training of forces of the Popular Movement for the Liberation of Angola in Cuba. In 1967, Castro declared Nicaragua "ripe for revolution" and allowed Radio Havana to give the FSLN insurgency considerable publicity.[18] U.S. officials possessed evidence of Cuban support for guerrilla movements in Bolivia, Colombia, and Venezuela.[19]

Within Castro's ongoing efforts, many Americans saw Moscow's hand at work. During a meeting of the Special Group (Counterinsurgency), CIA Director John McCone pointed to statements by the Soviets in 1965 that they supported "wars of liberation" in Latin America. McCone believed that Moscow had targeted Venezuela, Colombia, Guatemala, Honduras, and Paraguay for subversive activities. Although he conceded that the Communist threat was still in an "embryonic stage" in most countries, it could grow rapidly under the guidance of trained guerrilla cadres.[20]

The actual form that some future insurgency might take was unclear. Armed revolution was at best a problematic means for communism to gain a foothold in Latin America. A U.S. intelligence report released in early 1967 commented, "Ironically, what happened in Cuba has had something of the effect of an inoculation against revolution elsewhere in the area; indeed, Che Guevara himself has made the point that, because one Cuba happened, the chances of a second Cuba have become smaller rather than greater."[21] In the aftermath of the Cuban Revolution, many Latin American regimes had retooled their internal security infrastructures, in most cases with direct U.S. assistance, and had proven capable of preventing violent insurrections before they could emerge. McCone himself admitted that the prospects for armed insurgencies presently active were "not bright."[22]

Political subversion posed an entirely different challenge, however. By the mid-1960s, the Soviets had taken deliberate steps to support broad popular alliances that avoided premature revolutionary actions. In a policy reminiscent of the "popular front" approach of the 1930s, they emphasized political struggles that were expressed under democratic slogans and pursued coalitions with noncommunist elements that, in some instances, included elements of the Latin American military. Publicly, Moscow depicted Castro as an aberrant factor in traditional Latin American communism. Privately, Soviet leaders were able to win Castro's temporary agreement that he would support insurgencies only if invited by the Communist party of a host country. In 1965, the State Department's Bureau of Intelligence Research reported the noticeable progress of the popular-front model in Colombia, Chile, and Uruguay. Rebels in Guatemala at the time also began to stress a broader political approach to their insurgency.[23]

Nor was the Soviet Union the only potential sponsor for such a tactic. Intelligence information available as early as June 1964 reported extensive Chinese sponsorship of Latin American revolutionaries. In meetings that included Mao Tse-tung himself, the Chinese insisted that Latin American Communists reconstruct their ties with peasants, urban workers, government officials, and the military. "Without exception," U.S. officials noted, "the Chinese complimented the Peruvian Communist leaders on their program and progress and told the other leaders to follow Peru's example."[24] Addressing the internal friction experienced by the Ecuadoran Communist Party, Chinese leaders recommended the abandonment of ideological factionalism based upon loyalty to Peking in favor of the reconstruction of a disciplined, coherent membership. In an exchange with Peruvian dissidents, Mao allowed that although a slow mobilization of guerrilla forces was possible, it faced formidable U.S. opposition and had to be coupled with the growth of legitimate political organizations in order to ultimately succeed.[25]

The complex nature of this politicomilitary subversion deeply disturbed American officials. Here was an approach to disrupting both stability and American influence that preyed upon economic difficulties and concurrent social and political divisions, an atmosphere one report described as the "malaise," that affected at least twelve Latin American countries perceived to be vulnerable to revolution. Among those most immediately threatened—the Dominican Republic, Bolivia, Haiti, Guatemala, Honduras, and Panama—were a significant number of Central American nations.[26]

Interestingly, American observers believed that the primary revolutionary actors of concern were not those from the left side of the political spectrum, but those from the right. In this context, the excesses of a reactionary military regime would serve as the spark for a general uprising. Building upon popular resentment of corruption, nepotism, and the uncontrolled use of state-sponsored terror, dissident groups could succeed simply by feeding violent outbursts and manipulating the general public toward their own proffered solutions. Using the time-honored popular-front technique, Communists could capture dissident groups regardless of their affiliation and prevail in revolutions with minimal risk to themselves.[27] Essentially, U.S. policy makers recognized the potential for another Dominican situation, in which "there would be little in the social fabric of the society to prevent the Communists from moving quickly to gain influence" or, over the longer term, to develop "the capability effectively to exploit a coup initiated by other forces."[28]

The basic question posed to American policy makers was how to prevent this situation short of a massive, well-publicized invasion by conventional military forces.

In fact, such a question had been posed in May 1964 during a joint review of military policy for Latin America conducted by the Departments of State and Defense and the Bureau of Budget. The basic objective proposed was relatively simple and focused on the need for a "precise and realistic definition of U.S. defense objectives (including intelligence requirements) in Latin America."[29] Hemispheric defense, a long-standing American goal in the postwar period, was abandoned as impractical and unnecessary. In its place, the joint review recommended continued support for internal security and civic action.

Executing this basic objective provided an important opportunity to not only provide material support for Latin American security, but also a measure of influence in its final use. U.S. policy makers understood that advisors ultimately accompanied new weapons systems and materiel, continuing a relationship between militaries in the hemisphere that stretched back for decades. Soldiers, in effect, were seen as ideal vehicles to promote the political reforms necessary to undermine the appeal of the popular front. The committee noted, "The significance of the Latin American military in its influence upon internal political affairs and the social and economic structure is so extensive as to warrant special attention." It would be "helpful to recognize that military hardware and expertise can be legitimately and effectively used in pursuit of purely political, as well as defense, goals and that when they are so used we should not feel compelled to justify their use on military grounds."[30]

To further this idea, the committee recommended the creation of a Military Advisory and Assistance Group in every Latin American nation. In 1964, many countries still retained the old system of service missions that had existed for much of the century. In most cases, the service missions were paid for by host governments to serve their training needs and contained separate service-branch advisors who were paired off with their Latin American counterparts. Because it was by definition local in nature, the service-mission system lacked a clear command structure and was built upon redundant military branches that were often difficult to coordinate.[31]

A viable MAAG system could permit a greater degree of control over both aid and influence. The committee recommended increasing the number of contacts between American advisory missions and the Latin American military at all levels—from the high command to field-grade officers, junior officers, and enlisted personnel—so that the MAAGs could identify and establish relationships with what the study referred to as "military sub-groups in Latin American societies."[32] With this relationship in place, Americans could promote local self-help under U.S. direction, primarily in the form of civic action projects.[33] More important, the United States could also establish local relationships that would provide, at the very least, useful intelligence on local developments. In an interview conducted by Maxwell Taylor's Counterinsurgency Review Board in 1965, Joint Chiefs of Staff Chair Earl Wheeler commented that the country team was the best means for the United States to track plots against host governments.[34]

The United States was thus attempting to cultivate security under controlled conditions. It would find this policy severely tested during the 1960s, when many Latin American nations embarked upon a regional arms race. The issue itself had been a chronic problem during the previous decade and a particularly sore spot between

Washington and many Latin American countries. In 1958, for example, U.S. military grant aid to the hemisphere totaled $53 million. Military purchases for all Latin American countries, however, amounted to over $1.5 billion. In 1957, Brazil acquired a surplus British aircraft carrier and Peru bought its first modern submarines. The most popular items were jet aircraft, particularly supersonic fighters and bombers.[35] A few contemporaries protested the purchases, arguing that they detracted from economic development. Peruvian Finance Minister Pedro Beltran decried the new weapons, describing them as "expensive toys, already obsolete."[36]

Latin Americans believed that new weaponry and equipment were necessary to and dictated by the ongoing modernization of their militaries. Many military institutions, particularly those in the larger South American nations, already maintained relatively high levels of professionalization Younger officers received correspondingly high levels of training as their respective services incorporated increasingly complex weapons systems into front-line units. Many, according to one U.S. intelligence report, received better educations than most civilian university graduates in their countries. A primary interest of this new generation was in adapting new knowledge and technology to their institutions.[37] In other cases, modernization was driven by the practical need to upgrade existing equipment. This was most sorely felt in Latin American air forces, where aging fleets of prop-driven aircraft left over from World War II were no longer operable. In a letter to the State Department, the Chilean embassy cited the need to protect "our lines of communication," specifically the 3,000 miles of coastline vulnerable to disruption, a devastating prospect given the 12 million tons of Chilean cargo that were exported abroad in 1966 alone.[38] In other instances, the purchase of modern weapons was a question of prestige. Many Latin Americans argued that far less advanced countries in both Africa and Asia had received new equipment. The deluge of military items bound for South Vietnam after 1965 was a particular sticking point.[39] Nationalism clearly played a significant role in the acquisition of arms. Thomas Mann would remark in a 1968 interview that the Latin American military considered themselves "the guardians of the independence and the order of the hemisphere."[40] Restricting this province was an affront to national pride. As a consequence of these considerations, during the period between 1965 and 1968 outlays for defense spending rose dramatically in some countries. Peru increased its average defense spending by 12.3 percent during the period. Brazil (11.9%) and Venezuela (6.3%) also registered substantial annual gains.[41]

Circumventing this trend became an important objective during the Johnson presidency. First, Washington embarked upon an informal diplomatic effort to discourage the French and British, the most aggressive arms marketers, from approaching potential Latin American clients.[42] Second, following the recommendation in NSAM 297, the administration proposed that the United States "actively discourage" the purchase of "non-essential prestige equipment" in the hemisphere.[43] In a 1964 memo to the Departments of State and Defense and the Agency for International Development, McGeorge Bundy challenged the level and direction of military expenditures in Latin America. The problem, according to Bundy, was not so much the absolute quantity of arms purchased, but their qualitative impact on individual Latin American nations: "It really seems debatable whether these units are essential to internal security, harbor defense and coastal patrol. On the other hand, they weigh heavily on the budgets of the countries concerned." Bundy wanted to cut down or eliminate U.S. support for what he considered nonessential programs (i.e., big-ticket weapons) and encourage instead military units that promoted other areas more directly related to stability.[44]

Both State and Defense disagreed with this assessment. The State Department contested the idea that military spending had an adverse impact on Latin America. In a reply to Bundy, the special assistant to the secretary, Benjamin H. Read, argued that annual growth rates largely offset the impact of military outlays on social and economic development. On the whole, military expenditures affected on average only about 2 percent of total gross national product in most countries, the exceptions being Peru (3.5%) and the Dominican Republic (4.1%).[45] State Department officials further asserted that any consideration of aid reduction could cause a lapse of influence. Assistant Secretary of State for Inter-American Affairs Jack Vaughn claimed that without the United States overseeing the region's civil–military budgets, overall expenditures would lose their equilibrium. In other words, according to this somewhat labored logic, maintenance of increasing military assistance was essential to long-range economic development.[46] To those in the State Department who were closer to the topic, the prospect of creating a comprehensive policy that could be applicable to Ecuador and Argentina seemed problematic at best. Vaughn commented that, even if U.S. officials could come to an agreement, the final document "probably would not say anything."[47] He noted as well that it was impossible to foresee results of such a policy. One distinct outcome was that it would produce no results at all.

The Defense Department took a somewhat more subtle approach to the issue. The Office of International Security Affairs agreed that Latin American military spending was poorly proportioned, noting that Latin American militaries spent, on average, 64 percent of their budgets on pay and allowances and only 9 percent for "force improvement."[48] However, this granted, McNamara's initial recommendation to the White House, delivered in June 1965, was that Bundy's policy "should be delayed until some indefinite time in the future."[49]

Failing at this task, McNamara attempted to fob off the Bundy request by building it into a long-range defense plan for Latin America. In the summer of 1965 he proposed a "gradual, selective and controlled phasedown" of MAP materiel grants, an abolishment of maintenance and overhaul items between 1967 and 1969, and a gradual elimination of "investment items" from 1969 to 1971.[50] For the most part, McNamara's strategy prevailed because it offered substantive change to Bundy and a plan to accomplish the latter's goals, while it mitigated existing institutional efforts over a relatively long (five years) period of time.

In the meantime, American efforts to float a trial balloon for a hemispheric disarmament conference were rebuffed by most of the larger South American nations. President Fernando Belaunde Terry of Peru reacted vehemently against the U.S. proposals, arguing that disarmament was unrealistic for nations interested in carrying out realistic training in the preparation of their militaries. New equipment, moreover, was useful to counter the guerrilla threat and promote civic action as these forces conducted their training.[51]

The outcome of these efforts was a mixed bag of policy decisions that had little real impact on Latin American rearmament. A clear example was the controversy over the F-5 fighter. In 1966, Argentina, Chile, Brazil, and Peru all expressed interest in purchasing the F-5 Freedom Fighter, a twin-engined jet produced by the United States for export. Initially, American officials attempted to defer the sale with an offer of the older A-4B. Many countries appeared willing to accept the offer. Although Argentina had already begun talks with the French for the possible purchase of the Mystére jet as early as 1965, it eventually accepted the American deal.[52] Unfortunately, deliveries were disrupted by shipments of available A-4Bs to South Vietnam. Up to ninety aircraft had been available in 1965, but many had already been diverted to the Saigon government when the initial offer was made to Buenos Aires.[53] As a substitute, Washington offered older F-86 fighter jets of Korean War vintage.

Many South American nations saw this last-minute change as a betrayal of good faith and immediately shifted their sights abroad to solicit weapons from European arms markets. The chief of the Chilean Air Force openly scoffed at the offer of U.S. F-86s to be "immoral and almost an insult." His nation turned to Great Britain for the purchase of twenty-one Hawker Hunters in a $16-million package that included five years worth of spare parts and training support.[54] Peru decided to seek out French Mirage-5 supersonic fighter-bombers and ordered twelve in October 1967.[55] From Santiago, the U.S. military attaché reported rumors that Venezuela was interested in the purchase of Saab aircraft from Sweden.[56]

Faced with these alarming alternatives, Washington reversed its policy regarding the F-5 in late 1967 and offered the aircraft to Argentina, Chile, Brazil, Venezuela, and Peru. Brazil immediately announced its decision to buy both fifteen F-5s and fifteen Mirages, but later retracted the latter effort under U.S. pressure. Yet despite a major policy concession, European armament companies continued to make inroads in South America. England offered antitank missiles as part of its aircraft package deals. France would sell Peru seventy-eight AMX-13 tanks in 1968. Argentina acquired thirty of the same vehicles and concurrently negotiated a contract with the Société Francaise de Matérial de la Armée to arrange the joint manufacture of the AMX tank for export.[57]

At the conclusion of the Johnson administration, American officials continued to wrestle with the dual problems of meting out military assistance in a rational manner and gaining a degree of influence with client nations through its use. The F-5 sale was a major concession to the former, without any substantive linkage to the latter. It revoked what had been a hard line taken against the inclusion of sophisticated weaponry in the hemisphere and added supersonic jets to an already large inventory of U.S. equipment made available to Latin American militaries. As events demonstrated, the United States became one supplier among many who competed in an open market for prospective clients.

The F-5 sale also illustrated the difficulties that Washington faced when it came to exercising political influence within the realm of military assistance. U.S. policy makers recognized that a worst-case scenario in any Latin American country consisted of unchecked political subversion conducted in concert with armed insurgency. The basic charge to these individuals was to construct meaningful counterinsurgency policies within their respective host nations. However, its was an open question as to how to influence the course of client governments if the United States withdrew support for military purchases, an important condition given the nature of Latin American governments in the mid-1960s. In late 1967, for example, the United States maintained relations with six outright military regimes (i.e., Argentina, Brazil, Bolivia, Nicaragua, Paraguay, and El Salvador) and a number of others in which the military dominated internal affairs. (e.g., Peru, Venezuela, Ecuador, Guatemala, and the Dominican Republic).[58] In practical terms, the threat of an arms embargo eliminated a fundamental military relationship and any prospect of progress in civil–military affairs, rendering the coordination of MAAG efforts toward political reform moot. As the F-5 story unfolded, it essentially vindicated the State Department and its early assertion that the United States had to maintain a basic means to influence Latin American nations. Unfortunately, keeping this one door open closed opportunities in other important areas.

EXPANDING THE COUNTERINSURGENCY MISSION IN CENTRAL AMERICA

The military leg of the Alliance for Progress grew considerably in Central America during the Johnson era, prompted by determined insurgent movements in every country except Costa Rica. Despite significant efforts to stamp out guerrillas, particularly in Guatemala and Nicaragua, armed bands persisted in the hinterlands of the isthmus. Initially, the Defense Department supplemented U.S. military missions in Central America by deploying advisors from the 7th Special Forces Group stationed at Ft. Bragg, North Carolina. However, as the policy community discussed the need for a more permanent means to coordinate counterinsurgency policy, the Pentagon authorized the creation of the 8th Special Forces Group in April 1963. Based in Ft. Gulick in the Panama Canal Zone, the 8th SFG became the nexus and primary protagonist of U.S. counterinsurgency doctrine in the region during the 1960s. Between 1962 and 1967, 600 Special Forces mobile training teams were dispatched to nineteen Latin American countries. In 1965 alone, Special Forces personnel were able to train 41,000 Latin America soldiers. Of these missions, El Salvador and Guatemala received the largest number of American advisors.[59]

The 8th Special Forces Group joined an already formidable system of American training facilities in the Canal Zone. In 1963, U.S. instructors operated both the School of the Americas and the Jungle Warfare Training Center at Ft. Sherman. These institutions primarily emphasized military basics. Weapons training, small-unit tactics, and land navigation comprised the majority of instruction.[60] However, as this effort gained momentum, Johnson administration officials wanted the inclusion of additional topics related to civil–military relations. McGeorge Bundy requested a revision of curriculum taught in the Canal Zone to include an emphasis on democracy, public administration, and related subjects.[61]

The Defense Department was reluctant to include this type of training in the regime offered to Latin American students. The department maintained that its purview among the "more developed" nations of Latin America, those whose police operated outside the traditional military, was limited to traditional military topics.[62] It would be dangerous, according to a 1965 report by the assistant secretary of defense for international affairs, to blur the line between police and military functions. His case was reinforced by existing doctrine. According to American policy, instruction on civil–military relations fell to the Agency for International Development's Office of Public Safety, the office actually tasked with improving local internal security programs in Latin America. In July 1962, AID formally established an Inter-American Police Academy at Ft. Davis in the Canal Zone and graduated more than 600 police officers from fifteen Latin American countries in its first eighteen months of operation.[63]

Subsequent training programs conducted in the Canal Zone and by U.S. mobile training teams would continue to include counterinsurgency instruction, but treat it as a military rather than a civilian topic and place greater emphasis, for example, on small-unit operations in the field instead of civic action. American advisors would train a generation of ranger, special forces, and light infantry units (e.g., the Guatemalan *Kaibiles* or the Salvadoran *Cazadores*) designed to engage guerrillas in direct combat rather than address the fundamental sources of popular support that sustained them. This rather narrow pursuit of counterinsurgency was driven by a simple consideration. According to historian Michael McClintock, the United States was willing to envisage terror as a method to combat insurgency: "The innovation," in other words, "was in the generalized subordination of the tactics and techniques of counterinsurgency to the fundamental principle of fighting like with like."[64]

As it constructed internal security training doctrine, the United States placed even greater emphasis on creating a collective Central American security program. In part, this effort was dedicated to overcome the decades of mutual distrust that had dominated relations within the isthmus since its independence. More pointed, U.S. officials wanted to assimilate Central American militaries into their own counterinsurgency system, a system designed to coordinate local forces against regional subversion and insurgency. Such a structure was designed to parallel and subordinate itself to the centralization of the Military Advisory and Assistance Groups, accepting standardized training and equipment in exchange for greater cooperation between rival militaries.

The end product of this work was the creation of the Consejo de Defensa Centro Americana in early 1964. The organization was designed so that member nations (Costa Rica did not join) could cooperate in military training, conduct joint counterguerrilla operations, share intelligence related to regional security, and coordinate regional plans with the Inter-American Defense Board. A Permanent Commission of Central American Defense handled the daily requirements of planning, budgets, and internal procedures. Overall leadership of the council fell to Guatemala's minister of defense.[65]

CONDECA served as a conduit for U.S. advisors to Central America throughout the decade. Officially, a total of 122 military group and military attachés served in the region by 1967 and were involved in a broad array of technical instruction, logistical support, intelligence gathering, and training activities. Under CONDECA, the United States deployed a series of Counter-Insurgency Mobile Training Teams to advise local forces in both ground and air operations.[66]

CONDECA also organized an extensive array of joint training operation. In July 1965, Central American units participated in HALCON VISTA, a coastal surveillance and intercept exercise.[67] A year later, regional forces combined again to train company-size ground units in Honduras as part of "Operation Centro-America." The U.S. Military Group commander in Managua, Colonel William P. Francisco, described the efforts as "extremely valuable from a military training aspect as well as promoting closer ties and working arrangements between the armed forces of Central America." In his report to the embassy, Francisco noted as well the universally positive comments he received from the Nicaraguan National Guard, citing in particular junior officers' enthusiasm about the opportunity to train with and meet officers of other nations.[68]

The evolution of U.S. counterinsurgency doctrine in Guatemala offers a number of insights regarding both the extent of American aid and the impact of its influence. The original insurgent threat to Guatemala in the 1960s was, ironically, the creation of American covert efforts against Castro. Operation Zapata, the abortive effort to invade Cuba and topple communism, failed to overturn the government in Havana, but succeeded in promoting rebellion in the lower ranks of the Guatemalan officer corps after the Bay of Pigs invasion.[69] These young leaders considered U.S. sponsorship of the Cuban exile brigade as interference with their country's sovereignty and an insult to national pride. Within their ranks, anti-Americanism and anti-Communism were held in equal balance.[70] Their proposed solution, albeit poorly articulated, was to use the military as a means to reform the Guatemalan political system and return it to the post–1945 reform era. Dissatisfaction erupted in an abortive coup attempt against the regime of Miguel Ydigoras Fuentes in November 1960.[71]

Dissent lingered beyond the initial failure of rebellion. Two officers, Marco Antonio Yon Sosa and Luis Turcios Lima, returned to Guatemala in 1961 to continue their efforts against the pro-American Ydigoras government. Both had received their training at American installations in the Canal Zone and Ft. Benning, Georgia. Forming an uneasy political alliance with the Communist Guatemalan Workers Party, they created the Movimiento Revolucionario 13 de Noviembre and began a series of guerrilla raids in early 1962 in the Sierra de los Minas, a mountainous region in the northeastern part of Guatemala.[72] For the most part, the rebels kept their activities relegated to small-scale attacks against government facilities and infrastructure, while distributing propaganda throughout the countryside, a deliberate attempt to emulate the *foco* concept by sparking local population to join their cause as victories began to accumulate in their favor. In this effort, the rebels received direct assistance from Cuba.[73]

The *foco* largely failed as a tactic in the Guatemalan rebellion. Although the rough country of the northeast offered excellent terrain for guerrilla operations, it was a poor choice as the political fountainhead of a revolution. Illiterate and apathetic *campesinos* failed to rally around MR-13's crude slogans. Moreover, the unsophisticated cadres that attempted to cultivate local villages generated little interest among the predominantly Indian population of the Sierra de los Minas. The rebellion was further handicapped by constant bickering between Turcios Lima and Yon Sosa as well as by internal splits between MR-13 and the PGT over the conduct of the military campaign. Nevertheless, the movement gained considerable ground by 1966, openly confronting small army units in the field and capturing a number of small arms after skirmishes with government forces. By 1966, the total number of rebels numbered approximately 500, ten times the number Che Guevara would later lead in Bolivia.[74]

Government countermeasures against the rebellion initially foundered on the political intrigues that surrounded the Ydigoras government. For its own part, the United States briefly pulled away from Guatemala after a successful 1963 coup against Ydigoras that installed Colonel Enrique Peralta Azurdia as president. Accordingly, U.S. military aid to Guatemala decreased from $2.6 million in 1963 to $1.1 million in 1965.[75] This policy was reversed only after the pro forma election of Julio César Méndez Montenegro by the Guatemalan legislature in May 1966.

A moderate, Montenegro initially attempted to assuage Guatemala's internal strife with an amnesty program, an offer spurned by rebels and the Guatemalan military alike, the latter answering with "Operation Zacapa" in October 1966.[76] The operation was a three-stage effort to defeat the insurgency in the field, first beginning "search and destroy" missions against rebel strongholds, then supplementing these sweeps with paramilitary forces at the village level, and following this with a series civic action projects.[77] Airmobile units were deployed into the Sierra de los Minas for the first time, trained and supervised by American personnel. This enhanced capability was further reinforced by a system of *comisionados*, temporary civilian militiamen, who supervised local public order and organized military conscription. By the end of 1966, they numbered 9,000 and were supported in turn by the Policia Militar Ambulante, a 1,000-man force that, according to its charter, shall

lend assistance, in cases of emergency, to the owners or administrators of estates, haciendas, agricultural lands, forests and all rural properties . . . observe all activity that tends to inflame passions among the peasant masses or in the rural communities and, when necessary, repress through legitimate means any disorder that should occur.[78]

A disturbing development that coincided with this campaign was the appearance of quasimilitary right-wing death squads in the months that followed Méndez Montenegro's election. The so-called *Mano Blanca* appeared late in 1966 and was followed over the next year and a half by twenty additional organizations. Frequently acting in concert with the *comisionados*, who served to identify potential victims, the death squads purged both rebel sympathizers and potential political opponents of the Montenegro regime.

Most of the rebellion against the government was simply crushed under the sheer weight of these overlapping forces. Some 8,000 people were killed between November 1966 and March 1967 in attacks on what the government euphemistically described as the guerrilla's "social base."[79] A civic action program, undertaken under "Plan Piloto" in February 1967, followed in the wake of this carnage as more of an afterthought. In the end, a form of peace returned at an enormous price to the rural population.

The course of events in Guatemala illustrated the substantial effectiveness and disturbing limits of Central American internal security policy. Militarily, U.S. assistance performed almost too well against the Guatemalan insurgency. U.S. Special Forces teams succeeded in creating a counterpart institution in the form of the *Kaibiles* (Tigers) which served well in the function of light infantry, but also garnered a well-earned reputation for ruthlessness against the civilian population. The Office of Public Safety managed the creation of a formidable internal security infrastructure, but spawned in its wake a parallel, quasi-official system devoted to rooting out and killing the political opposition.

Political reform, indeed any substantive attempts at political suasion in favor of a more moderate course, were sacrificed in pursuit of a national security plan. In a situation with meaningful parallels to the conflict in South Vietnam, the "big war" in the field took precedence over pacification efforts.[80] In Guatemala, this priority reinforced the institutionalization of illiberal, repressive elements emplaced after the overthrow of Arbenz in 1954 and promoted armed rebellion against the regime well into the next decade.

INSURGENT ACTIVITY IN NICARAGUA

For most of the 1960s, the Nicaraguan insurgency could be best described as sporadic and ineffectual. In the early years of the decade, guerrillas failed to recreate the Cuban *foco* in the northern and central zones of the country. In 1963, for example, the Frente Sandinista de Liberacion Nacional tried to rally support in the Bocay region of northeastern Nicaragua, but was defeated by the isolation of the area and the lack of support offered by the predominantly Miskito population.[81] The extent of the National Guard's reach in the western half of the country also discouraged many would-be rebels. Realizing the significant obstacles at hand, most dissidents vested their faith in the electoral process, at least until the January 1967 protests in Managua.

Groups on the fringe of Nicaraguan politics, such as the FSLN, persisted in their attempts to subvert the Somoza regime, however. Between 1963 and 1967, the Sandinistas devoted their attention to the construction of an urban guerrilla network. The arrest of two members of the FSLN and confiscation of weapons on the Costa Rican border in December 1966 led the U.S. embassy to speculate that Communists might attempt to take advantage of political tension in the upcoming elections to foment violence.[82] Sandinistas gained little support from the urban poor, but made a number of inroads in the student population through the Frente Estudiantil Revolucionario. Tentative political contacts were made with disaffected members of the Liberal and Conservative parties, whose membership sometimes offered oblique support to the FSLN through their advocacy of the FER and other student groups.[83] Fernando Agüero Rocha claimed in the aftermath of the January 1967 riots that some Conservatives might join the FSLN if Somoza continued arrests of party members. His compatriots in the Nicaraguan National Assembly portrayed FSLN guerrillas as idealistic students. Intelligence reports also indicated that Sandinistas had met with Conservative leaders in May 1967, although American analysts speculated that Agüero gave passing support to the FSLN simply in order to embarrass the Somozas.[84] In the final analysis, the Sandinista's urban movement failed to generate substantial political support.

Perhaps realizing the limitations of the urban strategy, the FSLN began the transition back to a rural campaign against Managua in 1966. They coined their new strategy the *guerra popular prolongada*, in effect a continuation of the Cuban *foco* idea, albeit with the expectation that it would be conducted over a much more extended period of time.[85] The FSLN began organizing a guerrilla force around Pancasan, near Matagalpa, and were able to sustain military operations there for a number of weeks. Although contemporary observers noted signs of greater tactical aptitude, the rebels were routed in a series of clashes with *Guardia Nacional* units in August 1967 that resulted in the death of Sandinista leader Silvio Mayorga. FSLN leaders recognized the obvious military defeat, but portrayed the event as a moral victory against the Somozas.[86] In September 1967, attempting to build upon their earlier success against the rebels, the Guardia shifted operations north into the Isabela Mountains near the Honduran border. At the conclusion of an operation that pushed thirty FSLN guerrillas into the neighboring country, Anastasio Somoza announced to the U.S. and Nicaraguan press that the guerrilla threat had been "exterminated."[87]

He was wrong. After a series of bombings directed against Liberal politicians and a *Guardia* officer's home in October, some American analysts openly speculated that the FSLN had reverted to urban terrorism.[88] Later that month, the Somoza government announced that reliable intelligence information indicated that the FSLN and the Frente Estudiantil Revolucionario were planning to "unleash a wave of violence" in the city of Leon. The U.S. Defense attaché, according to the U.S. embassy, later "confirmed the substance of these reports."[89]

The Sandinistas' ability to sustain their war against the Somoza regime worried American officials. In a memorandum to Secretary Rusk, the State Department's Bureau of Intelligence and Research warned,

It is difficult to estimate the size, organization and potential of the FSLN, because nearly all of the available information comes from one source—the National Guard. However, there are strong indications that the FSLN has the potential to continue its efforts to organize a significant level of insurgency. The FSLN hard core is determined; the majority of its guerrillas are probably still at large; its urban and support mechanisms—although bruised—have not been broken. Moreover, the FSLN can probably continue to count on support from Cuba and it maintains links with other anti-Somoza groups in Nicaragua. The FSLN must contend with one of Central America's most efficient security forces, the Nicaraguan National Guard, but the Guard is not a large organization and its resources would be strained by a widespread, well-dispersed guerrilla insurgency.[90]

The report proved prophetic. Less than a month after it was released, National Guard units killed four FSLN members in a Managua raid that also seized arms and alleged lists of recruits as well as officials targeted for assassination.[91] The *Guardia* continued its campaign against suspected dissidents into 1968, when *La Prensa* reported the January arrest of eight accused Communists in Masatepe.[92]

U.S. military support for Nicaraguan counterinsurgency programs proved to be much more tentative and conditional than the assistance given to Guatemala. At the San Salvador conference of Central American Ministers of Government on 14 January 1964, U.S. officials were approached by Nicaragua's representative, Dr. Lorenzo

Guerrero, who "made a strong presentation" regarding the fact that his country was the only one at the meeting that did not receive police assistance from the United States. Later that night, Captain Franklin Wheelock, an advisor to Anastasio Somoza, made the case to American delegates representing the Office of Public Safety that Nicaragua "urgently needed" support for internal security. Specifically, Wheelock requested "commodity assistance" in the form of vehicles and radio equipment. The U.S. officials present referred the Nicaraguan officer back to the embassy in Managua, but restated the basic conditions for public safety aid: (1) The country had to have permanently assigned U.S. military advisors, and (2) U.S. officials had to complete a survey of the host nation's police organization, its administration, operation, and personnel.[93]

The American embassy in Managua conducted the review one year later. Officials focused in particular on the police function of the *Guardia*, noting that approximately one half of its 5,800 soldiers were directly engaged in police activities. The report commented that National Guard personnel actually assigned police duties were poorly trained and equipped to deal with either criminal activities or political subversion. Most of the police in Managua were assigned to traffic control. In fact, crime, and its concurrent impact on social stability, appeared to be the more serious challenge to U.S. interests. Gangs reportedly "operated with ease in Managua and some of the other larger towns." Ambassador Aaron Brown's final recommendation was that one public safety officer be assigned to the U.S. mission in Nicaragua.[94]

A military assistance plan followed the embassy report in 1966. Primarily, it endorsed measures dedicated to building Nicaragua's conventional military forces. The report drew criticism almost immediately from Ted Brown, Chief of the Office of Public Safety for Latin America. Brown commented that the twenty-two American military advisors stationed in Nicaragua were "thinking in terms of tanks and heavy military equipment rather than the more useful and effective civil police equipment." Moreover, he argued that the military's preference for bayonets in civil disturbances made it "difficult indeed to build the image of the National Guard as a Public Service organization."[95] Although the State Department did not concur with the specifics of Brown's report, it did balk at the monetary requirement of additional U.S. assistance for internal security. The estimated costs of military aid for fiscal year 1969 ($1.9 million) and fiscal year 1970 ($1.8 million) were 50-percent higher than 1967 funding levels. Policy makers in Washington flatly rejected the embassy's claim that the "most serious immediate security problem is relative lack of law and order."[96]

Planning and financing considerations aside, the United States remained extremely circumspect about the interaction of security assistance and internal Nicaraguan political affairs. Recently declassified documents reveal that both the State Department and the U.S. embassy in Nicaragua were extremely skittish about upsetting the political climate in Managua by offering any type of military aid that might be misconstrued as support for the Somoza regime. This fear was exemplified in the lengthy debate over a cable from Joint Chiefs of Staff Chairman Earl Wheeler to Anastasio Somoza in 1967. Specifically, the topic of the cable dealt with an invitation Wheeler had received to Somoza's inauguration ceremony, planned for May of that year. Wheeler declined the offer, citing the constraints of a busy schedule, but offered his "best wishes for success in his undertakings as chief of state of a good American neighbor."[97] State Department officials immediately voiced their objections to the term "best wishes," claiming that the Wheeler cable could be used by the regime "for publicity purposes."[98] For more than a week civilian officials reiterated the need to remove the unwanted phrase as it might imply an endorsement of the questionable 1967 election. In the end, Wheeler simply removed the reference in a final draft to the U.S. Defense attaché in Managua, conceding in principle to his diplomatic counterparts the risks contained in the phrase.[99]

In many respects, the contrast between U.S. treatment of the Nicaraguan and Guatemalan insurgencies could not have been more pronounced. The Guatemalan guerrilla movement was certainly larger and posed a greater threat to internal stability, but so too did the Guatemalan military. The fact that MR-13, the Fuerzas Armadas Rebeldes, and other Guatemalan insurgents were able to generate some momentum during the Dominican crisis marked them as a danger at a time when the United States was willing to commit substantial resources to the problem of subversion. The creation of the "counter-insurgency state," to use James Dunkerley's term, followed in the wake of this hard line.[100]

More important were the similarities between the two countries. The respective political transitions that placed Schick and Méndez Montenegro into office were stage-managed affairs that created the veneer of political legitimacy, assuring U.S. policy makers that they might offer the foundation for future reform, however far off. In both cases, American policy makers shied away from further direct political involvement via the military or other third-party political organizations. Once satisfied that the respective regimes were non-Communist and pro-American in their alignment, the United States left them to pursue "self-help" at home, and to take responsibility for the results.

CONCLUSIONS

In late 1967, U.S. officials in the so-called Special State–Defense Study Group undertook a basic reevaluation of Latin American policy. Comprised of such notables as Deputy Defense Secretary Paul Nitze, Chairman of the Joint Chief of Staff Earl Wheeler, and CIA Director Richard Helms, it was chaired by Edwin Martin, a former official from the Kennedy administration, then ambassador to Brazil.[101] The "Martin Study," as it became know, was charged to "identify and analyze U.S. national interests in [the] area; propose U.S. objectives; and recommend strategy and specific lines to promote attainment of objectives, for general period, 1968–1973."[102] Interestingly, despite the number of senior officials present in its membership, the report produced no great departures from the current policy regime and essentially endorsed a stay-the-course approach to future hemispheric relations. In one important area, however, the Martin Study conceded the need for the United States to provide supersonic aircraft to Latin America. Future sales policies, it recommended, should be made with an eye more favorable to political than military criteria.[103]

In the meantime, the insurgencies in Central America persisted. In Guatemala, the surviving elements of MR-13 and the FAR no longer functioned as cohesive guerrilla movements in the field and increasingly reverted to the same terrorism and use of selective assassinations as the death squads that pursued them. Nicaraguan rebels took a different sort of route in the late 1960s. By 1968, the FSLN had largely ceased to exist as a military organization. However, as Dunkerley has pointed out, the Sandinistas managed to survive as a coherent political movement, one built upon a pragmatism produced by bitter experience.[104] The FSLN of the next decade would benefit enormously from the substantive debate, if not its resolution, produced by the failure of the *foco* in Nicaragua.[105]

Aid and influence were clearly decoupled as far as the United States was concerned in Nicaragua, for two reasons. First, American officials who were part of the country team were sufficiently wary of the domestic political bramble bush to give the very idea of exercising influence a wide berth. If anything, the debate over the Wheeler cable exemplifies the degree to which both diplomats and soldiers tried to avoid even the smallest entanglement with the Somoza regime. Second, influence also ran aground on the notable preference within the *Guardia Nacional* for internal security over civic action.[106] Steven Ropp's research on *Guardia* attendees of the School of the Americas noted that few demonstrated an interest in training that discussed social reform or political development. Instead, most students surveyed viewed Communist subversion as the primary challenge to their nation's future stability.[107] Despite deliberate American attempts to the contrary, there was no "generational change" from within the lower ranks of the Nicaraguan officer corps.

NOTES

1. James T. Patterson, *Grand Expectations: The United States, 1945–1974* (New York: Oxford University Press, 1996), 524–561.

2. A. J. Bacevich, *The Pentomic Era: The U.S. Army between Korea and Vietnam* (Washington, D.C.: National Defense University Press, 1986), 88–100; Richard A. Aliano, *American Defense Policy from Eisenhower to Kennedy: The Politics of Changing Military Requirements, 1957–1961* (Athens: Ohio University Press, 1975). See also Maxwell Taylor, *Swords and Plowshares* (New York: W. W. Norton, 1972).

3. Paul Kennedy, *The Rise and Fall of Great Powers: Economic Change and Military Conflict from 1500 to 2000* (New York: Vintage Books, 1989), 384.

4. Warren W. Hassler, *With Shield and Sword: American Military Affairs, Colonial Times to the Present* (Ames: Iowa State University Press, 1982), 375.

5. Allan R. Millett and Peter Maslowski, *For the Common Defense: A Military History of the United States of America* (New York: The Free Press, 1994), 656.

6. "Jungle Faculty," *Newsweek*, 6 March 1961, 33.

7. Ibid.

8. Memorandum for the President from David Bell (AID), "New Directions in Foreign Aid," 9 December 1964, Lyndon Baines Johnson Library (hereafter LBJ), White House Central File, Confidential File, Subject File, Foreign Affairs, Box 46.

9. U.S. Department of State and Department of Defense, *Proposed Mutual Defense and Development Programs, FY 1966*, LBJ, National Security File (hereafter NSF), Agency File, Box 1.

10. U.S. Office of the President, *Foreign Assistance Program: Annual Report to Congress, Fiscal Year 1965*, LBJ, NSF, Agency File, Box 1.

11. Statement, Robert S. McNamara (Secretary of Defense) before the House Foreign Affairs Committee in Support of the FY Military Assistance Program, 11 March 1965, National Archives

and Records Administration (hereafter NARA), Records Group 59 (hereafter RG 59), Deputy Assistant Secretary of State for Politico–Military Affairs, Office of Operations, Subject Files, 1961–68, Lot 67D195, Box 19.

12. Morris H. Morley, *Washington, Somoza, and the Sandinistas: State and Regime in U.S. Policy toward Nicaragua, 1969–1981* (New York: Cambridge University Press, 1994), 39.

13. NSAM 283, "U.S. Overseas Internal Defense Training Policy and Objectives," 13 February 1964, NARA, R G 59, General Records of the Department of State, National Security Action Memoranda (hereafter NSAM) Files, 1961–1968, Box 7.

14. NSAM 297, "Latin American Military Aid," 22 April 1964, NARA, RG 59, National Security Action Memoranda Files, 1961–1968, Box 7.

15. Letter, Brigadier General John W. Vogt (Director, Policy Planning Staff) to Jeffrey C. Kitchen (Deputy Assistant Secretary of State for Politico-Military Affairs), 2 March 1964, NARA, RG 59, Deputy Assistant Secretary of State for Politico-Military Affairs, Office of Operations, Subject Files, 1961–68, Lot 66D117, Box 13.

16. Ibid.

17. Memorandum, Jeffrey C. Kitchen (Deputy Assistant Secretary of State for Politico-Military Affairs) to George Ball (Undersecretary of State), "Coordination within the State Department in Connection with Military Sales Efforts," 23 June 1964, NARA, RG 59, Deputy Assistant Secretary of State for Politico-Military Affairs, Office of Operations, Subject Files, 1961–68, Lot 67D195, Box 21.

18. Memorandum, Thomas L. Hughes (Bureau of Intelligence and Research) to Dean Rusk, "Nicaraguan Insurgency Still Smolders," 19 October 1967, NARA, Subject–Numeric File, 1967–69, Box 2178. See also John Shy and Thomas W. Collier, "Revolutionary War," in *Makers of Modern Strategy: From Machiavelli to the Nuclear Age*, ed. Peter Paret (Princeton, N.J.: Princeton University Press, 1986), 849–852.

19. Tad Szulc, *Fidel: A Critical Portrait* (New York: Avon Books, 1986), 668–674; see also Memorandum, Covey T. Oliver (Assistant Secretary of State for Inter-American Affairs) to Walt W. Rostow, "Counterinsurgency Developments in Latin America," 7 September 1967, LBJ, NSF, Country File, Latin America, Box 9.

20. Memorandum for the Record, Minutes of the Meeting of the Special Group (CI), 8 April 1965, NARA, Records Group 286 (hereafter RG 286), USAID, Office of Public Safety, Numerical File, 1956–74, Box 6.

21. U.S. Central Intelligence Agency (CIA), Board of National Estimates, Special Memorandum no. 1-67, "Latin American Insurgencies Revisited," 17 February 1967, LBJ, NSF, Country File, Latin America, Box 3.

22. Memorandum for the Record, Minutes of the Meeting of the Special Group (CI), 8 April 1965.

23. Department of State, Bureau of Intelligence and Research, Research Memorandum RSB-121, "Moscow's Evolving Doctrine for Latin America," 26 October 1965, NARA, RG 286, USAID, Office of Public Safety, Numerical File, 1956–74, Box 7.

24. CIA, Intelligence Information Cable, "Chinese Communist Party Advice to Latin America Communist Revolutionary Leaders, 25 June 1964, LBJ, NSF, Country File, Latin America, Box 2.

25. Ibid.

26. CIA, Office of Current Intelligence, Intelligence Memorandum, "Instability in Latin America," 18 May 1965, LBJ, NSF, Country File, Latin America, Box 2.

27. Memorandum for the Record, Minutes of the Meeting of the Special Group (CI), 5 November 1965, NARA, RG 286, USAID, Office of Public Safety, Numerical File, 1956–74, Box 7.

28. U.S. CIA, "Instability in Latin America," 18 May 1965.

29. U.S. Department of Defense and Department of State, Bureau of Budget, *Joint Study of the Defense Department Representation Abroad: Report for Latin America*, May 1964, LBJ, NSF, Country File, Latin America, Box 2.

30. Ibid.

31. Ibid.

32. Ibid.

33. Memorandum, Maxwell D. Taylor (Counterinsurgency Review Board) to Earl Wheeler (Chairman, JCS), 13 October 1965, NARA, Records Group 218 (hereafter RG 218), Records of the U.S. Joint Chiefs of Staff, Box 106.

34. Memorandum, U.S. Joint Chiefs of Staff, Office of the Special Assistant for Counterinsurgency and Special Activities, "Review of Counterinsurgency Activities," 12 November 1965, NARA, RG 218, Records of the U.S. Joint Chiefs of Staff, Box 106.

35. Michael D. Gambone, *Eisenhower, Somoza, and the Cold War in Nicaragua, 1953–1961* (Westport, Conn.: Praeger, 1997), 190–195.

36. Memorandum of Conversation, Roy R. Rubottom and Pedro Beltran, 23 October 1957, NARA, Record Group 59, Lot 59D573, Box 3.

37. U.S. CIA, Directorate of Intelligence, Special Report, Weekly Review, "Assessment of Latin American Military and Arms Needs," 23 December 1966, LBJ, NSF, Country File, Latin America, Box 2.

38. Letter, Embajada de Chile to the Department of State, "Chile and the 'Armaments Race' in Latin America," 1 November 1966, NARA, RG 59, Subject–Numeric File, 1964–66, Box 1655.

39. U.S. CIA, "Assessment of Latin American Military and Arms Needs," 23 December 1966.

40. Interview, Thomas Mann, 4 November 1968, LBJ, Oral History Collection, 20.

41. *SIPRI Yearbook of World Armaments and Disarmament, 1968/69* (New York: Humanities Press, 1970), 57.

42. Memorandum, Jack Vaughn (Assistant Secretary of State for Inter-American Affairs) to George Ball, "European Arms Sales to Latin Americans" 19 April 1965, NARA, RG 59, Deputy Assistant Secretary of State for Politico-Military Affairs, Office of Operations, Subject File, 1962–66, Box 6.

43. NSAM 297, 22 April 1964.

44. Memorandum, McGeorge Bundy (Special Assistant for National Security Affairs) to State, Defense, and AID, 8 October 1964, LBJ, NSF, Country File, Latin America, Box 2.

45. Memorandum, Benjamin H. Read (Special Assistant to the Secretary of State) to McGeorge Bundy, "Latin American Military Aid," 2 September 1964, NARA, RG 59, NSAM Files, 1961–68, Box 7.

46. Memorandum, Allen to Jack Vaughn (Assistant Secretary of State for Inter-American Affairs), "Study on U.S. Policies toward Latin American Military Forces," 15 March 1965, NARA, RG 59, Subject–Numeric File, 1964–66, Box 1656.

47. Letter, Jack Vaughn (Assistant Secretary of State for Inter-American Affairs) to Edwin M. Martin (Ambassador to Brazil), 4 August 1965, NARA, RG 59, Subject–Numeric File, 1964–66, Box 1656.

48. Office of the Assistant Secretary of Defense for International Security Affairs, "U.S. Policies toward Latin American Military Forces," 25 February 1965, LBJ, NSF, Country File, Latin America, Box 2.

49. Memorandum, Robert S. McNamara to McGeorge Bundy, 11 June 1965, NSF, Country File, Latin America, Box 2.

50. Ibid.

51. Cable, Embassy (Lima) to State, 24 August 1966, NARA, RG 59, Subject–Numeric File, 1964–66, Box 1655.

52. *SIPRI Yearbook of World Armaments and Disarmament*, 58–60.

53. Memorandum, Sandy M. Pringle to Adams, "Argentine Aircraft Procurement," 29 March 1965, NARA, RG 59, Deputy Assistant Secretary of State for Politico-Military Affairs, Office of Operations, Subject File, 1962–66, Box 6.

54. Cable, U.S. Defense Attaché (Santiago) to Department of the Air Force, 16 September 1966, NARA, RG 59, Deputy Assistant Secretary of State for Politico-Military Affairs, Office of Operations, Subject Files, 1962–66, Box 6.

55. "The Latin American Arms Race," *Economist*, 2 November 1967, 1–4.

56. Cable, U.S. Defense Attaché (Santiago) to Department of the Air Force, 16 September 1966.

57. Ibid.; *SIPRI Yearbook of World Armaments and Disarmament*, 59.

58. "The Latin American Arms Race," *The Economist: Foreign Report*, pp. 1–4.

59. Michael McClintock, *Instruments of Statecraft: U.S. Guerrilla Warfare, Counter-Insurgency, Counter-Terrorism, 1940–1990* (New York: Pantheon Books, 1992), 187–222; Charles M. Simpson, *Inside the Green Berets: The First Thirty Years, A History of the U.S. Army Special Forces* (Novato, Calif.: Presidio Press, 1983), 82–83.

60. U.S. Department of the Army, Jungle Warfare Training Center Brochure, Ft. Sherman, Canal Zone, n.d., JFK, NSF, Departments and Agencies, Box 269; Walter LaFeber, *Inevitable Revolutions: The United States in Central America* (New York: W. W. Norton, 1984), 151–153.

61. Memo, Bundy to State, Defense , and AID, 8 October 1964.

62. Office of the Assistant Secretary of Defense for International Security Affairs, "U.S. Policies toward Latin American Military Forces," 25 February 1965.

63. Edwin Lieuwen, *U.S. Policy in Latin America: A Short History* (New York: Praeger, 1967), 102–104.

64. McClintock, *Instruments of Statecraft*, 216.

65. John H. Coatsworth, *Central America and the United States: The Clients and the Colossus* (New York: Twayne, 1994), 106–108; Cable, U.S. Army Attaché (Nicaragua) to the Department of the Army, 28 April 1965, NARA, RG 59, Subject–Numeric File, 1964–66, Box 1654.

66. Letter, William B. Macomber (Assistant Secretary of State for Congressional Relations) to J. W. Fulbright, 31 October 1967, NARA, RG 59, Subject–Numeric File, 1967–69, Box 2109.

67. Cable, Embassy (Managua) to State, 12 July 1965, NARA, RG 59, Deputy Assistant Secretary of State for Politico-Military Affairs, Office of Operations, Subject Files, 1961–68, Lot 67D195, Box 19.

68. Cable, Embassy (Managua) to State, 22 June 1966, NARA, RG 59, Subject–Numeric File, 1964–66, Box 1654.

69. Trumbull Higgins, *The Perfect Failure: Kennedy, Eisenhower, and the CIA at the Bay of Pigs* (New York: W. W. Norton, 1987), 74, 104. See also Luis Aguilar, ed., *Operation Zapata: The "Ultrasensitive" Report and Testimony of the Board of Inquiry on the Bay of Pigs* (Frederick, Md.: University Publications of America, 1981).

70. Willard F. Barber and C. Neale Ronning, *Internal Security and Military Power: Counterinsurgency and Civic Action in Latin America* (Columbus: Ohio State University Press, 1966), 127–131.

71. Douglas S. Blaufarb and George K. Tanham, *Who Will Win? A Key to the Puzzle of Revolutionary War* (New York: Crane Russak, 1989), 91–99; Coatsworth, *Central America and the United States*, 90–121.

72. Blaufarb and Tanham, *Who Will Win?* 95–96.

73. Ibid., 95. See also Matt D. Childs, "An Historical Critique of the Emergence and Evolution of Ernesto Che Guevara's Foco Theory," *Journal of Latin American Studies* 27 (1995): 593–624.

74. James Dunkerley, *Power in the Isthmus: A Political History of Modern Central America* (New York: Verso, 1988), 444–461.

75. U.S. Department of Defense, Department of State, *Joint Study of the Defense Department Representation Abroad*; U.S. Department of Defense, Office of the Assistant Secretary of Defense for International Security Affairs, "MAP Review Meeting on 26 October 1964," 23 October 1964, NARA, RG 59, Deputy Assistant Secretary of State for Politico-Military Affairs, Office of Operations, Subject Files, 1961–68, Lot 66D117, Box 13. See Michael McClintock, *The American Connection: State Terror and Popular Resistance in Guatemala*, vol. 2 (London: Zed Books, 1985), 49–82.

76. Douglas S. Blaufarb, *The Counterinsurgency Era: U.S. Doctrine and Performance, 1950 to the Present* (New York: The Free Press, 1977), 52–60; Carlos Caballero Jurado and Nigel Thomas, *Central American Wars, 1959–1989* (London: Osprey, 1990), 8–11; Simpson, *Inside the Green Berets*, 81–86.

77. Blaufarb and Tanham, *Who Will Win?* 97.

78. Dunkerley, *Power in the Isthmus*, 446.

79. Ibid., 447.

80. Guenther Lewy, *America in Vietnam* (New York: Oxford University Press, 1978), 77–126. See also Jeffrey J. Clarke, *Advice and Support: The Final Years* (Washington, D.C.: Center of Military History, 1988).

81. Claribel Alegria and D. J. Flakoll, *Nicaragua: la revolucion sandinista, Una Cronica politica, 1855–1979* (Mexico, D.F.: Ediciones Era, S.A., 1982), 166–196; Dunkerley, *Power in the Isthmus*, 239.

82. Cable, Embassy (Managua) to State, 29 December 1966, NARA, RG 59, Subject–Numeric File, 1964–66, Box 2514.

83. Cable, Embassy (Managua) to State, 22 May 1964, NARA, RG 59, Subject–Numeric File, 1964–66, Box 2512.

84. Memorandum, Hughes to Rusk, "Nicaraguan Insurgency Still Smolders," 19 October 1967.

85. Liza Gross, *Handbook of Leftist Guerrilla Groups in Latin America and the Caribbean* (Boulder, Colo.: Westview Press, 1995), 125–127.

86. Steven Palmer, "Carlos Fonseca and the Construction of Sandinismo in Nicaragua," *Latin American Research Review* 23 (1988): 91–109.

87. Cable, Embassy (Managua) to State, 8 October 1967, NARA, RG 59, Subject–Numeric File, 1967–69, Box 2177.

88. Cable, Embassy (Managua) to State, 19 October 1967, NARA, RG 59, Subject–Numeric File, 1967–69, Box 2177.

89. Cable, Embassy (Managua) to State, 29 October 1967, NARA, Subject–Numeric File, 1967–69, Box 2177.

90. Memorandum, Hughes to Rusk, "Nicaraguan Insurgency Still Smolders," 19 October 1967.

91. Cable, Embassy (Managua) to State, 11 November 1967, NARA, RG 59, Subject–Numeric File, 1967–69, Box 2177.

92. Cable, Embassy (Managua) to State, 20 January 1968, NARA, RG 59, Subject–Numeric File, 1967–69, Box 2177.

93. Memorandum, Johnson F. Monroe (Office of Public Safety) to Byron Engle (Director, Office of Public Safety), "Nicaragua Public Safety Assistance," 24 January 1964, NARA, RG 286, USAID, Office of Public Safety, Country File, Box 91.

94. Cable, Embassy (Managua) to State, 3 July 1965, NARA, RG 59, Subject–Numeric File, 1967–69, Box 486.

95. Memorandum, Ted Brown (Chief, Office of Public Safety, Latin America) to Byron Engle (Director, Office of Public Safety), "Military Assistance Plan for Nicaragua," 1 August 1966, NARA, RG 286, USAID, Office of Public Safety, Country File, Box 91.

96. Cable, State Department to Embassy (Managua), 12 May 1967, NARA, RG 59, Subject–Numeric File, 1967–69, Box 2111.

97. Cable, Chairman, Joint Chiefs of Staff to U.S. Defense Attaché Office (Managua), 25 April 1967, NARA, RG 218, Records of the U.S. Joint Chiefs of Staff, Box 33.

98. Cable, State to Embassy (Managua), 27 April 1967, NARA, RG 218, Records of the U.S. Joint Chiefs of Staff, Box 33.

99. Cable, Chairman, Joint Chiefs of Staff to U.S. Defense Attaché Office (Managua), 28 April 1967, NARA, RG 218, Records of the U.S. Joint Chiefs of Staff, Box 33.

100. Dunkerley, *Power in the Isthmus*, 456

101. Cable, State to all ARA Posts, 25 October 1967, NARA, RG 59, Subject–Numeric File, 1967–69, Box 2111.

102. Memorandum, Covey T. Oliver (Assistant Secretary of State for Inter-American Affairs) to Nicholas Katzenbach (Undersecretary of State), "Recommendations for Handling of the 'Martin Study,'" 30 April 1968, NARA, RG 59, Subject–Numeric File, 1967–69, Box 2111.

103. Ibid.

104. Dunkerley, *Power in the Isthmus*, 239.

105. Palmer, "Carlos Fonseca and the Construction of Sandinismo in Nicaragua," 91–109.

106. Dunkerley, *Power in the Isthmus*, 455–460; Blaufarb and Tanham, *Who Will Win?* 98.

107. Steven C. Ropp, "In Search of the New Soldier: Junior Officers and the Prospect of Social Reform in Panama, Honduras, and Nicaragua" (Ph.D. diss., University of California, Riverside, 1971), 121–133; see also Steven C. Ropp, "Goal Orientation of Nicaraguan Cadets: Some Applications for the Problems of Structural/Behavioral Projection in Researching the Latin American Military." *Journal of Comparative Administration* 4 (1972): 107–116.

CHAPTER 6

Recapturing Economic Reform

To all the hemisphere we say: Let the pace be quickened. Time is not our ally.
Lyndon Johnson, 1966

As the Alliance for Progress moved forward, the afterglow of Punta del Este began to diminish, replaced by a growing public chorus of skepticism regarding its cost and direction. In the wake of accumulating commitments at home and in Southeast Asia, critics of the Johnson administration openly questioned the utility of economic assistance to Latin America. Faced with these obstacles, American officials needed to refashion economic assistance in a manner that would reduce its cost and provide some measurable way of demonstrating its progress. The Central American Common Market seemed to be one possible means of accomplishing this. Initially, the CACM proved more than adequate to spur regional economic growth through its reduction of barriers to trade. Problems later emerged over the structure of development and the preferences of the individual participants. Despite the prospect of declining U.S. assistance and the common market's difficulties, Nicaragua appeared to have a strong economy at mid-decade. Bolstered by strong coffee and cotton production, it had embarked on a broad diversification of industry and manufacturing. Yet even with the impressive array of statistics indicating progress, Nicaragua could not escape the same systemic economic problems that plagued Central America.

When Lyndon Johnson became president in 1963, he confronted an American assistance policy plagued by criticism at home and abroad. Many observers concluded that the Alliance for Progress, already burdened by the unresolved mistakes of the previous two years, was unsalvageable.[1] Covey T. Oliver, the assistant secretary of state for inter-American affairs during the latter part of the Johnson administration, attributed this problem to what he called the "Death Syndrome" in Latin America. Oliver believed that hemispheric leaders were fixated on the Dallas assassination and saw it as a sign of the symbolic and substantive death of the *Alianza* despite statements to the contrary by their American counterparts.[2]

The domestic political front seemed equally discouraging. According to the Agency for International Development's deputy administrator for operations, Frank M. Coffin, U.S. assistance programs were "in trouble in Congress." Capitol Hill demanded new procedures that minimized waste and duplication and placed a higher premium on self-help and private enterprise. Under legislative pressure, loan terms were hardened to include higher interest rates over shorter periods of time. Congress also demanded and received changes in grant and loan policies that required recipient nations to procure 80 percent of their goods and services from American suppliers, double the 1961 standard. "The irony," according to Coffin, "is that at the very time when the planning and execution of aid is better than ever before, the general view is that nothing has changed in ten years."[3]

Caught in the wake of a growing body of demands, conditions, and requirements, administration policy makers doggedly defended the past and began to consider significant changes for the future. In testimony before the Senate Foreign Relations Committee in April 1966, Dean Rusk reminded lawmakers,

Too often, I think, we let immediate crises and headlines obscure the very real progress that is being made in so many parts of the world. This is often called the "quiet battle," and it is a battle of which all Americans can be proud. As the President said in his Foreign Aid Message, "We still never know how many crises have been averted, how much violence avoided, or how many minds have been won to the cause of freedom in these years."[4]

Yet in the same testimony, Rusk also repeated an administrative line that emphasized self-help as a "fundamental fact" of America's economic assistance policy.[5]

Assurances like these generally failed to assuage the congressional reaction against the Alliance for Progress, particularly in the last months of the Kennedy administration. A report offered by Hubert H. Humphrey in 1963 attempted a balanced approach to the issue. On the positive side, the document recognized in a somewhat backhanded manner "solid, but spotty progress" in the areas of health, housing, education, and agriculture. What is striking about the Humphrey report was its consideration of the vast scale of the work still undone, particularly in the slums, "which fester in almost every Latin American city and in much of the countryside."[6]

Critics of the administration picked up on this theme. Raymond F. Mikesell, a professor of economics at the University of Oregon and consultant for the Senate Foreign Relations Committee, was mildly optimistic about the Alliance, suggesting that "certain positive achievements" had been made in its relatively short lifespan. The "majority of the leaders and of the articulate electorate appear to identify themselves with the fundamental aims of the program and 'Alianza para el Progreso' has become a symbol and a basis for positive economic and social philosophy for the moderate members of a number of political and economic groups within the individual countries." On a more tangible level, basic shortcomings remained: "However, I believe it is safe to say that in few, if any, of the Latin American countries, has the broadly based rate of economic growth and individual well-being equivalent to the two and a half per cent growth goal of the Punta del Este Charter been achieved."[7] Specifically, Mikesell cited the chronic problem of low savings rates and insufficient foreign investment. Moreover, primitive technology and a constant shortage of managerial talent inhibited productivity in both industry and agriculture. Inflation ravaged many countries. Between 1964–1965 and 1965–1966, most Latin American economies had failed to achieved the 2.5-percent growth in per capita GDP established as the standard at Punta del Este in 1961. In reality, during the entire 1961–1965 period, Latin American per capita GDP increased at an annual rate of only 1.8 percent.[8]

As the alliance appeared to lose momentum, so too did congressional support for its continuation. When legislators concluded deliberations on the AID budget for FY1967, they cut it from $2.46 billion to $2.14 billion. The agency's portion designated for the Alliance for Progress was reduced from $543 million to $503 million. Certain efforts, such as the war in South Vietnam, received supplemental assistance from other departments (e.g., Defense). Latin America, however, was on its own.[9]

To this list of obstacles that sat before the Johnson administration were added the concerns voiced by many Latin Americans themselves. Juscelino Kubitschek's protests in mid-1963 regarding the politicization of U.S. assistance have been noted in Chapter 3.[10] What gained these accusations even more traction among Latin Americans was the Johnson administration's blatant use of aid to manipulate local governments in the furtherance of U.S. interests. The earliest case in point involved American support of the Brazilian military's coup against the government of Joao Goulart in March 1964. While American warships stood off the coastline as part of Operation Uncle Sam, AID funneled assistance to the individual state governments of Brazil, completely bypassing the capital. Additional aid followed to support the military regime that ruled in its place for the remainder of the decade.[11]

Domestic and foreign criticism compounded extensive internal structural difficulties suffered by the alliance. In a letter to AID Administrator David Bell, a staffer reflected on the difficulties in coordinating the activities of participating American agencies with multilateral organizations such as the International Cooperation Administration and the Development Loan Fund. Additional problems emerged that were produced by the diverse regional structure of foreign-aid administration. Rarely did the fragile mix of political, social, and economic conditions produce in one portion of Latin America (e.g., the southern cone) policies that could be applied with relevance in another part of the hemisphere. Cumulatively, American assistance represented an endless, ongoing juggling act that required U.S. officials to "strike the delicate balance between regional and Mission autonomy on the one hand and consistent Agency-wide policies and procedures on the other."[12]

Lyndon Johnson's mission was a reflection of this balancing effort, albeit on a much broader scale. On the one hand, the president was forced to fight off an accumulating array of opponents to the alliance with an even more tangible list of answers. Efficiency and cost-effectiveness would become well-worn bywords. Administration officials would consistently argue after 1964 that U.S. aid, as a percentage of the federal budget and GDP, had steadily diminished during the past decade and a half, with the per capita cost of assistance diminishing from $30.52 in 1949 to $17.51 in 1966.[13] Second, policy makers would concurrently attempt to wean aid recipients away from American assistance or, failing that, find alternatives to it. The real dilemma in this exercise was meeting commitments made to Latin America in the recent past, commitments that would require substantial amounts of aid regardless of its source.

DEVELOPMENT POLICY RETRENCHMENT

Throughout the early 1960s, American policy makers accepted the utilitarian, structuralist concepts that defined post–1945 assistance policy.[14] Past paradigms as presented by Max F. Millikan, Adolf Berle, and Walt Rostow retained considerable traction during the Kennedy–Johnson transition and were accepted as viable solutions to the ongoing problem of Third World development, just as they had a generation earlier in Western Europe. The solution to poverty was the incorporation of the free market and the transplantation of proven managerial and technical expertise. Once established, these would produce both prosperity and a concurrent foundation for derivative political freedoms. The conventional wisdom circa 1964 held, in other words, that economic pluralism would cultivate a similar degree of political diversity. Generally, Americans placed considerable credence in the fundamental belief that free-market institutions could facilitate free political values and structures.

The one factor that did change considerably was the emphasis on finding a different means to achieve this singular end. Within the Johnson administration at the beginning of 1964 there was a growing acceptance that more centralized host states and private corporate entities could facilitate economic development in the place of bilateral aid.[15] Private investment could serve in the same capacity as public assistance, supplementing or, in some cases, replacing U.S. funding lost to congressional budget cuts. Consequently, in practice, the intermediate goal of American foreign assistance changed from an emphasis on social infrastructure development that had been pursued in 1961 to a much different focus on building the economic infrastructure necessary to cultivate foreign private investment and multilateral assistance.[16]

Mann Doctrine as expressed in early 1964 was the product of this basic reconsideration of the aid structure. In fact, prior to Mann's selection as assistant secretary of state for inter-American affairs, the Commerce Department had already endorsed "a major shift in emphasis of the foreign assistance program toward broader involvement of other Government agencies and the private sector."[17] In a memorandum to George Ball's committee on foreign aid, the department made the case that splitting off assistance functions, as opposed to the "lumping" that occurred under AID, would make future aid more "politically saleable" to Congress. It would also have the advantage, Commerce officials believed, of making projects more acceptable to recipient countries if they were not directly identified with the United States.[18]

AID vehemently disagreed with this strategy in February 1964. David Bell in his own memo to the Ball committee, argued that the United States should retain unified organization of assistance under his agency. Bell noted that existing congressional consideration of assistance was already divided into two manageable parts, with military aid under the Department of Defense and civilian aid under the purview of the State Department. He did concede, however, that U.S. policy makers should consider channeling more aid through international institutions. Bell also admitted that the American aid program needed to place additional stress on the transition from "soft" (low-interest, long-term) loans and grants to normal trade and capital-investment practices, citing the successful leap made by countries like Japan, Spain, and Lebanon from direct assistance to the free market.[19]

American officials subsequently began to shift larger amounts of assistance toward long-term development projects, particularly infrastructure, electrical power, planning, and management training. According to the FY1965 AID program, this type of assistance comprised 52 percent of total American aid, more than double the 1961 figure. The end goal was to increase the transition to self-support by enabling the Third World to attract private capital. Consequently, U.S. policy placed increasing emphasis on private loans instead of direct bilateral grants, furthering the process of self-sufficiency or, at the very least active, encouraging participation in the global marketplace as an alternative to American aid.[20]

The type and amount of assistance a country received was also dependent on its proximity to the Communist threat. Not surprisingly, the bulk of "supporting assistance" (emergency funds) went to Asia. In 1966, 88 percent of supporting assistance found its way to four countries (Korea, Laos, Vietnam, and Jordan). Two-thirds of military assistance was spent on countries located on the periphery of the Soviet Bloc (Greece, Turkey, Pakistan, Iran, Laos, Vietnam, Thailand, the Philippines, Korea, and Taiwan).[21]

For its own part, Latin America lived in "the shadow of Communist Cuba," away from the imminent threat posed by Moscow. In the Western Hemisphere, America's goal was to address "the historic gulf between the very rich and the very poor, and trying, at 'one minute to midnight' to bridge the gulf with reforms, self-help and development within the Alliance for Progress." Consequently, approximately one-quarter (23%) of total U.S. economic assistance was dedicated to Latin America. In terms of per capita assistance, the region had the largest AID contribution ($2.59) of any place in the world. By 1965, American administrators had created self-help projects in eleven Latin American countries, devoting particular attention to tax collection, housing, land reform, electrical power, and road construction.[22] Washington also encouraged the inclusion of Organization of Economic Cooperation and Development countries in Latin American development programs. Between 1962 and 1964, Austria, France, Germany, Italy, Japan, The Netherlands, and England contributed more than $99 million in technical assistance to Latin America (see Table 6.1).[23]

In order to gauge the effectiveness of this effort, the Agency for International Development undertook an extensive review of American assistance policy in late 1965. The key to success, according to AID Director David Bell, was self-help. However, Bell added the important caveat that alliance programs could only be assessed against "appropriate self-help standards."[24] In its 1965 *Summary Presentation to Congress*, AID noted that land reform projects "have begun" in Venezuela, Colombia, Chile, Central America, Panama, Uruguay, and Brazil. Large-scale self-help housing projects in fifteen countries had constructed 220,000 units for 1.5 million people. Potable water and sewage systems had been built to serve more than 18 million people. Perhaps most important was the fact that national development plans had been submitted by eight Latin American countries.[25]

The emphasis on self-help also helped establish the yardstick American policy makers used to measure success. In its *Summary Presentation to Congress*, AID indicated that it "had had to adapt its programs to specific problems, to the stage of development, to the capabilities, and to the performance of Alliance partners." There was, in other words, no single standard to objectively evaluate progress toward any *Alianza* objective. Chile and Colombia, for example, had made "clear responses under Alliance criteria," but seemed to be the exceptions rather than the rule in Latin America.[26] American officials appeared to be specifically interested not in the results of particu-

Table 6.1
Economic Assistance to Latin America, 1963–1966 (US$ millions)

	1963	1964	1965	1966
U.S.				
Agency for International Development	552	613	532	647
Ex-Im Bank	67	170	166	226
Food for Peace	174	339	113	202
Social Progress Trust Fund	127	42	101	24
Miscellaneous U.S. Sources (Peace Corps, Inter-American Highway, etc.)	<u>79</u> 999	<u>83</u> 1,247	<u>284</u> 1,196	<u>288</u> 1,387
International				
Inter-American Development Bank	191	131	240	369
International Bank for Reconstruction and Development	123	258	212	375
International Development Association	11	12	18	8
U.N. Technical Assistance	12	20	15	14
U.N. Special Fund	19	16	32	46
U.N. Children's Emergency Fund	10	9	7	5
International Finance Corporation	10	7	10	24
European Economic Community	<u>6</u> 382	<u>10</u> 463	<u>8</u> 542	<u>11</u> 852
Total U.S. and International Assistance	1,381	1,710	1,738	2,239

Source: Office of Public Affairs, Bureau of Inter-American Affairs, Department of State, "Facts on Latin America's Development under the Alliance for Progress," April 1967, LBJ, NSF, Agency File, Box 5.

lar policies, but the degree of self-help undertaken by host nations. Although American advisors placed great emphasis on detailed planning and the creation of complete national development programs, they consistently gave credit to countries for "making basic preparations for reform."[27] Effort appeared equivalent to results.

The fundamental question of objective evaluation, however, was generally unaddressed at mid-decade. The original standards articulated in 1961 indicated a failure in many areas (e.g., education, health, social services, economic growth). As noted earlier, few Latin American countries could attain the Act of Bogota goal of 2.5-percent annual per capita GDP growth.[28] Yet few AID officials were willing to acknowledge the systemic difficulty in either measuring this important shortfall or creating comprehensive measures to address it. Nevertheless, the Johnson administration clung to the relationship between aid and development as the panacea for

Latin America. Progress toward development and reform, however haphazard and inconsistent, was progress nonetheless.

The 1967 Organization of American States summit was the culmination of American efforts to support the alliance during Johnson's presidency. It offered a final opportunity to refocus assistance policy. In a January memorandum to the president, Walt Rostow bluntly stated, "Latin America is at a crossroads." It had reached a point where the leaders of the hemisphere "need to be reassured at the Presidential level that we will not be distracted by other world problems from our long term commitment to work with them under the Alliance."[29] Moreover, it was a point at which the administration needed to recapture a degree of legislative initiative from Congress on the subject of foreign assistance. This was particularly pressing after Capitol Hill had cut the FY1967 assistance program from $2.4 billion to $2.1 billion, the largest cuts being made in technical assistance (from $231 million to $200 million) and the aid contingency fund (from $75 million to $35 million). Although the Alliance for Progress was relatively unhurt—U.S. support dropped from $543 million to $508 million—the administration wanted to arrest the trend.[30]

Johnson arrived at the summit prepared with concrete proposals to alter this trajectory. The "maximum package," Rostow's best-case scenario, included a commitment for the creation of a Latin American Common Market by 1980. Toward this end, the United States was prepared to offer up to $300 million over five years to an "Integration Fund" designed to provide "adjustment assistance," an increase by $50 million annually to the Inter-American Bank's Special Operations Fund for infrastructure, and an increase by $900 million for education and agriculture over five years to raise the latter 2 percent above the annual population growth.[31] American representatives also appeared willing to be more flexible as to where U.S. assistance was spent (excluding Japan and Europe). In return, the United States expected initiatives from host Latin America nations to cultivate private investment, negotiate major multinational development projects, and forego "sophisticated, expensive military equipment."[32] Johnson was particularly insistent on a clear Latin American commitment to self-help measures that matched increased U.S. assistance.[33]

The measures discussed by the president sparked some disagreement from within his administration. The Treasury Department argued that the Inter-American Development Bank should handle the proposed Integration Fund rather than the United States so as to avoid accusations that this latest policy was a simple cat's paw designed to strengthen American influence. At AID, William Gaud "strongly opposed" the recommendation for additional educational and agricultural funding, openly worrying that Congress would approve the money "at the expense of other areas." For his own part, Rostow's stood on the side of history and warned that the stakes involved were reminiscent of the alliance's heyday in 1961: "The issue boils down to whether you wish to exploit this historic moment to get Latin Americans to move boldly on integration, and thereby put your stamp on it, or whether you prefer to let nature take its course."[34]

William Gaud was right to worry about continued congressional opposition to the alliance. In March 1967, the House Foreign Affairs Committee grilled Rusk on the proposed $1.5-billion increase in assistance to Latin America. Peter H. B.

Freylinghuysen was particularly adamant about the prospect of spending such a massive amount of additional money after years of substantial commitments to the hemisphere. Johnson managed to assuage problems briefly in a private 16 March meeting with Democratic leaders, and brokered a House resolution "to support the allocation of significant additional resources" prior to the OAS summit. The measure passed on a vote of 234 to 118. He was less successful in the Senate, where Wayne Morse caustically described such a vote as another Tonkin Gulf Resolution. Blocked by Morse and a substantial number of senators, Johnson abandoned efforts at a joint congressional resolution.[35]

Further setbacks followed hard on the heels of Johnson's return from Latin America. In its deliberations on the FY1968 budget, legislators decided to allow foreign assistance to revert back to annual authorizations rather than multiyear appropriations allowed during the Kennedy administration. "The net effect of all this," AID administrator William Gaud would comment in a later interview,

is very unfortunate, I think, because this is an agency, which you might say, jumps from cliff to cliff. It's a crisis agency, and there's always before Congress and always before the American people the possibility that we will not have an AID program. And an AID program should be a long-term proposition if it is to achieve its ends. This is a very disastrous, a very unfortunate, state of affairs.[36]

These problems were compounded by Johnson's tendency, when frustrated by setbacks, to micromanage American policy in general and assistance policy in particular. As Doris Kearns has discussed in her examination of the Great Society, the president's inclination for problem solving often led him to intervene at points in the policy process where he assumed personal dynamism would become an adequate substitute for bureaucratic cooperation. His handling of both the air and ground war in Vietnam was emblematic of this approach. In Latin America, it became common practice that any program loan in excess of $5 million or any project loan of more than $10 million required the president's personal authorization.[37]

At the conclusion of 1967, Covey T. Oliver offered an official post mortem on the alliance and the economic state Latin America. He noted that one significant and increasingly recurrent problem was the fact that regional exports had flattened out, held back by low global prices for basic commodities. The driving force behind privately supported development appeared to be faltering. Despite this, Oliver was optimistic. The year had shown a "steady but modest economic gain for Latin America as a whole and related signs of growing political stability and stronger democratic institutions throughout the hemisphere."[38] According to the assistant secretary of state, U.S. aid for the fiscal year ending in June 1967 had contributed $563 million to this trend, a new high in annual volume. Multilateral assistance had also increased. The Inter-American Development Bank had loaned $396 million to Latin America, surpassing the record of $212 million in the previous year.[39]

Other sources were less sanguine about the future. In February 1968, the National Advisory Council on International Monetary and Financial Policies presented a proposal for a $1-billion increase in "ordinary capital," which would be made available through the Inter-American Development Bank for loans. Although the dollar amount was significant, the terms under which loans would progress were even more important. "Ordinary capital" referred to capital available for loans at normal market rates.[40] Essentially, the council's proposal called for additional "hard loans" to Latin Americans at market interest rates of 7.75 percent over periods ranging from seven to twenty years. These would supplement hard loans totaling over $900 million that had already been granted by the IADB between 1959 and 1967.[41]

At a time when it was apparent that Latin American economic development had begun to bog down, the Johnson administration was prepared to embrace an economic policy reminiscent of the Eisenhower era. It was a decision based upon contemporary realities. By 1968, distracted by the war in Vietnam, stymied by eroding public and Congressional support, officials found themselves actively contemplating options that had been condemned as both too limited and damaging to the Latin American economy a decade earlier.[42]

THE COMMON MARKET STUMBLES

In 1965, the Agency for International Development described the Central American Common Market as "a model of economic integration, not only for Latin American but for other developing areas as well."[43] At mid-decade it appeared that the institutional structure created during the Kennedy era was serving as an adequate building block for the dual objectives of free trade and economic integration.[44] Other improvements in the CACM followed. The Permanent Secretariat for Economic Integration and the Central American Bank for Economic Integration, created in 1961, were followed by the Central American Clearing House and the Regional Office for Central America and Panama, a subcomponent of the Agency for International Development.[45] Together, these organizations promoted regional cooperation in projects that included a transportation system, home mortgage financing, telecommunications, and grain storage facilities. By 1966, with the exception of certain government monopolies (e.g., alcohol) and commodities controlled by international agreements (e.g., coffee), almost all intraregional trade restrictions in Central America had been removed.[46]

At least initially, the common market succeeded in promoting both trade and growth. By the mid-1960s, however, momentum had slowed. Projected growth rates for member nations in 1967 were at best modest. Nicaragua's GNP grew at the highest rate (5.8%), while El Salvador (3.0%) and Guatemala (2.5%) made lesser gains. Honduras saw a net decline of 1.4 percent.[47] One major problem experienced by all the common market nations was population growth. With a burgeoning birth rate that in most years exceeded 3 percent, Central American economies were hard pressed to maintain pace with the growing burdens of housing, feeding, and educating new citizens each year, much less pursue new economic enterprises. Of all the Central American nations, only Nicaragua appeared to be an exception to this rule (see Table 6.2).

As the decade progressed, other more systemic problems with the CACM also emerged. Uneven regional growth plagued the common market. An expressed and often repeated goal of the CACM was "balanced development," something that of-

Table 6.2
GNP Change in Central America, 1963–1967

	GNP % Change				GNP Per Capita % Change			
	63-64	64-65	65-66	66-67	63-64	64-65	65-66	66-67
Costa Rica	3.4	7.0	6.5	3.2	-0.5	3.1	2.8	-0.6
El Salvador	7.8	4.1	5.7	5.9	4.6	0.7	2.2	2.7
Guatemala	6.6	7.4	6.4	2.2	3.2	3.7	3.0	-0.1
Honduras	3.1	6.8	6.2	-1.4	0.0	3.6	3.0	-4.5
Nicaragua	8.0	9.1	5.8	5.8	4.3	5.0	2.7	2.8

Source: Memorandum, Joseph A. Silberstein (Director, Office of Regional Economic Policy, Bureau of Inter-American Affairs), "Growth Rate Trends for 1967 in Latin America," 2 August 1967, LBJ, NSF, Country File, Latin America, Box 3.

ten proved very difficult to achieve in practice.[48] Guatemala continued to control the largest portion of regional production in Central America. Honduras constantly complained that the concentration of industry in Nicaragua and Guatemala directly hurt its ability to compete within the common market and attract foreign investment.[49] Perhaps most important was the basic fact that despite significant diversification efforts, Central America as a region remained highly dependent on export agriculture and high commodity prices. In 1964, for example, all five Central American countries derived more than 30 percent of their GDP from agriculture.[50] The downturn of global commodity prices that began in the late 1960s proved to be a serious problem for the common market. Trade deficits also remained a concern. Two countries (Nicaragua and Honduras) ran deficits in 1966; three (Nicaragua, Honduras, and Costa Rica) in 1968.[51]

The Central American Common Market also did little to foster balanced development within member countries. Regional integration directly generated 60,000 new jobs between 1958 and 1972 and 71,000 to 95,000 indirect jobs. Despite contemporary predictions, this growth could not maintain pace with the number of rural jobs lost to agricultural consolidation.[52] The most profitable new export ventures, particularly cotton and cattle, were capital-intensive enterprises that did not translate readily into employment. Nor did the emerging manufacturing sector immediately translate into opportunities for the mass of unskilled labor that dominated the regional labor pool. Urban unemployment, already a chronic problem, worsened throughout the region.[53]

The bureaucratic delays produced by the individual Central American governments also hurt the common market. In part, these were caused by treaty language that had been deliberately left ambiguous in order to gain widespread acceptance in the late 1950s and early 1960s. The ratification requirements contained in the 1958 Integration Industries Convention delayed some trade protocols for as long as two years. Moreover, the restrictions that determined foreign capital participation, integration, industry status, and other factors often became hopelessly muddled and often served as a deterrent to private investors.[54] Coordination became even more difficult when CACM members failed to submit basic development guidelines. By 1966, only Honduras had produced a national development plan for consideration by AID.[55]

At a 1966 meeting of the Central American Economic Council, Nicaraguan Minister of the Economy Silvio Arguello argued that his country's exports should receive preferential status within the CACM. Arguello complained that the common market had left Nicaragua "dangerously dependent" upon a few agricultural commodities, while Nicaraguan purchases helped build industry in other nations.[56] To drive their point home, the delegation threatened to withdraw Nicaragua from the common market if the problem remained unaddressed. The embassy reported that the government in Managua was under considerable pressure by industrial and commercial interests to win some sort of boost in regional competition. Free trade had indeed proved to be problematic for Nicaraguan entrepreneurs. The elimination of restrictions on interregional trade had spiked Nicaragua's commercial deficit at $8.4 million in 1965.[57]

The complaints, while part of the normal course of business within the common market at the time, pointed to a much deeper degree of discord within the Nicaraguan private sector. Throughout 1966, editorials in both *La Noticia* and *Novedades* had taken repeated slaps at the Schick administration for its labor policies and its approach to the CACM. Entrepreneurs claimed that higher costs, particularly in the textile, cosmetics, and processed-food industries, made Nicaraguan goods less competitive. They would also protest, moreover, that many Central American trading partners were imposing special taxes and fees, not officially categorized as duties, on Nicaraguan goods.[58]

These problems were best expressed in a 6,000-word report presented by the Nicaraguan Chamber of Industries in August of 1966. Primarily the product of Arnoldo Ramirez Eva, general manager of Metales y Estructuras, S.A., a steel-fabricating firm in the Managua area, and all five Central American countries, the report made a reasoned case for the government to intervene in favor of the domestic industrial sector. It criticized Managua for a lack of a "national industrial policy" and specifically heaped scorn upon the Nicaraguan Ministry of Economy, whose membership was tasked with coordinating policy within the CACM, but who spent more time traveling abroad than building relationships with local business. The report pointed out the obvious need for more and cheaper electrical power and water, and a more modern infrastructure. It accused CACM members of blocking Nicaraguan products with arbitrary barriers (e.g., registration and transit charges, the registration of patents and trademarks) and slowly completing necessary daily coordination (e.g., clearing bank drafts). What perhaps gave the Ramirez report its greatest traction was the fact that METASA was partly owned by Luis Somoza.[59]

The U.S. embassy dismissed the report because it reflected an ongoing "tendency on the part of Nicaraguan businessmen to look to everything else as a source of their ills rather than themselves," and saw the protests as "a weak rationalization of the fact that many of them are less efficient than their counterparts in other CACM countries."[60] American officials in Managua at the time considered the threat to withdraw from the common market to be a bluff. Nevertheless, Nicaraguan criticism persisted. During a November 1967 speech inaugurating the Central American Economic Council, Anastasio Somoza spoke frankly regarding the ongoing problems of the common market, referring to "the dilatory practices, the evasive tactics, and the anomalies in the execution of integration agreements create a situation which sooner or later will endanger the very existence of integration."[61]

Unfortunately, although most of the problems identified within the CACM were the product of basic systemic failures, the preferred solution was to seek increased funding rather than even nominal reform efforts. In 1967, the Agency for International Development requested a $20-million loan to the Central American Bank for Economic Integration as a supplement to the $16 million already paid into the fund by Central American nations. The intent of the fund was to allow the Central American Integration Fund (established in 1965) to expand its lending activity for road construction, telecommunications, and grain storage. In principle, it was intended to promote self-help within the common market structure. Politically, the loan represented a "prompt response" to the commitments made by Lyndon Johnson during the OAS meeting held that year.[62] Additional promises of cooperation followed soon after. At a 5 July 1968 meeting of Central American nations in San Salvador, a joint declaration was issued by the participating presidents to adopt measures "speeding up the economic and social development of their countries and of Central America as a whole."[63] What followed was reminiscent of early speeches made by Lyndon Johnson regarding the accomplishments of the *Alianza*. The summit claimed success in providing "millions of textbooks," "malaria eradication efforts," "efforts to harmonize labor legislation," and "personnel training activities." Little was said regarding the status of integration itself. In a statement remarkable for its qualified language, the declaration proclaimed that Central Americans finally possessed "a legal and institutional framework that constitutes a basis for stimulating the process of reconstruction of their regional unity."[64]

There was little parity between the overinflated rhetoric that accompanied Central American summitry and the growing depths of the economic problem faced by the region. The primary engine of growth, agricultural exports, had begun to stumble badly by mid-decade, exacerbating already tense relations within the common market. In the meantime, manufacturing and industrial projects, intended to provide a degree of economic balance, import substitution, and labor diversification, were mired in the politics of economic self-interest. At a time when systemic reform or, at the very least, compromise was essential to the continued viability of the CACM, Central American nations appeared headed toward more conflict.

NICARAGUA: A NEW FIVE-YEAR PLAN

As the Central American Common Market began to bog down, it seemed that Nicaraguan economic development would continue uninterrupted from years past. The country entered 1964 bolstered by a record growth. The gross domestic product increased by 7.9 percent in 1964, compared to 7.4 percent in 1963. According to the

Inter-American Development Bank, average GDP growth between 1960 and 1965 was 8.2 percent, while per capita production rose at an annual rate of 5.2 percent, more than double the standard established by Punta del Este in 1961, and despite an annual population growth rate of 3.2 percent.[65] Nicaraguan per capita income stood at 2,086 cordobas ($298) in 1964, a 20-percent increase since 1954, and higher than either Guatemala or El Salvador.[66]

The foundation of the Nicaraguan economy was strong in 1965. The cotton crop, an economic mainstay, had survived drought in early 1963 and floods later that year and produced 350,000 bales, exceeding the previous crop by 35,000 bales. In 1965–1966, 5,080 producers cultivated cotton, more than triple the number fifteen years earlier.[67] Foreign trade also increased more than 10 percent, from $90.2 million in 1964 to over $100 million the following year. The cotton–coffee–cattle triad continued to dominate the economy, comprising 48.6 percent of GDP in 1964.[68]

New enterprises also emerged by the middle of the decade. The industrial sector grew at a 10.6-percent rate between 1959 and 1964, and 8 percent between 1965 and 1969. In 1953, Nicaragua had 1,575 manufacturing establishments, employing 18,899 people. By early 1965, 5,000 manufacturers employed more than 50,000 people. Light industry, particularly food processing and textiles, dominated these new ventures.[69] To a very large degree, industrial growth was one of the most notable success stories of the Schick government. Between September 1963 and September 1964, commercial bank credit available to domestic industry increased by 18 percent. Loans to agriculture, livestock, and industry expanded at a faster rate than overall credit expansion. By 1964, a total of 493.5 million cordobas ($70.5 million) had been spent on private-sector investments. In comparison, only 5.4 million cordobas were loaned to public entities.[70] Large-scale private investment from U.S. firms such as Westinghouse, Occidental Petroleum, Esso Standard Oil, the American Smelting and Refining Company, the United Fruit Company, and the Robinson Lumber Company followed in the wake of these Nicaraguan initiatives. Although most American businessmen admitted that there was considerable red tape to contend with in Nicaragua, most described the overall business climate in 1966 as "very good."[71]

During the August 1966 celebrations that marked the fifth anniversary of the *Alianza*, newspapers across the Nicaraguan political spectrum praised its accomplishments. There was good reason to rejoice. Nicaragua had attained the highest growth rates in Latin America, along with Costa Rica, Mexico, and Panama, from 1960 to 1969.[72] Both *La Prensa* and Anastasio Somoza's tabloid *Prensa Grafica* published a special alliance supplement prepared by the U.S. Information Service to mark the moment.[73] Taken within this buoyant context, the contemporary conventional wisdom questioned less the need for additional aid than whether more assistance was necessary at all.

Subsequent U.S. policy focused on two basic objectives. Not surprising, the embassy wanted to continue Nicaragua's high rate of growth and saw an opportunity in the strong economy to wean the country from U.S. assistance. The AID office in Managua was directed "to supplement and reinforce local initiatives." The general thrust of assistance followed this guideline, promoting training, planning, and management programs (see Table 6.3). Secondarily, American officials continued to pursue any means

Table 6.3
U.S. Aid to Nicaragua, 1958–1969 (US$ Thousands)

Project	Years Active	Estimated Total Cost
Agricultural Reform	1958-68	2,744
Industrial Management Training	1959-67	599
National Development Planning	1962-67	1,101
Manpower Planning	1964-69	496
Tax Administration Reform	1954-67	1,225
Rural Mobile Health	1963-67	1,011
Educational Planning	1955-1966	3,114
Educational Supplies	1965-67	227
Management Training Scholarships	1964-65	260
National Census	1962-65	549
Misc. Technical Support	1960-69	<u>1,337</u>
		12,663

Source: U.S. Department of State, Agency for International Development, "Program and Project Data Related to Proposed Programs—FY 1965, Region: Latin America," n.d., 185 195, LBJ, NSF, Agency File, Box 3.

possible to promote "democratic attitudes" in Nicaragua, seeing a tangible window of opportunity to translate free-market growth into political reforms. Yet despite the boom times that inhabited the country, American policy makers understood that these actions were a time-sensitive exercise. Current prosperity, driven by the relatively fragile export triad of coffee, cotton, and cattle, was unlikely to last.[74]

As the primary protagonist of the U.S. assistance program in Nicaragua, the Agency for International Development refined these objects further. Specifically, contemporary AID documents cited three goals for U.S. assistance: (1) technical cooperation with key Nicaraguan government agencies, (2) selected loans to industrial and agricultural production, and (3) infrastructure.[75] In 1964, AID financing assisted in the creation of the Corporation Nicaragüense de Inversiones. By 1963, the United States underwrote nearly $2 million in industrial development projects. Three years later, three-fifths of AID loans went to local industrial enterprises.[76] Overall, U.S. assistance supported a new rural credit union, teacher training centers, mobile health teams, food distribution, management training, and labor management programs. Additional American support also found its way to the Agricultural and Marketing Stabilization Agency, the National Bank, and the National Development Agency.[77]

A derivative benefit of this support was mounting pressure on the Somoza regime to address national development. As early as June 1964, the American country team asked Managua to introduce a five-year economic plan on par with what Anastasio Somoza Garcia had created with World Bank assistance ten years earlier.[78] In fact, the first steps toward a new national development program had been taken by the National Planning Office in 1963. In its report to the president, the Planning Office discussed the need to free Nicaragua from its dependence on agriculture, while improving its access to foreign markets. The report stressed that the most important prerequisite for economic success was internal cooperation, emphasizing the need for Nicaragua to make the transition from its "personalist" approach to domestic affairs to a more rational system. In a nod to the Kennedy administration, the report also addressed the need to cultivate a satisfactory environment for economic, political, and social development.[79]

The following year, in a speech made by Central Bank President Francisco Lainez, the Schick government presented what the embassy called "an authoritative statement on Nicaraguan economic policy." In it, Lainez called upon Nicaraguans to provide their effort, sacrifice, and efficiency to preserve the nation's future prosperity, citing the need for price stability and high employment levels. Lainez also took the opportunity to defend the bank's loan policies by saying that it was "only possible to obtain abundant and cheap credit by means of production, savings, and sacrifice and not by the easy route of unlimited monetary issuance."[80] Overall, the statement was hailed as a positive step by the U.S. embassy and many Nicaraguans, including members of the opposition Traditional Conservative Party.

Between 1963 and 1965, Managua assembled additional pieces of a comprehensive development program. The Central Bank increased credit to industry, provided more medium-term loans to the private sector, and funneled greater amounts of foreign commercial credit to Nicaraguan businesses.[81] Land reform, under the auspices of the Agrarian Reform Institute also accelerated. A Social Progress Trust Fund report noted that 30,000 farmers, approximately 30 percent of all land holders, either rented their property or held it illegally in 1965.[82] The IAN responded by granting 500 families titles to 8,000 acres in the first phase of a project that would eventually transfer 173,000 acres to Nicaraguan *campesinos*.[83]

These efforts finally coalesced into a distinct national development program in 1965. The "National Economic and Social Development Plan for Nicaragua" presented a comprehensive blueprint for the five-year span from 1965 to 1969. Its main objective was to maintain an average annual GDP growth rate of 7 percent. To produce this, the plan called for the familiar array of improvements in infrastructure and the diversification of agriculture, manufacturing, and industry. It projected a 6.4-percent growth rate for agriculture and an 11.8-percent rate for industry.[84]

Perhaps more important, the sheer scale of the plan served as a justification for more American aid. In 1966, the U.S. embassy rated Nicaragua's ability to produce development projects as "reasonably good." As a result, both the embassy and AID began to commit substantial amounts of U.S. assistance to the broad range of projects called for in the plan. Dollars began to flow into big-ticket items such as rural electrification ($450,000) and university assistance ($700,000), as well as a Ministry of Health program that provided $36,000 for family planning.[85] By 1967, the American country team had agreed to underwrite a $250,000 "demonstration" irrigation project, $150,000 for specialists in educational planning and administration, $90,000 for a study of future manpower needs in commerce and industry, and a $20,000 study of the impact of population growth on the economy and social structure.[86] The following year U.S. officials took up the cause of rural electric cooperatives. With the support of ambassador Kennedy Crockett, the Johnson administration provided a $10.2-million loan to the National Light and Power Company of Nicaragua that was dedicated to the construction of modern power facilities in the countryside. Such facilities purported to serve agricultural diversification and the Somoza regime's ongoing land-reform program. "Besides providing inexpensive electricity," AID official William S. Gaud commented, "the cooperatives should serve as centers of other activities and development programs and help to stimulate grass-roots democratic actions of its members." The U.S. assistance package for FY1968 also included $9.4 million for a "basic crop production" loan and $2.2 million for a "rural mobile health" program.[87] In a cable from the embassy in Managua to the State Department, U.S. officials remarked that they worried less about Nicaragua's ability to cultivate additional loans and grants than the strain implementing these myriad programs would place on existing manpower.[88]

At least initially, it appeared that the national development plan, bolstered by substantial assistance, was succeeding. Nicaragua enjoyed a record economic year in 1965, supported in no small measure by a cotton crop of an unprecedented 543,000 bales. Overall, exports rose 17 percent from the preceding year, producing important derivative benefits for both investors and the Schick government. In 1966, the Nicaraguan National Assembly was able to pass a record 583.7-million cordoba ($83.3 million) budget that allowed Managua to increase public-sector funding for development, defense, and social programs.[89] In terms of its proximity to the 1967 election, it could not have been better timed.

This bounty was short-lived, however. Drought in 1966 devastated export agriculture, particularly cotton. The 1967 harvest proved to be 10-percent smaller than the previous year. In 1966, the Nicaraguan GDP increased by a respectable 3.6 percent, but far below the average of 8.1-percent growth during the 1961 to 1965 period and, more important, a rate dangerously on par with population growth. American observers agreed that the Nicaraguan economy would not revisit previous levels of expansion in 1967, a conviction that deepened in 1968 when GDP rose by 5.5 percent.[90]

This financial whipsawing produced a disturbing effect in Nicaragua. In 1966, public-sector receipts, based largely upon traditional export growth, rose at an annual rate of 8 percent. That same year, the Managua regime increased public-sector expenditures by 16.5 percent.[91] In the context of contemporary Keynesian economics, this sort of pump priming was common practice at the time, no less in the Johnson administration itself. In terms of Nicaraguan economic realities, it proved an ominous development, given the fact that the country had become increasingly dependent on the public sector as its most dynamic element. Between 1960 and 1967, agriculture and livestock both proportionally declined as a part of the national economy, while industry and manufacturing increased only marginally. According to *Area Handbook for Nicaragua*, "government" was the most expansive sector of the economy, increasing as a percentage of the GDP from 5.7 to 8.6 percent between 1960 and 1967.[92]

As receipts began to erode, this engine began to sputter. Most alarming was the impact of profit repatriation on the Nicaraguan economy. According to the U.S. embassy, net external investment was a negative 764.1 million cordobas ($109.1 million) in 1966–1967. Gross public investment plummeted by 17 percent in 1966–1967, from 148.5 cordobas ($21.2 million) to 123.3 cordobas ($17.6 million), although this was due primarily to delays in implementation rather than a shortage of capital.[93] Nicaraguan concerns also focused on the trade deficit. On the fifth anniversary of the alliance, the country's balance-of-payments deficit was $12.2 million. It increased to $20.4 million only a year later (1967), driven primarily by $45.9 million in American imports and offset only partially by a favorable $32.2-million trade balance with Japan, Nicaragua's primary customer for cotton exports.[94]

What was often lost in the barrage of statistics that surrounded the alliance and concurrent Nicaraguan development efforts was not the systemic difficulties that began to plague both efforts after 1965, but, more important, the almost complete absence of any derivative economic benefits for the overwhelming mass of Nicaraguans. Although data regarding income distribution was spotty at best, the Social Progress Trust Fund recognized as early as its *Sixth Annual Report* in 1966 that "the effects of the economic boom of the past few years have not yet filtered down sufficiently to the mass of the population." Vast shortages of housing, sanitation, and health care remained an everyday problem throughout most of Nicaragua. The Nicaraguan Housing Institute, for example, managed to build a total of 6,000 new units of low-cost housing between 1961 and 1966, a notable achievement, but far behind urban demands as thousands poured into the cities along the Pacific coast and well short of the needs of the rural population.[95] Far from meeting local expectations, development seemed a distant hope to the average Nicaraguan, articulated in the arcane language of foreign advisors, beset by squabbling among the vested interests of local elites, and unable to effect a substantial change in the course of daily life.[96]

CONCLUSIONS

Despite accumulating evidence to the contrary, most Americans concerned with Central American policy appeared optimistic about the future as the Johnson administration came to a close. In a report to the president dated 14 November 1967, Assistant Secretary of State Covey T. Oliver saw the alliance as having moved beyond the initial grappling that marked its early years. Oliver characterized the alliance in "Phase II" of the "decade of urgency," a situation in which new and dynamic Latin American leadership would increasingly carry the burden of development into regional and local hands. He predicted the continued growth and eventual merger of LAFTA and the Central American Common Market into a "Latin American Common Market," which would serve as an autonomous agency for intraregional trade liberalization and tariff cuts.[97]

There were more important departures unacknowledged by Oliver, but not untouched by American policy. Throughout its term, the paradoxical problem for the Johnson administration was its unwillingness to turn its back on Latin America and its concurrent inability to win the congressional appropriations deemed necessary to promote hemispheric growth. By 1964, it took a hard-eyed realist like Thomas Mann to embrace the prospect of supplementing declining assistance budgets with private investment. At its root, Mann Doctrine foresaw the absolute necessity of using private capital as a means to not only provide aid, but to maintain American influence within the alliance. In the long term, administration officials assumed American policy could achieve the same large goals dictated by Punta del Este with different means.

Consequently, U.S. assistance policy reverted to what one historian has described as "neoconservativism," a difficult acknowledgement made by none other than Walt Rostow that "there were no miracles that Washington could perform to bring about accelerated economic and social progress."[98] In a rather remarkable shift in emphasis that conjured up images of John Foster Dulles rather than Adolf Berle, U.S. development efforts in Latin America shifted from achieving broad socioeconomic reform to securing the stability necessary to attract private capital.

In time, this proved to be a problematic construct. Extraregional trade, dictated by multinational corporations with an eye toward global market structures, warped itself toward basic raw materials and export agriculture. Central America's economy followed in the wake of this decision. Extraregional imports in 1966 comprised 81.6 percent of all Central American imports, down from 93.6 percent in 1960, but large nonetheless, and a clear indication of the degree to which the common market failed to achieve any significant economic autonomy.[99]

"Clientelism" came to dominate both Nicaragua and Central America. Rose Spalding has made the argument that Nicaraguans cooperated poorly in collective action, preferring instead "informal, individual communication with well-placed bureaucrats."[100] This was a reflection of not only intense internal rivalries, but the concurrent, overriding focus on external relationships with foreign private investors. The cultivation of export linkages became an end unto itself that interfered with the productive formulation of domestic policy. This cycle was essentially recreated in regional affairs. The political upheaval that marked all Central American countries except Costa Rica placed the military in a position of primacy in the 1960s and placed a premium on security.[101] A series of regimes emerged that did not per se resist economic integration. In fact, the security states created in Guatemala, El Salvador, and Nicaragua encouraged investors, but they did little that was necessary to create what Bulmer-Thomas describes as the "robust institutions capable of resolving major inter-country disputes."[102] In practice, economic competition between the individual members of the Central American Common Market added an important and dangerous edge to regional competition. The system as it existed by 1968 served better to fragment the region than to unite it behind a common purpose.

The real dilemma was not only "rewarding virtue," according to Albert O. Hirshman, but creating it. "In this fashion, then, aid is not seen in the role of rewarding virtue, but in the role, infinitely more difficult, of bringing virtue into the world."[103] The problem was that, in a series of policies based upon the free market, ones that had surrendered balanced multilateral development as a guiding principle, the only discernible yardstick of achievement was growth and profitability.

NOTES

1. William O. Walker, "Mixing the Sweet with the Sour: Kennedy, Johnson, and Latin America," in *The Diplomacy of the Crucial Decade: American Foreign Relations During the 1960's*, ed. Diane Kunz (New York: Colombia University Press, 1994), 59–66.

2. Interview, Covey T. Oliver, 2 December 1968, Lyndon Baines Johnson Library (hereafter LBJ), Oral History Collection, 27–28.

3. Frank M. Coffin, *Foreign Aid: Controversy and Reality* (Washington, D.C.: USAID, 1963), 1–10. John F. Kennedy Library (hereafter JFK) , Edwin R. Bayley Papers, Box 1.

4. Dean Rusk, Secretary of State, Statement before the Senate Foreign Relations Committee, 4 April 1966, National Archives and Records Administration (hereafter NARA), Records Group 59 (hereafter RG 59), Deputy Assistant Secretary of State for Politico-Military Affairs, Office of Operations, Subject Files, 1961–68, Lot 67D195, Box 20.

5. Ibid.

6. U.S. Senate, Committee on Appropriations and the Committee on Foreign Relations, *A Report on the Alliance for Progress* (Washington, D.C.: U.S. Government Printing Office, 1963), 2–7.

7. Letter, Raymond F. Mikesell to Wayne Morse, 15 May 1962, JFK, Jack N. Behrman Papers, Box 1.

8. Memorandum, Joseph A. Silberstein (Director, Office of Regional Economic Policy, Bureau of Inter-American Affairs), "Growth Rate Trends for 1967 in Latin America," 2 August 1967, LBJ, National Security Files (hereafter NSF), Country File, Latin America, Box 3; Inter-American Development Bank (IADB), Social Progress Trust Fund, *Seventh Annual Report, 1967* (Washington, D.C.: IADB, 1967), 1.

9. U.S. Department of State, Agency for International Development, Memorandum from William S. Gaud for the President, "Effect of Congressional Cuts on AID's Programs for FY 1967," 10 November 1966, LBJ, NSF, Agency File, Box 2.

10. Juscelino Kubitschek, "Report on the Alliance for Progress," 15 June 1963, JFK, Teodoro Moscoso Papers, Box 2; Memo, "Lleras and Kubitschek Reports on the Alliance for Progress," 3 July 1963, JFK, U.S. Department of the Treasury, Office of International Affairs, Box 14.

11. John H. Coatsworth, *Central America and the United States: The Clients and the Colossus* (New York: Twayne, 1994), 20, 110; Morris H. Morley, *Washington, Somoza, and the Sandinistas: State and Regime in U.S. Policy toward Nicaragua, 1969–1981* (New York: Cambridge University Press, 1994), 17; Benjamin Keen and Mark Wasserman, *A History of Latin America* (Boston: Houghton Mifflin, 1988), 372–377.

12. Letter, Seymour M. Peyser (Coordinator, Implementation Project) to David E. Bell (AID), 7 October 1963, JFK, Teodoro Moscoso Papers, Box 1.

13. U.S. Department of State, Agency for International Development, *Proposed Mutual Defense and Development Program, FY 1966, Summary Presentation to the Congress* (Washington, D.C.: U.S. Government Printing Office, 1966), 17, LBJ, NSF, Agency File, Box 1.

14. See, for example, Max F. Millikan and Walt W. Rostow, *A Proposal: Key to an Effective Foreign Policy* (New York: Harper and Brothers, 1957), and Walt W. Rostow, *The United States in the World Arena: An Essay in Recent History* (New York: Harper and Row, 1960).

15. Wilfred L. David, *The Conversation of Economic Development: Historical Voices, Interpretations, and Reality* (Armonk, N.Y.: M. E. Sharpe, 1997), 9–11, 91, 119.

16. R. Peter DeWitt, *The Inter-American Development Bank and Political Influence* (New York: Praeger, 1977), 48.

17. Letter, Jack N. Behrman to George W. Ball, 30 December 1963, JFK, Jack N. Behrman Papers, Box 1.

18. Ibid.

19. Memorandum, David E. Bell (AID) for Members of the Ball Committee, 11 February 1964, LBJ, White House Central File (hereafter WHCF), Confidential File, Subject File, Foreign Affairs, Box 46.

20. U.S. Department of State, Agency for International Development, *Proposed Mutual Defense and Development Program, FY 1965: Summary Presentation to Congress* (Washington, D.C.: U.S. Government Printing Office, 1965), 1–9, 21–29, LBJ, NSF, Agency File, Box 1. See also U.S. Department of State, *Proposed Mutual Defense and Development Program, FY 1966*, 2–4.

21. U.S. Department of State, *Proposed Mutual Defense and Development Program, FY 1966*, 5.

22. Ibid., 2, 7–9. See also U.S. Department of State, Agency for International Development, *Foreign Assistance Program, Annual Report to the Congress, Fiscal Year 1965* (Washington, D.C.: U.S. Government Printing Office, 1965), 1–23, LBJ, NSF, Agency File, Box 1.

23. Cable, USOECD (Paris) to Department of State, "Technical Assistance Programs of DAC Members in Latin America," 20 July 1965, NARA, Subject–Numeric File, Box 515; Diane B. Kunz, *Guns and Butter: America's Cold War Economic Diplomacy* (New York: The Free Press, 1997), 103–107.

24. Memorandum, David E. Bell (AID) to McGeorge Bundy, 20 October 1965, LBJ, NSF, Agency File, Box 5.

25. U.S. Department of State, *Proposed Mutual Defense and Development Program, FY 1965*, 49.

26. Ibid.

27. Memorandum, Jack H. Vaughn (AID) to David E. Bell (AID), "Performance of Latin American Countries in Relation to Aid," n.d., LBJ, NSF, Agency File, Box 5.

28. U.S. Department of State, *Proposed Mutual Defense and Development Program, FY 1965*, 47.

29. Memorandum, Walt W. Rostow to the President, 27 January 1967, LBJ, NSF, International Meetings and Travel File, Box 15.

30. Memorandum, William S. Gaud (AID) to the President, "Effect of Congressional Cuts on AID's Program for FY 1967," 10 November 1966, LBJ, NSF, Agency File, Box 2.

31. Memorandum, Rostow to the President, 27 January 1967.

32. Ibid.

33. Memorandum, William G. Bowdler (White House) to Walt W. Rostow, "Research Projects: The OAS Summit," 17 October 1967, LBJ, NSF, International Meetings and Travel File, Box 19.

34. Memorandum, Rostow to the President, 10 February 1967, LBJ, NSF, International Meetings and Travel File, Box 15.

35. Memorandum, Bowdler to Rostow, "Research Projects: The OAS Summit," 17 October 1967.

36. Interview, William S. Gaud, 26 November 1968, LBJ, Oral History Collection, 4.

37. Ibid., 5. Doris Kearns, *Lyndon Johnson and the American Dream* (New York: Harper and Row, 1976), 286–308. For scholarship discussing Johnson's role during the Vietnam War, see George C. Herring, *America's Longest War: The United States and Vietnam, 1950–1975* (New York: McGraw-Hill, 1996), 144, and Stanley Karnow, *Vietnam: A History* (New York: Viking, 1983), 541.

38. Memorandum, Covey T. Oliver (Assistant Secretary of State for Inter-American Affairs) to the President, 20 December 1967, LBJ, NSF, Agency File, Box 5.

39. Ibid.

40. National Advisory Council on International Monetary and Financial Policies, *Special Report to the President and to the Congress: On the Proposed Increase in the Ordinary Capital Resources of the Inter-American Development Bank*, February 1968, LBJ, WHCF, Subject File, International Organizations, Box 17.

41. Ibid. See also Letter, David Rockefeller (Council for Latin America, Inc.) to Dean Rusk, 17 April 1968, NARA, RG 59, Subject–Numeric File, 1967–69, Box 2113.

42. United Nations, Economic Commission for Latin America, *Economic Survey of Latin America, 1970* (New York: United Nations, 1972), 270–275.

43. U.S. Department of State, *Proposed Mutual Defense and Development Programs, FY 1965*, 50, 62–68.

44. William R. Cline and Enrique Delgado, eds., *Economic Integration in Central America* (Washington, D.C.: The Brookings Institution, 1978), 25–27.

45. Victor Bulmer-Thomas, *The Political Economy of Central America since 1920* (New York: Cambridge University Press, 1987), 174.

46. Cable, Embassy (San José) to State, 8 July 1966, NARA, RG 59, Subject–Numeric File, 1964–66, Box 789.

47. Memorandum, Silberstein "Growth Rate Trends for 1967 in Latin America," 2 August 1967.

48. Cline and Delgado, *Economic Integration in Central America*, 18.

49. Ibid., 40; Union Panamericana, Secretaria General de la Organizacion de los Estados Americanas, Comite de los Nueve, *Informe Sobre Los Planes Nacionales de Desarrollo y el Proceso de Integracion Economica de Centroamerica: Informe Presentado por el Comite Ad Hoc a los Gobiernos de las Republicas Centroamericanas* (Washington, D.C.: Comite de los Alianza para el Progreso, Augusto 1966), 36.

50. Organization of American States (OAS), *The Alliance for Progress and Latin American Development Prospects: A Five-Year Review, 1961–1965* (Baltimore: Johns Hopkins University Press, 1967), 11–13, 21.

51. Donald H. McClelland, *The Central American Common Market: Economic Policies, Economic Growth, and Choices for the Future* (New York: Praeger, 1972), 52–53.

52. James D. Cochrane, *The Politics of Regional Integration: The Central American Case* (New Orleans: Tulane University Press, 1969), 103; Cline and Delgado, *Economic Integration in Central America*, 164.

53. John Weeks, *The Economies of Central America* (New York: Holmes and Meier, 1985), 78; OAS, *The Alliance for Progress and Latin American Development Prospects*, 15, 20.

54. David E. Ramsett, *Regional Industrial Development in Central America: A Case Study of the Integration Industries Scheme* (New York: Praeger, 1969), 64–65.

55. U.S. Department of State, *Proposed Mutual Defense and Development Program, FY 1966*, 24.

56. Cable, Embassy (Managua) to State, 20 September 1966, NARA, Subject–Numeric File, 1964–66, Box 789.

57. Cable, Embassy (Managua) to State, 29 June 1966, NARA, RG 59, Subject–Numeric File, 1964–66, Box 789.

58. Ibid.

59. Cable, Embassy (Managua) to State, 20 August 1966, NARA, RG 59, Subject–Numeric File, 1964–66, Box 789; Cable, Embassy (Managua) to State, 3 July 1968, NARA, RG 59, Subject–Numeric File, 1967–69, Box 2177.

60. Cable, Embassy (Managua) to State, 29 June 1966; Cable, Embassy (Managua) to State, 19 September 1966, NARA, Subject–Numeric File, 1964–66, Box 789.

61. Cable, Embassy (Managua) to State, 22 November 1967, NARA, RG 59, Subject–Numeric File, 1967–69, Box 695.

62. Memorandum, William S. Gaud (AID) to the President, "Proposed A.I.D. Loan to the Central American Bank for Economic Integration," 21 June 1967, LBJ, NSF, Country File, Latin America, Box 3.

63. Memorandum, White House Situation Room to William G. Bowdler, 4 July 1968, LBJ, NSF, International Meetings and Travel, Box 22.

64. Ibid.

65. IADB, Social Progress Trust Fund, *Sixth Annual Report, 1966* (Washington, D.C.: IADB, 1966), 293; U.S. Agency for International Development, Bureau for Program and Policy Coordination, Office of Statistics and Reports, *A.I.D. Economic Data Book: Latin America* (Washington, D.C.: U.S. Government Printing Office, 1971), 2; Cable, Embassy (Managua) to State, 24 June 1965, NARA, Subject–Numeric File, 1964–66, Box 893.

66. U.S. Department of Commerce, Bureau of International Commerce, Overseas Business Reports, *Basic Data on the Economy of Nicaragua*, OBR 65-42 (Washington, D.C.: U.S. Government Printing Office, 1965), 4. Nicaraguan 1964 per capita income remained nearly 25-percent lower than in Costa Rica.

67. Rose J. Spalding, *Capitalists and Revolution in Nicaragua: Opposition and Accommodation, 1979–1993* (Chapel Hill: University of North Carolina Press, 1994), 36.

68. United Nations, Economic Commission for Latin America, *Economic Survey of Latin America, 1970*, 38.

69. Cable, Embassy (Managua) to State, 13 February 1964, NARA, Subject–Numeric File, 1964–66, Box 486; U.S. Department of Commerce, *Basic Data on the Economy of Nicaragua*, 10.

70. Cable, Embassy (Managua) to State, 28 October 1964, NARA, RG 59, Subject–Numeric File, 1964–66, Box 893.

71. Cable, Embassy (Managua) to State, 12 March 1966, NARA, RG 59, Subject–Numeric File, 1964–66, Box 893.

72. United Nations, Economic Commission for Latin America, *Economic Survey of Latin America, 1970*, 10.

73. Cable, Embassy (Managua) to State, 20 August 1966, NARA, RG 59, Subject–Numeric File, Box 2512.

74. Cable, Embassy (Managua) to AID (Washington), 10 June 1964, NARA, RG 59, Subject–Numeric File, 1967–69, Box 486.

75. U.S. Department of State, Agency for International Development, "Program and Project Data Related to Proposed Programs—FY 1965, Region: Latin America," n.d., 73, LBJ, NSF, Agency File, Box 3.

76. IADB, Social Progress Trust Funds, *Fourth Annual Report, 1963* (Washington, D.C.: IADB, 1964), 50, 91, 110; Richard W. O. Lethander, "The Economy of Nicaragua" (Ph.D. diss., Duke University, 1968), 359.

77. Jaime M. Biderman, "The Development of Capitalism in Nicaragua: A Political Economic History," *Latin American Perspectives* 10 (Winter 1983): 25–26.

78. See International Bank for Reconstruction and Development, *The Economic Development of Nicaragua* (Baltimore: Johns Hopkins University Press, 1954).

79. Oficina de Planificacion, Consejo Nacional de Economia, *Informe Parcial al Señor Presidente de la Republica* (Managua: Republica de Nicaragua, 1963), 1–14.

80. Cable, Embassy (Managua) to State, 30 December 1964, NARA, Subject–Numeric File, 1964–66, Box 486.

81. U.S. Department of Commerce, *Basic Data on the Economy of Nicaragua*, 17.

82. IADB, Social Progress Trust Fund, *Fifth Annual Report, 1965* (Washington, D.C.: IADB, 1965), 459.

83. Cable, Embassy (Managua) to State, 1 October 1967, NARA, RG 59, Subject–Numeric File, Box 2177.

84. Republica de Nicaragua, Consejo Nacional de Economia, Oficina de Planificacion, *Plan nacional desarollo economico y social de Nicaragua, 1965–1969* (Managua: Republica de Nicaragua, 1965); Consejo Nacional de Economia, Oficina de Planificacion, *Informe Anual de la Oficina de Planificacion, 1967–1968* (Managua: Republica de Nicaragua, 1968), I-1–I-3; IADB, *Sixth Annual Report, 1966*, 301.

85. Thomas C. Mann (Assistant Secretary of State for Inter-American Affairs) to the President, "A Report to the President on Alliance for Progress Activities, March–May 1964," April 1964, LBJ, NSF, Agency File, Box 4; Cable, Embassy (Managua) to State, 1 October 1967.

86. Cable, Embassy (Managua) to State, 27 May 1967, NARA, RG 59, Subject–Numeric File, 1967–69, Box 2177.

87. Memorandum, William S. Gaud (AID) to the President, 19 June 1968, LBJ, NSF, Country File, Nicaragua, Box 63.

88. Cable, Embassy (Managua) to State, 13 April 1966, NARA, RG 59, Subject–Numeric File, 1967–69, Box 486.

89. Cable, Embassy (Managua) to State, 12 February 1966, NARA, Subject–Numeric File, 1964–66, Box 486.

90. Cable, Embassy (Managua) to State, 15 June 1967, NARA, RG 59, Subject–Numeric File, 1967–69, Box 646. See also IADB, *Seventh Annual Report, 1967*, 219; *Eighth Annual Report, 1968* (Washington, D.C.: IADB, 1968), 235.

91. IADB, *Seventh Annual Report, 1967*, 222. See also Republica de Nicaragua, Banco Central de Nicaragua, Departamento de Estudios Economicos, *Boletin Trimestral, Julio–Setiembre, 1966*, no. 23 (Managua: Republica de Nicaragua, 1966), 65.

92. John Morris Ryan, Robert N. Anderson, Harry R. Bradley, Carl E. Nesus, Robert B. Johnson, Charles W. Hanks, Gerald F. Croteau, and Cathy C. Council, *Area Handbook for Nicaragua* (Washington, D.C.: U.S. Government Printing Office, 1970), 208.

93. Cable, Embassy (Managua) to State, 6 June 1968, NARA, RG 59, Subject–Numeric File, 1967–69, Box 646.

94. Cable, Embassy (Managua) to State, 25 April 1968, NARA, RG 59, Subject–Numeric File, 1967–69, Box 798.

95. IADB, *Sixth Annual Report, 1966*, 293; *Seventh Annual Report, 1967*, 223.

96. For an interesting sample of recent scholarship on this topic, see Margaret Randall, *Sandino's Daughters: Testimonies of Nicaraguan Women in Struggle* (New Brunswick, N.J.: Rutgers University Press, 1995).

97. Oliver, "The Alliance Moves On—A Report on Developments since the Summit Meeting," 14 November 1967.

98. Walker, "Mixing the Sweet with the Sour," 61–62.

99. Cable, ROCAP (Regional Organization for Central America and Panama) to State, 12 June 1968, NARA, RG 59, Subject–Numeric File, 1967–69, Box 696.

100. Spalding, *Capitalists and Revolution in Nicaragua*, 47–50.

101. Bulmer-Thomas, *The Political Economy of Central America since 1920*, 178.

102. Ibid.

103. Albert O. Hirschman and Richard M. Bird, *Foreign Aid: A Critique and a Proposal* (Princeton, N.J.: Princeton University Press, 1968), 9.

PART III

THE SYSTEM CRUMBLES, 1969–1972

CHAPTER 7

Nixon Doctrine and Latin America

In a democracy, policy is the public's business. I believe the President has an obligation to lay before the American people and its Congress the basic premises of his policy and to report fully on the issues, developments and prospects confronting the nation.

Richard Nixon, 1971

By recognizing fundamental American limitations at the conclusion of the 1960s, Richard Nixon restructured U.S. foreign policy and redrew the basic structure of the Cold War. Gone apparently was the American commitment to "bear the burden of a long twilight struggle" in its anti-Communist crusade. Replacing it was Nixon's emphasis on a strictly limited array of strategic objectives. Latin America fell well outside this new policy trajectory. Located within the southern tier of nations, it retained its value as a source of raw materials and a concern when American policy makers perceived instability or Communist influence. The heyday of the Alliance for Progress was over. In its place, Latin Americans began to seek paths separate from American hegemony. In Nicaragua, Anastasio Somoza Debayle took the reigns of power, the third member of his family to do so in twenty years. His rule proved problematic, hampered by his own ineptitude in maintaining the patronage system that served the dynasty, and increasingly at odds with a polity more willing to abandon the old arrangement of Nicaraguan political power.

For a great portion of Richard Nixon's political career, Latin America had been the site of both humiliation and frustration. Perhaps one of the most infamous moments in his career had come in 1958 when, as part of an ill-fated goodwill trip to the region, Nixon's motorcade was attacked in Caracas by an angry mob. Although the Eisenhower administration dismissed the attack as Communist inspired, it served to symbolize growing friction between the United States and many Latin American nations.[1] Two years later, during one of his televised debates with John F. Kennedy, Nixon was forced to keep his own counsel regarding the planned Bay of Pigs invasion while his opponent lambasted the White House for its lax policy on Castro's Cuba. As he prepared the way for a second campaign for the presidency in 1967, Nixon deliberately chose Latin America as the place to embellish his reputation as a world leader. In a well-publicized tour that visited Mexico, Peru, Chile, Argentina, and Brazil, he worked his way through what were generally enthusiastic crowds.[2]

Yet, Nixon's relationship with the region remained at best superficial throughout much of his presidency. When he entered office, Nixon was determined to chart a course between two prevalent aspects of U.S. foreign policy: Wilsonian internationalism and his own American version of *Realpolitik*.[3] He appeared prepared to recognize both the traditional leadership role America had embraced since World War I and the realistic limits of American power. The Nixonian worldview recognized that the Soviet Union and China, not Latin America, were key partners in a global system where sovereignty was defined by mutual self-interest, diplomacy would assume reciprocity between the major powers, and peace would become the product of mutual restraint.[4]

According to historian Michael Genovese, Nixon offered a "far-reaching, forward-thinking approach to foreign policy that had a momentous impact on the world."[5] It was the culmination of a career imbued with international affairs. From his participation as a freshman Congressman in 1947 on the Marshall Plan, to his famous "kitchen debate" with Khrushchev as vice president, to the contacts he made later during his years of self-enforced political exile in the mid-1960s, few presidents in the twentieth century appeared as prepared to understand the multiplicity of challenges to American hegemony by the time he assumed office in 1969.[6]

At the end of the decade, Nixon was forced to confront two unshakable realities: emerging nuclear parity with the Soviet Union and the rapidly approaching demise of American global economic dominance. In 1969 it was increasingly obvious to most observers of world affairs that neither the dollar nor America's nuclear arsenal could sustain the United States in a pluralistic world. Moreover, as one of the more perceptive witnesses to the era, Nixon saw the need to recapture a foreign policy that had been largely discredited in the public mind by the war in Vietnam. More important, Nixon also recognized an even greater imperative to reconstruct what many members of his own party believed was a rigid, reactionary ideology that avoided conflict with the real sources of the Cold War and assumed arbitrary boundaries of conflict. Franz Schurman has characterized Nixon as a president who saw "the struggle between democracy and Communism going on on many fronts, within each other's territory, with the battle lines ever shifting and the combat continuing even though battles have been won or lost—or drawn."[7] His was a time witnessing the end of the nation-state as a primary actor in international affairs, a period when multilateral economic and security concerns were the real currency of international relations.[8]

In its first months in office, the Nixon administration attempted to reverse what it considered to be the haphazard and reactive pursuit of American foreign policy. Nixon's national security advisor, Henry Kissinger, expressed particular concern that "crisis management" had become the rule rather than the exception under Kennedy and Johnson. This methodology, as applied to the Cuban missile crisis, had resulted in a success of sorts. It had not in Vietnam. Rather than react to events in a seemingly endless series of improvisations, Kissinger asserted the need to conduct policy that instead shaped world affairs in a rational manner and reflected consistent national interests.[9] Nixon agreed. On 18 February 1970, as part of his first annual report on foreign policy, the president attempted to make his intent explicit:

Our objective, in the first instance, is to support our *interests* over the long run with a sound foreign policy. The more the policy is based on a realistic assessment of our and others' interests, the more effective our role in the world can be. We are not involved in the world because we have commitments; we have commitments because we are involved. Our interests must shape our commitments, rather than the other way around.[10]

The historian in Kissinger saw his own time as an opportunity to revisit the rationalism of the post-Revolutionary eighteenth century, a time he considered to be a golden period of American diplomacy, when European-trained leaders such as Franklin and Jay deftly conducted the nation's business amidst an amazingly complex field of challenges and opportunities.[11] The more recent diplomatic history of the post–1945 era had seen what he described as a "burst of creativity" under Secretary of State George C. Marshall and George F. Kennan that had provided "one of the glorious moments of American history."[12] What had made each of these periods distinct was the contemporary policy makers' ability to separate the exercise of power and diplomacy into distinct and successive phases of activity. While the United States had not abandoned these measures in the 1960s, Kissinger believed that American leaders had lost sight of proportionality in their application, investing, for example, far too much effort and attention on the Vietnam War, while also placing far too much credence in the ability of conventional arms to win diplomatic objectives.[13]

As it unfolded, "Nixon Doctrine" became a combination of idealistic objectives coupled with pragmatic means to achieve them. Throughout his presidency, Nixon never lost his substantial faith in the power of the free market. Capitalism, from his perspective, served as a global engine of economic progress and a necessary prerequisite to free social and political institutions. Like many leaders of his generation, Nixon was confident that the process that had nurtured democracy and free markets in the United States and Western Europe could be replicated in other parts of the world if the proper components could be constructed and set in place.[14]

The pragmatic side of Nixon Doctrine, articulated during a speech made in Kansas City on 6 July 1971, addressed exactly where the United States would first support and defend these principles. Nixon placed the primary area of American interests in what he described as the "northern tier," a geographic region that included the United States, the USSR, China, Japan, and the Western European community.[15] For all intents and purposes, this "pentagonal strategy" was essentially an adaptation of Kennan's own theory regarding key strategic industrial areas of importance to American security twenty years earlier.[16] Nixon's argument called for a form of limited universalism that prescribed mutual dependence in a multilateral system that gave each major power a stake in preserving the peace. Trade would serve as the carrot, opening doors to old enemies (e.g., Communist China) and friends alike. Nuclear deterrence would remain the stick. In this latter case, the United States would respond to direct aggression by other nuclear powers, and expected the same in turn. Last, Nixon would, unlike his predecessors, be more circumspect about activity within the recognized spheres of influence possessed by the northern tier of nations.

Such a doctrine was designed to limit American power in both scope and application. Left unaddressed was the "southern tier," an enormous section of the globe that included Africa, the Middle East, southern Asia, and Latin America. Each, within the context of this new worldview, held a secondary position that might periodically become upgraded according to emergent crisis situations (e.g., the Yom Kippur War).

Nixon's greatest interest, however, was maintaining the U.S. sphere of influence in the southern tier rather than embarking upon fundamental changes to it.[17]

In terms of practical policy making, Nixon Doctrine contemplated a much more selective course for American foreign relations. Robert Osgood has described it in the following terms:

In short, this revised consensus envisions American material retrenchment without political disengagement—that is, continued American military preponderance at a lower level of effort and reduced risk of armed involvement—in the context of a multipolar configuration of diplomatic maneuver that restrains all participants.[18]

What followed after 1969 was a rather interesting dichotomy of progress and regress. The Nixon administration contemplated pragmatism among the new community of what it considered to be relevant nations. American ties with Communist China expanded into the unexplored territory of commerce and diplomacy. Washington was also able to reach a new *modus vivendi* with Moscow on the issue of strategic arms limitation. The degree of change among this tier of great powers fundamentally refashioned the nature of the Cold War. In contrast, American policy in other areas of the world stood stock still. Throughout much of the underdeveloped world, it retained the same dogmatism that defined U.S. foreign relations for much of the 1940s and 1950s. In these places, Nixon remained the cold warrior, intent on maintaining stability and American influence. In Africa, Asia, and Latin America, the Cold War continued, albeit in a more muted form, for U.S. hegemony in the place of communism.

NIXON DOCTRINE AND LATIN AMERICA

In the waning days of the Johnson administration, many departing senior officials, such as Robert McNamara and George Ball, reconsidered the nature of the Cold War and the basic premises that guided U.S. foreign policy. One of these individuals was Walt W. Rostow, a person who intimately understood both the theoretical and practical problems of American foreign relations. During a speech made at the National War College in May 1968, Rostow raised significant questions regarding American influence and its limits in what he described as "a profound rearrangement of world affairs."[19] More specifically, Rostow informed his audience that global influence had begun to significantly shift away from Moscow and Washington.[20] Both superpowers were confronting an increasing number of attempts by client states and allied countries throughout the world to reassert their national sovereignty. France's departure from NATO was still vivid in recent American memory; South Vietnamese recalcitrance at the negotiating table even more so. On the other side of the Iron Curtain, relations between the Soviet and Chinese governments continued to deteriorate, a fact reflected in the tense military situation along their common frontier. As Rostow spoke, the Soviet invasion that crushed Czechoslovakia's "Prague Spring" was only months away.[21]

In this era of increasing restiveness, Rostow argued that American policy makers needed to "maintain a balance of power within the world that is favorable to us" by forming policies that emphasized a "shared basis of responsibility" for the defense of U.S. interests.[22] He believed that while the United States should retain its primary leadership position in the Free World, it was becoming necessary for America to shift an additional burden of defense to its allies. The proposal, considering a retrenchment of American strategic interests, hearkened back to the Eisenhower administration's Mutual Security Program a decade earlier.[23] It would also predict Nixon's "Vietnamization" policy in 1969.[24]

Rostow's proposed model provided, for all intents, an accurate exposition to Nixon Doctrine in Latin America. Under the new president, the southern tier of nations in our hemisphere dwindled in importance. Subsequent policy addressed Latin America as a regional rather than a global concern, something clearly reflected in February 1969 when the administration issued National Security Study Memorandum 15, "Review of U.S. Policy toward Latin America." It considered five basic American priorities in the hemisphere: the U.S. posture toward "internal political developments," regional security requirements, development assistance strategy, trade and investment policy, and the role of multilateral organizations.[25] Throughout, the clear emphasis was on security, specifically with respect to the possibility of Communist influence in the region. In the administration's 1970 annual review of policy, "the Chile Problem" and "attempts by non-Western Hemisphere countries to interfere in [the] Western Hemisphere" occupied two-thirds of the space designated in the document for Latin America.[26]

In the meantime, the administration made considerable efforts to reassure less-developed nations in general and Latin Americans in particular that the administration was interested in their future. The 1970 policy review also suggested that the U.S. promote the theme of "Building a Generation of Peace" in 1970:

It now appears to be possible for this country to join with other countries of the world in building for a generation of peace. The structure of peace that we would help build would permit individuals and groups in all parts of the world to realize their potential and objectives while respecting the rights of other individuals and groups to do the same. This structure of peace would not be frozen but would foster constructive change to meet changing aspirations and circumstances.[27]

In his initial meetings with Charles A. Meyer, the new assistant secretary of state for inter-American affairs, and members of the Latin American diplomatic corps, Nixon stressed the need to maintain stability in order to encourage private investment and officially committed his administration to resolve conflicts between host governments and American multinational corporations. During a March 1969 meeting with Meyer and senior diplomats from Colombia, Mexico, Venezuela, and the Dominican Republic, Nixon attempted to assuage concerns regarding Peru's ongoing conflict with the International Petroleum Corporation and the possible imposition of the Hickenlooper amendment, a 1961 change to the Foreign Assistance Act that terminated economic assistance if American property was expropriated without compensation.[28] Afterward, Meyer dedicated himself to taking the president at his word. In a strident memo to Secretary of State William Rogers, Meyer addressed an upcoming session of the National Security Council in the following terms:

The meeting will be, at once, an opportunity for and a test of the Administration: an opportunity to arrest and reverse the deterioration of our relations with the other governments and peoples of the Hemisphere, and a test of the Administration's readiness to incur costs and risks, some in the international field but most in the domestic sector, and to invest considerable political capital in turning our relations with the Hemisphere around. The effort cannot be evaded or postponed, and the time is now.[29]

Contemporary intelligence reports concurred with Meyer's sense of urgency. A report issued by the State Department's Bureau of Intelligence and Research in October 1969 noted growing Latin American "frustrations" regarding the absence of economic development or U.S. economic assistance. This trend had contributed to the nationalization of American property in Chile and support of outright expropriation in Peru. It had also opened the door for increased contacts with Communist nations by countries interested in alternative export markets. By 1969, Peru had established full diplomatic relations with the USSR, Hungary, and Bulgaria. Venezuela had opened relations with Hungary and was discussing them with the Soviets. Bolivia and Ecuador had initiated diplomatic contacts with Czechoslovakia.[30] Although these economic ties were sometimes frustrated by the composition of Communist Bloc exports, which tended to rely on heavy industry, U.S. officials suspected that they could serve as the thin tip of the wedge that would open Latin America to future Communist influence.[31]

In light of these growing concerns, Nixon offered at least additional rhetorical attention to Latin America on 31 October 1969. In a somewhat sober account of future U.S. directions in the hemisphere, he promised a "posture of noninterference" and called for a new and "more equal" relationship between the United States and the nations to the south. Nixon promised a "decade of action and progress" and greater attention to multilateral relations.[32] The president proposed a partnership, according to a subsequent State Department memorandum, that would be "based upon lecturing less and listening more."[33] Latin American reactions to the message were generally positive. Brazilian officials commented on a "new tone of humility" in American policy. Colombian president Carlos Lleras Restrepo noted the speech's "enlightened, constructive and intelligent presentation of common tasks and common responsibilities in the hemisphere."[34] Venezuelan president Rafael Caldera offered his own support for the idea that the United States appeared prepared to cooperate rather than impose external standards on Latin America.[35]

Regional leaders were further encouraged by the release of the Rockefeller Report on 10 November. The capstone of an extensive study of Latin American economic needs and a intensive tour of the hemisphere, the report noted "a grim political and economic picture" and called for a host of immediate reforms, ranging from an increase in the U.S. sugar quota, to a "generous refinancing" of the region's growing foreign debt, to the removal of spending restrictions on direct American assistance, to a repeal of the Hickenlooper amendment. In a White House press conference that followed the announcement, Nixon added, "I believe that this report will see more of its recommendations implemented by acts than any report on Latin America ever made."[36]

However, underlying and undercutting promises of partnership was Nixon's anti-Communism. In fact, little had changed in Nixon's outlook from his earlier service during the Eisenhower administration. The president fundamentally believed in confronting communism to prevent its expansion. In the 1950s, he became an early advocate of what William Bundy has recently described as "pactomania," John Foster Dulles's practice of placing a heavy emphasis on collective defense.[37] Nixon was willing to argue in the wake of his 1958 Latin American tour that the administration should not allow democracy to stand in the way of relations with stable, pro-American, anti-Communist governments. He also recommended the use of covert propaganda against what the White House denounced as "Communists, hoodlums, and thrill seekers."[38] As plans to overthrow Castro moved forward in 1960, the vice president voiced his consistent support.[39]

As president, Nixon pressed for active intervention in nations that appeared willing to even consider a leftward turn. After 1970, policy makers struggled mightily to draw connections between Latin American political developments and Communist interests. In the election of Salvador Allende Gossens as president of Chile, the embassy in Santiago depicted a deliberate Soviet effort to "obtain the respectability and presence accorded a major world power."[40] Embassy officials in Moscow suggested that the Brezhnev regime was deriving considerable satisfaction from any perceived shift to the political left in South America. Editorials found in *Izvestiya* and *Pravda* applauded a new era of relations with Chile, as well as Ecuador, Bolivia, and Peru.[41] The Soviets seemed willing to conduct what one State Department intelligence paper described as a "low-profile and long-range policy" toward Latin American relations. This new "diplomatic offensive," apparently capped by the Allende election, appeared focused on a gradualist strategy that emphasized trade and political assistance without open support for armed conflict. Moscow had even managed rapprochement with Cuba on the question of armed revolution after Soviet Defense Minister A. A. Grechko visited Havana in November 1969.[42] One Soviet journalist, Sergo Mikoyan, whose father had been instrumental in forming the USSR's alliance with Cuba, speculated before a embassy official in Moscow that Latin America's advanced state of development made it a better field for competition between socialism and capitalism.[43]

An array of covert countermeasures followed the new Soviet "foothold" in Chile. In his memoirs, Nixon would later claim consistency with Johnson and Kennedy in the American effort to finance political opponents of the Allende government and promote anti-Allende propaganda.[44] Yet perhaps the best examples of Nixon's approach to communism in Latin America would appear later in the efforts orchestrated by the White House to overthrow Allende. The intensity of these measures were a marked departure from the Dominican invasion of 1965 or the more subtle covert U.S. efforts to encourage coups in El Salvador (1961), Guatemala (1963), and Brazil (1964).[45]

The immediate consequence of Allende's overthrow was to leave the impression throughout the world that the United States had reverted to a Eurocentric foreign policy, one that diminished the importance of the peripheral areas of the world. Old Cold War dogma now seemed to suffice as a measurement of U.S. policy in the Third World. American diplomats subsequently dispatched by the administration to posts in Latin America embodied its interest in preserving the old, anti-Communist order. Ambassador Turner

Shelton, who arrived in Nicaragua in 1970, became, according to Deputy Mission Chief Robert White, little more than the regime's primary "cheerleader."[46]

Few Latin Americans were oblivious to this course of events as it unfolded in the early 1970s. At the midpoint of Nixon's first term, a growing sense of impatience and betrayal increasingly marked Latin American attitudes toward the United States. A September 1971 editorial by the Costa Rican newspaper *La Prensa Libre* summed up the feelings of many in the hemisphere:

Most assuredly, the government of president Nixon is not to be characterized by a policy of drawing closer to Latin America. On the contrary, Mr. Nixon's policy has been marked by a negativeness and growing separativeness that is bringing to an end, the active and meaningful Panamericanism of John F. Kennedy.[47]

Many U.S. policy makers echoed concerns that the United States had failed to maintain pace with events or expectations in Latin America. In July 1971, U.S. AID official Frank Shakespeare wrote directly to Kissinger to emphasize the significant Soviet inroads made in the hemisphere. Although portions of the memorandum were obviously shaped by Cold War considerations, Shakespeare addressed what he considered to be serious substantive problems with U.S. Latin American policy. Proposed multilateral assistance funding remained blocked by congressional opposition and it appeared that the president was unwilling to expend the political capital necessary to force it to a vote. Unresolved tariff problems had been compounded by the administration's decision to take the United States off the gold standard that year. On a less tangible but no less important issue, Shakespeare also pointed out that presidential attention toward Latin America had begun to drift again, noting that there had not been a major policy address on the region since November 1969, nearly two years earlier.[48]

In his response, Kissinger recommended that the administration submit "generalized preferences legislation" to Congress in order to demonstrate its interest in Latin America. He also suggested a major policy statement on Latin American issues, possibly tied to the tenth anniversary of the Punta del Este Charter.[49] Shortly thereafter, in September 1971, an NSC interdepartmental study group conducted a review of U.S.–Latin American relations. It acknowledged the region's political and economic "fragility" and the accompanying sense within Latin America that it was incumbent upon the United States to provide favorable terms of trade and assistance in order to see individual nations through the difficult process of modernization. According to the study group, the primary U.S. challenge in Latin America was developing policies that would

reduce the causes and minimize the effects of radical/extremist and other forces that are inimical to our interests, while at the same time associating ourselves with constructive elements of change and otherwise maximizing the positive forces at work in these societies. Such actions will provide tangible evidence that we deem such change to be in or mutual benefit.[50]

Moreover, in an echo of a statement made by AID Administrator David Bell six years earlier, the report noted that it was important that U.S. policy makers not apply a universal standard to all Latin American nations.[51] The "differing importances of the nations of Latin America" required "differential bilateral approaches"; in effect, customized combinations of trade, aid, "political/psychological" programs, and military assistance.[52]

In its final conclusions, the report recommended no additional U.S. aid to Latin America. Private investment was deemed adequate to carry the burden of "constructive" change. Conversely, the study group recommended that American policy makers impress upon their Latin American counterparts the domestic political problems at work within the United States that placed distinct limits on foreign assistance. Official U.S. policy, therefore, became more an exercise in managing the style and interpretation of American action and less an effort to produce tangible results in the hemisphere.[53]

As the first Nixon administration concluded, hope remained that Latin America would regain some degree of priority in the upcoming year. In late October 1972, with all polls pointing to a Nixon landslide victory over Democrat George McGovern, administration officials began to speculate that the next administration might devote additional attention to unmet Latin American problems. From the Bureau of Inter-American Affairs, Mark B. Feldman speculated that the United States could enter into a "mature partnership" with the region, one characterized by assigning Latin America a higher priority in U.S. global policy and a degree of reciprocity in regional relations.[54] Hindsight tells us that Nixon, basking in the glow of his visit to China, preoccupied with the end stages of the war in Vietnam, and increasingly distracted by the Watergate scandal, had little time or energy to devote to his own hemisphere. All a contemporary observer had to do, however, was review the amount of aid offered by Washington to measure a continued downward trajectory. U.S. assistance as a proportion of total bilateral assistance to Latin America fell from 94.1 percent in 1970 to 44.7 percent in 1976.[55] Nixon Doctrine remained true to its original intent. At the start of the 1970s, most Latin American nations searching for additional U.S. leadership and aid would find themselves wanting.

CENTRAL AMERICA AT THE END OF THE 1960s

As U.S. attention moved toward crises abroad and at home, opposition to the status quo in Latin America began to crystallize. Throughout the 1960s, it had been one of America's often repeated objectives to forge a sense of commonality in the hemisphere. Whether through the device of collective security or the principles of free-market enterprise, the United States had hoped to create at least the basic framework of mutual interests among Latin Americans. However, when Washington ceased to remain the dedicated protagonist of such an effort, regionalism and, more important, national interests reasserted themselves.[56]

Redefining individual national sovereignty became a major preoccupation among scores of countries as the region untangled itself from American-imposed unity. What Latin America lacked, however, was an adequate non-American yardstick for this transition. Cuba clearly no longer served this role. Exhausted and introverted at the end of the decade, the Castro government's most compelling interest in 1970 was the national sugar harvest.[57] The political center also proved an equally problematic reference point. Eduardo Frei, long seen as the paragon of anti-Communist moderation, won numerous reforms in Chile that proved to be pyrrhic victories in too many cases. Prior to Allende's ascent, the Christian Democrat presided over wage increases and managed the proliferation of union organizations into the rural sector. The result had been a riptide of rising public expectations and growing uneasiness from within traditional landholding and business interests.[58] On the right, military institutions throughout Latin America took power in the late 1960s and began to explore alternative governments at least outwardly dedicated to popular reforms. A series of "self-proclaimed progressive military coups d'état" in Peru, Bolivia, Panama, and Ecuador reflected a general sense of institutional impatience with stagnant, corrupt civilian governance. The methods utilized by each varied broadly, from agrarian reform in Peru, to Bolivian General Alfredo Ovando's short-lived "revolutionary–nationalist" government, to Omar Torrijos' manipulative nationalism in Panama. Few were able to pursue even a form of political, economic, or social liberalization.[59] Taken as a whole, the Latin America's political spectrum had fragmented to a degree that defied any one single consensus power or revolutionary leader. In the wake of this political atomization, nations began to seek out their own paths.

Populism reasserted itself, fueled by a combination of both nationalist sentiment and emerging anti-Americanism. In Panama, the Torrijos regime that overtook civilian leadership in 1968 immediately began to challenge its American patron. Stoking resentment that had simmered since the flag riots almost ten years earlier, Torrijos made the status of the canal zone a unifying issue amongst the general population.[60] After he secured support for a new canal treaty at home, Torrijos took his campaign to other regional military governments, opening relations with both Castro and Allende, and won general acclaim for his initiative. Other nations challenged U.S. sovereignty in smaller ways. The archives of the State Department are filled with conflicting claims regarding the administration of a 200-mile territorial sea limit that caused no end of problems for American fishing fleets. By 1971, half of Latin America was involved in fishing-rights disputes with the United States, resulting in numerous seizures of American vessels.[61]

Unchecked by U.S. influence, conflicts between Central American nations re-emerged to a degree not seen since the 1950s. Many countries sought out a means to redress regional balance-of-power relationships, a process that combined open armed conflict to resolve bilateral disputes with requests for foreign intervention.[62] The best example of this was the 1969 Soccer War between El Salvador and Honduras. Essentially the product of an ongoing border conflict that had begun soon after independence from Spain, war had alternated with diplomacy for almost 150 years.[63] In the post–1945 period, the United States used the Organization of American States and the Rio Pact to keep a cap on open conflict. Animosity flared in May 1967 when the Salvadoran National Guard arrested a Honduran in the disputed border area. Firefights between military patrols on both sides erupted in the weeks that followed and culminated in dozens of casualties. Further mobilization along the border followed. In June 1969, after a series of riots at the World Cup qualifying matches between the two countries, thousands of Salvadoran immigrants were attacked by Honduran residents and driven across the border. On 27 June, El Salvador broke diplomatic relations with Honduras and halted all commerce with the nation. On 14 July, as violent clashes escalated, Salvadoran troops invaded Honduras and advanced to within seventy-five miles of Tegucigalpa. Honduras responded by bombing San Salvador and oil refineries in Acajutla.[64]

Warfare compounded already strained economic and political relations between the two countries. Ironically, these tensions were an unforeseen product of the Central American integration effort. As the Central American Common Market evolved, it became apparent that El Salvador enjoyed substantial economic growth, while Honduras registered consistent balance-of-payments deficits and a declining gross national product in the years immediately prior to the war.[65] In an effort to alleviate this disparity, Honduras imposed a 30-percent surcharge on Salvadoran manufactured goods and initiated a national campaign to encourage consumption of local products. Of even greater concern to Honduras were the provisions contained within the integration treaties signed after 1958 that permitted the free movement of individuals between common market nations. El Salvador had used this treaty to literally export its excess population to neighboring countries. By 1961, Salvadorans constituted 74 percent of all foreigners living in Honduras.[66] A Treaty of Migration, negotiated between the two countries in 1965 and ratified in 1967, provided for the expulsion of undocumented immigrants and applied to approximately 150,000 Salvadorans illegally living in Honduras. In 1968, Honduras passed its own internal law restricting the rights of legal immigrants to own land.[67] Combined, the overlapping problems of economic inequities, the ongoing border dispute, and the legal status of migrant populations created the dry tinder for the short, bitter war that began in the summer of 1969.

American and OAS intervention eventually ended the conflict in July 1969, but failed to satisfy any of its underlying causes. As the Organization of American States pursued diplomatic initiatives, the United States imposed an arms embargo that effectively choked off all military operations between the combatants and threatened both nations with an economic embargo. In the short term, the latter action made continued conflict impossible. Unfortunately, it only embellished the anti-American animus that characterized the aftermath of the war. The Salvadoran and Honduran militaries, trained in cooperation with U.S. advisors, claimed betrayal, citing American violation of security agreements designed to protect their territorial sovereignty. Included in the claims and counterclaims of atrocities in both sides' dedicated propaganda efforts was an underlying resentment of the United States that would linger for years to come.[68]

Amidst this tumult, the Catholic church added its own considerable voice to a growing body of criticism against the United States and the existing order in Latin America. The 1960s marked an important point of departure for the church as an institution. During most of the post–1945 period, the senior clergy had maintained a largely apolitical stance toward Latin America's ruling elite, scrupulously avoiding public breaks over even the most overt social, economic, or political abuses. However, as the list of problems suffered by the vast majority of the population accumulated, the church's position changed, motivated by the doctrinal initiatives of Pius

XII and Paul VI (e.g., *Mater et Magistra* in 1961), and a growing restiveness among lower-ranking priests and lay leaders. When the Medellin Episcopal Conference convened in 1968, the Latin American clergy was prepared to envisage a significant break with past tradition. During an event attended by Pope Paul VI himself, Latin American bishops committed themselves to the liberation of their people from neo-colonialism, imperialism, and "institutionalized violence." More pointed, in place of the moral and material vacuum produced by unmitigated capitalism and the ruthless defense of property over individual rights the church pressed forward with demands for social and economic welfare programs and political equity.[69] Inspired by Medellin, important segments of the church abandoned cooperation with the status quo in order to serve as a catalyst for both reform and revolution.

The Nicaraguan Catholic church closely paralleled this regional trend. Throughout most of its existence, Nicaraguan Catholic leaders had closely supported both the parties and leadership that preserved order and privilege. Each member of the Somoza family, in their own turns at the presidency, had enjoyed the willing and active endorsement of the country's Catholic bishops. According to John Kirk, until the early 1960s any mention of social or political ills by the clergy in official statements or sermons was a relatively rare occurrence.[70] This placidity was badly eroded by the mid-1960s, replaced by a growing sense of Christian activism that rejected the fatalism that permeated church teaching. As one member of the Solentiname Christian community, Manuel Alvarado, later recalled, "Religion taught us that we had to have a dictator there, for God has put him there, that we had to spend our time praying for this man to be healthy. That's what religion taught us, to accept the conditions of life that we had."[71] In the place of old beliefs, young priests like Ernesto Cardenal and Uriel Molina taught the peasant communities in Nicaragua that despite material disparities of wealth and political power, each individual possessed intrinsic value. As this doctrine spread, so too did "Christian base communities" like Cardenal's at Solentiname.[72]

Official criticism of the Nicaraguan church followed in the wake of the Medellin Conference. Between January and February 1969, the Encuentro Pastoral was held in Managua and attended by more than 250 members of the country's clergy, including three of Nicaragua's nine bishops. The event became a platform to criticize existing church practices. Without question, the most acerbic statement was delivered in a report written by the Jesuit priest Noel Garcia, who described the church hierarchy as "decrepit, conservative, stationary, advanced in age, apathetic, negative, disunited, hardly accessible to the public, some of whom have no idea about—or interest in—the hierarchy. It merely represents the desire to do nothing, merely repeating coldly and compulsively timeworn positions."[73] Only two years after the bloodshed that had tainted the 1967 presidential election, others questioned the church's fundamental relevancy in a time of socioeconomic upheaval.

Another three years would pass before the church presented an official response to the Encuentro Pastoral. In the Bishops' Pastoral Letter of 12 May 1972, the hierarchy abandoned traditional support of the Somoza regime, contradicting a 1950 church document that had stated that when Catholics obeyed the government, "they do not degrade themselves, but rather are performing an act which basically constitutes respect for God."[74] The Pastoral Letter was described by the U.S. embassy as an "indictment and a call for change" in Nicaragua. Church officials now openly aligned themselves with the opposition Traditional Conservative Party. In the emerging war of words between the Somoza-backed government and the clergy, church officials veered between moderation and outright attacks on the Managua government. During a July 1972 speech before the National University, Archbishop Obando y Bravo denounced the abuse of state power and called for greater social justice in Nicaragua, lamenting, "A situation of violence is crushing the masses. This violence conceals itself in oppression caused by unjust or corrupt structures and situations." Obando y Bravo recommended against physical violence and the application of "moral pressure" to the regime.[75] Other Catholic leaders proved to be less patient. Cardenal's mentor, Father Uriel Molina, formed the Christian Revolutionary Movement in 1972 with the avowed purpose of combining Marxist and Christian methodology to reform Nicaraguan society. That year, he opened contacts between his organization and the reemergent FSLN.[76]

To a large degree, the Latin America that ended the decade was more closely identifiable with its traditional past than with the shaky tutelage of the Alliance for Progress. The sheer number and type of governments struggling to retain control over domestic affairs or build power anew served as a testament to the political heterogeneity of the region. In another sense, the very existence of these institutions—spanning the political spectrum—was an even more telling commentary on the futility of American efforts to win anything but a grudging consensus on development or anti-Communism.

Perhaps more important, the diversity of rebellion against the status quo spanned the ideological spectrum to include an impressive array of national, economic, political, and religious standpoints. If there was any common cause to be found among these various movements, it was within a context that combined long-standing resentments: a backlash against the disparities produced by the foreign capitalism and a strong undercurrent of virulent anti-Americanism. The late 1960s essentially saw the birth of the coalition movements that would bedevil American policy makers in the 1970s and early 1980s.

In Central America itself, traditionally a region of considerable U.S. hegemony, local prerogatives also reasserted themselves. Old animosities, the product of old territorial disputes combined with roiling conflicts over equity within the common market, tore apart the superficial unity imposed upon the isthmus. Where the United States decided to intervene and win back a degree of stability, as was the case in the Soccer War, it was to end conflict and not address its underlying causes. These were left to Central America. Consequently, with the possible exceptions of Guatemala and Nicaragua, the region began to diverge markedly from its American patron.

THE SOMOZATO

At the conclusion of the 1960s, the youngest and least prepared Somoza took charge of an increasingly restive and divided country. As "Tachito" settled into office, a steady stream of official and unofficial concerns emerged regarding his ability to handle the complicated sociopolitical balancing act that often defined real power in Nicaragua. An embassy report in February 1969 remarked, for example, on the "marked decline" of the National Liberal Party "from the powerful, cohesive machine that helped bring Anastasio Somoza to power" to almost an afterthought.[77] The embassy noted further,

This neglect is not solely related to the fact that 1968–1969 are not election years, and thus a time when enthusiasm for a candidate wanes and when there are few, if any, jobs to dispense. Rather, it appears that President Somoza has little interest in maintaining a viable Liberal Party. The President is the Party's chief, yet he has done virtually nothing to build party cadres; has been reluctant to spend Government funds on Liberal Party organizing efforts; has often neglected party professionals in the allocation of Government jobs; and has even removed or sent abroad important and powerful party officials.[78]

Among those removed were Minister of Education Ramiro Sacasa Guerrero and Minister of Economy Arnoldo Ramirez Eva. Minister of Government Julio Quintana, a thorn in the family's side since the administration of Luis Somoza, was made ambassador to France.

Nicaraguan and U.S. officials alike speculated that Somoza simply wished to replace "old-line" Liberals with "efficient, technically qualified, and honest" advisors. Nonetheless, the embassy also openly worried that "President Somoza has shown an unfortunate tendency to insist on 'yes men'—and relatives and cronies—to serve as his advisors, and those with followings of their own or ideas of their own at variance with the President's have had to leave."[79] Moreover, the last ambassador to serve the outgoing Johnson administration, Kennedy M. Crockett, was also realistic enough to report in February 1969 that Somoza retained substantial faith in the *Guardia* to preserve his power.[80]

Even more pessimistic news followed. As early as September 1968, the embassy had reported on rumors that Somoza was considering a move to convene a constituent assembly that would revise the constitution so that he would be able to extend his existing term an additional three years. The foundation of this strategy appeared to be a power-sharing agreement with Conservative Party leaders that allowed them additional cabinet representation as well as seats in the national assembly.[81] Trial balloons floated by the regime soon followed these rumors. A 1969 pamphlet entitled "Paralelismo Historico" and published by Somoza's uncle, Dr. Luis Manuel Debayle, endorsed what he described as "the Somoza Doctrine of Government," a system in which a minority party would become a permanent member of a decision-making process overseen by the president. The pamphlet described this future situation as "a period of maturity" in which "opinions are projected about a common unity, and in which the parties cooperate in a free and rational atmosphere of reciprocal respect."[82] An editorial published in the *Frente Liberal Somocista*, managed by retired *Guardia* Colonel Eugenio Solorzano, argued that Somoza's plan of government was of such "colossal dimensions" that it required an "indefinite period," or at least two or three presidential terms, to be carried out.[83] Adding to American qualms was a December 1969 report by U.S. Military Group officer, Major Leoncio Estrada, on plans to form a "Constitutional Junta" in which Somoza would abolish Congress and replace it with a body comprised of "reliable GON military and a few civilians only." Somoza himself reportedly was canvassing the *Guardia Nacional* at large to see if the measure had support.[84] The Military Group commander considered this particular information to be "marginally reliable," although he added the caveat that its source had been "80% accurate" in the past.[85] Somoza muddied the waters even further during a March 1970 rally by saying that although he would not challenge the constitutional prohibition against a second term, ultimately "the representatives of the people and the people themselves" would decide the question of future governance. For the first time, Somoza mentioned a "national solution" to this issue, a statement that moved the U.S. embassy to speculate that a national coalition government would become Nicaragua's caretaker until his next presidential run in 1977.[86]

Somoza's rather transparent effort to extend his tenure in office inadvertently prompted vehement opposition within his own Liberal Party. Constructed around the ousted Ramiro Sacasa Guerrero, a faction of Liberal leaders acted as a traveling truth squad to the regime, holding rallies in Esteli and Granada to criticize the president. Both the events and the speeches were provided front-page coverage by *La Prensa* and quoted at length.[87] Somoza's own vice president, Alfonso Callejas Deshon, openly speculated in conversations with American officials that Somoza would attempt to amend the constitution or conduct an "auto golpe." For his own part, Callejas Deshon began to distance himself from an administration he found "increasingly bereft of purpose, quality, or understanding."[88] Substantively, these rebels offered no real challenge to Somoza from within his own party. During the December 1970 national convention of the Partido Liberal Nacionalista, Somoza-backed candidates were overwhelmingly chosen over their Sacasista challengers. As if to add insult to injury, Sacasa was removed as convention president and replaced by a pro-Somoza congressional deputy, while Callejas Deshon himself was dropped as a member of the Liberal Party Executive Committee.[89]

Taken together, these events marked a clear regression of governance in Nicaragua. The political machinery that had served the family so well for decades was in a poor state of repair by 1970, diminished by Anastasio Somoza's ham-fisted approach to party patronage, his increasingly overt reliance on the National Guard, and, most important, his seeming indifference to even the most superficial trappings of democratic government. The unfortunate product of these actions was to confirm earlier suspicions regarding his aptitude as president.

Fortunately for the continued viability of Somoza's clumsy regime, these serious shortcomings were offset to a degree by continued disarray from within Nicaragua's political opposition. For the most part, Conservatives fell among themselves after their failed 1967 electoral challenge, bitterly divided into fractious finger-pointing and contentious, sterile debate. At year's end, the party had split into three major elements, two led by Fernando Agüero and his old enemy Pedro Joachim Chamorro, and a third guided by Fernando Zelaya Rojas and José Joaquin Cuadra.[90] However, although the party separated into these groupings, control of it ultimately fell to the individual who maintained a hammerlock on the party's organization, from individual district delegates to the national executive committee. In November 1968, Agüero—bolstered by incumbency and a carefully cultivated patronage system—managed his own reelection as party president, thwarting a challenge for the office by the Chamorrista bloc. Unperturbed by the defeat, Chamorro moved immediately to organize his own Conservative offshoot, creating the Accion Nacional Conservadora in July 1969. The new party offered, according to the U.S. embassy, "less than a positive program, more of a series of criticisms of the present situation."[91] For his own part, Chamorro claimed for the ANC the grassroots issues of the Conservative rank and file: honesty in public service and attention toward social welfare, something he claimed—plausibly—that the traditional party had lost under Agüero's often demagogic tutelage. In private, Chamorro also approached the U.S. military attaché, Colonel Trevor Swett, and Defense attaché, Lieutenant Colonel William Watt, asking that they act as intermediaries to like-minded officers in the *Guardia Nacional*.[92]

The competition between these groups spilled out into the open during the debate over membership in the constituent assembly, a body proposed in 1970 by the regime to formulate a transitional government that would follow Somoza's term in office. Throughout the spring, Agüero stubbornly waited for a summons from Somoza. To U.S. officials, he claimed that the PCT would endorse a Liberal president as long as he was not Somoza or "a Somoza puppet." In the meantime, Agüero worried that Chamorro would attempt to trump him by initiating his own dialogue with the government.[93] Initial meetings between Somoza and PCT Secretary General Arnoldo Lacayo Maison finally began in May 1970 and were followed by a series of personal meetings between Somoza and Agüero in November.[94] For his own part, Chamorro welcomed the talks between the PCT leadership and their Liberal Party counterparts. As early as 1968, he had informed the embassy political officer, David W. Burgoon, that control of the party would revert to him by default if Agüero reached any agreement with the regime. He chided the PCT president for even considering collaboration, stating flatly, "No real Conservative would stay with Agüero after he sells out to the Government."[95] Editorials from *La Prensa* followed suit. However, despite increasing criticism from Chamorristas, Agüero moved forward, pressured by his party's leadership to come to an agreement with Managua in order to forestall any further loss of his political traction within the PCT. Talks regarding a power-sharing agreement continued, garnished by public announcements that Conservatives were also pursuing a series of reforms that would address the judicial system, elections, and landownership.[96]

The final product of these efforts was the Somoza–Agüero Pact. Signed on 28 March 1971, it represented Liberal–Conservative deal making in the best tradition of the regime's founder, Anastasio Somoza Garcia. In part, the agreement served as a platform for statements of principle for public consumption. Both parties agreed to "resolve their quarrels in a dialogue" and recognize the "diversification in power and electoral justice." Substantively, however, the pact required the creation of a national constitutional convention to revise the document and called for the election of a new National Assembly by February 1972. Once the legislature had been determined, an additional round of balloting would be held in May for a three-man "Executive Council," which would serve for a period of two and a half years until the next presidential election. Agüero insisted, and was allowed, to serve as the Conservative member of the new ruling troika.[97] At a meeting held during a state visit with Nixon in the White House Treaty Room, Somoza bragged that the pact would ensure political stability in Nicaragua for the next twenty years.[98]

As these events unfolded, the American country team made increasingly strained efforts to place the best face on events. During the 1969 review of the "Country Analysis and Strategy Paper for Nicaragua," the embassy acknowledged a "special relationship" between the two countries, one that had produced a situation in which U.S. prestige was very high among Nicaraguans at large and their leadership in particular. With the exception of "certain political issues," American officials concurred with Nicaragua's future direction and were prepared to offer "judicious and timely counsel at all levels." The embassy wanted to focus attention on alleviating the country's recent economic doldrums, while expressing confidence in "slow but perceptible progress toward greater political maturity."[99]

As time progressed, however, diplomats began to voice growing concerns regarding Nicaragua's tentative political stability and the negative impact Somoza's own leadership was having on the national political climate. Reports on the progress of the Somoza–Agüero Pact disturbed Americans. On the eve of elections for the National Assembly, Nicaragua was eerily calm and peaceful. Unlike the past contests of 1963 and 1967, there was almost no sign of the grandstanding or violence that normally plagued Nicaraguan politics. The Conservative opposition was described in one cable as "apathetic," and the general public "largely indifferent" to the outcome of the election. According to interviews with Conservatives, the PCT optimistically expected to received at best 25 percent of the vote, but was guaranteed 40 percent of assembly seats due to the pact. Both the ANC and Social Christians denounced the election as a farce, the PSC claiming that they represented "just a simple confirmation of that determined by the dictatorship."[100] The regime and members of Agüero's staff dismissed the comments as sour grapes. However, analysts and political desk officers in the U.S. embassy took the diminished voter turnout as an ominous sign and forecast little possibility of reform over the short term.[101]

Little changed as a result of the pact. Somoza personally named two-thirds of the ruling triumvirate after the May elections. Roberto Martinez, a former *Guardia* general and Minister of Defense assumed one position in the Executive Council. The second was taken by Nicaragua's minister of agriculture, Dr. Alfonso Lovo Cordero. The last, by prior arrangement, fell to Fernando Agüero Rocha. Their installation proved to be an impressive event. Ambassador Shelton cabled the State Department:

The Council hosted a gala, huge reception to commemorate its inauguration, allowing hundreds of Conservatives their first glimpse of the inside of *The Casa* [Presidential]—though many years ago some, including Dr. Agüero, had visited its cellars for interrogation. Shiny new limousines, swarthy bodyguards and stalwart Military Aides were assigned to the new Chief Executives who were seen going up and down the hill each day. The shingle was clearly out and the *Casa* was open for business, but nothing happened.[102]

Within a month of assuming power, the council was an object of public ridicule. It was ignored by both visiting officials and the various ministers of government, who gravitated to Somoza at his nearby La Curva residence out of simple habit and deference. In the normal conduct of daily business, the council was often summarily bypassed. During 27 May ceremonies for Armed Forces Day, the *Guardia Nacional* commander did not deem it an important matter to invite a single member. When, in June, IADB representatives met with Somoza, the ministers of finance and economy, and the secretary of the council, a *La Prensa* headline showed the former president presiding over the event and offered the headline "And the Junta, For What?" The situation was restored to a degree by the summer, when Somoza, rather ironically, issued orders from La Curva granting the Executive Council greater autonomy.[103]

It was not a meaningful concession. Few, if any, of the important offices in the Nicaraguan government were allowed to fall outside either Somoza's purview or that of the Liberal Party. In addition to the Ministry of Defense, the family retained control of the Ministries of Treasury, Economy, Foreign Relations, and Education.[104] The composition of the various vice ministers who occupied the second tier of administration also reflected Somoza's heavy hand. As was the case with the Executive Council, all were Somoza appointees. Again, both current and former National Guard officers—Dr. Justo Garcia Aguilar (Government), César Augusto Borge (Finance), Ernesto Rugama Nuñez (Education), and César Napoleon Suazo (Defense)—were present throughout the bureaucracy. Many were cronies of Jose R. Somoza in the Ministries of Government, Finance and Public Credit, Education, and Defense. This membership was leavened with the introduction of a number of young technocrats to key positions in the Ministries of Public Works, Economy, Industry and Commerce, and Agriculture.[105] It was with a somewhat forced optimism that the embassy reported on the situation in July 1972: "Although there has been no surge forward, there has significantly been no falling apart."[106]

CONCLUSIONS

Recent scholarship by James T. Patterson has described Nixon Doctrine as "a cynical and high-handed way of managing foreign affairs." The rationalism professed by Kissinger at the time and defended in his memoirs ever since has been depicted by Patterson and historians such as Joan Hoff as a policy riven with personal politics and the subjectivity of deeply flawed individuals.[107] Moreover, within the historical context of the Cold War, Nixon Doctrine offered few departures from the policies of John Foster Dulles. It did not tolerate the loss of additional countries to the Sino–Soviet Bloc any more than the Eisenhower administration had ten years earlier.

These criticisms offer only a narrow perspective of Nixon Doctrine. In its search to identify errors, contemporary scholarship overlooks one of the more important insights that Henry Kissinger brought to the practice of foreign policy: an understanding that mutual self-interest could become a transcendent element in international relations. Nuclear parity and America's economic decline brought with them uncertainty on both sides of the Iron Curtain and a period ripe to redefine the prevalent concerns regarding the security of all major powers. Nixon possessed the acuity to understand that the United States, if it acted first, could shape this definition. His first step, American rapproachment with China, served both parties' desire to create a balance against accumulating Soviet power. The subsequent easing of U.S.–Soviet tensions and the initiation of arms control negotiations after 1972 again reflected the desire of both sides to mutually seek out a new means to preserve their own security.

Mutuality of interest enabled the Nixon administration to set aside Cold War blinders in place since 1945.

The utility of this approach diminished drastically when applied to nonnuclear, underdeveloped nations. Here, the relevance of Kissinger's Western European model, with its heroic allusions to rational diplomacy and Realpolitik fared poorly if at all. Few Latin American leaders were required to worry about the nuclear balance of power. Instead, they confronted the hard-edged problems of economic development and internal political turmoil. This basic disconnect between the northern and southern tiers explains the observation of one scholar in 1973 that the less-developed nations of the world were proving much less tractable to outside manipulation by either the United States or the Soviet Union.[108]

In this context, many Latin American countries were poised, in large and small ways, to challenge U.S. hegemony. Recognizing the lack of importance given the hemisphere, Latin American leaders emerged from the late 1960s intent on filling the vacuum created by American imperial retreat.[109] The Nixon administration's intention to make an example of Allende backfired. Its role in his overthrow was interpreted throughout the hemisphere not only as the reactionary application of anti-Communism, but as a simple blow struck against the principle of Latin American sovereignty. In the longer term, intervention served only to stoke additional anti-Americanism in the hemisphere.

Patterson's categorization of cynical and highhanded policy making is more applicable to the Somoza regime and its handling of Nicaraguan political affairs after 1969. As president, Anastasio Somoza Debayle proved to be the least adept of the family when it came to managing his country, failing as a caretaker to the patronage system created by his father and preserved by his brother. For most of his tenure, Somoza was able to keep both his political opposition and the U.S. embassy guessing as to the means he would use to preserve the family dynasty. When he finally acted, the result was decidedly anticlimactic. At its best, the Somoza–Agüero Pact was an obsolescent instrument that preserved not even the fig leaf of coalition government. When first employed by the elder Somoza in 1950, it had fared poorly, spawning a decade of violence and cross-border invasions. A generation later, it would provoke an even worse result.

NOTES

1. Stephen E. Ambrose, *Eisenhower: The President*, vol. 2 (New York: Simon and Schuster, 1984), 464.

2. Stephen E. Ambrose, *Nixon: Triumph of a Politician, 1962–1972* (New York: Simon and Schuster, 1989), 111–112.

3. Frank Ninkovich, *The Wilsonian Century: U.S. Foreign Policy since 1900* (Chicago: University of Chicago Press, 1999), 48–77, 215–245; Paul Kennedy, *The Rise and Fall of the Great Powers: Economic Change and Military Conflict from 1500 to 2000* (New York: Vintage Books, 1989), 407–410.

4. Richard M. Nixon, "Asia after Vietnam," *Foreign Affairs* 46 (1967): 95–110; John R. Greene, *The Limits of Power: The Nixon and Ford Administrations* (Bloomington: Indiana University Press, 1992), 106–127; Alan M. Jones, "Nixon and the World," in *U.S. Foreign Policy in a Changing World: The Nixon Administration, 1969–1973*, ed. Alan M. Jones (New York: David McKay, 1973), 57.

5. Michael A. Genovese, *The Nixon Presidency: Power and Politics in Turbulent Times* (Westport, Conn.: Greenwood Press, 1990), 99.

6. Ibid., 102; Henry Kissinger, *The White House Years* (Boston: Little, Brown, 1979), 57.

7. Franz Schurman, *The Foreign Politics of Richard Nixon: The Grand Design* (Berkeley, Calif.: Institute of International Studies, 1987), 80.

8. See Richard M. Nixon, *United States Foreign Policy for the 1970's: Building for Peace* (New York: Harper and Row, 1971).

9. John Lewis Gaddis, *Strategies of Containment: A Critical Appraisal of Postwar American National Security Policy* (New York: Oxford University Press, 1982), 274–283.

10. Henry Kissinger, *Diplomacy* (New York: Simon and Schuster, 1994), 711–712.

11. Kissinger, *The White House Years*, 48–70. See Felix Gilbert, *To the Farewell Address: Ideas of Early American Foreign Policy* (Princeton, N.J.: Princeton University Press, 1961), 19–75. See also Forrest McDonald, *Novus Ordo Seclorum: The Intellectual Origins of the Constitution* (Lawrence: University of Kansas Press, 1985), 57–142.

12. Kissinger, *The White House Years*, 60.

13. For an interesting commentary on the immediate post–Vietnam period, see Hans J. Morgenthau, "The Lessons of Vietnam," in *The New Era in American Foreign Policy*, ed. John H. Gilbert (New York: St. Martin's Press, 1973), 13–20.

14. Genovese, *The Nixon Presidency*, 149; Gaddis, *Strategies of Containment*, 275.

15. Joan Hoff, *Nixon Reconsidered* (New York: Basic Books, 1994), 158.

16. George F. Kennan, *American Diplomacy, 1900–1950* (Chicago: University of Chicago Press, 1951).

17. Hoff, *Nixon Reconsidered*, 158–159.

18. Robert E. Osgood, "How New Will the New American Foreign Policy Be?" in *The New Era in American Foreign Policy*, ed. John H. Gilbert (New York: St. Martin's Press, 1973), 77.

19. Walt W. Rostow, "The United States and the Changing World: Problems and Opportunities Arising from the Diffusion of Power," Remarks at the National War College, Washington, D.C., 8 May 1968, Lyndon Baines Johnson Library (hereafter LBJ), National Security File (hereafter NSF), Name File, Box 7.

20. For an early example of this paradigm, see Walt W. Rostow, *The United States in the World Arena: An Essay in Recent History* (New York: Harper and Row, 1960).

21. Rostow, "The United States and the Changing World," 8 May 1968.

22. Ibid.

23. NSC 162/2, "Basic National Security Policy," 30 October 1953, in U.S. Department of State, *Foreign Relations of the United States, National Security Affairs, 1952–1954*, vol. 2 (Washington, D.C.: U.S. Government Printing Office, 1984), 554–597; U.S., President's Message to Congress on the Mutual Security Program, *The Mutual Security Program for Fiscal Year 1958: A Summary Presentation* (Washington, D.C.: U.S. Government Printing Office, 1957), 11.

24. See Jeffrey J. Clarke, *Advice and Support: The Final Years* (Washington, D.C.: Center of Military History, 1988).

25. National Security Study Memorandum 15, "Review of U.S. Policy toward Latin America," 3 February 1969, National Archives and Records Administration (hereafter NARA), Records Group 273 (hereafter RG 273), National Security Council File, Box 3.

26. National Security Study Memorandum 102, "The President's Annual Review of American Foreign Policy," 21 September 1970, NARA, RG 273, National Security Council File, Box 1.

27. Ibid.

28. Memorandum of Conversation, Richard Nixon, Secretary of State William P. Rogers, Foreign Minister Alfonso Lopez Michelson (Colombia), Foreign Minister Fernando Amiama Tio

(Dominican Republic), Foreign Minister Aristides Calvani (Venezuela), and Foreign Secretary Antonio Carrillo Flores (Mexico), "Latin American Policy," 31 March 1969, NARA, Records Group 59 (hereafter RG 59), Subject–Numeric File, 1967–69, Box 2110; U.S. Senate, *The Foreign Assistance Act of 1968: Hearings before the Committee on Foreign Relations* (Washington, D.C.: U.S. Government Printing Office, 1968), 21.

29. Memorandum, Charles A. Meyer (Assistant Secretary of State for Inter-American Affairs) to William Rogers, "NSC Meeting on Latin American Policy," 14 October 1969, NARA, RG 59, Subject–Numeric File, 1967–69, Box 2111.

30. U.S. Department of State, Director of Intelligence and Research, "The Situation in Latin America," 4 November 1969, NARA, RG 59, Subject–Numeric File, 1967–69, Box 2108.

31. Cole Blasier, *The Giant's Rival: The USSR and Latin America* (Pittsburgh: University of Pittsburgh Press, 1987), 48–74.

32. "President Urges Latins Take Lead to Spur Progress," *New York Times*, 1 November 1969, 1.

33. Memorandum, State Department to Henry Kissinger (National Security Advisor), "Implementation of President's October 31 Speech," 1 December 1969, NARA, RG 59, Subject–Numeric File, 1967–69, Box 2112.

34. U.S. Department of State, Director of Intelligence and Research, "Latin Americas Pleased with President's Speech but Apprehensive about New Relationship," 7 November 1969, NARA, RG 59, Subject–Numeric File, 1967–69, Box 2112.

35. Cable, Embassy (Caracas) to State, 20 February 1970, NARA, RG 59, Subject–Numeric File, 1970–73, Box 2434.

36. Tad Szulc, "Rockefeller's Latin Plan Faces Fire in Washington," *New York Times*, 10 November 1969, 1; Cable, State to All American Republic Diplomatic Posts, 11 November 1969, NARA, RG 59, Subject–Numeric File, 1967–69, Box 2108; Hoff, *Nixon Reconsidered*, 154.

37. William Bundy, *A Tangled Web: The Making of Foreign Policy in the Nixon Presidency* (New York: Hill and Wang, 1998), 9; Jones, "Nixon and the World," 17–19.

38. Letter, Robert Cutler to Richard M. Nixon, 20 June 1958, Dwight David Eisenhower Library, White House Office, Special Assistant Series, Chronological Subseries, Container 6; "President's View: Red Hands in Unrest Around the World," *U.S. News & World Report*, 23 May 1958, 96–97.

39. See Trumbull Higgins, *The Perfect Failure: Kennedy, Eisenhower, and the CIA at the Bay of Pigs* (New York: W. W. Norton, 1987). See also Michael McClintock, *Instruments of Statecraft: U.S. Guerrilla Warfare, Counter-Insurgency, Counter-Terrorism, 1940–1990* (New York: Pantheon Books, 1992).

40. Cable, Embassy (Santiago) to State, 29 March 1971, NARA, RG 59, Subject–Numeric File, 1970–73, Box 2435. In *The White House Years*, Kissinger devotes extensive attention to establishing Allende's Communist credentials.

41. Cable, Embassy (Moscow) to State, 4 February 1970, NARA, RG 59, Subject–Numeric File, 1970–73, Box 2435.

42. U.S. Department of State, Bureau of Intelligence and Research, "USSR–Latin America: Moscow Pursues a Low-Profile, Long-Range Policy," 17 April 1970, NARA, RG 59, Subject–Numeric File, 1970–73, Box 2435.

43. Cable, Embassy (Moscow) to State, 4 December 1973, NARA, RG 59, Subject–Numeric File, 1970–73, Box 2435.

44. Richard M. Nixon, *The Memoirs of Richard Nixon* (New York: Grosset and Dunlap, 1978), 489–490; Laurie Nadel, *The Great Stream of History: A Biography of Richard M. Nixon* (New York: Atheneum, 1991), 144–145.

45. Alain Rouquié, "The Military in Latin American Politics since 1930," in *Latin America: Politics and Society since 1930*, ed. Leslie Bethell (New York: Cambridge University Press, 1998), 167–172; Kissinger, *The White House Years*, 655–671.

46. Morris H. Morley, *Washington, Somoza, and the Sandinistas: State and Regime in U.S. Policy toward Nicaragua, 1969–1981* (New York: Cambridge University Press, 1994), 67.

47. Cable, Embassy (San José) to State, 22 September 1971, NARA, RG 59, Subject–Numeric File, 1970–73, Box 2434.

48. Memorandum, Frank Shakespeare (USAID) to Henry Kissinger (National Security Advisor), 2 July 1971, NARA, RG 59, Subject–Numeric File, 1970–73, Box 2434.

49. Memorandum, Theodore L. Eliot (Executive Secretary, Department of State) to Henry Kissinger (National Security Advisor), "Frank Shakespeare's July 2, 1971 Memorandum on Latin America," 17 July 1971, NARA, RG 59, Subject–Numeric File, 1970–73, Box 2434.

50. NSC-IG/ARA, "U.S. Policy towards the Nations of Latin America," 3 September 1971, NARA, RG 59, Subject–Numeric File, 1970–73, Box 2434. See also Hoff, *Nixon Reconsidered*, 159–162.

51. Memorandum, David E. Bell (AID) to McGeorge Bundy, 20 October 1965, LBJ, NSF, Agency File, Box 5.

52. NSC-IG/ARA, "U.S. Policy towards the Nations of Latin America," 3 September 1971.

53. Ibid.

54. Memorandum, Mark B. Feldman (Bureau of Inter-American Affairs) to Charles A. Meyer (Assistant Secretary of State for Inter-American Affairs), 24 October 1972, NARA, RG 59, Subject–Numeric File, 1970–73, Box 2434.

55. John H. Coatsworth, *Central America and the United States: The Clients and the Colossus* (New York: Twayne, 1994), 123–125.

56. Ralph Lee Woodward, *Central America: A Nation Divided* (New York: Oxford University Press, 1985), 271.

57. Jorge I. Dominguez, *Cuba: Order and Revolution* (Cambridge: Belknap Press of Harvard University Press, 1978), 173–180.

58. Paul W. Drake, *Labor Movements and Dictatorships: The Southern Cone in Comparative Perspective* (Baltimore: Johns Hopkins University Press, 1996), 117–141.

59. Rouquié, "The Military in Latin American Politics since 1930," 175–182. See also Brian Loveman and Thomas M. Davies, Jr., eds., *The Politics of Anti-Politics: The Military in Latin America* (Lincoln: University of Nebraska Press, 1989), 194–196.

60. U.S. Department of State, Bureau of Intelligence and Research, "Latin America: The Situation and Trends, 1969–1975; An Overview," 6 May 1971, NARA, RG 59, Subject–Numeric File, 1970–73, Box 2432.

61. U.S. Department of State, Bureau of Intelligence and Research, "Trends in Latin America," 8 October 1971, NARA, RG 59, Subject–Numeric File, 1970–73, Box 2432.

62. U.S. Department of State, Bureau of Intelligence and Research, "Latin America: Growing Ties—and Rivalries—among Neighbors," 23 August 1972, NARA, RG 59, Subject–Numeric File, 1970–73, Box 2432.

63. Honduras and El Salvador fought their first war in 1839. This inconclusive conflict was followed by an alternating series of diplomatic and military efforts in 1841, 1845, 1854, 1861, 1871, 1876, 1886, 1895, 1906, and 1916. See Royce Q. Shaw, *Central America: Regional Integration and National Political Development* (Boulder, Colo.: Westview Press, 1978), 129–165.

64. Ibid.

65. William R. Cline and Enrique Delgado, eds., *Economic Integration in Central America* (Washington, D.C.: The Brookings Institution, 1978), 25–27, 164. For a more specific analysis of Central American growth trends, see Memorandum, Joseph A. Silberstein (Director, Office of

Regional Economic Policy, Bureau of Inter-American Affairs), "Growth Rate Trends for 1967 in Latin America," 2 August 1967, LBJ, NSF, Country File, Latin America, Box 3.

66. Woodward, *Central America*, 274–275.

67. Ibid.

68. Shaw, *Central America: Regional Integration and National Political Development*, 163–164; Coatsworth, *Central America and the United States*, 126–130.

69. Edward A. Lynch, *Religion and Politics in Latin America: Liberation Theology and Christian Democracy* (Westport, Conn.: Praeger, 1991), 91–95; Benjamin Keen and Mark Wasserman, *A History of Latin America* (Boston: Houghton Mifflin, 1988), 554–555.

70. John M. Kirk, *Politics and the Catholic Church in Nicaragua* (Gainesville: University Press of Florida, 1992), 36–45.

71. Joseph E. Mulligan, *The Nicaraguan Church and the Revolution* (Kansas City, Mo.: Sheed and Ward, 1991), 76.

72. Sheldon B. Liss, *Radical Thought in Central America* (Boulder, Colo.: Westview Press, 1991), 192–195. See also Deane William Ferm, *Third World Liberation Theologies* (Maryknoll, N.Y.: Orbis Books, 1986), 8, 16–37. Cardenal would argue at the time that Socialist Cuba represented the best and most viable alternative to the soulless sociopolitical systems in control of the remainder of Latin America.

73. Kirk, *Politics and the Catholic Church in Nicaragua*, 53.

74. Mulligan, *The Nicaraguan Church and the Revolution*, 73.

75. Cable, Embassy (Managua) to State, 3 November 1972, NARA, RG 59, Subject–Numeric File, 1970–73, Box 2503.

76. Marta Harnecker, *Los Christianos en la Revolucion Sandinista: Del Verticalismo a la Participacion de las Masas* (Buenos Aires: Ediciones al Frente, 1987), 9–27; Liss, *Radical Thought in Central America*, 189.

77. Cable, Embassy (Managua) to State, 5 February 1969, NARA, RG 59, Subject–Numeric File, 1967–69, Box 2177.

78. Ibid.

79. Cable, Embassy (Managua) to State, 12 May 1969, NARA, RG 59, Subject–Numeric File, 1967–69, Box 646.

80. Cable, Embassy (Managua) to State, 5 February 1969.

81. Cable, Embassy (Managua) to State, 12 October 1968, NARA, RG 59, Subject–Numeric File, 1967–69, Box 2177.

82. Cable, Embassy (Managua) to State, 5 June 1969, NARA, RG 59, Subject–Numeric File, 1967–69, Box 2177.

83. Cable, Embassy (Managua) to State, 17 November 1968, and Cable, Embassy (Managua) to State, 9 February 1969, NARA, RG 59, Subject–Numeric File, 1967–69, Box 2178.

84. Memorandum, Major Leoncio Estrada (USMILGP) to Colonel Trevor W. Swett (Commander, US MILGP), "News of Interests," 15 December 1969, NARA, RG 59, Subject–Numeric File, 1967–69, Box 2178.

85. Memorandum, Colonel Trevor W. Swett (Commander, US MILGP) to Ambassador Crockett, 15 December 1969, NARA, RG 59, Subject–Numeric File, 1967–69, Box 2178.

86. Cable, Embassy (Managua) to State, 31 March 1970, NARA, RG 59, Subject–Numeric File, 1970–73, Box 2503.

87. Ibid.

88. Memorandum of Conversation, Alfonso Callejas Deshon and Robert E. White (Chargé de Affaires), 15 October 1970, NARA, RG 59, Subject–Numeric File, 1970–73, Box 2503.

89. Cable, Embassy (Managua) to State, 21 December 1970, NARA, RG 59, Subject–Numeric File, 1970–73, Box 2503.

90. Cable, Embassy (Managua) to State, 23 December 1967, NARA, RG 59, Subject–Numeric File, 1967–69, Box 2177.

91. Cable, Embassy (Managua) to State, 28 July 1969, NARA, RG 59, Subject–Numeric File, 1967–69, Box 2177.

92. Memorandum of Conversation, Pedro Joaquin Chamorro, Emilio Alvarez Montalvan, Colonel Trevor Swett (U.S. Milgroup), Lt. Colonel William Watt (Defense Attaché), and James E. Briggs (Embassy Political Office), 28 September 1969, NARA, RG 59, Subject–Numeric File, 1967–69, Box 2179.

93. Cable, Embassy (Managua) to State, 5 April 1970, NARA, RG 59, Subject–Numeric File, 1970–73, Box 2503.

94. Cable, Embassy (Managua) to State, 28 June 1970, and Cable Embassy (Managua) to State, 30 November 1970, NARA, RG 59, Subject–Numeric File, 1970–73, Box 2503.

95. Cable, Embassy (Managua) to State, 10 November 1968, NARA, RG 59, Subject–Numeric File, 1967–69, Box 2177; Memorandum of Conversation, Pedro Joaquin Chamorro and David W. Burgoon (Embassy Political Officer), 21 November 1968, NARA, RG 59, Subject–Numeric File, 1967–69, Box 2177.

96. Cable, Embassy (Managua) to State, 30 December 1969, NARA, RG 59, Subject–Numeric File, 1967–69, Box 2177; Cable Embassy (Managua) to State, 30 November 1970.

97. Cable, Embassy (Managua) to State, 6 April 1971, and Cable, Embassy (Managua) to State, 22 April 1971, NARA, RG 59, Subject–Numeric File, 1970–73, Box 2503.

98. Memorandum of Conversation, Richard Nixon, Anastasio Somoza Debayle, and Alexander Haig, 2 June 1971, NARA, RG 59, Subject–Numeric File, 1970–73, Box 2504.

99. Cable, Embassy (Managua) to State, 9 February 1969, NARA, RG 59, Subject–Numeric File, 1967–69, Box 2179. See also Embassy (Managua) to State, "Country Analysis and Strategy Paper for Nicaragua," 25 January 1971, NARA, RG 59, Subject–Numeric File, 1970–73, Box 2503.

100. Cable, Embassy (Managua) to State, 4 February 1972, NARA, RG 59, Subject–Numeric File, 1970–73, Box 2503.

101. Cable, Embassy (Managua) to State, 18 January 1970, NARA, RG 59, Subject–Numeric File, 1970–73, Box 2503.

102. Cable, Embassy (Managua) to State, 7 July 1972, NARA, RG 59, Subject–Numeric File, 1970–73, Box 2503.

103. Ibid.

104. Cable, Embassy (Managua) to State, 6 April 1972, NARA, RG 59, Subject–Numeric File, 1970–73, Box 2503.

105. Cable, Embassy (Managua) to State, 24 May 1972, NARA, RG 59, Subject–Numeric File, 1970–73, Box 2503.

106. Cable, Embassy (Managua) to State, 7 July 1972.

107. James T. Patterson, *Grand Expectations: The United States, 1945–1974* (New York: Oxford University Press, 1996), 745.

108. Robert E. Osgood, "How New Will the New American Foreign Policy Be?" 72–75.

109. Coatsworth, *Central America and the United States*, 122–131.

CHAPTER 8

The New Balance of Military Power

If history teaches anything it is that there can be no peace without equilibrium and no justice without restraint.

Henry Kissinger

Tyrants do not represent nations, and liberty is not won with flowers.

Augusto César Sandino

American military policy in the Nixon era was a reflection of growing parity with Soviet power and increasing domestic criticism of U.S. deployments abroad. Moscow's pursuit of a massive nuclear weapons program established parity with the United States by 1970 and forced a basic reevaluation of American strategic capabilities. In the latter case, the Nixon White House dueled with legislators as Congress began to reassert its authority in both strategic planning and appropriations. The end result of this increasingly combative relationship was a reduction in defense budgets and new limits on American military capabilities. Latin American militaries, in the meantime, continued to assert their prerogatives over the political direction and defense of their respective nations. By the late 1960s, their influence extended into regional affairs as the larger nations of South America offered increasing military assistance to their smaller neighbors. Conversely, in Nicaragua the Somoza regime struggled to retain control over the National Guard. Distracted by the difficulties of domestic politics and limited by declining economic fortunes, Anastasio Somoza discovered growing factionalism at the core of his government's power structure.

As the 1960s drew to a close, the United States found itself in an era of approaching strategic military parity, a situation that fundamentally challenged American hegemony on a global scale. This situation was the primary product of massive Soviet military expenditures during the decade. Between 1960 and 1969, Moscow more than doubled its outlays for defense, from $36.9 billion to $89.8 billion. These budgets spurred the rapid growth of conventional forces, particularly the country's first legitimate blue-water navy since the Russo–Japanese War.[1]

More important in American eyes was the exponential increase in Soviet nuclear capability, a result of massive expenditures on strategic rocket forces. After its humiliation at the hands of the United States during the Cuban Missile Crisis, the USSR abandoned its "minimum deterrence" strategic posture in favor of eliminating American nuclear dominance. When Nixon first took office, the United States possessed 1,054 ICBMs, 656 submarine-launched ballistic missiles (SLBMs), and 540 B-52s equipped to deliver nuclear weapons. In comparison, the USSR commanded approximately 1,200 ICBMs, 200 SLBMs, and 200 long-range bombers.[2] The newest additions to this inventory, the SS-9 "Scarp" and SS-11 "Sego" strategic nuclear missiles, offered a degree of range, accuracy, and "throw-weight" (25 megatons in the case of the SS-9) that truly alarmed American military leaders.[3] In 1970, the Strategic Air Command informed Nixon that the Soviets had the capability to damage the United States in a first strike to the point that American retaliation would not produce equal destruction.[4]

Cumulatively, these Soviet advances, coupled with additional steps to deploy ICBMs in hardened, dispersed silos and maintain them at a high degree of readiness, caused American policy makers to shed a number of strategic preconceptions by the end of the decade. "Minimum deterrence" joined "damage limitation" on the ash heap of American war planning.[5] Consequently, by 1969, it appeared that Washington was prepared to shift its approach to strategic defense, engaging in diplomatic efforts at managing parity rather than the continued preservation of strategic superiority. Subsequent discussion in the American policy-making community focused more on limiting substantive developments in antiballistic missile systems, improvements in MIRV technology, and Soviet experiments with a "fractional orbital bombardment system."[6] The end product of this policy of mitigation was the first Strategic Arms Limitation Treaty in 1972. According to the agreement, the United States would limit its ICBMs to 1,054, while the Soviets retained 1,618 intercontinental missiles. SALT I also held American submarine-launched missiles at 710 in forty-four boats and allotted the Soviets 950 in sixty-two submarines.[7]

Although by 1972 the Nixon administration was prepared to concede the hard reality of a genuine strategic nuclear balance of power, the path to this conclusion was neither clear nor easy. As a new arrival to the White House, Nixon initially offered mixed messages regarding U.S. military priorities. On the one hand, he appeared ready to offer a new doctrine that could reconcile American strategic commitments with its diminishing capabilities. The redeployment of American forces from Southeast Asia to more important regions (i.e., Western Europe) seemed to be a logical first step in this direction. However, the new president also counseled that a significant contraction of American military involvement in global affairs might create dire circumstances for the country. During the commencement address at the Air Force Academy in June 1969, Nixon warned, The "danger to us has changed, but it has not vanished. . . . The aggressors of this world are not going to give the United States a period of grace in which to put our domestic house in order. . . . There is no advancement for Americans at home in a retreat from the problems of the world."[8]

The Air Force Academy speech was meant as a statement of principle, an acknowledgment that security was not a function of changing domestic political circumstances. It was designed to reassure American allies that the United States would honor its treaty obligations. In broader terms, the speech was also a reflection of the difficulties the administration faced in applying Nixon Doctrine. Within the confines of the Oval Office, the policy appeared to be a rational, clear-cut approach for a reorienting America to lead a changing world. However, throughout his presidency, Nixon would be bedeviled by the practical problems produced by the conflicting needs to both preserve American credibility abroad and prioritize American military commitments. Any contraction of American power could be construed as a failure either by the still potent Cold War hawks in both political parties or by Moscow, eventualities Nixon wanted to avoid at all costs. Throughout most of his first term, the president labored, not always successfully, to satisfy both sides of the policy debate, alternating attempts to delegate some military responsibilities to American allies (e.g., through the promotion of Vietnamization) with overt demonstrations of military might (e.g., the 1972 Christmas bombing). The sum total of these efforts was to a produce a muddled indication of American strategic objectives.

In the meantime, the Air Force Academy speech provoked a firestorm of debate within Congress that further bogged down the administration. Many Democrats had lauded Nixon Doctrine when it was announced in March 1969, particularly the provisions calling for a substantial reduction of the U.S. role in South Vietnam. Not surprising, they reacted with alarm when the president pressed forward with requests for new assistance appropriations later that summer. Senator Frank Church noted in July 1969,

The greatest danger to our democracy . . . is not that the Communists will destroy it, but that we will betray it by the very means chosen to defend it. Foreign policy is not and cannot be permitted to become an end in itself. It is, rather, a means toward an end which in our case is not only the safety of the United States but the preservation of her democratic values.[9]

Others questioned not the administration's ultimate objectives, but the fact that the chief executive continued to exert primary control over American foreign policy. Senator Albert Gore, Sr., of Tennessee remarked after the Air Force Academy speech,

I know of no one in the Senate who has questioned the need for a strong defense. It seems to me that it is a little too fashionable around Washington these days to assume that only the President, or perhaps his Secretary of Defense, has responsibility with respect to the security of the country. . . . The security of the country is a matter for which responsibility is shared by Congress and the President.[10]

In the aftermath of the Air Force Academy speech, the Senate Foreign Relations Committee convened an Ad Hoc Subcommittee on U.S. Security Agreements and Commitments. Chaired by Stuart Symington, who had served as secretary of the air force under Harry Truman, its purpose was to begin "an independent study of the extent of U.S. commitments and the political and financial costs of maintaining U.S. bases overseas."[11] In real terms, the Symington Committee served as the first point of demarcation in an increasingly bitter struggle to reshape and delimit American foreign policy according to Congressional prerogatives, one that would see the questions of appropriations and strategic objectives subsumed by a larger debate over authority. In the wake of this ongoing conflict, defense spending would begin a marked decline, contracting by 37 percent overall between 1968 and 1974.[12]

As the struggle between the chief executive and Congress unfolded, it fundamentally altered the formation and conduct of American military policy. Most apparent was the more belligerent attitude adopted by the White House toward Congress in the first year of Nixon's presidency. After an initial honeymoon period prompted by troop withdrawals from South Vietnam, the discourse between the Oval Office and Capitol Hill dissolved into a constant drum beat of administrative stonewalling and legislative criticism. A September 1969 letter from Carl Marcy, the chief of staff of the Senate Committee of Foreign Relations, to Henry Kissinger reflected "a feeling of frustration among members of the Committee." "Putting it more bluntly but in broader terms," Marcy wrote, "There is a growing feeling that the development in recent years of the position you occupy has had the effect of moving the Committee one more step away from having either an influence on foreign policy decisions, or knowing the ingredients that are being put into them."[13]

The spectacle of administration officials testifying before Congress became a commonplace affair after public revelations of U.S. military incursions into Laos and Cambodia. As the tempo of these investigations increased, Nixon instructed his principle subordinants to adopt a hard line toward the legislature. In an August 1971 memorandum addressed to both Melvin Laird and William Rogers, Nixon asserted that the president "has the responsibility not to make available any information and material which would impair the orderly function of the Executive Branch of Government, since to do so would not be in the public interest."[14] Referring to inquiries made by the Senate Foreign Relations Committee into basic planning data for American military assistance, the president determined that it was not in the public interest to divulge such information and ordered the Departments of State and Defense to refuse congressional requests not first officially cleared by the White House.[15] The Senate Foreign Relations Committee responded in October by cutting Military Assistance Program funding from $705 million to $565 million. Military assistance to Latin America was limited to only $10 million.[16]

Within this context, the American approach to foreign military assistance changed, particularly with respect to the underdeveloped areas of the world. In this specific arena, Nixon Doctrine became a basic effort to relegate the cost and responsibility for security to the host country somehow without undercutting American leverage. National Security Decision Memorandum 76, "The New U.S. Foreign Assistance Program," articulated the general philosophy that "the United States, through its assistance programs, should henceforth seek to support the initiatives of other countries and the international development institutions rather than seek to dominate the development process."[17] American efforts, in other words, were better spent modernizing and improving proxies who could preserve U.S. military assets for larger strategic confrontations. A 1971 statement by undersecretary of state U. Alexis Johnson accurately summarized this new emphasis, which, in many respects, closely resembled the military assistance policies of the Eisenhower administration: "Effective policing is like 'preventative medicine.' The police can deal with threats to internal order in their formative states. Should they not be prepared to do this, 'major surgery' would be needed to redress these threats. This action is painful and expensive and disruptive in itself."[18]

Unfortunately, the growing array of congressional restrictions on military assistance made the pursuit of this policy difficult at best. Between 1971 and 1973, funds for military credit assistance were reduced from $743.4 million to $541 million.[19] In order to sidestep this limitation, the administration promoted foreign military assistance through an increase in direct U.S. military sales, reversing long-standing American policy that encouraged credit purchases. Consequently, foreign military sales to underdeveloped countries jumped from $422 million in 1970 to $5,058.5 million three years later.[20] The administration further supplemented Third World internal security by expanding existing facilities for foreign military trainees in the U.S. military school system. By 1970, 22,000 foreign military students received instruction in both the United States and its overseas bases, an increase from 16,000 in 1968.[21]

Nowhere were these trends more apparent than in Latin America. When Nixon took office, no plausible Soviet nuclear or conventional threat existed in the hemisphere. Moreover, after nearly a decade of counterinsurgency efforts, only the remnants of earlier guerrilla movements remained active in a handful of countries. For all intents, the military leg of the Alliance for Progress was a dramatic success.

In fact, the policy itself had succeeded almost too well. According to a 1970 report by the State Department's Bureau of Intelligence and Research, the Latin American military constituted a "preeminent political force," and was described as "the strongest national institution," and the "ultimate political arbiter" in the hemisphere.[22] At the conclusion of the decade, military governments dominated governments in nearly every nation in Latin America. With the rare exceptions of Costa Rica or Colombia, soldiers institutionally and politically dominated their civilian counterparts.

At a very fundamental level, the existence of these military and military-dominated governments provoked a renaissance for the American military assistance program. According to a 1965 congressional report, American officers stationed in Brazil were there with the express purpose of "exerting U.S. influence and retaining the current pro-U.S. attitude of the Brazilian Armed Forces."[23] Four years later, after an extensive tour of Latin America that culminated in a well-publicized report, Nelson Rockefeller encouraged the use of U.S. advisory groups in low-profile efforts to influence their military counterparts. This practice would allow the United States, according to a 1970 House Committee on Foreign Affairs report, to retain a "generally favorable influence on the various host military establishments and to meet their aspirations." The committee also noted,

By physically removing themselves from the host military commands, the MAAG's and Milgroups can contribute to several practically and psychologically important objectives, including (1) enhancing the self-confidence of the host military, (2) discouraging over-identification of U.S. personnel with their foreign military counterparts, and (3) lowering the U.S. "profile" generally in the military affairs of MAP recipient countries.[24]

Administration policy closely followed these recommendations. In a memorandum regarding military assistance ceilings in Latin America, William P. Rogers advised the president,

The degree of our responsiveness to legitimate Latin American military requirements has an important bearing on our ability to maintain influence with both civilian and military leaders in a broad spectrum of issues. In recent years, our inability to respond favorably to such requests has been interpreted by the Latin American Governments, be they civilian or military, as evidence of a lack of concern for the area or a patronizing attitude.[25]

Weapons sales became either a means to strengthen already reliable allies or served as a balm for fragile relationships. In July 1971, in an effort the sway anti-Allende elements in the Chilean military, the Nixon administration approved $9 million in credits for the purchase of paratroop equipment and C-130 military transport aircraft.[26] Throughout the first administration, the State Department consistently recommended that the United States adopt a more flexible weapons-sales policy, restore cuts in grant assistance, and increase the total number of military advisors stationed in Latin America proper.[27]

The actual political role these advisors would assume was the point of minor controversy within the American diplomatic community. A State Bureau of Intelligence and Research study in 1971 noted the lack of preparedness of many resident Military Group officers to act as agents of U.S. policy beyond their specific military duties. The embassies in both Bogota and Tegucigalpa pointedly made an apolitical approach to military assistance a deliberate standard for their respective country teams.[28] In contrast, the U.S. ambassador to Chile made it his business to act as a primary agent in the administration's intervention against the Allende government.[29] Overall, however, there was no one consistent practice that guided military assistance in Latin America.

One proffered solution to this problem was the creation of a regional organization responsible for internal security. In 1969, the Rockefeller Report had posited the idea that the United States sponsor a civilian-directed "Western Hemisphere Security Council." This council would ostensibly construct policy that addressed the correlation between growing socioeconomic problems and the reversion to violence, essentially in an attempt to prevent the root causes of rural insurrection and the emerging problem of urban terrorism.[30] More specifically, the proposed organization would address the escalating problem that terrorism—particularly kidnapping and assassination—posed to American citizens and diplomats residing in Latin America.[31]

Once announced, the security council proposal attracted widespread public criticism throughout the hemisphere. Thirteen of the twenty-three governments surveyed by embassy staffs in Latin America and the Caribbean rejected the idea out of hand. Only two nations, Nicaragua and Paraguay, offered their unconditional support.[32] The security council plan died, lacking even the remotest interest in comprehensive regional security under U.S. sponsorship. In one respect, its failure was a reflection of its irrelevance. Existing programs offered by U.S. AID and the Office of Public Safety were more than adequate to the task proposed by the Rockefeller Report. Conversely, the overwhelming rebuke offered by the Latin American nations themselves was a stinging reminder that U.S. institutional influence had reached a point of near saturation.

Washington's continuing struggle over the issue of Latin American weapons procurement was another cause for concern and a pointed indication of America's loosening grip on hemispheric military affairs. By the time Nixon assumed office, prior concerns regarding the sale of European weapons and the concurrent danger of a regional arms race had been superseded by demands that U.S. policy provide the American arms industry at least equal access to Latin American buyers. According to the Department of Commerce, Chile and Venezuela offered a potential market for $100 million in weapons sales alone.[33] The scale of foreign competition had certainly increased by the end of the decade. Between 1965 and 1970, arms suppliers in Western Europe and Canada provided almost $1 billion in military equipment to Latin America (see Table 8.1). The United Kingdom was the largest supplier to the hemisphere, accounting for $590 million of total sales, followed by France, Canada, Germany, and Italy. Other nations, such as The Netherlands (transport planes), Belgium (small arms), Spain (patrol boats), and Switzerland (armored cars), provided munitions and materiel in smaller amounts.[34] Modern jets, particularly the French Mirage supersonic fighter, dominated sales that included 200 combat and training aircraft, 138 tanks, 12 destroyers, and 6 submarines. European arms agents utilized what the State Department called "aggressive and imaginative salesmanship," which offered low-interest loans, long-term repayment schedules, and special concessions on local licensing arrangements.[35]

This deluge of weapons produced an interesting trickle-down effect throughout Latin America. Once they managed to meet their primary modernization goals, many countries proved perfectly willing to export their obsolescent surplus to less well endowed neighbors. Major South American nations in particular provided increasing amounts of equipment and weaponry to Central America and the Caribbean at the end of the 1960s. The embassy in Caracas reported in April 1970 that Venezuela was preparing to sell El Salvador ten F-86K jet fighters and 1 million rounds of linked 0.50-caliber ammunition. The State Department speculated that the sale was arranged as a rebuke to the United States and its arms embargo against Honduras and El Salvador following the Soccer War.[36]

Table 8.1
Arms Sales to Latin America, 1965–1970 (US$ Millions)

	1965/66	1967	1968	1969	1970	Total
United Kingdom	42.9	16.0	29.1	154.7	350.0	592.7
France	6.4	46.0	15.6	3.0	59.0	130.0
Canada	1.6	20.6	32.9	70.0	0.0	125.1
Italy	0.0	2.4	4.0	52.0	0.0	58.4
West Germany	6.5	3.6	0.0	27.8	7.3	45.2
Netherlands	0.0	0.0	18.0	3.2	2.0	23.2
	57.4	88.6	99.6	310.7	418.3	974.6

Source: U.S. Department of State, Bureau of Intelligence and Research, "Third-Country Arms Sales to Latin America," 9 February 1971, NARA, RG 59, Subject–Numeric File, 1970–73, Box 1763.

Years before Watergate would cripple his presidency, Richard Nixon had begun to discover that the era of a true "imperial presidency" was rapidly drawing to a close. Challenged abroad by Soviet nuclear rearmament, Western European economic growth, and the escalating expectations of the underdeveloped world, the United States found its power abroad circumvented by forces unprecedented in the post-1945 period. At home, as it was bombarded with congressional hearings and campus protests, the White House faced escalating skepticism regarding the absolute goals of its foreign policy and the means it proposed to achieve them. Combined, these restrictions forced the administration into a period of incrementalism that belied its deteriorating control over American foreign affairs. Gone were the days when the United States could forge sweeping treaties that could produce the collective global security under its leadership. Instead, the United States adopted a strategic posture that depended upon cooperation as its guiding principle. Nixon's overtures to China, the SALT I negotiations with the Soviet Union retrenchment, Vietnamization, and a host of other major initiatives all recognized new limits on American hegemony. Military assistance policy in the Third World followed suit.

Most Latin American nations were perfectly cognizant of this fact and appeared prepared to exploit it to their advantage. Despite loudly expressed American concerns regarding economic cost and the real risk of regional war, Latin American rearmament continued unabated. Moreover, by 1970, it appeared that persistent Latin American demands for additional U.S. military aid had finally paid off. Rather than threaten reprisals, American leaders were prepared to join a regional arms race, competing with European companies in a nascent attempt to reconstruct U.S. influence. The end product of this policy was an era of open-ended support for purportedly anti-Communist, military-dominated regimes that promised reform in exchange for additional military assistance. What remained a significant question mark was the Nixon administration's ability to guide this change in ways that preserved both U.S. influence and Latin American stability.

CENTRAL AMERICAN MILITARY AFFAIRS AT THE END OF THE 1960s

The late 1960s represented the apogee of military power in Latin America. Sixteen military interventions took place between 1961 and 1969. A successive series of coups against civilian power in Brazil (1964), Argentina (1966), and Peru (1968) produced, according to one State Department report in August 1969, "The military's control of government in the three countries, which include half the area's population, and their determination to retain power for an indefinite term have been widely regarded as placing in question the future of constitutional representative government in Latin America."[37]

Overall, the motives for military intervention varied only slightly from country to country. The universal problem for civilian governments at the start of the 1960s had been achieving broad and, in too many cases, overoptimistic social and economic reforms. The pronouncements offered by the Kennedy and Johnson administrations, via the Alliance for Progress, had served to expand expectations throughout the hemisphere. A general sense of impatience prevailed in many nations, and, by the mid-1960s, Latin American military leaders began to share public discontent with civilian corruption, incompetence, and constant political infighting.[38] General Juan Carlos Ongania of Argentina expressed the thoughts of many officers in 1966:

> During the last few years, we have been witnesses to a contradictory process between the conduct of politics and the exigencies of the national reality. With the mechanism for representation damaged, the popular will was rendered impotent and the far-reaching changes so vitally needed became merely wishes. The armed forces constituted the medium of legitimate expression of that popular will which had been isolated through cunning. From that point, this revolutionary unanimity and consent were expressed in our history only when it was necessary to make a decision about the national destiny.[39]

The military in this context would therefore serve as both an agent of modernization and the most adequate expression of the "popular will." After their respective takeovers, Argentina, Brazil, and Peru all announced sweeping national reforms. The juntas that ruled Brazil and Argentina publicly made the case that they had gotten their countries "moving again in terms of economic growth," according to one State Department report. Many contemporary policy makers and academics largely agreed, claiming that the newer generation of contemporary officers who had come to power in the 1960s was a breed apart from older Latin American military leaders. This generation enjoyed the benefits of what was, in many cases, the best technical and civilian training in Latin American history. The assumed derived benefit of this was a less conservative and reactionary body of leaders than those who had dominated many countries in the 1940s and 1950s.[40]

The following is a breakdown of the military role in Latin American government:[41]

Military Interventions (Date of Action)	Military-Based Regimes (Term of Office)	Constitutional Governments (Date Initiated)
Argentina (1962, 1966)	Argentina (1962–1963, 1966–)	Chile (1932)
Bolivia (1964)	Bolivia (1964)	Colombia (1932)
Brazil (1961, 1964)	Brazil (1964–)	Costa Rica (1949)
Dominican Republic (1962, 1963, 1965)	Dominican Republic (1963–1965)	Mexico (1930)
Ecuador (1961, 1963)	El Salvador (1931–)	Uruguay (1938)
El Salvador (1961)	Guatemala (1963–1966)	Venezuela (1959)
Guatemala (1963)	Honduras (1963–)	
Honduras (1963)	Ecuador (1963–1966)	
Panama (1968)	Nicaragua (1936–)	
Peru (1962, 1968)	Panama (1968–)	
	Paraguay (1954–)	
	Peru (1962–1963, 1968–)	

As military intervention in the civilian sector grew, Latin American military institutions continued their own separate evolution, particularly with respect to interregional military cooperation. For years, military training and procurement had been the province of powers foreign to Latin America. Prior to World War II, Germany, France, and Spain accounted for the bulk of a substantial advisory effort. In the postwar period, the United States dominated the region through the Rio Pact. Between 1950 and 1970, American agencies trained 54,270 Latin American servicemen in facilities in both the United States and the Canal Zone and provided $750 million in instruction and equipment assistance.[42]

Interregional military cooperation also began to grow. This relationship existed between major donors (Argentina, Brazil, and Mexico) and major recipients (Bolivia, Paraguay, Ecuador, and Central America). Chile, Mexico, Brazil, and Peru all maintained advisory efforts throughout Latin America. Brazil had military missions in nine countries by 1972. Argentina had thirteen. According to a Bureau of Intelligence and Research report, the Salvadoran military had invaded Honduras in 1969 using a contingency plan drawn up by Chilean military advisors. Some nations received aid from multiple sources. Nicaragua enjoyed military assistance from Mexico, Guatemala, El Salvador, Venezuela, and Peru. For its own part, Brazil supplied planes, small arms, and equipment to each nation that hosted a military mission. Between 1968 and 1970, almost 700 Latin American military personnel received training through regional military programs.[43]

Although cooperation flourished in some parts of Latin America, there was also significant evidence of sharpening regional military rivalries. Contained within the populist movements that swept through Latin America in the 1960s was the reassertion of rivalries dating back to the previous century. Animosity marred bilateral relations between Venezuela and Colombia, Argentina and Paraguay, and Chile and Peru.[44] In many cases, conflicts dormant since the 1950s gained a new lease on life. Interference in the internal affairs of neighbors once again became the rule of the day rather than the exception. Rumors flew in 1969 of Salvadoran efforts in a plan to assassination Anastasio Somoza Debayle.[45] Somoza himself actively supported Guatemalan armed forces candidates in that country's 1970 election and allowed his *Guardia Nacional* to intervene against a coup attempt by Salvadoran junior officers in 1972.[46] Clearly, the situation surrounding the Soccer War was far from an aberration.[47]

THE SPOILS OF VICTORY

When Anastasio Somoza Debayle came to power in 1967, the state and the military were integrated to a degree unprecedented since his father held office more than a decade earlier. However, once in power, "Tachito" proved to be much less adept at running the country than either the family's founding patriarch or his older brother Luis. Interestingly, the one area where he proved to be particularly untalented was in the maintenance of military loyalty, the true key to power in Nicaragua.[48]

A clear trend that emerged after his electoral "victory" in 1967 was Somoza's infatuation with politics at the expense of his *Guardia*. For years, Somoza the soldier had been sequestered by his father and brother within the Nicaraguan military under the watchful eyes of senior officers loyal to the family. At certain moments, particularly in 1954, 1956, and 1959, he had been able to act decisively against armed opponents of the regime.[49] However, as a distinctly military authority, final decision-making authority was denied to him. After his father's death, the youngest Somoza began to test the limits of this authority, deliberately blurring the line between his office as *Jefe Director* of the *Guardia* and true political leadership. He dabbled in the political arena, arranging and orchestrating his own *homenajes* and conducting years of pseudo-political campaigning.

His ascension to the office of president ended these years of waiting. As the chief executive of Nicaragua, Somoza was finally free to engage his family's critics in a public arena. In the years immediately following his election, Somoza took great pains to prove himself a political *jefe* equal in capacity to his earlier military experience. The Conservative Party led by Fernando Agüero was more than willing to oblige his desire for political combat. As campaigns over policy evolved into the bitter exchange of recriminations that characterized much of Nicaraguan political discourse, the cumulative effect was to steal time and attention away from the military, an institution Somoza considered loyal, but whose needs he devoted decreasing attention to as the years passed. The immediate demands of military patronage were seconded to Somoza's political ambitions, a distraction that began to separate the *Jefe Director* from his own soldiers.

Complaints regarding this inattention reached Colonel Trevor W. Swett, the U.S. Military Group commander, early in Somoza's presidency. Swett was approached by the *Guardia* chief of staff, Brigadier General Julio Morales, with significant concerns that while Somoza frequently interfered in daily military operations, he offered little guidance regarding its long-term operations. When reports of possible corruption within the *Guardia* Commissary, an office that annually managed almost $5.4 million in goods and services, reached the president's office, they went unanswered for months. In desperation, Somoza's aides approached the U.S. Military Group commander at a reception in December 1969, asking him to provide "needed hard advice" to Somoza regarding professional standards in the National Guard.[50]

Factions within the Guard began to emerge from this vacuum. As early as October 1968, Francisco Lainez, a former Somoza confidant and president of Nicaragua's Central Bank, related disturbing cleavages that had begun to appear within the military. Lainez, considered by the embassy to be an "accurate and well-informed observer," offered what he considered to be "present serious dangers" to Nicaraguan stability, citing in discussions with U.S. officials the absence of effective day-to-day leadership on the part of Somoza and the emergence of three factions within the National Guard. One was led by Colonel José Agurto, the Departmental Commander of Leon who enjoyed the loyalty of a combination of officers in outlying rural areas as well as within Somoza's own military staff. This group included Colonel Edmundo Rocha (departmental commander in Chinandega), Colonel Federico Prado (departmental commander Nueva Segovia), Colonel Ernesto Rugama (chief of laws and public relations on the General Staff), and Colonel Manuel Lopez (adjutant to the president). A second faction formed around Quartermaster General Colonel Guillermo Noguera. Nicknamed El Coro de los Angeles, it included a number of logistics officers who controlled the daily maintenance of equipment and armament throughout the Guard. A third group centered around Jose R. Somoza, commander of the president's body-guard unit.[51] In his report to the ambassador, Swett commented that "Jose R. had improved the 1st Presidential Battalion so greatly that the *Jefe Director* was worried about all the military capability that Jose R. controls."[52] Although described as "entirely dependable" by the U.S. Military Group, Lainez expressed real concern that Jose Somoza would use his key position to arrange a quick coup against the regime.[53]

Somoza was not oblivious to the challenges emanating from the National Guard. During a 5 December 1969 speech before approximately 1,000 *Guardia* members and their families at a gala celebration of his birthday, Somoza offered a "pep talk" to his soldiers. Stressing the need for the *Guardia* to stay together "no matter what," according to one American observer, the *Jefe Director* expressed his support of constitutional limits on presidential succession. Somoza also discussed the Central American Common Market and made pointed references to Salvadoran abuses of existing trade agreements that had damaged the Nicaraguan economy.[54] Taken as a whole, the address was an appeal for stability that combined the president's new role as a statesman with his old military comrades desire to protect the country's future.

Somoza also understood the limited impact of these blandishments and moved rapidly to offer the *Guardia* modern equipment as a sop for their continued allegiance. In 1971, under pressure from the Air Force, he began discussions with the United States for the purchase of A-37 jets and OV-10 observation aircraft. To American officials, Somoza demanded parity with the Guatemalan Air Force, which had already acquired similar planes from the United States. Privately, he understood that the aircraft themselves represented prestige items useful to assuage senior Air Force leaders.[55]

Unfortunately, these time-tested methods of dispensing military patronage staggered under a series of economic setbacks, particularly with respect to declining coffee and cotton prices. As the export-led boom of the 1960s slowly ground to a halt, the regime found itself unable to follow through with the purchase of either jet fighters or observation aircraft to upgrade the Air Force in mid-1972. Even worse, the traditional cushion offered by U.S. military credit assistance effectively vanished after 1970, caught in the wake of congressional budget cuts.[56] The energy crisis of 1973–1974 was a simple endpoint to the story, serving to severely limit Managua's remaining ability to rearm.

Guardia corruption proved to be an equally intractable problem. A major scandal became public in May 1969 when the GN Paymaster's Office was accused of misappropriation of funds. In its report on the Somoza administration's first two years in office, the U.S. embassy commented,

But long entrenched attitudes are slow to change; there are continuing and highly publicized examples of brutalities committed by the Guardia personnel. . . . Moreover, Guardia personnel continue the institutionalized practice of systematic rake-offs from both legal and shady civilian operations, and no apparent efforts are underway to eliminate or restrict the practice.[57]

The revelations themselves could not have come at a worse time. As the *Guardia* proved itself an increasingly clumsy obstacle to justice, crime rates surged throughout logical baggage that had retarded its popular appeal.[68] The revised FSLN was more than willing to consider cooperation with grassroots organizations such as the Jesuit-led Comité Evangélico de Promocion Agraria.[69] Perhaps most important, the Sandinista shift to urban enclaves, regardless of its overall effectiveness, carried the revolution to the bulk of the Nicaraguan population and increased its exposure, nearly a decade before the massacres at Masaya, Leon, and Diriamba, to the corruption, ineptitude and heavy-handedness of the *Guardia Nacional.*

This latter problem deeply disturbed the American country team stationed in Managua. During a 1970 assessment of the Somoza regime, the embassy recommended significant increases in funding for improvements in the civil police and public safety policy. Of the 1,900 *Guardia* members assigned to police duties, only 378 had received minimum (i.e., 100 to 250 hours) of law enforcement training. In order to rectify this situation, U.S. officials wanted an additional $600,000 devoted to improved technical training, maintenance, communications, riot control, and "crime detection" techniques.[70]

Over the longer term, the embassy also wanted to promote a higher professional standard within the Nicaraguan police and believed that U.S. assistance could contribute toward this end. American training programs, in combination with the presence of U.S. advisors at all levels, offered the possibility of exposure to civil–military relations based on the democratic model. The advisory effort could therefore perform the secondary, albeit important task, of encouraging Managua "to develop more democratic concepts of responsible and human police administration." Such training would "enable the *Guardia* to have a first line of public safety defense against urban terrorism, and otherwise to cope with the increasing mobility of the civilian populace."[71]

However, because Nicaragua lacked a Public Safety Project run by U.S. AID, this mission initially fell to the military assistance group. Not surprisingly, American officers stationed in Managua saw the task at hand as largely a military problem, in part because police functions had long been the province of the *Guardia Nacional.* They lauded the Somoza administration's "consistently firm stand against communist subversion," while recognizing the growing threat of the armed insurrection (the FSLN) and its infiltration of legal political parties as well as the enlisted ranks of the *Guardia.* For the most part, these officers seconded rural insurgency to urban terrorism as the primary threat to the country and devoted their energies to the improvement of the existing security infrastructure. According to U.S. military officials, the 450 *Guardia* troops assigned to police duties in Managua were entirely inadequate to deal with crime, let alone a dedicated terrorist effort.[72] Most of the recommendations that followed focused primarily on structural reforms and planning rather than a basic reconstruction of civil–military relations.

It was not until early 1971 that the Agency for International Development made the first tentative steps toward civilian-directed internal security assistance. The United States was represented by Gunther Wagner, the new director of the Office of Public Safety. His Nicaraguan counterpart was Colonel Francisco Rodriguez Somoza, chief of Managua's police and the president's cousin. Wagner optimistically claimed in a letter to U.S. AID in February that "our program in this 'Virgin Territory' has definitely found acceptance and I am confident, that our involvement will be most challenging and rewarding."[73]

the country. Managua proper, and most other major cities, were deluged w
of thefts, assaults, and a broad array of felonies committed against citizen:
ists alike.[58]

Compounding these difficulties was the continued persistence of
Sandinista de Liberacion Nacional. Although existing intelligence estim:
total membership at only 150 in 1971, the Sandinistas were identified a
dangerous subversive threat to Nicaragua.[59] In fact, it was a desperate ti
FSLN as an organization. Rural clashes, such as one in northwest Mataga
1970, diminished in size and intensity as Sandinista units were defeate
reeling toward the cities in search of sanctuary.[60] There, the National Gua
defeated sporadic Sandinista attacks on government employees and offices i
and the provincial towns of Masaya, Grenada, Corazo, and Rivas.[61] Subsequ
conducted by the Office of National Security resulted in a series of arre
FSLN members and much of their clandestine network of supporters. .
December 1968, the *Guardia* had penetrated and seriously damaged the
infrastructure located inside the Nicaraguan National University.[62] By 1969
was reduced to sporadic raids, bank robberies, and hijackings.[63]

The real dilemma for the Sandinistas was their inability to create mass s
their cause. Despite its considerable growth during the Alliance for Pro;
Nicaragua lacked what could accurately be described as either a rural o
proletariat. Seasonal labor occupied the majority of the rural population
for example, cotton plantations required only 23,000 permanent workers
Manufacturing and industrial labor, while on the increase during the
1960s, occupied perhaps one-tenth of the workforce and was not a domir
At best, the country possessed what Doreen Massey has described a
proletariate."[64]

Internal squabbling plagued the armed anti-Somoza bloc. In 1969, wh
ing in Havana to celebrate the tenth anniversary of the Cuban Revoluti
Fonseca Amador continued a war of words with the Nicaraguan Socialist
lier, the PSN weekly *La Tribuna* had denounced Che Guevara for not h
true Marxist–Leninist line in his approach to Latin American revolutioi
responded with his own broadside at the PSN, denouncing it and Nicarag
munist Party regulars as nothing more than "bourgeoisie political experts.
cious as the debate appeared to the outside layman, it did point to some
crisis of purpose inside the FSLN itself. The fundamental question for the S
as expressed by Regis Debray, was the need to find a means to revitalize co
in a Latin American context, a search that required the effective comb
socialist ideology and nationalism.[66] While the FSLN groped toward an an;
logical fissures began to appear, ones that would later lead to the divis
movement into the Tendencia Proletaria, the Guerra Popular Prolongada
and the Tendencia Tercerista.[67]

The FSLN would eventually emerge with a coherent strategy to win
popular support and the initiative in its war against the Somoza regii
Dunkerley has observed that the reverses of the early 1970s left the Sandin
nizationally leaner, more focused, more disciplined, and prepared to jettisoi

However, the two countries made only minor progress toward a concrete country security program. By August 1971, the Office of Public Safety was able to report marginal improvements in the training, organization, and administration of the Managua police department. In part, this was the product of Wagner's own inexperience. His posting to Managua was only his second assignment in the Office of Public Safety. Although he was provided the requisite briefings and introductory processing that any new member of the U.S. country team received, he was a neophyte when it came to the inner workings of the Nicaraguan military. Wagner was vastly unprepared to win the cooperation of any one part of the *Guardia* or its leader. Somoza remained key to any operational changes. As *Jefe Director*, the president retained control of all police, intelligence, and military activities. His minister of defense remained largely a symbolic member of the cabinet, responsible for Nicaragua's inefficient national telephone system, the postal service, and port facilities.[74]

Within this atmosphere, internal security reform was captured by the desire to promote positive political relations. When William P. Rogers received a diplomatic note from the Nicaraguan ambassador to the United States in August of 1970, in itself a breach of protocol, requesting 8 million rounds of 0.30-caliber ammunition, 2.5 million rounds of 0.45-caliber ammunition, practice grenades, and practice mortar rounds, the State Department approved the request.[75] Two years later, in March 1972, ambassador Turner Shelton approved an increase in the FY1974 Military Assistance Program for helicopters, justifying the brief spike in aid as a temporary expedient counterbalanced by its positive impact on U.S. relations with Nicaragua.[76] The very nature of the Nicaraguan requests themselves illustrated how much distance remained between the *Guardia* and the subtleties of internal policing or effective civil–military relations. Despite calls for additional riot training and the accumulation of nonlethal equipment, the Nicaraguan military remained fixated on the conventional military instruments that had preserved its power for decades.

At points, the United States appeared willing to tolerate Nicaragua efforts to entirely bypass the Office of Public Safety. In May 1971, the State Department received reports from London that the Somoza government had sought out advice from the United Kingdom on counterinsurgency training. When informed of the development, OPS Director Byron Engle noted that the United States would have no problem with foreign security operations acting within Nicaragua, commenting that it was "much better the UK than someone else."[77]

The earthquake that destroyed much of Managua in December 1972 was a devastating commentary on both the *Guardia Nacional* and American military assistance effort in Nicaragua. The Guard, as well as most of the country's civil service, collapsed when confronted with the disaster that enveloped the nation's capital. According to conservative estimates, more than 10,000 died and 20,000 were injured during the brief but savage event. Three hundred thousand were made homeless. In the aftermath of the quake, work crews cremated bodies where they found them. Few escaped the stench of death that permeated the rubble.[78]

Amidst this chaos, the Guard disintegrated into a collection of mobs intent on looting what remained of downtown Managua, while their *Jefe* retreated to his personal residence. All three of Managua's jails were destroyed, freeing more than 400 inmates. No attempt was made to recapture them. Of the few units that remained at their posts, many Guardsmen were reluctant to fire on civilian looters. A *Guardia* lieutenant interviewed in the immediate aftermath of the quake claimed, "But we can't shoot people who have lost everything they have."[79]

For their own part, American officials were surprised and appalled at a military run amok. When it became blatantly apparent that local agencies could neither administer emergency relief to the hundreds of thousands of civilian refugees of the earthquake nor guarantee the safety of the private organizations that tried to do so, U.S. troops from the Canal Zone and CONDECA member nations were dispatched to restore order.[80] The Nicaraguan military's simple inability to preserve stability or save the prostrate capital, and its absolute dependence on outside powers, marked the nadir of the *Guardia*.

CONCLUSIONS

During the Nixon administration, U.S. policy makers scrambled to redefine security policy at a time when political capital and budgetary support were at a premium. American policy makers were forced to abandon the largess that had characterized the two earlier administrations. The glory years of a nuclear capability built upon MacNamara's thousand Minuteman missiles and across-the-board increases in conventional forces were over, spent on the battlefields of Southeast Asia.[81]

Replacing them was a defense policy tied to a complex formula that utilized measured amounts of aid, diplomacy, and prioritized commitments. Clearly, the team Nixon constructed to maintain this balancing act, including the president himself, were as formidable a grouping of policy makers as in any period of American history. Joan Hoff's commentary on Nixon's own conceptual grasp of U.S. diplomacy is well taken. It is indeed arguable that a great mind such as Kissinger's traveled in the wake of his president.[82] Regardless, their combined efforts were able to win back only a degree of coherence and focus to American security interests. NATO, China, and strategic arms diplomacy regained their perch in the official conventional wisdom.

Yet in other areas around the world outside this arena, American defense policy was on much less sure footing. The battles fought by the United States in the Third World after Vietnam were relegated to conflicts designed to preserve American influence. During this dawning era of limits, American leaders were hard pressed to cultivate proxies willing to pursue U.S. interests in the far-off corners of the world. In many respects, and not without some small degree of irony, the situation Nixon presided over closely resembled that of his mentor, Dwight D. Eisenhower, a generation earlier.

Unfortunately, the Nixon administration was even more hard pressed to find an effective means by which it could exercise its interests while maintaining its influence in the Third World. According to the conventional wisdom of the time, weapons transfers created influence within military governments intent of modernization, prestige acquisitions, or regional arms races. Weapons sales, credit assistance, and military advisory missions all offered highly positive means to promote friendly relations with any American ally. All offered the prospect of influence without overt intervention.

However, when the United States attempted to flex its muscle and exercise a degree of leverage purchased by this policy, the system performed very poorly in Latin America, if at all. Any American threat of an arms embargo meant very little in a hemisphere literally awash in modern weapons systems and rival allied nations intent on promoting their own individual wares. Any threat of withdrawal was easily deflected. Moreover, as his assistance appropriations shrank with each fiscal year, Nixon found himself struggling to maintain any measure of equilibrium amidst these challenges. His administration's preference for military sales rather than credit was a point of departure marking an increased U.S. dependence on the preferences of the purchaser, not on its own influence.

The evolution of U.S. security policy in Latin America offers an excellent illustration of the administration's dilemma. In nearly every instance that the military intervened to take control of civil government in Latin America, it did so because of professional contempt for civilian institutions. Whether driven by raw ambition or simple sincerity, military leaders saw themselves as the proper guardians of national sovereignty and polity.[83] Given this basic intent, it was highly unlikely that American demands would fail to suffer resistance or obstruction. The string of military and military-dominated governments that controlled most of Latin America were indeed receptive to U.S. military aid without concrete conditions. However, when U.S. policy makers attempted to use assistance as a fulcrum for meaningful changes, the relationship was easily abandoned in favor of third-party sales with no conditions.

The situation in Nicaragua mirrored this trend. At the conclusion of Nixon's first term, it was clear that the *Guardia Nacional* remained Nicaragua's most influential military and political institution. After nearly a decade of combat against the guerrilla threat, it had prevailed. Warfare in the countryside had been superseded by police work within the cities of the Pacific coast against an adversary reduced to bank robberies and random assassination attempts. What remained for Nicaragua's soldiers was presiding over their victory.

However, as the Guard's mission changed to address a new urban environment, its ability to develop and use new doctrine did not. It was unable to alter its "management of violence," to borrow a phrase from Robert H. Holden.[84] Civil policing, the focus of this new emphasis, continued to be a ham-fisted exercise, characterized by chronic corruption, brutal treatment of the population at large, and indifference toward change. Over the longer term, the *Guardia* proved able to hurt the Sandinista movement, but it never developed the capability to destroy new Sandinista networks that reinvigorated the FSLN in the early 1970s. Nor was it able to successfully separate the Sandinistas from the civilian population as a whole.

Arguably, this situation was created and maintained by the *Guardia*'s own success at dispensing with rivals of the Somoza regime. With its position secure, the military gradually dissolved into small, bickering groups that battled over the small power vacuums created by Anastasio Somoza's inattention to all parts of his family's regime. Nicaragua in 1972 represented more a polyhierarchy of competing *caudillos* than a coherent government. The craven weakness of the Guard during the earthquake that year revealed to Nicaraguans and the world the depths of the institution's self-interest and fundamental incompetence.

The American country team was one witness to this failure. A review of the cable traffic emanating from Managua after 1969 indicates that there was little question in the minds of U.S. officials that basic reforms were essential to bolster the *Guardia's* effectiveness, especially in the areas of police work and internal security. Very little action followed these reports. In part, inertia was the product of Gunther Wagner's inexperience with the arcane avenues of Nicaraguan internal affairs and local suspicion regarding his office's purpose.[85] To a much greater degree, however, this hesitancy was the product of a basic and somewhat contradictory American desire to not sacrifice influence for the sake of leverage. The embassy was willing to rationalize local obstruction and departures from normal protocol (e.g., the solicitation of British counterinsurgency experts) for the expressed purpose of cultivating productive long-term relations. Again, the regime's performance in the aftermath of the Managua earthquake illustrated to all observers the fallacy of this approach.

NOTES

1. Paul Kennedy, *The Rise and Fall of the Great Powers: Economic Change and Military Conflict from 1500 to 2000* (New York: Vintage Books, 1989), 384–399; J. E. Moore, "The Soviet Navy," in *The Soviet War Machine: An Encyclopedia of Russian Military Equipment and Strategy,* ed. Ray Bonds (New York: Chartwell Books, 1976), 114–126.

2. Stephen E. Ambrose, *Rise to Globalism: American Foreign Policy since 1938* (New York: Penguin Books, 1991), 242.

3. John Prados, *The Soviet Estimate: U.S. Intelligence Analysis and Russian Military Strength* (New York: Dial Press, 1982), 183–199; James E. Dornan, "Strategic Rocket Forces," in *The Soviet War Machine: An Encyclopedia of Russian Military Equipment and Strategy,* ed. Ray Bonds (New York: Chartwell Books, 1976), 207–210.

4. Allan R. Millett and Peter Maslowski, *For the Common Defense: A Military History of the United States of America* (New York: The Free Press, 1994), 595.

5. Lawrence Freedman, "The First Two Generations of Nuclear Strategists," in *Makers of Modern Strategy: From Machiavelli to the Nuclear Age,* ed. Peter Paret (Princeton, N.J.: Princeton University Press, 1986), 746–761; Prados, *The Soviet Estimate,* 192.

6. Prados, *The Soviet Estimate,* 190.

7. Millett and Maslowski, *For the Common Defense,* 596.

8. *Global Defense: U.S. Military Commitments Abroad* (Washington, D.C.: Congressional Quarterly Service, 1969), 66.

9. Ibid., 65.

10. Ibid., 66.

11. Ibid., 69.

12. Millett and Maslowski, *For the Common Defense,* 594, 656.

13. Letter, Carl Marcy to Henry A. Kissinger, 23 September 1969, National Archives and Records Administration (hereafter NARA), Richard M. Nixon Presidential Materials Collection (hereafter RMN), White House Central File (hereafter (WHCF), Subject File, Box Box 20.

14. Memorandum, Richard M. Nixon to the Secretary of State and the Secretary of Defense, 30 August 1971, NARA, RMN, WHCF, Subject File, Box 20.

15. Ibid.

16. Memorandum, Jack F. Lehman (Office of the White House) to Henry Kissinger, 14 October 1971, NARA, RMN, WHCF, Subjects, Box 20.

17. NSDM 76, "The New U.S. Foreign Assistance Program," 10 August 1970, NARA, Records Group 273, Records of the National Security Council, National Security Decision Memoranda, Box 1.

18. U. Alexis Johnson, "The Role of Police Forces in a Changing World," *State Department Bulletin*, 13 September 1971, 282.

19. Michael T. Klare, *Supplying Repression: U.S. Support for Authoritarian Regimes Abroad* (Washington, D.C.: Institute for Policy Studies, 1977), 13. See also U.S. Senate, Committee on Banking, Housing, and Urban Affairs, *Financing Foreign Military Sales* (Washington, D.C.: U.S. Government Printing Office, 1978), 29. The Johnson administration, for example, saw its foreign-aid appropriations requests slashed by 33.8 percent in 1964. Kennedy had his requests for foreign aid cut by 18 percent and 18.4 percent in 1962 and 1963, respectively. See *Evolution of Foreign Aid, 1945–1965* (Washington, D.C.: Congressional Quarterly Service, 1966), 25.

20. Klare, *Supplying Repression*, 40; Harold J. Clem, *Collective Defense and Foreign Assistance* (Washington, D.C.: Industrial College of the Armed Forces, 1968), 34.

21. Miles D. Wolpin, *Military Aid and Counterrevolution in the Third World* (Lexington, Mass.: Lexington Books, 1972), 144.

22. U.S. Department of State, Bureau of Intelligence and Research, "Latin America: U.S. Influence on the Latin American Military," 5 January 1971, NARA, Records Group 59 (hereafter RG 59), Subject–Numeric File, 1970–73, Box 1764.

23. Wolpin, *Military Aid and Counterrevolution in the Third World*, 20.

24. U.S. House, Committee on Foreign Affairs, Subcommittee on National Security and Scientific Developments, *Reports of the Specific Study Mission to Latin America on Military Assistance Training and Developmental Television* (Washington, D.C.: U.S. Government Printing Office, 1970), 21.

25. Memorandum, William P. Rogers to the President, "Waiver of Regional Ceiling on Military Assistance and Sales to Latin America," 19 June 1973, NARA, RG 59, Subject–Numeric File, 1970–73, Box 1763.

26. "The Politics of Leverage," *Time*, 12 July 1971, 29.

27. U.S. Department of State, "Latin America: U.S. Influence on the Latin American Military," 5 January 1971.

28. Ibid.

29. Henry Kissinger, *The White House Years* (Boston: Little, Brown, 1979), 653–664.

30. U.S. Department of State, Director of Intelligence and Research, "Latin America: Guerrillas and Terrorists Primarily a Disruptive, Not a Revolutionary Threat," 8 April 1970, NARA, RG 59, Subject–Numeric File, 1970–73, Box 2433.

31. Memorandum, William P. Rogers to Richard M. Nixon, "Rockefeller Report Recommendations," 22 November 1969, NARA, RG 59, Subject–Numeric File, 1967–69, Box 2112; U.S. Department of State, Bureau of Intelligence and Research, "Latin America: New Terrorist Threat—Assassination of Diplomats," 9 October 1970, NARA, RG 59, Subject–Numeric File, 1970–73, Box 2433.

32. Memorandum, "Rockefeller Recommendation for Western Hemisphere Security Council—Country Attitudes," 6 February 1970, NARA, RG 59, Subject–Numeric File, 1970–73, Box 2434.

33. Harold B. Scott (Acting Assistance Secretary of Commerce for Domestic and International Business) to U. Alexis Johnson (Undersecretary of State for Political Affairs), "Sales of Military Equipment to Developing Countries," 28 April 1971, NARA, RG 59, Subject–Numeric File, 1970–73, Box 1763.

34. U.S. Department of State, Bureau of Intelligence and Research, "Third-Country Arms Sales to Latin America," 9 February 1971, NARA, RG 59, Subject–Numeric File, 1970–73, Box 1763.

35. Ibid.; U.S. Department of State, Bureau of Intelligence and Research, "Latin America: The Outlook for Arms Spending," 5 March 1973, NARA, RG 59, Subject–Numeric File, 1970–73, Box 1763.

36. Cable, State Department to U.S. Embassy (Caracas) and U.S. Embassy (San Salvador), "Central American Arms Purchases," 30 April 1970, NARA, RG 59, Subject–Numeric File, 1970–73, Box 1763.

37. U.S. Department of State, Director of Intelligence and Research, "The New Militarism in South America: Agent for Modernization?" 28 August 1969, NARA, RG 59, Subject–Numeric File, 1967–69, Box 2109.

38. Ibid.

39. Brian Loveman and Thomas M. Davies Jr., eds., *The Politics of Anti-Politics: The Military in Latin America* (Lincoln: University of Nebraska Press, 1989), 195.

40. U.S. Department of State, "The New Militarism in South America: Agent for Modernization?" 28 August 1969; U.S. Department of State, Director of Intelligence and Research, "Trends in Latin America," 8 October 1971, NARA, RG 59, Subject–Numeric File, 1970–73, Box 2432. See also Samuel P. Huntington, *Political Order in Changing Societies* (New Haven, Conn.: Yale University Press, 1968), 192–263; Philippe C. Schmitter, ed., *Military Rule in Latin America: Functions, Consequences, and Perspectives* (London: Sage, 1973); David Collier, ed., *The New Authoritarianism in Latin America* (Princeton, N.J.: Princeton University Press, 1979); Guillermo O'Donnell, Philippe C. Schmitter, and Laurence Whitehead, eds., *Transitions from Authoritarian Rule: Comparative Perspectives* (Baltimore: Johns Hopkins University Press, 1986); Karen L. Remmer, "The Politics of Economic Stabilization: IMF Standby Programs in Latin America, 1954–1984," in *Money Doctors, Foreign Debts, and Economic Reforms in Latin America: From the 1890s to the Present*, ed. Paul W. Drake (Wilmington, Del.: Scholarly Resources, 1994), 175–202; Brian Loveman, *For la Patria: Politics and the Armed Forces in Latin America* (Wilmington, Del.: Scholarly Resources, 1999), 165–226.

41. U.S. Department of State, Director of Intelligence and Research, "The New Militarism in South America: Agent for Modernization," 28 August 1969, NARA, RG 59, Subject–Numeric File, 1967–69, Box 2109.

42. U.S. Department of State, Bureau of Intelligence and Research, "Latin America: Growing Ties—and Rivalries—among Neighbors," 23 August 1972, NARA, RG 59, Subject–Numeric File, 1970–73, Box 2432.

43. Ibid.

44. Ibid.

45. Memorandum, U.S. Military Group Nicaragua to the Ambassador, "Conversation with the Chief of Staff," 17 December 1969, NARA, RG 59, Subject–Numeric File, 1967–69, Box 2178.

46. Morris H. Morley, *Washington, Somoza, and the Sandinistas: State and Regime in U.S. Policy toward Nicaragua, 1969–1981* (New York: Cambridge University Press, 1994), 39.

47. Memorandum, Rogers to the President, "Waiver of Regional Ceiling on Military Assistance and Sales to Latin America," 19 June 1973.

48. For a discussion of this "maintenance," see Michael D. Gambone, *Eisenhower, Somoza, and the Cold War in Nicaragua, 1953–1961* (Westport, Conn.: Praeger, 1997), 105–130.

49. See Patricia Taylor Edmisten, *Nicaragua Divided: La Prensa and the Chamorro Legacy* (Pensacola: University of West Florida Press, 1990).

50. Memorandum, U.S. Military Group Nicaragua to the Ambassador, "Contact Report," 15 December 1969, NARA, RG 59, Subject–Numeric File, 1967–69, Box 2178.

51. Memorandum of Conversation, Francisco Lainez (ex-Central Bank President) and David W. Burgoon (Embassy Political Officer), 1 October 1968, NARA, RG 59, Subject–Numeric File, 1967–69, Box 2177.

52. Memorandum, U.S. Military Group Nicaragua to the Ambassador, "Contact Report," 15 December 1969.

53. Memorandum, U.S. Military Group Nicaragua to the Ambassador, "MILGP Contact Reports," 16 December 1969, NARA, RG 59, Subject–Numeric File, 1967–69, Box 2178.

54. Memorandum, U.S. Military Group Nicaragua to the Ambassador, "Contact Report," 15 December 1969.

55. Cable, Embassy (Managua) to State, 24 March 1971, and Letter, Anastasio Somoza Debayle to Lieutenant General George M. Seinious (Deputy Assistant Secretary of Defense for Security Assistance), 22 July 1972, NARA, RG 59, Subject–Numeric File, 1970–73, Box 1776.

56. Memorandum, Chris C. Pappas (PM/MAS) to Billings (DOD/DSSA), "Request to Purchase OV-10 Aircraft," 31 July 1972, and Cable, Embassy (Managua) to State, 14 February 1973, NARA, RG 59, Subject–Numeric File, 1970–73, Box 1776.

57. Cable, Embassy (Managua) to State, "The Somoza Administration's First Two Years," 12 May 1969, NARA, RG 59, Subject–Numeric File, 1967–69, Box 2178.

58. Cable, Embassy (Managua) to State, 12 May 1969, NARA, RG 59, Subject–Numeric File, 1967–69, Box 646.

59. Cable, Embassy (Managua) to State, "Country Analysis and Strategy Paper for Nicaragua," 25 January 1971, NARA, RG 59, Subject–Numeric File, 1970–73, Box 2503.

60. Cable, Embassy (Managua) to State, 18 June 1970, NARA, RG 59, Subject–Numeric File, 1970–73, Box 2503.

61. Morley, *Washington, Somoza, and the Sandinistas*, 62.

62. Cable, Embassy (Managua) to State, 12 January 1969, NARA, RG 59, Subject–Numeric File, 1967–69, Box 2178.

63. Ibid.; Cable, Embassy (Managua) to State, 5 November 1969, NARA, RG 59, Subject–Numeric File, 1967–69, Box 2178.

64. Doreen Massey, *Nicaragua* (Philadelphia: Open University Press, 1987), 8–9. See also Rose J. Spalding, *Capitalists and Revolution in Nicaragua: Opposition and Accommodation, 1979–1993* (Chapel Hill: University of North Carolina Press, 1994), 32–62.

65. Cable, Embassy (Managua) to State, 12 January 1969.

66. Regis Debray, *Revolution within the Revolution? Armed Struggle and Political Struggle in Latin America* (New York: Monthly Review Press, 1967), 19–25.

67. Steven Palmer, "Carlos Fonseca and the Construction of Sandinismo in Nicaragua," *Latin American Research Review* 23 (1988): 91–109.

68. James Dunkerley, *Power in the Isthmus: A Political History of Modern Central America* (New York: Verso, 1988), 239–247. See also Juan Bosch, "An Anti-Communist Manifesto," in *Regis Debray and the Latin American Revolution*, ed. Leo Huberman and Paul M. Sweezy (New York: Monthly Review Press, 1968), 96–105.

69. Michael Dodson and Laura Nuzzi O'Shaughnessy, *Nicaragua's Other Revolution: Religious Faith and Political Struggle* (Chapel Hill: University of North Carolina Press, 1990), 124–125.

70. Cable, Embassy (Managua) to State, 18 January 1970, NARA, RG 59, Subject–Numeric File, 1970–73, Box 2503; Cable, Embassy (Managua) to State, 27 August 1971, NARA, RG 59, Subject–Numeric File, 1970–73, Box 573.

71. Ibid.

72. Cable, Embassy (Managua) to State, 9 February 1969, NARA, RG 59, Subject–Numeric File, 1967–69, Box 2179; Cable, Embassy (Managua) to State, 21 May 1971, NARA, RG 59, Subject–Numeric File, 1970–73, Box 2503.

73. Letter, Gunther O. Wagner (USAID/OPS Managua) to Byron Engle, (Director, OPS), 23 February 1971, NARA, Records Group 286, USAID Office of Public Safety, Latin America, Countries, Nicaragua, Box 91.

74. Cable, Embassy (Managua) to State, "The Somoza Administration's First Two Years," 12 May 1969; Cable, Embassy (Managua) to State, 27 August 1971.

75. Letter, Guillermo Sevilla Sacasa (Ambassador to the United States) to William P. Rogers, 10 August 1970, NARA, RG 59, Subject–Numeric File, 1970–73, Box 1776.

76. Letter, Turner Shelton to John R. Breen (Country Director, ARA-LA/CEN), 24 March 1972, NARA, RG 59, Subject–Numeric File, 1970–73, Box 2434.

77. Cable, Embassy (London) to State, 25 May 1971, NARA, RG 59, Subject–Numeric File, 1970–73, Box 2503.

78. Dunkerley, *Power in the Isthmus,* 234–236; Taylor, *Nicaragua Divided,* 56.

79. "The Managua Earthquake: How a City Died," *Newsweek,* 8 January 1973, 28.

80. Dunkerley, *Power in the Isthmus,* 235.

81. For an excellent study of the absolute economic costs of the war, see Robert Warren Stevens, *Vain Hopes, Grim Realities: The Economic Consequences of the Vietnam War* (New York: New Viewpoints, 1976).

82. Joan Hoff, *Nixon Reconsidered* (New York: Basic Books, 1994).

83. Frederick M. Nunn, *The Time of the Generals: Latin American Professional Militarism in World Perspective* (Lincoln: University of Nebraska Press, 1992), 206–210.

84. Robert H. Holden, "Constructing the Limits of State Violence in Central America: Towards a New Research Agenda," *Journal of Latin American Studies* 28 (1996): 435–459.

85. Cable, Embassy (Managua) to State, 11 May 1971, NARA, RG 59, Subject–Numeric File, 1970–73, Box 573. Pedro Joaquim Chamorro offered a constant barrage of "extremely negative" editorials regarding Wagner's job performance and public appearances.

CHAPTER 9

The Approaching Economic Crisis

A nation, like a person, has to have a certain inner drive in order to succeed. In economic affairs, that inner drive is called the competitive spirit.

Richard Nixon, 1971

This report is geared to action. For Latin American countries can no longer put off the decision to take deliberate steps to influence the course of their economic and social development if they are to overcome serious handicaps which the passage of time is more likely to aggravate than to remedy.

Raul Prebisch, 1971

The end of the decade saw a dissipation of U.S. economic hegemony in concert with its dwindling nuclear superiority. Nixon's presidency faced a new era of limits, not self-imposed, but the product of America's weakening global economic position. The greatest challenge to American power in the post-Vietnam period was not simply the maintenance of nuclear parity with the Soviet Union, but the construction of an economic foundation that would underpin it. By the end of the 1960s, the Central American Common Market was in shambles. Plagued by trade imbalances and an ongoing dependency on primary commodities, the common market devolved into bickering and finger-pointing by 1970. The dream of integrated progress seemed to be at an end. For the Somoza regime, the decline of the common market was but one indication of its own economic difficulties. Coffee and cotton prices suffered in 1969, prompting concerns about a Nicaraguan recession. More disturbing was the regime's apparent lack of a strategy to combat the problem. The start of the 1970s was an important point of departure for the Somoza government, one that demanded either a comprehensive response to address economic growth or the surrender of some state autonomy to private-sector initiatives.

AMERICAN DECLINE AND RETRENCHMENT

Richard Nixon's tenure as president coincided with a precipitous decline in the economic underpinnings of the country. Unambiguous problems were apparent almost from the outset of his administration. Unemployment rose dramatically, from 3.6 percent in 1968 to 5.8 percent by 1971.[1] When Nixon defeated Humphrey at the polls, inflation stood at 4.7 percent, low in comparison to later standards, but twice the average annual rate for the period from 1956 to 1967.[2] At the start of the 1970s, U.S. leaders and the public alike would see the emergence of "stagflation," a problem that would plague the American economy for nearly a decade.

As is often the case with presidential administrations, Nixon's dilemma was primarily the product of an accumulation of problems that neither Kennedy nor Johnson had treated during their respective tenures. In Kennedy's case, economic policy was diverted by crises abroad and congressional obstruction. While better versed in domestic affairs and able to complete many Kennedy initiatives in 1964, Lyndon Johnson demonstrated little interest afterward in constructing a legitimate means to sustain his Great Society programs.[3] Consequently, it fell to Richard Nixon to address shortcomings in both domestic and foreign economic policy and find adequate measures to sustain U.S. economic prosperity.

One of the first challenges Nixon had to face was the changing structure of the global economy. According to research conducted by Walt Rostow, world industrial production nearly doubled between 1963 and 1973.[4] However, the greatest proportion of this growth occurred outside the United States. The respective economic "miracles" experienced by Germany and the rest of Western Europe (with the exception of Britain) marked the region as one of the fastest growing economic areas in the postwar period. Between 1950 and 1970, European gross domestic product grew at an average annual rate of 5.5 percent. At 7.9 percent, industrial production grew even faster. Japan saw an equally dramatic economic resurgence. Between 1950 and 1973, gross domestic product grew at an average annual rate of 10.5 percent.[5] In the wake of Japanese expansion, America saw its control of industries such as shipbuilding, steel, and automobiles come under siege by the start of the 1970s.

Added to this disturbing trajectory was rapidly advancing competition from the Third World. This particular region saw its share of global manufacturing increase from 6.5 percent in 1953 to 12.3 percent in 1970, primarily in light manufacturing businesses such as textiles and food processing.[6] Global growth in specific sectors had an almost immediate impact on the U.S. economy. Former American bastions of textile processing in the South suffered considerably when placed in direct competition with Mexico, Singapore, South Korea, and Indonesia.[7]

Cumulatively, these forces caused both the U.S. global market share and the American balance-of-payments situation to deteriorate considerably throughout the 1960s. The continuing contraction of American wealth was most apparent in the decline of American gold reserves, which had held steady prior to 1957, but fell significantly afterward, from $17.8 billion in 1960 to $10.9 billion in 1968.[8] This flow was exacerbated further by capital flight from the United States to Europe and Asia as American investors followed cheap labor and lucrative investments and remained overseas. The end product of this movement was an American net liquidity deficit that averaged $3.2 billion between 1961 and 1970. Domestic economic initiatives often backfired and served to worsen this already bad situation. The Nixon administration's earliest attempts to address the recession at home prompted even worse capital flight. When the White House and an amenable Federal Reserve agreed to lower interest rates, a massive capital flow began to higher rates of return in Europe. Consequently, the net liquidity deficits for the first three quarters of 1971 increased from $10.4 billion, to $22.8 billion, to $39.6 billion.[9]

The economic dynamics created by the Vietnam War added another important layer to Nixon's burden in 1969. The war arrived in 1965 at a time when the American economy had reached approximate full capacity and full employment. The already burgeoning machine that drove American productivity was fed even more as a result of defense orders for Southeast Asia. This spending remained in the procurement pipeline for years. Subsequently, when he assumed office, Nixon inherited a seriously overheated economy. Perhaps more important, American overseas defense spending turned, in the words of Paul Kennedy, "the flow of dollars exported into a flood."[10] According to Commerce Department figures, Vietnam led the way in U.S. defense expenditures, registering an 800-percent increase between 1964 and 1969. Overall, American military spending abroad during this half decade increased by 68.6 percent.[11]

The cumulative effect of all these crises was the collapse of the postwar monetary system. In his testimony before the congressional Joint Economic Committee in June 1969, one of the primary architects of this system, Dean Acheson, placed the issue in plain context:

The Bretton Woods agreements which were made for commerce were not designed to support military exchange arrangements. They just were not designed for that and we cannot do it. So we have a lot of makeshift agreements by which the Germans purchase arms or one thing and another. . . . I am all in favor of foreign trade . . . imports as well as exports. But you cannot take a lot of imports, pay a lot of dollars to support troops, and also make American capital available in the world without going broke. You cannot do it. It just will not work under the rules we have.[12]

By August 1971, it was clear that the American economy stood at the crossroads of a genuine crisis. No longer was the country able to chart the economic course of the world, or its own.

Nixon's programmatic response to this situation developed in parallel with the administration's effort to return rationality to American foreign affairs. As president, Nixon brought an important understanding of global trade from his experience in the Wall Street firm of Nixon, Mudge, Rose, Guthrie, and Alexander. In an interview with historian Joan Hoff, he noted the need to overcome a reluctance in the diplomatic community to let foreign policy promote international commerce: "Unlike the ignoramuses I encountered among economic officers at various embassies in the 1950's and 1960's, I wanted to bring economics to foreign service."[13]

To this end, he created the Council on International Economic Policy in early 1971. Led by Peter G. Peterson, the president of the Bell and Howell Company of Chicago, CIEP was charged with preparing a report on the changing nature of the world economy and possible American policy options for the near future. For his own part, Peterson did not believe that a single cause could explain the contemporary problems suffered by the American economy. In his 1971 report, *The United States in the Changing World Economy*, he attributed the current situation to increasing energy needs, inadequate growth of U.S. productivity, rapidly increasing labor costs, and excess domestic inflation. The most prevalent reason for America's dire economic straits was her trading partners' tendency to grant preferential treatment to agriculture and local industries at the expense of American exports. The obvious long-term solution to this, according to Peterson, was free trade and greater American access to foreign markets. At no point was defense spending or Vietnam mentioned in his discourse.[14]

The dramatic series of policy decisions announced by the administration in August 1971 reflected the primary obstacles identified by the Peterson report if not its long-term solutions. When Nixon introduced his "New Economic Policy" on 15 August it was, for all intents, a policy of American economic retrenchment. To meet the chronic problems of inflation and recession, it mandated a ninety-day freeze on wages and prices and a 10-percent "Job Development Credit" for investment in new equipment. To offset the cost of the tax cut, Nixon ordered a $4.7-billion reduction in the federal budget, with most of this amount taken from federal revenue-sharing programs. The president also announced the appointment of a Cost of Living Council to foster agreements between management and labor in discussions on wage and price stability. Regarding foreign commerce, Nixon's NEP tended to adopt protectionist measures designed to respond in kind to the preferential treatment that stymied American trade. His plan introduced an across-the-board 10-percent surcharge on imports. U.S. foreign aid was also cut by 10 percent. Most dramatic was the suspension of the convertibility of the dollar to gold. Toward this particular end, Nixon vowed that he was "determined that the American dollar must never again be a hostage in the hands of international speculators."[15]

Nixon reaped considerable domestic benefits for his decisions in August 1971. On the day following the speech, the New York Stock Exchange traded a record 31 million shares.[16] Inflation and unemployment responded favorably, if briefly, to the measures taken and declined in the last quarter of the year to 4 percent and 5.1 percent, respectively. Domestic pundits generally applauded the White House for its initiative. The lead editorial in the *New York Times* on 16 August commended the president for rejecting the "do-nothing approach that immobilized the country and sapped the national will."[17] Donald R. Burns, president of the National Association of Business Economists, commented, "The President attacked the three biggest problems facing business—inflation, the balance of payments and the dollar crisis. I would say that total output—the country's gross national product measured in terms of real physical output—should move up in the months ahead at a faster rate than expected."[18]

The longer-term international implications of the NEP were less compelling. American allies were stunned by the decisions announced, made with virtually no attempt at consultation. Countries that held considerable dollar reserves, particularly West Germany and Japan, were taken completely by surprise when the gold convertibility policy was announced and lost heavily in currency markets. More important, American credibility suffered in the aftermath of Nixon's NEP speech. The simple fact of the 10-percent cut in foreign aid cast a large shadow over American commitments abroad. More pointed, the very nature of Nixon's unilateral action itself disturbed allies, who began to doubt American support for multilateral economic institutions. Their concern appeared justified. A careful reading of the Peterson report reveals references to international trade mechanisms only to the extent that they were either outmoded or biased against the United States.[19]

Sustaining the NEP with concrete policies over the long run was equally problematic. While Nixon endorsed the principle of free trade and open markets, little followed in the way of concrete proposals toward that end. At most, the White House appeared content to pursue bilateral economic agreements rather than a fundamental revision of multilateral institutions called for by Peterson. Moreover, Nixon was a hands-off president with respect to international economic policy and foreign aid. Soon after taking office, he rescinded Lyndon Johnson's standing requirement that PL480 agreements and U.S. AID project loans over $10 million and U.S. AID program loans over $5 million receive presidential approval.[20] At the Treasury Department, George Schultz became the "deputy president for economic matters" and Nixon's key advisor in all economic matters until the creation of the Council on Economic Policy in 1972. Unfortunately, Schultz's advice on matters of foreign trade and assistance, and later John Connally's at Treasury, was seriously handicapped by a simple lack of experience. Conversely, in cases where CIEP attempted to offer the president its counsel on these issues, it found itself effectively nullified by Henry Kissinger, who regularly expressed his disinterest in international economics, but who also feared CIEP at turns when it appeared to eclipse his influence on foreign policy.[21]

The last item is a curious omission in the career of Richard Nixon. For all his vaunted expertise in international affairs, particularly in crafting the "linkages" that married concrete international actions with equally specific American responses, Nixon essentially failed to incorporate political economy into the arsenal of methods intended to create leverage for the service of U.S. international interests. Gabriel Kolko is correct in asserting that foreign aid was an increasingly popular option for Nixon given the escalating degree of domestic scrutiny that followed American foreign policy after 1969.[22] However, as an option, it remained on the periphery of policy, subverted by the distractions of the 1972 reelection campaign and the bitter bureaucratic infighting that characterized both the White House and his partnership with Kissinger.

"NEW" FOREIGN ASSISTANCE POLICY

One of Nixon's first acts as president was to order a comprehensive review of U.S. foreign aid policy. The study, begun in January 1969, considered the overlapping issues of "the political aspects of aid, the costs and benefits of different types of aid, and the costs and benefits of different aid levels."[23] In subsequent memoranda, administration officials left little doubt that aid still retained utility. The NSC considered assistance essential to "assure military security and economic support for a limited number of exposed allies." Secondarily, aid would also allow the United States to "participate politically in the development of the main poor countries" and "accelerate development in the third world" for humanitarian reasons and "improve chances for world order."[24]

American policy makers were realistic enough to understand that aid would not buy lasting friendships and could inadvertently produce tension. However, the administration could ill afford to disregard its importance: "Unless the United States continues a substantial program of development lending and technical assistance, development just won't happen on a broad scale—even under optimistic assumptions about self-help by the poor countries and about contributions from other rich countries."[25]

The question left begging was how the United States would maintain contemporary levels of assistance to both its primary allies and prospective clients in the underdeveloped world. Policy makers in the National Security Council argued that the minimum amount necessary to support the U.S. Agency for International Development for FY1969 was $1.3 billion, with a "high option" of $2.3 billion, increasing to $2.9 billion by FY1974.[26] Unfortunately, this plan was counterbalanced by congressional concerns that foreign assistance was exacerbating the outflow of gold and the U.S. balance-of-payments problem. In testimony before the House, the acting administrator of U.S. AID, Rutherford M. Poats, noted that his agency accounted for approximately $150 million in gold outflow, a figure offset by repayment and the repurchasing of American goods and services with foreign aid. He assured legislators that the "net impact of AID expenditures on the balance of payments seems to be essentially zero."[27] However, given the contemporary political climate, even a modest program of new direct assistance appeared unlikely.

In its place, the administration developed a plan for the United States to serve as a broker for foreign assistance and investment rather than its primary protagonist. According to National Security Decision Memorandum 76, "The New U.S. Foreign Assistance Program," written more than a year after Nixon's first presidential directive, "The United States, through its assistance programs, should henceforth seek to support the initiatives of other countries and the international development institutions rather than seek to dominate the development process." Key to development assistance policy was the desire to channel responsibility to multilateral institutions "as soon as practicable, in light of the capabilities of the institutions and without raising the U.S. share in them."[28] The administration placed particular emphasis on garnering additional contributions from Western European allies for the International Bank for Reconstruction and Development and the International Monetary Fund.[29] Secondarily, albeit important, the administration also pursued a more important role for the private sector in international economic development policy. NSDM 76 proposed the creation of a "U.S. Development Corporation," comprised of both public and private officials, that would administer bilateral lending programs and "rely heavily on the efforts of the international institutions to provide the broad framework and country programs within which it considers individual loans."[30] In addition, American policy makers contemplated the use of multinational corporations as vehicles for U.S. interests. In Peterson's lengthy report to the president, multinationals figured prominently as a means to manage investments and capital transfers. Looking toward the future, he called for policies that would not only cooperate with business by cultivating exports and balance overseas investment with the concerns of U.S. organized labor, but would also but guard against inappropriate taxation and expropriation.[31]

The first administration consequently proved to be a lean time for recipients of direct American foreign assistance. Although net new economic and technical aid and new economic credits would increase between 1970 to 1972, from $3 billion to $3.6 billion, Southeast Asia, particularly Nixon's "Vietnamization" program, would absorb the lion's share of U.S. assistance. Overall, total American direct foreign assistance declined from 1968 to 1971, rebounding, ironically, after Nixon's August 1971 speech (see Table 9.1). Other systemic changes in American foreign economic assis-

Table 9.1
U.S. Foreign Economic Assistance, 1967–1974 (US$ millions)

	Total	Loans	Grants
1967	3,942	1,662	2,281
1968	4,103	1,835	2,267
1969	3,524	1,340	2,185
1970	3,676	1,389	2,288
1971	3,442	1,299	2,143
1972	3,941	1,639	2,301
1973	4,118	1,391	2,726
1974	3,906	1,150	2,756

Source: U.S. Department of Commerce, Bureau of the Census, *Statistical Abstract of the United States: 1975* (Washington, D.C.: U.S. Government Printing Office, 1975), 807.

tance were more pointed in their effect on aid recipients. In July 1972, Henry Kissinger announced a 37-percent reduction in overseas U.S. AID personnel.[32] As early as the end of the administration's first year, the United States would see its quantitative and qualitative commitment to foreign assistance retreat.

While Washington reapportioned its priorities, Latin America was finishing out a remarkable decade of economic expansion. In 1969, the Agency for International Development estimated that the growth rate of Latin America GNP was 6.7 percent, with per capita income increasing at a rate of 3.5 percent. Annual average industrial growth had surged forward at a formidable 6.5 percent between 1965 and 1969.[33] Productivity had become increasingly diversified. As a region, agriculture comprised 15 percent of total GNP, outmatched by manufacturing (22%), trade and finance (24%), and services (23%). Latin America's infrastructure had also made major strides forward. Electrical power output almost doubled between 1961 and 1968, from 68,840 million kwh to 116,260 million kwh.[34] On its face, it appeared that the hemisphere had made great strides toward the original goals set down at Punta del Este in 1961.

Despite these accomplishments, significant problems persisted in Latin America. Among the many issues that affected the region, the population explosion in Latin America was perhaps its greatest obstacle to success. Nations such as Mexico (3.5%), El Salvador (3.5%), Venezuela (3.4%), and Ecuador (3.4%) led the world in average annual population growth between 1960 and 1973. According to a State Department study, at the 1968 GNP per capita growth rate of 2.6 percent, it would take twenty-seven years to double the level of per capita income. Population growth also far outpaced national and local efforts to provided adequate housing, sanitation, and education.[35] Solving this one challenge would be the essential predicate for a host of social and economic reforms in Latin America.

From the outset, the Nixon administration understood very well the critical role played by the United States in Latin America's success or failure. As it contemplated changes in overall U.S. foreign assistance policy, the White House also ordered a

February 1969 review of U.S. policy in Latin America and scheduled a series of missions by Nelson Rockefeller for the summer of that year. Rockefeller's visits, according to William Rogers, were intended "as serious appraisals of the future course of the Alliance for Progress."[36]

While the policy process ground forward, trade emerged as the preference of choice to meet Latin America's socioeconomic challenges. An NSC report offered in late 1970 described commerce as the "overriding consideration" in U.S. foreign policy in Latin America.[37] There were numerous advantages to this approach. By the late 1960s, American trade with the hemisphere, albeit diminished from the postwar decade, was still dominant. In 1968, the United States accounted for 33.7 percent of Latin American exports, just ahead of Western Europe (32.2%). Similarly, Latin America purchased 38.4 percent of its imports from U.S. sources.[38] American producers heavily influenced the import of autos, petroleum, steel, plastics, and electronics.[39] An assistance policy presaged by American import superiority offered an important means to indirectly maintain influence without the concurrent costs to the U.S. budget.

The administration consequently placed a much heavier emphasis on delegating the responsibility for development to multilateral agencies whose mission was securing and promoting private investment in the hemisphere. In late 1969, the State Department proposed an "Inter-American Finance Corporation" for the financing of "high risk long payment projects."[40] American officials also lent their support for an Overseas Private Investment Corporation, an agency that would act as a clearinghouse for foreign capital and Latin American companies.

As it was gradually applied in Latin America, this policy produced a secondary but important offshoot. R. Peter Dewitt has observed that the use of multilateral agencies controlled by the United States allowed Washington to exercise influence without the absolute political or economic cost of assistance. The Inter-American Development Bank, in which the United States controlled more than 50 percent of the votes in 1969, became a widely recognized vehicle for American policy, but allowed Washington at least a fig leaf of multilateralism in regional economic development policy.[41] However, as U.S. policy began to defer responsibility for development from official to private sources, American contributions to the IADB began to significantly diminish. By 1973, the United States enjoyed a bare plurality among the top five lending nations to the bank, with Germany, Japan, and Switzerland providing an increasing amount of available capital (see Table 9.2).

Direct economic assistance persisted primarily for the sake of political suasion and secondarily as a means to promote economic development. American policy makers were concerned that any reduction in direct aid levels would be interpreted as a retreat from the Alliance for Progress and the region. Subordinated to this were more practical concerns that an interruption in American aid would also reduce progress on infrastructure projects and technical progress. Initially, the Nixon administration proposed $606 million in aid to Latin America for FY1970, granting the bulk to Brazil, Chile, and Colombia.[42] To supplement this amount, U.S. representatives offered a number of limited proposals at the annual meeting of the Inter-American Economic and Social Council in 1970. They also agreed to reduce some tariffs on Latin American products, particularly seafood, fruits, and vegetables, and approved

Table 9.2

Capitalization of the Inter-American Development Bank Top Five Lending Nations, 1969–1973 (US$ millions)

	United States	West Germany	Latin America	Italy	Japan	Switzerland	Total
1969	405.0 (50.8%)	125.7 (15.7%)	63.7 (7.9%)	72.0 (9.0%)	28.0 (3.5%)	n.a.	796.5
1970	479.1 (52.3%)	151.4 (16.5%)	75.1 (8.2%)	72.0 (7.8%)	n.a.	36.6 (3.9%)	915.1
1971	460.3 (45.2%)	169.3 (16.6%)	79.1 (7.7%)	76.3 (7.4%)	n.a.	59.9 (5.8%)	1,017.8
1972	448.3 (39.4%)	227.5 (20.0%)	77.3 (6.7%)	n.a.	85.9 (7.5%)	79.4 (6.9%)	1,137.4
1973	434.5 (34.4%)	267.1 (21.2%)	83.3 (6.6%)	n.a.	122.4 (9.7%)	116.9 (9.2%)	1,259.6

Sources: Inter-American Development Bank (IADB), *Tenth Annual Report, 1969* (Washington, D.C.: IADB, 1970), 19; *Eleventh Annual Report, 1970* (Washington, D.C.: IADB, 1971), 22; *Annual Report, 1971* (Washington, D.C.: IADB, 1972), 21; *Annual Report, 1972* (Washington, D.C.: IADB, 1973), 26; *Annual Report, 1973* (Washington, D.C.: IADB, 1974), 18.

steps to ease the terms of PL480 sales to Latin America, but would not budge on increased import quotas for key commodities (e.g., coffee, sugar, and beef).[43]

Despite its consistent emphasis on the utility of capitalism as the best means to assist Latin America, the Nixon administration could not avoid many of the basic rules that governed the free exchange of goods and services between nations. Perhaps the most important was the law of comparative advantage. No single Latin American country nor any of the various trading blocs in place by 1969 could effectively compete with the United States in the production of finished or semifinished goods. Consequently, as initiatives in support of private enterprise unfolded, there was also a concurrent, negative relationship between U.S. capital investment and the remittance of profits from Latin America. Between 1960 and 1968, more than $4.2 billion left the Latin American economy.[44] Trade imbalances would persist into the next decade and significantly worsen after the oil crisis of the early 1970s.

Nor could this policy assuage congressional concerns that increasing American investments in Latin America would not prompt additional attempts at expropriation. In fact, the literature of the period, as well as the documents exchanged between the White House and Congress, are notable for their references to the Hickenlooper Amendment to the Foreign Assistance Act of 1961, its explicit threat to cut aid after expropriation, and the constant repetition of the ongoing conflict between Peru and the International Petroleum Corporation.[45]

The market structure and legislative concerns aside, the administration's emphasis on the private market was also important to the extent that it spurred independent Latin American efforts to redress the challenge of economic development. By the end of the 1960s, most Latin American nations, both individually and collectively, had begun to pursue new trading relationships, particularly with the European Economic Community and Japan. The EEC's position was already strong within the region, second only to the United States as a source of trade for Latin America. More important, the trade balance with the EEC was also very favorable to Latin America, which maintained surpluses from 1966 to 1968. Primary commodities exports such as coffee, beef, maize, and cotton enjoyed significant growth during the decade. Copper exports soared by 418 percent between 1958 and 1969.[46]

This bounty slowed considerably by 1969, however, when the EEC began to place an increasing number of tariff barriers on "temperate-zone" products that competed with those of its member nations. Wheat and beef suffered in particular. The import price for beef into the European Economic Community was $68 per hundred kilograms, almost double the world price of $38.82.[47] The entry of the United Kingdom into the EEC, bringing with it African states whose tropical products competed with those of Latin America, compounded this problem.[48] Despite an almost continuous series of meeting held between Latin American and European diplomats between 1960 and 1970, negotiations fundamentally failed to provide a substantive resolution to the continuing erosion of trade or a host of other smaller problems. Bilateral efforts to negotiate preferential trade agreements, such as those initiated by Argentina in October 1968 and February 1969, also made little progress toward opening European markets.[49]

The situation dictating Latin American trade with Japan differed somewhat from that of Western Europe. As an economic partner, Japan clearly represented enormous potential for the hemisphere as a whole. Between 1956–1958 and 1966–1968, regional exports to Japan rose from $248 million to $593 million, increasing at an average annual rate of 9.1 percent. By 1970, total exports amounted to $900 million, representing a more rapid growth rate than any other part of the Free World.[50] Between 1966 and 1968, Japan purchased more raw materials from Latin American sources than the United States, particularly lumber, hardwoods, cotton, iron ore, and mineral products. The value of coffee imports to Japan alone increased from $18 million in 1961 to $49 million in 1969. Japanese imports of iron ore climbed from an average annual figure of $83 million in 1956–1958 to a staggering $969 million by 1969.[51]

Yet Japanese trade policies were often unsatisfactory to the Latin American community in ways that were quite different from the EEC. Most frustrating to the region was the fact that trade was primarily limited to a relatively restricted range of raw materials. Without question, the economic symbiosis between the basic commodities produced by the hemisphere and new Japanese light industries was a boon to both sides. Central American cotton enjoyed its considerable success in the 1960s largely because of the Japanese market. However, Japan proved extremely reluctant to allow light manufactures from Latin America to compete with its home industries. As a result, Latin American manufacturing exports to Japan grew only slowly and faced formidable import restrictions.

For its own part, the region made excruciatingly slow progress toward a Latin American Free Trade Association. At its annual meeting in Caracas in December 1970, LAFTA members agreed to postpone the deadline for the culmination of a free-trade area from 1973 to 1980. In part, these delays reflected a generally held fear of foreign domination, particularly in the form of multinational corporations that were active throughout the hemisphere. Argentina, Brazil, and Mexico all expressed reservations about integration decisions made outside their respective political jurisdictions.[52]

By 1972, it was clear that the fundamental nature of American assistance to the Western Hemisphere had changed, as had the economic structure of Latin America itself. During the Nixon era, assistance to Latin America consistently declined until 1971, whereupon it rebounded to a level approaching the Johnson administration (see Table 9.3). However, even this commitment was qualified by the growing reliance of American assistance on loans rather than grant aid. By 1974, nearly 88.7 percent of U.S. assistance to the region came in the form of loans. Although the shrinking amount of U.S. grant aid did not directly account for the drastic increase in Latin American public debt—outstanding external public-sector debt grew from $7.1 billion in 1960 to more than $20.2 billion ten years later—it did force the region into an increasing reliance on the private sector to sustain its continued economic development. Between 1968 and 1970, credit provided from private sources to Latin America rose from $361 million to $952 million, in contrast to an average of $229 million between 1961 and 1965.[53]

Washington also exercised little effort with regard to the various obstacles to trade that had begun to block Latin American exports at the end of the 1960s. The American leadership appeared unwilling to address more than the most superficial features of commodity agreements and U.S. import quotas. More important, the administration, locked within its own currency crisis between 1969 and 1971, was unable to leverage any meaningful trade concessions from Japan or the EEC on behalf of Latin America. By 1970, the region's share of global exports had declined to 5 percent, down from 6.9 percent in 1960.[54] Improved intraregional trade offered a poor alternative to this downward trend. As the 1970s began, the hemisphere was forced to shoulder the heavy burdens of an increasingly insular and indebted economic structure.

Table 9.3
U.S. Assistance to Latin America, 1967–1974 (US$ millions)

	Total	Grants	Loans	%Loans
1967	1,102.5	215.8	886.7	80.4%
1968	1,080.0	189.8	890.2	82.4%
1969	644.2	151.2	493.0	76.5%
1970	685.1	223.6	461.5	67.3%
1971	647.5	157.5	490.0	75.6%
1972	1,007.3	184.1	823.2	81.7%
1973	896.0	144.2	751.8	83.9%
1974	1,216.2	137.1	1,079.1	88.7%

Source: James W. Wilkie, David E, Lorey, Enrique Ochoa, eds., *Statistical Abstract of Latin America*, vol. 26 (Los Angeles: UCLA Latin American Center Publications, 1988), 698.

THE CENTRAL AMERICAN
COMMON MARKET IN CRISIS

By the start of the 1970s, the varying strategies attempted in Central America during the preceding two decades had produced, at best, a problematic prosperity. On the positive side, integration had led to significant Central American economic expansion. Intraregional trade increased from $33 million in 1960 to $258 million in 1968, one-quarter of the total for Central America.[55] In 1968 alone, trade within the Common Market grew by 22 percent.[56] The region also made substantial strides in manufacturing and import-substitution industrialization. The ratio of value added to GDP by manufacturing rose from 13.2 percent to 17.2 percent between 1960 and 1971. Overall, average annual growth rates for manufacturing remained formidable for much of the 1960s, at 7.9 percent from 1966 to 1969 and 5.9 percent from 1969 to 1971.[57]

However, despite an impressive degree of diversification, Central American economies remained highly dependent on traditional exports. Coffee, cotton, bananas, sugar, and cattle garnered the bulk of revenue for most nations. In 1970, for example, Costa Rica depended upon these five commodities for 91 percent of its total extraregional exports. El Salvador (91.1%), Guatemala (86.5%), Honduras (71.9%), and Nicaragua (77.9%) all enjoyed a similar dependency.[58]

Other warning signs also appeared by 1970. Growth clearly began to slow by the end of the decade. Average annual GDP gains slid from 6.0 percent between 1961 and 1966 to 5.3 percent between 1969 and 1971. Although still comparatively high, these numbers were substantially undercut by the explosive increase of Central America's population. During the 1966 to 1971 period, the growth rate of per capita income actually declined from 2.6 percent to 2.1 percent. By 1972, manufacturing growth was also down, as was the growth rate of exports.[59]

A series of accumulating problems had produced this situation. Foremost was the excessive reliance on export agriculture and primary commodities exports as main sources of revenue. Built upon this narrow pillar, Central American economies were openly vulnerable to fluctuations in global primary commodity markets. The general downward trend in food and raw materials prices from 1966 to 1968 hurt the region more so than comparable areas with greater economic diversity.[60]

A second problem was the chronic inability of Central American countries to absorb excess labor in the transition from agriculture to manufacturing, or to compensate for employment lost in the shift of many national economies to the export sector. Light manufacturing centers could not absorb the thousands of rural workers who sought out the higher wages they offered or who were displaced by the burgeoning, land-intensive cattle industry. Coffee and cotton were two enterprises that required large work volumes only during brief annual harvest seasons. At the close of the 1960s, all CACM countries struggled with the dual difficulties of unemployment and seasonal underemployment. "Open" unemployment—that is, unemployment that officials could accurately measure statistically—was estimated at between 8 and 15 percent in 1971.[61]

A third important concern, well documented in scholarship by Victor Bulmer-Thomas and Frederick S. Weaver, was the overall financial cost absorbed by the Central American Common Market to encourage trade, regional integration, and devel-opment. In order to assuage the various local export interests in CACM countries, agricultural inputs and many other goods were excluded from tariff lists.[62] Intraregional import duties were also cut in order to encourage Common Market production. As a consequence, governments in all participating countries suffered significant losses in revenue. Nicaragua saw its customs revenues decline for three years in a row from 1967 to 1969.[63] For the most part, no comparable sources of revenue (e.g., income tax, property tax) took the place of import duties. Despite years of American efforts to the contrary, tax reform remained a consistently unmet goal during most of the 1960s. Fundamental administrative weakness and widespread evasion remained the norm throughout much of the Common Market. Over time, many governments were forced to borrow in order to meet annual budget requirements. According to the State Department, the area's external public debt increased at an average annual rate of 16 percent between 1966 and 1971.[64]

The problem of capital outflow and the relationship between direct foreign invest-ment and profit repatriation also severely handicapped Central American develop-ment. From the very start of the Common Market itself, when Central American nations agreed to not establish minimum local ownership of integrated industry stocks, foreign investors took a dominant position in many sectors, dictating industrial in-puts and drawing profit without regulation, both often to the disadvantage of CACM nations.[65]

A final, hidden cost to Central America was contained in the gradual shift from the "social infrastructure" projects originally sponsored by the Alliance for Progress at its outset to economic infrastructure programs later in the decade.[66] The well-intentioned potpourri of social reforms proposed in the optimistic days of 1961 were gradually displaced by the more identifiable requirements of economic development. The familiar assortment of technical assistance in economic management and infra-structure development took precedence over education, health, and housing projects. The shift was intended to allow a greater absorption of capital investment and, con-sequently, a greater degree of per capita prosperity. Development proponents in the United States and Central America consoled themselves with their original function-alist theories and continued to argue that the benefits of growth would eventually trickle down to the population at large.[67]

The Central America Common Market proved unable to solve these or myriad other problems. One of the market's primary objectives, balanced development, proved extremely difficult in practice, thwarted by continuous trade imbalances between member nations. In principle, CACM countries had been encouraged to pursue free-trade agreements and cooperate in economic integration projects of regional interest. However, as Cline and Delgado have observed, these two ideas—free competition and regional integration—proved to be mutually exclusive and contradictory.[68] The pursuit of free trade often led to competition and redundancy. Common Market members with less-developed industries, such as Honduras, complained loudly about the compara-tive advantages enjoyed by Nicaragua and Guatemala.[69] Efforts to industrialize cre-ated significant debt with little concurrent return. The ratio of debt service to exports increased most rapidly in Nicaragua and Guatemala, the region's most aggressively diversifying economies. Moreover, import substitution had reached a practical saturation point by 1972. According to U.S. reports, there were simply not enough new industries to build in Central America, the CACM having explored the limits of light industry and manufacturing in food processing, textiles, and chemicals.[70]

Central American leaders struggled constantly but unsuccessfully with these challenges as the 1960s drew to a close. Conferences dedicated to resolving the various inequities within the CACM became commonplace annual occurrences. In May 1968, Central American ministers of finance met in Costa Rica to discuss the balance-of-payments problem within the CACM and managed to hammer out what became known as the San José Protocol. The agreement, approved in June by all countries except Costa Rica, established import surcharges of 30 percent on goods outside of the Common Market and proposed to terminate the competitive granting of tax exonerations that were crippling regional integration. A month later, when all five Central American presidents met with Lyndon Johnson during his visit to the isthmus, they reiterated their support of a common front on trade.[71]

Real cooperation appeared to be short-lived, however. Despite their convivial rhetoric, none of the Common Market's members stepped forward to offer a compromise that would address the significant trade imbalances that existed within the organization. Nor could the CACM, with its bulky administrative organization and vague lines of jurisdiction and enforcement, win collective commitments from its members. Nicaragua, which ran a consistent trade deficit with the CACM for every year between 1961 and 1970 and Honduras, which experienced a similar problem from 1965 to 1970, began to bridle under this regime.[72]

Nicaragua acted first to resolve the situation. On 21 June 1968, Managua unilaterally imposed the San José Protocol and added a 5-percent sales tax on all Central American goods not covered by the agreement. Along the Nicaraguan border, customs officials began to demand immediate payment of the new tax. Traffic jams involving hundreds of trucks jammed highways for days afterward. The remaining CACM members immediately filed protests against the action, charging that the tax was discriminatory and in violation of the 1960 General Treaty of Central American Economic Integration.[73] Less than a year later, on 1 March 1969, Nicaragua again unilaterally introduced a tariff against Central American imports, claiming that other members were interfering with the import of Nicaraguan agricultural products. Nicaraguan officials also expressed great dissatisfaction with the price and quality of industrial products available within the CACM, complaining that they were not competitive with goods outside the Common Market.[74] From his office in Managua, Anastasio Somoza justified this decision by blaming his domestic budget difficulties on the CACM. In a conversation with Edward W. Coy, the U.S. AID mission director to Nicaragua, the president claimed that a loss of revenues caused by the CACM had forced him to fire 5,000 government employees in order to maintain his existing expenditures. Particular vitriol was reserved for El Salvador and Guatemala, which Somoza accused of "bleeding" the more prosperous members of the market.[75] In response to his provocation, the remaining four countries of the Common Market introduced their own countertariffs against Nicaraguan exports. Managua consequently began to boycott meetings of the Economic Council of the CACM. Negotiations ground to a halt by the summer.

The Soccer War between Honduras and El Salvador followed hard on the heels of this deadlock. Once the war began, the shipment of goods between the belligerents ceased. As the conflict dragged on, Honduras blocked the movement of Salvadoran goods south to other CACM members. The standoff that followed the brief, bitter conflict placed the remaining three countries in the quandary of either purchasing goods from outside the Common Market and suffering applicable tariffs on exports outside the CACM or waiting out a settlement between Honduras and El Salvador.[76] This situation was further complicated when Honduras, miffed that its basic grievances were still unaddressed by the Common Market, abruptly dropped out of the organization in December 1970.

The crisis continued well into the following year. By that time, the reversion to a four-member Common Market without Honduras had become the de facto standard. In an attempt to resuscitate the union, the rump CACM formed a "Normalization Commission" to discuss measures necessary to regain the former status quo. The primary obstacle to progress was Honduras's continuing insistence that its border dispute was directly tied to reintegration into the CACM. Progress was slow.[77] In the meantime, it was obvious that Honduras was too lucrative a trading partner to ignore. Between 1964 and 1968, all of the "neutral three" not involved in the Soccer War had markedly improved their trade with the country. The annual rate of increase of imports from Nicaragua (32.5%), Costa Rica (39.9%), and Guatemala (25.2%) to Honduras during this period was too important to abandon entirely. Replacing Honduran trade to El Salvador also appeared to be a significant opportunity.[78]

The neutral three nations scrambled to maintain some sort of equilibrium in the wake of Honduras's decisions. Some sought out bilateral trade treaties. Nicaragua agreed to a treaty with Honduras worth $12 million in trade between the countries.[79] Other nations began constructing unilateral protections for their economies. Costa Rica, which had enjoyed its only trade surplus with Honduras before the latter's departure from the Common Market, accused the remaining membership of dumping exports and unfair competition. By mid-1971, San José began to institute *fianzas* on major categories of imports from other CACM countries. El Salvador and Guatemala reacted by imposing additional import restrictions on Costa Rican imports.[80]

Throughout much of the 1960s, the Central American Common Market had been a successful, if fragile, creation. The organization was competitive in times of rapid growth, something that defined much of the situation during the decade.[81] Steady increases in primary commodity prices served to bolster all members, despite their unsteady efforts at import substitution and diversification. However, the comparatively marginal status of the CACM, defined by its expensive, inefficient manufacturing sector and overreliance on export agriculture, made it vulnerable to increasing energy costs or dramatic fluctuations in the global price structure.

The bulky instrument that was the CACM also militated against its effectiveness. In part, it proved unable to serve the goals of a common market because its policies were fundamentally contradictory. Balanced development could not easily coexist with the dynamic of competing, free-market economies. In practice, intranational competition overwhelmed the paper-thin veneer of the Common Market. Economic rivalry too easily became a mechanism of long-standing disputes between traditional regional enemies. A State Department cable commented in June 1971,

The recent events involve not only the interests and welfare of nations but also the prestige and positions of Ministers. It is unfortunate that the latter concerns may sometimes have more effect on policy decisions than the former. On this aspect one can only hope that the personality clashes and recriminations will not blind the decision makers to what is now at stake in Central America.[82]

That same year, Raul Prebisch would complain that Latin America lacked the proper "dynamism" to further its own economic progress. His analysis, which focused specifically on advances in technology, the use of labor, and capital formation, was strictly true, particularly so with respect to Central America. It was not for a lack of energy and leadership that the isthmus did not advance. One of the most formidable obstacles to Central American growth remained the region itself, in the energy misapplied to endemic bickering and constant political maneuvering.[83]

NICARAGUAN ECONOMIC RETRENCHMENT

In many respects, Nicaragua was a model economy at the close of the Alliance for Progress. With an annual average growth rate of 9.9 percent between 1969 and 1971, the country witnessed a marginal decline from the first half of the 1960s, but still far outperformed most other countries in the region.[84] By 1970, the Nicaraguan GNP had almost doubled from the start of the decade, from $372 million to $728 million.[85] Its terms of trade also appeared to be on solid footing. Victor Bulmer-Thomas has observed that Nicaragua was the only member of the Central American Common market to see its share of the global economy increase during the Alliance for Progress years.[86]

However, like much of Latin America, Nicaragua experienced a number of seemingly intractable difficulties that hampered development and cast serious doubt upon its future prosperity. Despite its strong economic momentum, the country did not escape the short-term problems created by Common Market conflicts. After the tariff battles and the Soccer War, definite signs of strain began to appear in the economy, particularly with respect to the link between the marked decline in trade and bank deposits. By 1970, commercial loans to entrepreneurs began to dry up. In Managua, rumors flew about the nation's major banks calling in their outstanding notes in order to recover some of their losses.[87]

Larger, systemic problems in the Nicaraguan economy also began to appear. The continued dominance of export agriculture proved to be an entrenched reality in 1970 and a point of substantial vulnerability. Cotton stumbled badly in the 1969–1970 growing season. Production plummeted from 402,000 bales in 1969 to 297,500 the following year, with revenues declining to an eight-year low of $34.3 million. Coffee, the country's second-largest export earner, also contracted, from $23 million in 1968 to $20 million in 1969.[88] According to the U.S. embassy, Nicaragua was in "an economic recession of serious proportions" by mid-1969.[89] The financial impact of this decline upon the regime was immediate. The Somoza government submitted an alarmingly austere budget for 1969, proposing across-the-board cuts in the judiciary (13.9%), public works (19.9%), the Ministry of Economy, Industry, Commerce (17.7%), and defense (2.2%).[90]

For the average Nicaraguan, the economic news was much worse. Matched against a formidable increase in annual population (2.6% from 1960 to 1973), per capita growth proved to be a paltry 0.5 percent in 1969. Moreover, the ongoing transition of the Nicaraguan economy from agriculture to manufacturing and services failed to absorb excess labor or provide an increase in the standard of living. In fact, real wages actually declined by 25 percent between 1967 and 1975. By 1970, Nicaragua had a higher percentage of landless rural families (34%) than any other country in Central America.[91]

After 1969, the Somoza regime dedicated considerable effort to resurrecting the economy from its doldrums. One proposal involved official sponsorship of internal development as a means to restart growth. In April 1969, a new credit institution, the Corporacion Financiera de Oriente, was created with the objective to develop the departments of Masaya, Granada, Carazo, and Rivas. Subscribed at $357,000, its purpose, according to the U.S. embassy, was "to arrest the present capital flow from the region to Managua."[92] Francisco Lainez, ex-president of the Central Bank and a regime foe, was appointed as a member of the board of directors.

On a broader level, Anastasio Somoza attempted to borrow a page from his father's playbook by ordering the creation of a central planning authority that would oversee national economic development. In March 1971, the administration announced the creation of a new National Office of Planning. Its primary purpose was to determine the priorities, goals, and conditions applied to foreign investment and coordinate ongoing private businesses with central government programs and autonomous agencies. The U.S. AID office in Managua proved skeptical about this initiative, noting that the Somoza government was "not organized to prepare projects and programs requiring external assistance and still must rely almost completely on foreign assistance agencies."[93] American officials were particularly disturbed by the strict limits that would be placed on the Planning Office's budget. According to the Somoza regime, only 25 percent of its annual requirement would be taken from central government revenues. The FY1972 budget provided for 356,000 cordobas of the 1.4 million cordobas required by the agency. An additional quarter was to be drawn from the Central Bank. The remainder was supposed to be derived from the budgets of autonomous government agencies.[94] In practice, however, as the U.S. country team rightly pointed out, rival components of the regime refused to cooperate in the furtherance of the National Office of Planning. The Instituto de Fomento Nacional, which had been created as the lead development agency in 1953 and had overseen tax policy, foreign investment strategy, infrastructure projects, and industrial diversification, saw the new organization as an interloper. Subsequent cooperation was limited.[95]

The tentative nature of Nicaragua's transitory government also seriously undercut coherent economic planning. When the three-man Executive Council was formed as a temporary, power-sharing arrangement between Liberal and Conservative rivals, long-range economic planning was lost in an almost constant jockeying for political advantage. One significantly adverse product of this conflict was its impact of the country's loan portfolio. In 1971, Nicaragua held $16 million in undisbursed U.S. AID loans and $26 million in undisbursed loans from the Inter-American Bank. Unable to spend its existing assistance, Nicaragua was a poor candidate for additional loans. In their place, the regime was forced to pursue what U.S. AID described as an "ad hoc" process of small grants won by individual agencies (e.g., the Ministry of Education and the Ministry of Public Works) acting on their own initiative.[96]

Managua was consequently badly positioned to criticize American economic assistance policy to Nicaragua or solicit any changes in it. As early as 1969, the regime complained, often bitterly, that domestic U.S. inflation was having an adverse effect on interest rates and production costs in Nicaragua. The Nicaraguan Chamber of Commerce appealed directly to the embassy to consider lifting restrictions on Nicaraguan meat imports and increasing import quotas for sugar.[97] Help was not forthcoming.

For the most part, the U.S. embassy kept its distance from Nicaraguan economic policy. American officials were well aware that Nicaragua'a access to foreign loans was dominated by the United States. International organizations provide the bulk (71.7% in 1970) of assistance to the country. Within this field, the Agency for International Development was the most important source, offering more than one-third of the funds available to Nicaragua. Commercial banks, in contrast, provided less than one-quarter of the total.[98] Despite this, in its annual "Country Analysis and Strategy Paper for Nicaragua" in February 1969, the embassy recommended that the United States's "task is not basically to change GON [government of Nicaragua] views but rather to provide judicious and timely counsel at all levels of the GON."[99]

Over the long term the country team actually planned to reduce the U.S. role in Nicaragua. U.S. AID cut back its mission in 1971, abolishing the positions of population officer, food and agriculture officer, and deputy multi-sector officer. The tax reform program was also phased out after eight years of "intensive activity."[100] New projects included an export-promotion and industrial-development project intended to coordinate private investors in the Chamber of Industries with the Export Promotion Section of the Central Bank of Nicaragua. In its 1971 annual report, U.S. AID/ Nicaragua also altered the general philosophy of its loan program. Rather than advance specific projects, which had been the mainstay of American assistance policy for most of the decade, the office decided to embrace a "broader approach" that involved aid to complete economic sectors:

This will be contingent upon the Mission being able to unite the human resources available in the private and government sectors in such an approach, as the success of a sector loan depends upon the host country's ability to organize itself to develop, administer and implement the more complete and broader requirements of a sector loan.[101]

In the future, officials argued that U.S. AID should serve as the "catalyst" in the effort to promote private investment rather than allow Americans to continue as the primary protagonist for Nicaraguan economic development.

The 1972 earthquake that devastated much of Managua significantly reinforced this basic direction. On 23 December, in the space of only thirty seconds, some thirty-six city blocks—half of the total city area—in the heart of the country's capital were destroyed. More than 50,000 homes were lost. Preliminary estimates of damage went as high as $600 million. Approximately half of the nation's gross national product was disrupted and approximately one-quarter of its manufacturing capability was eliminated. More than half of the government's sources of revenue were lost in the disaster.[102]

According to the embassy's "feel" in April 1973, the country was already on the road to recovery. Manufacturing activity had recovered considerably and some industrial production had attained prequake levels. Only months after the catastrophe, the domestic market had begun compensating for the loss of productivity in the capital metropolitan area. A Nicaraguan Chamber of Industries survey reported that firms operating outside of Managua saw their sales increase by 148 percent. More important, agriculture and most of the country's infrastructure were largely untouched by the quake. Cotton, cattle, coffee, and sugar, bolstered by a good season in 1973, took the lead in the economic reconstruction of the country.[103]

In order to accomplish this, the business community in Nicaragua largely bypassed the central government to make policy decisions on its own. A November 1973 embassy cable reported that "many, if not most, Nicaraguan businessmen have been more self-confident, more aggressive, more receptive to change and much more outspoken."[104] This confidence was rooted in the autonomy exercised by the "Private Sector Emergency Committee," which emerged in the immediate aftermath of the quake. During the chaotic weeks that followed the earthquake, when Anastasio Somoza bunkered in his official residence and civil and military agencies unraveled, the committee became a point of contact for the government as well as a conduit for specific official assistance. For months, it was the sole provider of information on the state of local commerce and industry. The committee, not the regime, was also the first agency that dispatched representatives to Common Market countries to reestablish contacts during reconstruction.

The creation of the Private Sector Emergency Committee was an interesting confluence of past policy and immediate need. In the years preceding 1972, both the U.S. embassy and the Somoza regime had made deliberate efforts to encourage greater assertiveness in the Nicaraguan private sector. At the start of 1973, circumstances forced Nicaraguan entrepreneurs to the forefront of not only economic recovery, but public policy as well. By the late summer, local business leaders could point to a tentative recovery with justifiable pride. In August, imports, exports, and net international reserves were at record levels. Coffee exports that month had already surpassed total 1972 levels. Cotton exports were not far behind.[105]

In the eyes of the Nicaraguan business community, however, the Somoza family never recovered the degree of dominance it held prior to December 1972. The regime was able to recapture relief efforts with the creation of the Office of Coordination and Implementation of National Reconstruction Programs later in 1973, gaining in the process a $16.7-million loan from the Inter-American Development Bank to facilitate its administrative efforts.[106] As revelations of scandal blanketed the Somoza government throughout the year following the earthquake, it lost whatever remnants of prestige that it still held among the leading families of the nations. This loss of confidence was the product of not only the regime's unashamed corruption, but the growing realization that it could not provide the requisite stability sought by the Nicaraguan private sector, a factor that would nurture the first elements of a united opposition against the Somoza family later in the 1970s.[107]

CONCLUSIONS

In many respects, the year that marked Richard Nixon's arrival in the White House was an interesting echo of his past. In 1969, as in 1953, American policy makers were in the process of concluding a bitter and divisive war in Asia. At the end of the 1960s, as was the case fifteen years earlier, a restive Congress and the public clamored for a return to the domestic priorities of peace and prosperity.

There were, of course, important differences that also defined the two periods. Foremost was the basic nature of the world itself in 1969 and America's place in it. The end of the decade saw a dissipation of U.S. economic hegemony in concert with its dwindling nuclear superiority. Nixon's presidency, unlike Dwight D. Eisenhower's, faced a new era of limits, not self-imposed, but the product of America's weakening global economic position. The greatest challenge to American power in the post-Vietnam period was not simply the maintenance of nuclear parity with the Soviet Union, but the construction of an economic foundation that would underpin it.

Unfortunately, in constructing this response, Nixon largely abandoned a coherent, long-term strategy in favor of immediate political benefits that would embellish his chances for reelection in 1972. Diane Kunz's observation that Nixon was the "destroyer of Bretton Woods" is pointed to the extent that his desire for a second term clearly outmatched his interest in the ramifications of the decisions announced in August 1971.[108]

Strategic guidance for U.S. foreign economic policy subsequently languished in the early 1970s. Nixon's admission in his 15 October 1969 speech that "the decisions on how far and how fast this process of integration goes are not ours to make" was not rhetorical.[109] Throughout his first term, neither the White House nor any other single official body exercised primary leadership in coordinating domestic and foreign economic policy or establishing long-term objectives. The trickle-down effect of this policy became increasing noticeable in the meantime. A February 1971 conference that called for twenty-one U.S. AID mission directors from Latin America was designed as a public showpiece of the president's dedication to the Alliance for Progress. Behind the scenes, its primary purpose was to "boost sagging morale in the AID organization."[110]

The new trajectory was poorly timed for events in Central America at the conclusion of the 1960s. By 1969, the Central American Common Market was forced to contend with the unaddressed short-term economic consequences of regional integration, import substitution, and export-led growth. The structuralist policies promoted by the Alliance for Progress and the Economic Commission for Latin America had indeed led to fantastic growth rates. Yet for all the optimism that had accompanied progress, neither U.S. nor Latin American policy makers had proven adept enough to fine tune development internally or on a regional scale to meet problems that began to surface. The unanswered questions of trade imbalances, industrial redundancy, and a whole host of related social problems effectively neutralized the promising statistics offered each year by the Common Market and host agencies like U.S. AID and the Inter-American Development Bank.[111] Moreover, as an institution, the Common Market proved completely inadequate to reach quick decisions or foster regional compromise in the face of these challenges. In part, its limitations were structural. Balanced development within the CACM had never implied that it would have the authority to mandate unpopular measures such as tax reform, wage increases, or rural land redistribution. In a larger sense, however, the Common Market foundered on long-standing national animosities within the isthmus that economic integration did not mitigate and, conversely, overwhelmed and militated against the reasonable conduct of business.

At the end of the 1960s, Nicaragua had reached its own economic watershed. After the years of ceaseless bickering and the debacle that had followed the Honduras–Salvadoran Soccer War, the prospects of growth led by development and regional integration had considerably dimmed. As this realization dawned, pressure on the regime from all sectors of the country increased in their intensity. Business elites worried about the future of the Common Market. The urban poor grew increasingly restive in the slums that surrounded Managua, Masaya, Jinotepe, and a host of other cities. As president, Anastasio Somoza Debayle could not afford to forestall meaningful alternative policies that could capture popular expectations and prolong Nicaraguan prosperity. The situation was, in many respects, similar to the one his own father had faced at the conclusion of the Korean War, a time when new structuralist development theories offered the promise of sustained growth and improved social stability.[112]

But Somoza Debayle had no plan. In point of fact, Somoza's efforts to consolidate his own political base came at the expense of attention to strategic economic planning. His appointment of technocrats in key ministries after 1969 was largely offset by the absence of an overall vision. Moreover, the progressively more oblique approach to advice and economic assistance adopted by Turner Shelton and the U.S. embassy (a 1971 U.S. AID report recommended, for example, that basic tax reform fall under IMF sponsorship) served only to embellish policy drift in Nicaragua.[113] Consequently, both the regime and its U.S. sponsor were willing to envisage a greater degree of delegation within the Nicaraguan economy by default.

The 1972 earthquake served as the final point of departure for many Nicaraguans. In the wreckage of Managua, the regime demonstrated not only its unwillingness, but its blatant inability to plan and successfully prosecute Nicaraguan economic policy. More important to the longevity of the regime was its paralysis in the months after December 1972. Nature itself had stripped away the various cushions that had protected the Somoza family, exposing the basic incompetence of its leader to provide future prosperity.

NOTES

1. James T. Patterson, *Grand Expectations: The United States, 1945–1974* (New York: Oxford University Press, 1996), 737; "Nixon's New Economic Policy," *U.S. News & World Report*, 30 August 1971, 16.

2. John Morton Blum, *Years of Discord: American Politics and Society, 1961–1974* (New York: W. W. Norton, 1991), 403.

3. Diane B. Kunz, *Guns and Butter: America's Cold War Economic Diplomacy* (New York: The Free Press, 1997), 97–98.

4. Walt W. Rostow, *The World Economy: History & Prospect* (Austin: University of Texas Press, 1978), 247–286, 662. See also Paul Kennedy, *The Rise and Fall of the Great Powers: Economic Change and Military Conflict from 1500 to 2000* (New York: Vintage Books, 1989), 414.

5. Kennedy, *Rise and Fall*, 417, 421. See also Ryutaro Komiya and Motoshige Itoh, "Japan's International Trade and Trade Policy, 1955–1984," in *The Political Economy of Japan*, vol. 2, ed. Takashi Inoguchi and Daniel I. Okimoto (Stanford, Calif.: Stanford University Press, 1988), 173–224.

6. Kennedy, *Rise and Fall*, 415.

7. Richard E. Barrett and Soomi Chin, "Export-Oriented Industrializing States in the Capitalist World System: Similarities and Differences," in *The Political Economy of the New Asian Industrialism*, ed. Frederic C. Deyo (Ithaca, N.Y.: Cornell University Press, 1987), 23–43.

8. Gabriel Kolko, *Confronting the Third World: United States Foreign Policy, 1945–1980* (New York: Pantheon Books, 1988), 2.

9. Robert Warren Stevens, *Vain Hopes, Grim Realities: The Economic Consequences of the Vietnam War* (New York: New Viewpoints, 1976), 113.

10. Kennedy, *Rise and Fall*, 434.

11. Stevens, *Vain Hopes, Grim Realities*, 106.

12. Ibid., 120.

13. Joan Hoff, *Nixon Reconsidered* (New York: Basic Books, 1994), 166–173.

14. Peter G. Peterson, *The United States in a Changing World Economy*, vol. 1 (Washington, D.C.: U.S. Government Printing Office, 1971), ii, 4.

15. "President's Economic Policy in His Own Words," *U.S. News & World Report*, 30 August 1971, 64; Stephen E. Ambrose, *Nixon: Triumph of a Politician, 1962–1972* (New York: Simon and Schuster, 1989), 458; Blum, *Years of Discord*, 406.

16. Ambrose, *Nixon*, 459.

17. "Call to Economic Revival," *New York Times*, 16 August 1971, 26.

18. "Nixon's New Economic Policy," 17.

19. Peterson, *The United States in a Changing World Economy*, 3–13.

20. National Security Decision Memorandum 10, "AID and PL 480 Commitments," 11 April 1969, National Archives and Records Administration (hereafter NARA), Records Group 273 (hereafter RG 273), Records of the National Security Council (hereafter NSC), National Security Decision Memoranda (hereafter NSDM), Box 1.

21. Hoff, *Nixon Reconsidered*, 166–173.

22. Kolko, *Confronting the Third World*, 216–220.

23. National Security Study Memorandum 4, "U.S. Foreign Aid Policy," 21 January 1969, and National Security Study Memorandum 15, "Review of U.S. Policy toward Latin America," 3 February 1969, NARA, RG 273, NSC, National Security Study Memoranda (hereafter NSSM), Box 2.

24. Memorandum, Jeanne W. Davis (NSC Secretariate) to Richard Pedersen (State), 18 March 1969, RG 273, NSC, NSSM, Box 2.

25. Ibid.

26. Ibid.

27. Letter, Rutherford M. Poats (AID Acting Administrator) to Henry A. Kissinger, 21 January 1969, NARA, Richard M. Nixon Presidential Materials Collection (hereafter RMN), White House Central File (hereafter WHCF), Subject File, Box 11.

28. National Security Decision Memorandum 76, "The New U.S. Foreign Assistance Program," 10 August 1970, NARA, RG 273, NSC, NSDM, Box 1.

29. Memo, Economic Assistance by Other Free Nations to LDC's, Task Group 4, 2 April 1959. Dwight David Eisenhower Library, Joseph Dodge Papers, Box 1; International Bank for

Reconstruction and Development (IBRD), *Policies and Operations* (Washington, D.C.: IBRD, 1957), 121.

30. NSDM 76, "The New U.S. Foreign Assistance Program," 10 August 1970.

31. Peterson, *The United States in a Changing World Economy*, 29–30.

32. U.S. Department of Commerce, Bureau of the Census, *Statistical Abstract of the United States: 1975* (Washington, D.C.: U.S. Government Printing Office, 1975), 803–807; Memorandum, Henry A. Kissinger to Richard M. Nixon, "Meeting with John Hannah, Administrator, AID," 24 July 1972, RMN, WHCF, Subject File, Box 11.

33. U.S. Agency for International Development (AID), Bureau for Program and Policy Coordination, Office of Statistics and Reports, *A.I.D. Economic Data Book: Latin America* (Washington, D.C.: U.S. Government Printing Office, 1971), 4; United Nations, Economic Commission for Latin America, *Economic Survey of Latin America, 1970* (New York: United Nations, 1972), 10, 38.

34. United Nations, *Economic Survey of Latin America, 1970*, 16.

35. James W. Wilkie, David E. Lorey, and Enrique Ochoa, eds., *Statistical Abstract of Latin America*, vol. 26 (Los Angeles: UCLA Latin American Center Publications, 1988), 71; U.S. Department of State, Bureau of Intelligence and Research, "The Population Explosion in Latin America," 12 January 1970, Records Group 59 (hereafter RG 59), Subject–Numeric File, 1970–73, Box 3075.

36. Memorandum, Rutherford M. Poats (Acting AID Administrator) to the Secretary (Rogers), "Postponement of Presentation Testimony on Foreign Assistance Legislation," 19 February 1969, RG 273, NSC, NSSM, Box 2.

37. NSC Undersecretaries Committee, "Secretary Stans' Report on his Latin American Trip," 10 December 1970, NARA, RG 59, Subject–Numeric File, 1970–73, Box 762.

38. Kenneth Ruddle and Mukhtar Hamour, *Statistical Abstract of Latin America: 1970* (Los Angeles: UCLA Latin American Center Publications, 1971), 338–339.

39. United Nations, *Economic Survey of Latin America, 1970*, 302.

40. Memorandum, William P. Rogers to Richard M. Nixon, "Rockefeller Report Recommendations," 22 November 1969, NARA, RG 59, Subject–Numeric File, 1967–69, Box 2112; National Security Decision Memorandum 37, "U.S. Position for the Special Meetings of the Inter-American Economic and Social Council," 27 January 1970, NARA, RG 273, NSC, NSDM, Box 1.

41. R. Peter DeWitt, *The Inter-American Development Bank and Political Influence* (New York: Praeger, 1977), 52.

42. Memorandum, Davis to Pedersen, 18 March 1969.

43. National Security Decision Memorandum 30, "U.S. Position for the Special Meetings of the Inter-American Economic and Social Council," 5 November 1969, NARA, RG 273, NSC, NSDM, Box 1.

44. United Nations, *Economic Survey of Latin America, 1970*, 288.

45. Memorandum of Conversation, Richard Nixon, Secretary of State William P. Rogers, Foreign Minister Alfonso Lopez Michelson (Colombia), Foreign Minister Fernando Amiama Tio (Dominican Republic), Foreign Minister Aristides Calvani (Venezuela), and Foreign Secretary Antonio Carrillo Flores (Mexico), "Latin American Policy," 31 March 1969, NARA, RG 59, Subject–Numeric File, 1967–69, Box 2110; U.S. Senate, *The Foreign Assistance Act of 1968: Hearings before the Committee on Foreign Relations* (Washington, D.C.: U.S. Government Printing Office, 1968), 21; Kunz, *Guns and Butter*, 136.

46. United Nations, *Economic Survey of Latin America, 1970*, 309–312.

47. Ibid., 332.

48. Ibid., 313–314.

49. Ibid., 319, 325.

50. Ibid., 336–337. Latin American exports to socialist countries increased by an average annual rate of 19.6 percent, a figure produced primarily by Cuban sugar exports to the Soviet Union.

51. Ibid., 339, 348.

52. Memorandum, Theodore L. Eliot (State Department Executive Secretariate) to Henry A. Kissinger, "United States Support for Latin American Integration," 17 July 1970, NARA, RG 59, Subject–Numeric File, 1970–73, Box 762.

53. Wilkie, Lorey, and Ochoa, *Statistical Abstract of Latin America*, 698; Inter-American Development Bank (IADB), *Annual Report, 1971* (Washington, D.C.: IADB, 1972), 10.

54. Ibid., 667.

55. William R. Cline and Enrique Delgado, eds., *Economic Integration in Central America* (Washington, D.C.: The Brookings Institution, 1978), 59.

56. Cable, Regional Office for Central America and Panama(ROCAP)/Guatemala to State, 28 January 1969, NARA, RG 59, Subject–Numeric File, 1967–69, Box 696.

57. Cable, ROCAP/Guatemala, "Growth Trends in the Central American Common Market (CACM), 1960–1971," 1 December 1972, NARA, RG 59, Subject–Numeric File, 1970–73, Box 812.

58. Victor Bulmer-Thomas, *The Political Economy of Central America since 1920* (New York: Cambridge University Press, 1987), 188.

59. Cable, ROCAP/Guatemala, "Growth Trends in the Central American Common Market," 1 December 1972.

60. Rostow, *The World Economy,* 248–249. According to Rostow, the index for food and raw materials prices (1963 = 100) dropped from 105 in 1966 to 102 in 1968.

61. Cline and Delgado, *Economic Integration in Central America*, 126–128, 252; Cable, ROCAP/Guatemala, "Growth Trends in the Central American Common Market," 1 December 1972.

62. Frederick S. Weaver, *Inside the Volcano: The History and Political Economy of Central America* (Boulder, Colo.: Westview Press, 1994), 169.

63. Cable, Embassy (Managua) to State, 12 June 1969, NARA, RG 59, Subject–Numeric File, 1967–69, Box 798.

64. Bulmer-Thomas, *The Political Economy of Central America since 1920*, 181–183.

65. Weeks, *Economies of Central America*, 92; Cline and Delgado, *Economic Integration in Central America*, 33.

66. DeWitt, *The Inter-American Development Bank and Political Influence*, 48.

67. Wilfred L. David, *The Conversation of Economic Development: Historical Voices, Interpretations, and Reality* (Armonk, N.Y.: M. E. Sharpe, 1997), 115, 119; Wilkie, Lorey, and Ochoa, *Statistical Abstract of Latin America*, 141. Daily caloric intake in Latin America, for example, increased only marginally (2.4%) from 1966–1968 to 1969–1971.

68. Cline and Delgado, *Economic Integration in Central America*, 18–25.

69. Ibid., 154–155.

70. Cable, ROCAP/Guatemala, "Growth Trends in the Central American Common Market," 1 December 1972.

71. Cable, ROCAP/Guatemala to State, 28 January 1969.

72. Bulmer-Thomas, *Political Economy of Central America*, 195.

73. Royce Q. Shaw, *Central America: Regional Integration and National Political Development* (Boulder, Colo.: Westview Press, 1978), 103–128.

74. Memorandum, John P. Walsh (State, Acting Executive Secretary) to Henry A. Kissinger, "Dispute within the Central American Common Market," 25 March 1969, NARA, RG 59, Subject–Numeric File, 1967–69, Box 696.

75. Memorandum, Edward W. Coy (U.S. AID) to Kennedy M. Crockett (U.S. Ambassador, Nicaragua), "Additional Points Made by President Somoza at Lunch on December 11," 13 December 1968, NARA, RG 59, Subject–Numeric File, 1967–69, Box 696.

76. Cable, Embassy (Managua) to State, 11 October 1969, NARA, RG 59, Subject–Numeric File, 1967–69, Box 696.

77. Cable, Embassy (San Salvador) to State, 25 June 1971, and Cable, ROCAP/Guatemala to State, 28 December 1971, RG 59, Subject–Numeric File, 1970–73, Box 812.

78. Cable, ROCAP/Guatemala to State, "Current Situation in the Central American Common Market," 23 June 1971, NARA, RG 59, Subject–Numeric File, 1970–73, Box 812.

79. Cable, Embassy (Managua) to State, 10 July 1971, NARA, RG 59, Subject–Numeric File, 1970–73, Box 812.

80. Cable, ROCAP/Guatemala to State, "Current Situation in the Central American Common Market," 23 June 1971.

81. John Weeks, *The Economies of Central America* (New York: Holmes and Meier, 1985), 69.

82. Cable, ROCAP/Guatemala to State, "Current Situation in the Central American Common Market," 23 June 1971.

83. Raul Prebisch, *Change and Development—Latin America's Great Task: Report Submitted to the Inter-American Development Bank* (New York: Praeger, 1971), 3–22.

84. Cable, ROCAP/Guatemala, "Growth Trends in the Central American Common Market," 1 December 1972.

85. U.S. AID, *A.I.D. Economic Data Book: Latin America*, 231–234.

86. Bulmer-Thomas, *The Economic History of Latin America since Independence*, 291.

87. Cable, Embassy (Managua) to State, 28 October 1969, NARA, RG 59, Subject–Numeric File, 1967–69, Box 696.

88. Cable, Embassy (Managua) to State, 4 December 1971, NARA, RG 59, Subject–Numeric File, 1970–73, Box 770; U.S. AID, *A.I.D. Economic Data Book: Latin America*, 235.

89. Banco Central de Nicaragua, Departamento de Estudios Economico, *Boletin Semestral, Enero–Junio 1972*, no. 43 (Managua: Banco Central de Nicaragua, 1972), 62, 76, 80; Cable, Embassy (Managua) to State, 12 May 1969, NARA, RG 59, Subject–Numeric File, 1967–69, Box 2178.

90. Cable, Embassy (Managua) to State, 15 December 1968, NARA, RG 59, Subject–Numeric File, 1967–69, Box 798.

91. Morris H. Morley, *Washington, Somoza, and the Sandinistas: State and Regime in U.S. Policy toward Nicaragua, 1969–1981* (New York: Cambridge University Press, 1994), 41, 51; U.S. AID, *A.I.D. Economic Data Book: Latin America*, 14; Wilkie, Lorey, and Ochoa, *Statistical Abstract of Latin America*, 71.

92. Cable, Embassy (Managua) to State, 26 June 1969, NARA, RG 59, Subject–Numeric File, 1967–69, Box 798.

93. Inter-American Development Bank, *Annual Report, 1972* (Washington, D.C.: IADB, 1973), 61; U.S. AID/Nicaragua, *FY1973 Program Submission*, July 1971, NARA, RG 286, Records of the Agency for International Development, Office of Public Safety, Latin America, Country File, Nicaragua, 1957–1974, Box 90.

94. Cable, Embassy (Managua) to State, 5 August 1971, NARA, RG 59, Subject–Numeric File, 1970–73, Box 2503.

95. Michael D. Gambone, *Eisenhower, Somoza, and the Cold War in Nicaragua, 1953–1961* (Westport, Conn.: Praeger, 1997), 54–58.

96. U.S. AID/Nicaragua, *FY1973 Program Submission*, July 1971.

97. Cable, Embassy (Managua) to State, 26 May 1969, NARA, RG 59, Subject–Numeric File, 1967–69, Box 646. See also U.S. Agency for International Development, Bureau for Pro-

gram and Policy Coordination, *The Nature and Impact of the International Market for Sugar*, discussion paper no. 24 (Washington, D.C.: AID, 1971), 3, 11, 14.

98. Organizacion de los Estados Americanos, Consejo Interamericano Economico y Social, Comité Interamericano de la Alianza para el Progreso, Subcomite del CIAP Sobre Nicaragua, *Situacion, Principales Problemas, y Perspectivas del Desarollo Economico y Social de Nicaragua* (Washington, D.C.: Secretaria General de la Organizacion de los Estados Americanos, 1973), 124.

99. Cable, Embassy (Managua) to State, 9 February 1969, NARA, RG 59, Subject–Numeric File, 1967–69, Box 2179.

100. U.S. AID/Nicaragua, *FY1973 Program Submission*, July 1971.

101. Ibid.

102. Memorandum, Maurice J. Williams (AID) to the President, "Special Report on Emergency Relief for the Managua Disaster," 8 January 1973, NARA, RMN, WHCF, Subject File, Box 11.

103. Cable, Embassy (Managua) to State, 12 April 1973, NARA, RG 59, Subject–Numeric File, 1970–73, Box 770.

104. Cable, Embassy (Managua) to State, 28 November 1973, NARA, RG 59, Subject–Numeric File, 1970–73, Box 770.

105. Cable, Embassy (Managua) to State, 28 December 1973, NARA, RG 59, Subject–Numeric File, 1970–73, Box 770.

106. IADB, *Annual Report, 1973* (Washington, D.C.: IADB, 1974), 57–58.

107. James Dunkerely, *Power in the Isthmus: A Political History of Modern Central America* (New York: Verso, 1988), 235–247.

108. Kunz, *Guns and Butter*, 192.

109. Memorandum, Eliot to Kissinger, "United States Support for Latin American Integration," 17 July 1970.

110. Memorandum, Al Haig (White House) to Dave Parker (White House), "Latin American AID Mission Directors' Conference, February 24–26," 20 February 1971, RMN, WHCF, Subject File, Box 11.

111. IADB, *Economic and Social Progress in Latin America: External Debt: Crisis and Adjustment, 1985 Report* (Washington, D.C.: IADB, 1985), 125–137.

112. Gambone, *Eisenhower, Somoza, and the Cold War in Nicaragua, 1953–1961*, 46–58.

113. U.S. AID/Nicaragua, *FY1973 Program Submission*, July 1971.

CHAPTER 10

Conclusions

At the start of the 1970s, revolution flourished as never before in Latin America. Its root causes, observable in the outright destitution and disenfranchisement of millions that had arguably grown, a fact not lost on a new generation of rebels regaining purchase throughout the region. This was no less true in Central America, where the remnants of revolutionary groups that had survived the 1960s reinvented themselves around new constituencies in order to survive. New revolutions appeared where old struggles diminished. Despite the devastating blows landed by the Guatemalan military and U.S. military advisors in the late 1960s, local insurgents persisted long enough to form the Ejercito Guerrillero de los Pobres (Guerrilla Army of the Poor) in the 1970s, and were able to launch major offensives in the department of Quiché by the middle of the decade. In El Salvador and Nicaragua, rejuvenated rebel movements also reemerged to challenge the status quo.

Revolution was equally evident in the ongoing tendency of Latin American militaries to exercise coup d'état against civilian institutions. Salvador Allende Gossen's brutal overthrow in 1973 was only the most outstanding example of an ongoing practice that dominated the regional political process. That same year, El Salvador saw the election of José Napoleon Duarte overturned by senior military officers, sparking more than ten years of electoral fraud and bloodshed.[1] With the exception of one brief period in 1971–1972, the military essentially ruled Honduras from 1963 to 1981.[2] In Nicaragua, 1972 saw the government pass from Anastasio Somoza Debayle to a sham civilian troika that still included the dictator. Real power, however, remained at the feet of the *Guardia Nacional*.

After ten years of effort, the dispatch of thousands of advisors, and the expenditure of millions of dollars in aid and still more billions in investment, fundamental stability still eluded the hemisphere. What had caused this situation to exist? Where had the Alliance for Progress fallen short? What had leaders in the United States, Central America, and Nicaragua failed to understand? Two separate, albeit complementary answers offer some degree of insight.

THE CHANGING NATURE OF REVOLUTION

Challenges to Latin American stability were a fluid constant throughout the 1960s, one that defied easy categorization. They existed in the burgeoning demographic problems of the vast urban shanty towns that surrounded every major city. They appeared in the expectations of the elites, whose interests were tied to new economic sectors, elites who challenged the old oligarchy. They existed in the multiplying political movements that arose out of a generally held desire to transcend the traditional boundaries of political discourse in Latin America.

Communism was an obvious revolutionary culprit, but one that underwent its own evolution during the decade. The apparent failure of Cuban communism to spread far beyond its borders did not signal the end of its ideological utility to Latin American rebels.[3] Indigenous communism flourished in separate movements throughout Central America. It grew in El Salvador under the legitimate auspices of the Union Democratica Nacionalista. It persisted in Nicaragua in the form of the Movilizacion Republicana, the Partido Socialista Nicaragüense, the Frente Sandinista de Liberacion Nacional, and a host of small student movements. Borrowing in part from the popular-front tactic of the late 1930s, moderate Communist factions pursued alliances with other members of the Latin American left, particularly fellow Christian Democrats. It was an alliance of these two ideologies that led to Duarté's election in 1972. In Nicaragua, especially at the conclusion of the 1960s, the FSLN found a common purpose with the more radical elements of the Catholic church in Nicaragua. These alliances proved to be critical to the longevity of Central American communism. They created the necessity that party cadres translate Marxism into the local lexicon. Urban unions cared more about wages than the intricacies of political ideology. Christian base communities discussed land reform and moral justice. By embracing coalitions with contemporary opponents of the status quo, Communists were able to tailor their message to a broadening range of constituents.

The use of violence in Central American also evolved during the 1960s. The failure of the Cuban *foco* model led, after a brief period of uncertainty at mid-decade, to new innovations in the art of revolutionary warfare. Long rural campaigns to indoctrinate an inert peasantry gave way to more selective urban operations. The proliferation of kidnappings, assassinations, and raids were intended to take advantage of the relatively little attention spent by counterinsurgency doctrine on the city. The police and military units created by U.S. advisors were rural constructs, built around experiences in Vietnam, Malaya, and the Philippines. They were at sea in the significantly different operating environment of the twentieth-century metropolis. Moreover, urban guerrilla operations also had the potential for a greater political impact on a much more concentrated audience. A bold, dramatic act could potentially galvanize popular support. The successful 1974 FSLN ransom of key Somoza supporters was a milestone that exposed the impotency of the regime and, in the throngs that turned out to cheer the rebels, its unpopularity.

Over the long term, the militarization of Latin America proved to be a greater threat than communism could ever produce. Local military establishments, reinforced by modern equipment and American advisors, became the most proximate threat to their own citizenry, serving in too many cases as blunt instruments of state power that failed to distinguish between friend and foe. At the conclusion of the 1960s, the gap between civilians and the military had grown more pronounced. All areas of life were affected in the process. Cable traffic from U.S. military advisors in Managua repeatedly expressed concerns regarding the increase of common crime, the product of a persistent lack of professionalization within the *Guardia* and its ever-increasing tendency toward graft and corruption. On the other end of the spectrum, in Guatemala, the security infrastructure produced the deaths and imprisonment of thousands of innocent civilians.

The impact of this process on political institutions was equally destructive. The perceived utility of military power, and the increasing tendency toward military intervention in civil affairs, came at the expense of both civilian leadership and democratic institutions. For many Latin American senior officers, intervention appealed to common sense: Partisan bickering between traditional parties and political latecomers was seen as an obstacle to progress. The seemingly momentary political cost of intervention to preserve public order was seen as an unfortunate but necessary step toward eventual democracy. In the meantime, the lingering problem for Latin Americans was that militaries rarely identified the point at which adequate stability would allow a transition back to civilian rule. As the years progressed, military occupation of power became a continuous end unto itself.[4]

Regional militarization proved to be a significant obstacle to U.S. influence in Latin America. The fact that the United States spent millions on the modernization and rearmament of Latin America created little suasion with its military leadership. Latin American commanders received the best training that the U.S. military school system could provide in the hope that immersion would somehow transfer the American civil–military ethic and lead to the creation of an apolitical institution. This effort backfired on its American sponsors. Professional training provoked within regional militaries the constant search for betterment and a sense that the U.S. military was a peer and not a mentor. Latin American officers came to resent Washington's unwillingness to provide first-line arms and equipment, seeing this policy as an arbitrary effort to limit the impact of military assistance. Consequently, rather than adhere to the selective U.S. arms embargo, Latin Americans learned to look abroad to U.S. allies, who were perfectly happy to ply the hemisphere with their own newest-model weaponry. As a result, Washington soon found itself forced into free competition in the global arms market. By 1969, the Nixon administration had abandoned all hope of control for open competition with England, France, and other nations intent on rearming the hemisphere.

In a much broader sense, the 1960s also reflected a revolution of expectations created by the Alliance for Progress. Foremost among these was the hope that the socioeconomic status of both participating nations and individual Latin Americans would improve. Contemporary advances in science, communications, and medicine offered the tantalizing possibility that Latin America could abandon the practices of a stagnant past and enter into a community of truly modern nations. Growth indeed proved to be real and dramatic. Manufacturing, industry, and agriculture all improved, both in terms of the quality of products and productivity itself. Infrastructure, management, education, and health care made substantial strides forward. At least superficially, it appeared that Latin America might be moving toward Rostow's "take-off" stage of development.

Instead, development was neither balanced nor universal. The explosive population growth that was commonplace to the region proved to be a permanent check on macroeconomic growth. The structure of growth was equally problematic. Few nations were able to diversify far beyond the primary commodities of the previous century. National planning remained hostage to fluctuations in commodity prices. For those who tried to move beyond this straitjacket, the costs of import-substitution industrialization rapidly outweighed its benefits. As this system began to falter, attempts to bolster the free-market model, through tariff reductions and other devices, only managed to seriously undercut public revenues. As the 1970s began, debt became a fixed point on the Latin American landscape. Dependence grew, expanding to include not only include the United States, but other advanced nations in Europe and Asia.

Revolutionary challenges to Nicaragua multiplied throughout the 1960s. National politics offered one clear indication that change had arrived. At the start of the decade, the Somoza brothers found themselves besieged by a burgeoning number of challengers disinterested in the old order. Members of their own Liberal Party openly questioned the Somozas' ability to lead, a practice unheard of in their father's day. More to the point, in every electoral cycle of the 1960s, the Somozas faced a dissident group from within their own core constituency. The stable, reliable foundation enjoyed by the family for nearly thirty years was rapidly eroding. The evolution of the Conservative Party proved to be even more dramatic. Gone were the *caudillos* who had controlled the traditional opposition, replaced by youthful insurgents prepared to envisage both a new populist charter and the political coalitions necessary to achieve it. Moreover, as events in 1967 indicated, Conservatives also appeared prepared to embrace electoral violence to a degree unseen since the end of World War II. In this environment, the Nicaraguan left, although not initially strong, found it could gain purchase and allies as the two major parties bludgeoned each other. Student organizations, trade unions, and the church all began to build core constituencies that would prove critical to the revolution that would sweep through the country in the 1970s.

Military threats to the Somoza regime also underwent a substantial evolution during the 1960s. Cuban *foquismo* was an obvious failure in Nicaragua. The *Guardia Nacional* was able to deliver a drubbing to would-be revolutionaries for years, nearly wiping out the FSLN in the process of its counterinsurgency operations. These victories proved to be pyrrhic in the long run, however. They produced, on the one hand, a surviving core element of guerrillas better able to both formulate political strategy and prosecute future military operations against Managua. Defeat, in other words, produced a de facto professionalization of the Sandinistas. The 1970s would see a much more sophisticated revolutionary effort on their part, one that combined the cultivation of political ties with a growing list of regime opponents and a more carefully husbanded military campaign. In another important sense, the initial successes experienced by the Nicaraguan National Guard against the FSLN diminished its interest in the nonmilitary aspects of the Alliance for Progress. Civic action, aside from the showcase affairs created for American consumption, never accompanied the rather heavy-handed use of force. At the start of the 1970s, the *Guardia* was essentially the same anachronistic institution it had been thirty years earlier, efficient in arms but not in its ability to understand or address the political and socioeconomic causes of rebellion.

As was the case throughout Central America, within Nicaragua the Alliance for Progress created both impressive development and greater expectations. In many respects the country was a showcase for developmentalism. Its trade, both within the Central American Common Market and among a growing international clientele, was a remarkable success story. Nicaraguan agriculture and industry were also causes for optimism, managing to both diversify and make substantial gains in productivity. However, the Somoza regime was unable to translate this prosperity into material gains for most Nicaraguans. The old landed elites, particularly those directly tied to the family, dominated new business enterprises, a fact that caused no small degree of dissonance among younger entrepreneurs. For the bulk of the citizens outside this circle, the quality of life was at best problematic. Housing shortages plagued the country, especially in the rapidly growing cities of the Pacific coast. Illiteracy remained chronically high. In the poor *barrios* of Jinotepe and Matagalpa, the Sandinistas would find dry tinder. Perhaps more fundamental, the many disparities between progress and poverty discredited the alliance and the faith that development could produce a measurably better quality of life in Nicaragua, a realization that opened even more doors for proponents of revolution.

THE FAILURE OF CAPTURE

By the early 1970s it was clear that the Alliance for Progress had failed to keep pace with threats to Latin American stability. When announced, it had promised a commitment by all parties concerned to pursue a series of universal solutions to the systemic problems of the hemisphere. A decade later, it had proven to be a clumsy vehicle, riven with faults that were the product of both the individual parts that made up the alliance and its overall conceptual foundation.

The United States, for a variety of reasons, proved to be a poor sponsor to Latin America. During the heady days of the first Punta de Este conference, northern American leaders were abundantly confident that the reconstruction of Latin America, spanning a potpourri of diverse categories, was not only possible, but achievable within the ten-year span of the proposed Alliance for Progress. The sheer number of goals set characterized an overriding sense that the program could promote development and security on a broad front. It was an ambitious, even arrogant agenda, but one plagued by critical flaws.

Primary among these was the U.S. leadership's failure to translate its developmental theories into workable policies. The European model of development, forged during the formation of the Truman Doctrine and the creation of the Marshall Plan, had wildly succeeded in rebuilding prosperous, anti-Communist American allies. Many of the transplants from the Marshall Plan era who worked for the Kennedy administration, particularly Adolf Berle, made the faulty assumption that the same methodology that had created NATO and the European Economic Community could be reapplied to Latin America. American policy makers were especially optimistic that this process would quickly progress in larger, comparatively more sophisticated nations like Mexico, Brazil, or Chile. They recognized that Central America would absorb more time and effort, but remained confident that the same development model held for the isthmus as well. This proved to be a serious miscalculation for the simple reason that Latin America did not contain the same social, economic, and political infrastructure that had allowed for success in Western Europe. Throughout the 1960s, Latin American political and military institutions resisted efforts to hammer them into new unfamiliar forms. In part, slow progress was a matter of choice. An irony of the alliance lies in the fact that Latin American resistance to U.S. policy initiatives actually stiffened as time went on. Efforts to rally the hemisphere against Cuba or for the Dominican intervention drew an increasingly louder chorus of criticism. Unlike the heyday of the Cold War in the 1950s, Pan-Americanism orchestrated from Washington produced a diminishing echo throughout the hemisphere a generation later.

The Rostow–Millikan development model that assumed a transition of free-market practices to democratic values proved even more tenuous when applied to Latin America. It was a vague paradigm that did not define political empowerment or suggest the precise measures necessary to achieve it. On the ground, American policy makers could agree that democracy should become an inclusive, universal standard. Using economic aid to somehow create this endpoint was another matter entirely. Instead, the various embassy teams assigned to Latin America allowed economic assistance to move ahead, focusing on the concrete products of growth and the myriad difficulties of managing it. These issues, because they were tangible and could be measured and reported, occupied the greater proportion of American attention.[5] Over time, economic statistics were offered to infer progress over a much broader social and political spectrum than could be realistically applied.

The lack of experience within each of the successive American administrations compounded these problems. In *The Best and the Brightest*, David Halberstam offered this characterization of McGeorge Bundy, a key member of the Kennedy White House: "He was bright and he was quick, but even this bothered people around him. They seemed to sense a lack of reflection, a lack of depth, a tendency to look at things tactically, functionally and operationally rather than intellectually; they believed Bundy thought that there was a straight line between two points."[6]

Bundy, like many of his contemporaries, lacked a detailed understanding of Latin America, its history, its culture, or its internal politics. Regional experts, such as Arthur Schlesinger Jr., maintained extensive relationships with ruling elites, but not with the political echelons descending from the presidential palace. Consequently, those outside of power, comprised of a diverse variety of interests and ideologies, were often simply lumped into the category of "antiregime" or "anti-American" when they spoke out against the alliance. The failure to discern the many internal dynamics affecting Latin America and the tendency to describe them in simplistic, doctrinaire Cold War terms effectively crippled U.S. policy and further isolated the United States from Latin America.

America's accumulating distraction with international crises was a final strike against the Alliance for Progress. As the record indicates, the brief Kennedy administration served as a momentary period of focus. Yet even this president felt the constant pull of foreign affairs that carried greater weight, policies in need of articulation, and agencies that demanded greater coordination. Bobby Kennedy once remarked to Stanley Karnow when asked about the growing importance of Vietnam early in the administration, "Vietnam . . . We have thirty Vietnams a day here."[7] Subsequently, badly needed course corrections to the alliance never surfaced in the shadow of constant demands in other arenas. Domestic affairs captured Lyndon Johnson's attention. Torn between the successful pursuit of his Great Society and the Vietnam War, Johnson had little time for Latin America. His late attempts at summitry near the end of his presidency were a sad commentary on the region's priority. Nixon's distraction differed in terms of its cause if not its effect. As president, Nixon saw the world in a manner more akin to John Foster Dulles than Dean Rusk or George C. Marshall, a place where geopolitical relevance gravitated to the bipolar (or tripolar) construction of global power. Secondary regions were treated with policy dedicated to minimizing risk through covert (e.g., in the case of Allende) or overt (e.g., in the case of armaments) proxies. At the conclusion of his presidency, U.S. policy toward Latin America more closely resembled that of the first Eisenhower administration, characterized by a clear reticence to promote dramatic economic, political, or social reform.

In sum, in the years after the announcement of the Alliance for Progress, American policy underwent what could be best described as a consistent deevolution. The Kennedy administration, determined to make its mark in the Third World at a key juncture in the Cold War, set the bar high, expressing its policy as a set of universal principles it could neither accurately articulate nor adequately pursue. Its successors, saddled with an enormous commitment of resources and prestige, did little more than maintain an expensive assortment of policies that received only sporadic comprehensive guidance. As time wore on and America found itself tested by an accumulation of major problems, a list that grew to include the war in Vietnam, the decline of the dollar, Soviet nuclear parity, and a host of other items, U.S. policy in Latin America lost its focus and became intent instead on extrication from the responsibilities engendered by the alliance.

For its own part, Central America adapted poorly to the Alliance for Progress. Part of its problem was structural. What contemporary advocates of the *Alianza* asked the region to attempt was a significant and speedy restructuring of virtually every internal institution it possessed. Economies based upon export agriculture were pushed to diversify into new industries and balance this development on a regional scale never before attempted. Democratic institutions were offered for wholesale adoption in a region where, with the exception of Costa Rica, the observance of an open political discourse was something discussed only in theory during the twentieth century. At its foundation, Central America lacked the political, economic, or social infrastructure to support the alliance. Traditional practices became significant obstacles to modernization on virtually every front. American sponsorship could not prevent the military in Guatemala, Honduras, or El Salvador from arbitrarily exercising its authority over civilian government in the 1960s. Nor could American aid facilitate a degree a political tolerance necessary for opposition groups to gain traction in legitimate electoral processes. Economic programs, such as proposals to reform domestic taxation policies, met with significant resistance from traditional elites. Despite the best efforts of its sponsor and itself, much of Central America remained mired in the amber of its past.

Other difficulties were produced by the Central American states. While U.S. influence in the region was formidable, it could not guarantee total compliance with the high-minded principles embraced at Punta del Este in 1962. After a point, Central American nations sometimes simply refused to conform to change as a matter of deliberate choice. Consequently, meaningful regional cooperation became an American chimera. Long-held national rivalries blocked attempts to build a workable consensus in either the Central American Common Market or the Central American Defense Council. The shrill rhetoric that accompanied Common Market policy debates in the late 1960s drowned out American appeals to embrace cooperation that would lead to balanced development. Central American support for collective security was periodic at best. Each military was willing to take advantage of American training facilities and assistance, a fact indicated by the thousands of officers and enlisted ranks sent to the School of the Americas. Active participation in U.S. policy initiatives was another matter. While the Dominican intervention garnered individual offers of military support, a more systemic degree of common effort eluded the U.S. military in Central America for most of the 1960s.

More to the point, these efforts were not simply a matter of rivalry or institutional prerogative, but a partial backlash against U.S. sponsorship of the alliance. Many Central American nations gladly accepted aid that reinforced the status quo. They resented, however, the nation-building programs attempting to alter the existing power structure. Demonstrations of self-interest took many forms, both subtle and more overt. In many cases, the host nation could determine the pace and direction of alliance programs. Police and military assistance, for example, normally made more progress than civic action projects. Physical improvements to internal infrastructure that supported local economic elites—ports, roads, and electrification—normally took precedence over public housing, education, and health care. In instances where an open divergence between U.S. and Central American interests took place, the break was more dramatic. The outpouring of nationalist sentiment that accompanied the Soccer War in 1969 was as much an expression of a local animosities as it was a reaction against U.S. intervention to resolve the conflict. Afterward, American efforts to resuscitate the Common Market faced increasingly recalcitrant clients in Honduras and El Salvador.

In total, these barriers to reform produced an environment in which economic, military, and political power grew increasingly distorted over time. Without the necessary counterbalances supported by the alliance—electoral reform, military professionalization, increased social services—internal schisms over wealth and political access became more pronounced and more dangerous. Central America exited the decade more volatile than it had entered it.

Nicaragua was a problematic receptacle for the alliance and its basic principles. U.S. embassy officials attempting to make the state more conducive to reform found themselves opposed by a Somoza regime intent on the maintenance of its own power and influence. This system was tolerable for Americans and some Nicaraguans as long as it produced economic growth and, for a brief period, it worked. Nicaragua was one of five Latin American republics able to increase its share of world trade in the 1960s.[8] Moreover, the system worked as well when it promised a degree of enfranchisement for the Conservative Party and tolerance of the regime's critics. Unfortunately, this period passed with the departure of Luis Somoza from the presidency. Even before he prevailed in the 1967 election, Anastasio Somoza Debayle discarded any efforts at flexibility, reverting to the old-style system of patronage and the tried-and-true tactics of coercion and foreign cultivation. In an important sense, Nicaragua saw its own deevolution in the 1960s.

In the meantime, while Managua became mired in Somoza family's hubris, regime opponents began to unify. The chronic deterioration of Nicaragua's economic system, coupled with popular identification of the regime as a "predatory state," unified previously diverse groups into progressively larger coalitions as the decade wore on.[9] The creation of the Union Nacional Opositora in 1966 was a harbinger of greater challenges to the regime in the future. Traditional dissidents, a restive entrepreneurial class, and the leftist fringe were all perched on the brink of open cooperation when the 1972 earthquake occurred.

In this atmosphere, the optimism and energy of Punta del Este seemed distant, the ideas naïve. The specter of revolution, however, remained and continued to confound leaders in the United States and Latin America. Both would enter the 1970s contemplating new forms of instability with seemingly fewer means to meet them.

NOTES

1. Edward S. Herman and Frank Brodhead, *Demonstration Elections: U.S.–Staged Elections in the Dominican Republic, Vietnam, and El Salvador* (Boston: South End Press, 1984), 17–54, 93–152.

2. James Dunkerley, *Power in the Isthmus: A Political History of Modern Central America* (New York: Verso, 1988), 540–560.

3. Matt D. Childs, "An Historical Critique of the Emergence and Evolution of Ernesto Che Guevara's *Foco* Theory," *Journal of Latin American Studies* 27 (1995): 593–624; Tad Szulc, *Fidel: A Critical Portrait* (New York: Avon Books, 1986), 661–672.

4. See David Collier, ed., *The New Authoritarianism in Latin America* (Princeton, N.J.: Princeton University Press, 1979).

5. Raul Prebisch, *Change and Development—Latin America's Great Task: Report Submitted to the Inter-American Development Bank* (New York: Praeger, 1971), 3–22.

6. David Halberstam, *The Best and the Brightest* (Greenwich, Conn.: Fawcett, 1969), 76.

7. Ibid., 98.

8. Victor Bulmer-Thomas, *The Economic History of Latin America since Independence* (New York: Cambridge University Press, 1994), 291.

9. Morris H. Morley, *Washington, Somoza, and the Sandinistas: State and Regime in U.S. Policy toward Nicaragua, 1969–1981* (New York: Cambridge University Press, 1994), 53.

Bibliography

ARCHIVAL RESOURCES

The National Archives and Records Administration,
College Park, Maryland

Richard M. Nixon Presidential Materials Collection

White House Central File

Records Group 59

General Records of the Department of State, Bureau of Inter-American Affairs, Office of
Central American and Panamanian Affairs (ARA/OAP), Subject and Country Files,
Lot Files, 63D127, 64D310, 65D159, 66D131
General Records of the Department of State, Central Decimal File, 1960–1963
General Records of the Department of State, Deputy Assistant Secretary of State for Politico-
Military Affairs, Office of Operations, Subject Files, 1962–1966
General Records of the Department of State, Executive Secretariat, Records Relating to Cabi-
net Meetings, 1953–1965
General Records of the Department of State, Miscellaneous Memoranda Relating to the Mili-
tary Defense Assistance Program and Related Activities, 1959–1963
General Records of the Department of State, National Security Action Memoranda Files,
1961–1968
General Records of the Department of State, Presidential and Secretary of State Official
Exchanges of Correspondence, 1961–1966
General Records of the Department of State, Records of Robert Komer, 1948–1968, Lot
69D303
General Records of the Department of State, Subject–Numeric File, 1964–1969
General Records of the Department of State, Subject–Numeric File, 1970–1973

Records Group 218

Records of the U.S. Joint Chiefs of Staff, Records of the Chairman, Gen. Earl G. Wheeler,
1964–1970

Records Group 273

Records of the National Security Council

Records Group 286

Records of the Agency for International Development, Office of Public Safety, Latin America,
Country File, Nicaragua, 1957–1974

The John Fitzgerald Kennedy Library, Boston, Massachusetts

White House Central Files
President's Office Files
National Security Files
U.S. Department of the Treasury Records
U.S. Central Intelligence Agency, Printed Materials
Edwin R. Bayley Papers
Jack N. Behrman Papers
David E. Bell Papers
McGeorge Bundy Papers
Robert H. Estabrook Papers
Max F. Millikan Papers
Teodoro Moscoso Papers
Arthur M. Schlesinger Papers

The Lyndon Baines Johnson Library, Austin, Texas

National Security File
White House Central Files
White House Central Files, Confidential File
Office Files of White House Aides
Oral History Collection
Papers of George Ball
Papers of H. Barefoot Davis

The Nettie Lee Benson Collection, University of Texas, Austin

PRIMARY SOURCES

Banco Central de Nicaragua. Departmento de Estudios Economicos. *Boletin Trimestral, Julio–Setiembre, 1966.* No. 23. Managua: Banco Central de Nicaragua, 1966.
———. *Boletin Semestral, Octubre–Diciembre, 1966.* No. 24. Managua: Banco Central de Nicaragua, 1966.
———. *Boletin Semestral, Enero–Junio, 1972.* No. 43. Managua: Banco Central de Nicaragua, 1972.
Consejo Interamericano Economico y Social. *La Marcha de la Alianza para el Progresso, 1962–1963.* Washington, D.C.: Union Panamericana, 1964.
Inter-American Development Bank (IADB). *Social Progress Trust Fund Agreement.* Washington, D.C.: IADB, 1961.
———. *Tenth Annual Report, 1969.* Washington, D.C.: IADB, 1970.
———. *Eleventh Annual Report, 1970.* Washington, D.C.: IADB, 1971.
———. *Annual Report, 1971.* Washington, D.C.: IADB, 1972.
———. *Annual Report, 1972.* Washington, D.C.: IADB, 1973.
———. *Annual Report, 1973.* Washington, D.C.: IADB, 1974.
———. *Economic and Social Progress in Latin America: External Debt: Crisis and Adjustment, 1985 Report.* Washington, D.C.: IADB, 1985.
Inter-American Development Bank. Social Progress Trust Fund. *First Annual Report, 1961.* Washington, D.C.: IADB, 1961.

————. *Second Annual Report, 1962.* Washington, D.C.: IADB, 1962.

————. *Third Annual Report, 1963.* Washington, D.C.: IADB, 1963.

————. *Fourth Annual Report, 1964.* Washington, D.C.: IADB, 1964.

————. *Fifth Annual Report, 1965.* Washington, D.C.: IADB, 1965.

————. *Sixth Annual Report, 1966.* Washington, D.C.: IADB, 1966.

————. *Seventh Annual Report, 1967.* Washington, D.C.: IADB, 1967.

————. *Eighth Annual Report, 1968.* Washington, D.C.: IADB, 1968.

Inter-American Foundation (IAF). *Annual Report, 1977.* Rosslyn, Va.: IAF, 1978.

International Bank for Reconstruction and Development (IBRD). *The Economic Development of Nicaragua.* Baltimore: Johns Hopkins University Press, 1954.

————. *The World Bank and the IDA in the Americas.* Washington, D.C.: IBRD, 1962.

Naciones Unidas. Comision Economica para America Latina. *Analisis y Proyecciones del Desarrollo Economico: IX El Desarrollo Economico de Nicaragua.* New York: Naciones Unidas, 1966.

Organization of American States (OAS). *The Alliance for Progress and Latin American Development Prospects: A Five-Year Review, 1961–1965.* Baltimore: Johns Hopkins University Press, 1967.

————. *Declaration of the Presidents of America: Meeting of American Chiefs of State, Punta del Este, Uruguay, 12–14 April 1967.* Washington, D.C.: General Secretariat of the Organization of American States, 1967.

Organization of American States. Departments of Economic and Social Affairs. *The Alliance for Progress and Latin-American Development Prospects: The Five-Year Review, 1961–1965.* Baltimore: Johns Hopkins University Press, 1967.

Organization of American States. Inter-American Economic and Social Council. *The Alliance for Progress: Its First Year, 1961–1962.* Washington, D.C.: OAS, 1963.

Organizacion de los Estados Americanos, Consejo Interamericano Economico y Social, Comité Interamericano de la Alianza para Progreso, Subcomite del CIAP Sobre Nicaragua. *Situacion, Principales Problemas, y Perspectivas del Desarrollo Economico y Social de Nicaragua.* Washington, D.C.. Secretaria General de la Organizacion de los Estados Americanos, 1973.

Pan American Union. Department of Economic Affairs. *Economic Survey of Latin America, 1962.* Baltimore: Johns Hopkins University Press, 1964.

————. *Latin America: Problems and Perspectives of Economic Development, 1963–1964.* Baltimore: Johns Hopkins University Press, 1966.

Republic of Nicaragua. Nicaraguan Industrial Promotion Office. *Nicaragua in the Central American Common Market.* New York, 1966.

Republica de Nicaragua. Consejo Nacional de Economia. Oficina de Planificacion. *Estadisticas del Desarrollo Economico de Nicaragua: 1960–1967, Programacion Global.* Managua: Consejo Nacional de Economia, Oficina de Planificacion, 1968.

Republica de Nicaragua. Direccion General de Estadistica y Censos.

————. *Boletin de Estadistica, 1964.* No. 10. Managua: Republica de Nicaragua, 1964.

————. *Comercio Exterior de Nicaragua por Productos.* Managua: Republica de Nicaragua, 1968.

Republica de Nicaragua. Ministerio de Economia. *Noticias Nacionales y Actividades de las Dependencias del Ministerio de Economia.* No. 23. Managua: Republica de Nicaragua, 1966.

Republica de Nicaragua. Ministerio de la Guerra, Marina y Aviacion. *Memoria del Ministerio de la Guerra, Marina y Aviacion.* Managua: Republica de Nicaragua, D.N., 1956.

————. *Memoria del Ministerio de la Guerra, Marina y Aviacion.* Managua: Republica de Nicaragua, D.N., 1957.

Republica de Nicaragua. Oficina de Planificacion. Consejo Nacional de Economica. *Informe Parcial al Señor Presidente de la Republica.* Managua: Republica de Nicaragua, July 1963.

————. *Informe Anual de la Oficina de Planificacion, 1967–1968.* Managua: Republica de Nicaragua, August 1968.

Republica de Nicaragua. Recaudador General de Aduanas. *Memoria de la Recaudacion General de Aduanas por el Periodo del 1 de Enero al 31 de Deciembre de 1961.* Managua: Republica de Nicaragua, 1962.

Union Panamericana. Secretaria General de la Organizacion de los Estados Americanas. Comite de los Nueve. *Informe Sobre Los Planes Nacionales de Desarrollo y el Proceso de Integracion Economica de Centroamerica: Informe Presentado por el Comite Ad Hoc a los Gobiernos de las Republicas Centroamericanas.* Washington, D.C.: Union Panamericana, Comite de los Alianza para el Progreso, 1966.

United Nations. Economic Commission for Latin America. *The Economic Development of Latin America and Its Principle Problems.* New York: United Nations Publications, 1950.

————. *Annual Report, 24 May 1959–29 May 1960.* New York: United Nations, 1961.

————. *Economic Survey of Latin America: 1970.* New York: United Nations, 1972.

U.S. Agency for International Development (USAID). Bureau for Latin America. *The Charter of Punta del Este.* Washington, D.C.: U.S. Government Printing Office, 1961.

————. *Latin American Growth Trends: Seven Years of the Alliance for Progress.* Washington, D.C.: USAID, 1967.

U.S. Agency for International Development. Bureau for Program and Policy Coordination. Office of Statistics and Reports. *A.I.D. Economic Data Book: Latin America.* Washington, D.C.: U.S. Government Printing Office, 1971.

————. *Determinants of Use of Special Drawing Rights by Developing Nations.* AID Discussion Paper No. 27. Washington, D.C.: U.S. Government Printing Office, 1971.

————. *Fiscal Incidence in Empirical Studies of Income Distribution in Poor Countries.* AID Discussion Paper No. 25. Washington, D.C.: U.S. Government Printing Office, 1971.

————. *Growth of Exports and Income in the Developing World: A Neoclassical View.* AID Discussion Paper No. 28. Washington, D.C.: U.S. Government Printing Office, 1971.

————. *The Nature and Impact of the International Market for Sugar.* AID Discussion Paper No. 24. Washington, D.C.: U.S. Government Printing Office, 1971.

————. *Payments Arranged for Less Developed Countries: The Role of Foreign Assistance.* AID Discussion Paper No. 26. Washington, D.C.: U.S. Government Printing Office, 1971.

U.S. Agency for International Development. Statistics and Reports Division. *U.S. Overseas Loans and Grants and Assistance from International Organizations: Obligations and Loan Authorizations, July 1, 1945–June 30, 1966.* Washington, D.C.: U.S. Government Printing Office, 1967.

U.S. Department of Commerce. Bureau of International Commerce. Overseas Business Reports. *Investment in Nicaragua.* OBR-62-14. Washington, D.C.: U.S. Government Printing Office, 1962.

————. *United States Trade with Major World Areas, January–December, 1963.* OBR 64–48. Washington, D.C.: U.S. Government Printing Office, 1964.

————. *United States Trade with the 19 Latin American Republics, 1959–1963.* OBR 64–121. Washington, D.C.: U.S. Government Printing Office, 1964.

————. *Basic Data on the Economy of Nicaragua.* OBR 65-42. Washington, D.C.: U.S. Government Printing Office, 1965.

————. *Market Indicators for Latin American Republics.* OBR 65-41. Washington, D.C.: U.S. Government Printing Office, 1965.

———. *Market Profiles — The Latin American Area.* OBR 66-37. Washington, D.C.: U.S. Government Printing Office, 1966.

———. *Foreign Trade of the Central American Common Market, 1963–64.* OBR 66-41. Washington, D.C.: U.S. Government Printing Office, 1966.

———. *Market Indicators for Latin America.* OBR 67-74. Washington, D.C.: U.S. Government Printing Office, 1967.

———. *The International Investment Position of the United States: Developments in 1968.* OBR 69-60. Washington, D.C.: U.S. Government Printing Office, 1969.

———. *Latin American Economic Integration: Implications for U.S. Business.* OBR 69-7. Washington, D.C.: U.S. Government Printing Office, 1969.

———. *United States Foreign Trade Annual, 1962–68.* OBR 69-2. Washington, D.C.: U.S. Government Printing Office, 1969.

———. *U.S. Foreign Trade by Quarters, January–March 1967—January–March 1969.* OBR 69-24. Washington, D.C.: U.S. Government Printing Office, 1969.

U.S. Department of Commerce. Bureau of the Census. *Statistical Abstract of the United States: 1975.* Washington, D.C.: U.S. Government Printing Office, 1975.

———. *Historical Statistics of the United States: Colonial Times to 1970.* Washington, D.C.: U.S. Government Printing Office, 1976.

U.S. Department of Commerce. Business and Defense Services Administration. *Copper Quarterly Industry Report* 5 (Spring–Summer 1960). Washington, D.C.: U.S. Government Printing Office, 1960.

U.S. Congress. Committee on Foreign Affairs. *Collective Defense Treaties: With Maps, Texts of Treaties, a Chronology, Status of Forces Agreements, and Comparative Charts.* Washington, D.C.: U.S. Government Printing Office, 1967.

U.S. Congress. Joint Economic Committee. Subcommittee on Inter-American Economic Relationships. *Economic Developments in South America.* Washington, D.C.: U.S. Government Printing Office, 1962.

———. *Private Investment in Latin America.* Washington, D.C.: U.S. Government Printing Office, 1964.

U.S. Department of State. *Report to Congress on the Mutual Security Program for the Fiscal Year 1960.* Washington, D.C.: Department of State, 1961.

———. *Foreign Relations of the United States, 1961–1963, American Republics.* Vol 12. Washington, D.C.: U.S. Government Printing Office, 1996.

U.S. Senate. Committee on Banking, Housing, and Urban Affairs. *Financing of Foreign Military Sales.* Washington, D.C.: U.S. Government Printing Office, 1978.

U.S. Senate. *The Foreign Assistance Act of 1968: Hearings before the Committee on Foreign Relations.* Washington, D.C.: U.S. Government Printing Office, 1968.

SECONDARY SOURCES

Aguilar, Luis, ed. *Operation Zapata: The "Ultrasensitive" Report and Testimony of the Board of Inquiry on the Bay of Pigs.* Frederick, Md.: University Publications of America, 1981.

Ai Camp, Roderic, ed. *Democracy in Latin America: Patterns and Cycles.* Wilmington, Del.: Scholarly Resources, 1996.

Alba, Victor. *Alliance Without Allies: The Mythology of Progress in Latin America.* New York: Praeger, 1965.

Alegria, Claribel, and D. J. Flakoll. *Nicaragua: la revolucion sandinista, Una Cronica politica, 1855–1979.* Mexico City, D.F.: Ediciones Era, S.A., 1982.

Alexander, Robert J. "New Directions: The United States and Latin America." *Current History* 42 (1962): 65–70.

Allan, Pierre, and Kjell Goldman, eds. *The End of the Cold War: Evaluating Theories of International Relations*. Boston: Martinus Nijhoff, 1992.

Alvarado Martinez, Enrique. *El pensamiento politico nicaragüense: de los ultimos años*. Managua: Editorial y Lit. Artes Graficas, 1968.

Alvarez Montalvan, Emilio. *Las Fuerzas Armadas en Nicaragua: Sinopsis Historica, 1821–1994*. Managua: J. E. Arellano, 1994.

Ambrose, Stephen E. *Nixon: Triumph of a Politician, 1962–1972*. New York: Simon and Schuster, 1989.

———. *Rise to Globalism: American Foreign Policy since 1938*. New York: Penguin Books, 1991.

"American Guerrillas," *Time*, 10 March 1961, 19.

Ameringer, Charles D. *The Democratic Left in Exile: The Antidictatorial Struggle in the Caribbean, 1945–1959*. Coral Gables, Fla.: University of Miami Press, 1974.

———. *Don Pepe: A Political Biography of José Figueres of Costa Rica*. Albuquerque: University of New Mexico Press, 1978.

———. *U.S. Foreign Intelligence: The Secret Side of American History*. Lexington, Mass.: Lexington Books, 1990.

———. *The Caribbean Legion: Patriots, Politicians, Soldiers of Fortune, 1946–1959*. University Park: Pennsylvania State University Press, 1996.

Anderson, Thomas P. *Politics in Central America: Guatemala, El Salvador, Honduras, and Nicaragua*. Westport, Conn.: Praeger, 1988.

Apter, David E. *Rethinking Development: Modernization, Dependency, and Postmodern Politics*. London: Sage, 1987.

Ball, M. Margaret. "Latin America and the Balance of Power." *Current History* 40 (1961): 193–224.

Barber, Willard F., and C. Neale Ronning. *Internal Security and Military Power: Counterinsurgency and Civic Action in Latin America*. Columbus: Ohio State University Press, 1966.

Barry, Tom. *Low Intensity Conflict: The New Battlefield in Central America*. Albuquerque, N.M.: Resources Center, 1986.

Beede, Benjamin R. *Intervention and Counterinsurgency: An Annotated Bibliography of the Small Wars of the United States, 1898–1984*. New York: Garland, 1985.

Beschloss, Michael R. *The Crisis Years: Kennedy and Khrushchev, 1960–1963*. New York: Edward Burlingame, 1991.

Bethell, Leslie, ed. *Latin America: Politics and Society since 1930*. New York: Cambridge University Press, 1998.

Beverley, John, and Marc Zimmerman. *Literature and Politics in Central American Revolutions*. Austin: University of Texas Press, 1990.

Biderman, Jaime M. "The Development of Capitalism in Nicaragua: A Political Economic History." *Latin American Perspectives* 10 (Winter 1983): 7–32.

Blasier, Cole. *The Giant's Rival: The USSR and Latin America*. Pittsburgh: University of Pittsburgh Press, 1987.

Blaufarb, Douglas S. *The Counterinsurgency Era: U.S. Doctrine and Performance, 1950 to the Present*. New York: The Free Press, 1977.

Blaufarb, Douglas S., and George K. Tanham. *Who Will Win? A Key to the Puzzle of Revolutionary War*. New York: Crane Russak, 1989.

Bloomfield, Richard J., and Gregory F. Treverton, eds. *Alternative to Intervention: A New U.S.–Latin American Security Relationship*. Boulder, Colo.: Lynne Rienner, 1990.

Blum, John Morton. *Years of Discord: American Politics and Society, 1961–1974*. New York: W. W. Norton, 1991.

Bonds, Ray, ed. *The Soviet War Machine: An Encyclopedia of Russian Military Equipment and Strategy*. New York: Chartwell Books, 1976.

Booth, John A., and Thomas W. Walker. *Understanding Central America*. Boulder, Colo.: Westview Press, 1989.

Brands, H. W. *The Wages of Globalism: Lyndon Johnson and the Limits of American Power*. New York: Oxford University Press, 1995.

Bulmer-Thomas, Victor. *The Political Economy of Central America since 1920*. New York: Cambridge University Press, 1987.

———. *The Economic History of Latin America since Independence*. New York: Cambridge University Press, 1994.

Bundy, William. *A Tangled Web: The Making of Foreign Policy in the Nixon Presidency*. New York: Hill and Wang, 1998.

Caballero Jurado, Carlos, and Nigel Thomas. *Central American Wars, 1959–1989*. London: Osprey, 1990.

Cadorette, Curt. *From the Heart of the People: The Theology of Gustavo Gutiérrez*. Oak Park, Ill.: Meyer Stone Books, 1988.

Cardenal, Ernesto. *The Gospel in Solentiname*. Maryknoll, N.Y.: Orbis Books, 1976.

Cardoso, Fernando Henrique, and Enzo Faletto. *Dependency and Development in Latin America*. Berkeley and Los Angeles: University of California Press, 1979.

Castro, Daniel, ed. *Revolution and Revolutionaries: Guerrilla Movements in Latin America*. Wilmington, Del.: Scholarly Resources, 1999.

Childs, Matt D. "An Historical Critique of the Emergence and Evolution of Ernesto Che Guevara's *Foco* Theory." *Journal of Latin American Studies* 27 (1995): 593–624.

Clem, Harold J. *Collective Defense and Foreign Assistance*. Washington, D.C.: Industrial College of the Armed Forces, 1968.

Cline, William R., and Enrique Delgado. *Economic Integration in Central America*. Washington, D.C.: The Brookings Institution, 1978.

Close, David. *Nicaragua: Politics, Economics, and Society*. London: Pinter, 1988.

Coatsworth, John H. *Central America and the United States: The Clients and the Colossus*. New York: Twayne, 1994.

Cochrane, James D. *The Politics of Regional Integration: The Central American Case*. New Orleans: Tulane University Press, 1969.

Cohen, Warren I. *The Cambridge History of American Foreign Relations: America in the Age of Soviet Power, 1945–1991*. Vol. 4 New York: Cambridge University Press, 1993.

Cohen, Warren I., and Nancy Bernkopf Tucker, eds. *Lyndon Johnson Confronts the World: American Foreign Policy, 1963–1968*. New York: Cambridge University Press, 1994.

Collier, David, ed. *The New Authoritarianism in Latin America*. Princeton, N.J.: Princeton University Press, 1979.

Committee on Economic Development. *Economic Development of Central America*. New York: CED, 1964.

Cooper, Frederick, Florencia E. Mallon, Steve J. Stern, Allen F. Isaacman, and William Roseberry. *Confronting Historical Paradigms: Peasants, Labor, and the Capitalist World System in Africa and Latin America*. Madison: University of Wisconsin Press, 1993.

Crawley, Eduardo. *Nicaragua in Perspective*. New York: St. Martin's Press, 1979.

Cullather, Nick. *Secret History: The CIA's Classified Account of Its Operations in Guatemala, 1952–1954.* Stanford: Stanford University Press, 1999.

Dallek, Robert. *Flawed Giant: Lyndon Johnson and His Times, 1961–1973.* New York: Oxford University Press, 1998.

David, Wilfred L. *The Conversation of Economic Development: Historical Voices, Interpretations, and Reality.* Armonk, N.Y.: M. E. Sharpe, 1997.

Debray, Regis. *Revolution within the Revolution? Armed Struggle and Political Struggle in Latin America.* New York: Monthly Review Press, 1967.

DeWitt, R. Peter. *The Inter-American Development Bank and Political Influence.* New York: Praeger, 1977.

Dodson, Michael, and Laura Nuzzi O'Shaughnessy. *Nicaragua's Other Revolution: Religious Faith and Political Struggle.* Chapel Hill: University of North Carolina Press, 1990.

Dominguez, Jorge I. *Cuba: Order and Revolution.* Cambridge: Belknap Press of Harvard University Press, 1978.

Drake, Paul W. *Labor Movements and Dictatorships: The Southern Cone in Comparative Perspective.* Baltimore: Johns Hopkins University Press, 1996.

———, ed. *Money Doctors, Foreign Debts, and Economic Reforms in Latin America: From the 1890s to the Present.* Wilimington, Del.: Scholarly Resources, 1994.

Dreier, John C., ed. *The Alliance for Progress: Problems and Perspectives.* Baltimore: Johns Hopkins University Press, 1962.

Dunkerley, James. *Power in the Isthmus: A Political History of Modern Central America.* New York: Verso, 1988.

"Eighteen Examples of Growing Worry for U.S. Business." *U.S. News,* 27 June 1960, 62–63.

Everingham, Mark. *Revolution and Multiclass Coalition in Nicaragua.* Pittsburgh: University of Pittsburgh Press, 1996.

Evolution of Foreign Aid, 1945–1965. Washington, D.C.: Congressional Quarterly Service, 1966.

Falcoff, Mark, and Robert Royal, eds. *Crisis and Opportunity: U.S. Policy in Central America and the Caribbean.* Washington, D.C.: Ethics and Public Policy Center, 1984.

Fauriol, Georges, ed. *Security in the Americas.* Washington, D.C.: National Defense University Press, 1989.

Ferm, Deane William. *Third World Liberation Theologies.* Maryknoll, N.Y.: Orbis Books, 1986.

Findling, John E. *Close Neighbors, Distant Friends: United States Central American Relations.* Westport, Conn.: Greenwood Press, 1987.

Fowler, Will. *Ideologues and Ideologies in Latin America.* Westport, Conn.: Greenwood Press, 1997.

Fuentes Mohr, Alberto. *La creacion de un mercado comun: Apuntes historicos sobre la experiencia de Centroamérica.* Buenos Aires: Instituto para la integracion de America Latina, 1973.

Gaddis, John Lewis. *Strategies of Containment: A Critical Appraisal of Postwar American National Security Policy.* New York: Oxford University Press, 1982.

———. *We Now Know: Rethinking Cold War History.* New York: Clarendon Press, 1997.

Gemmill, Harry. "How to Lose Sales: Gringo Grip on Latin Markets is Loosened by Pushing Up Prices." *Wall Street Journal,* 29 May 1959, 1.

Genovese, Michael A. *The Nixon Presidency: Power and Politics in Turbulent Times.* Westport, Conn.: Greenwood Press, 1990.

Gerschenkron, Alexander. *Economic Backwardness in Historical Perspective: A Book of Essays.* Cambridge: Belknap Press of Harvard University Press, 1962.

———. *Continuity in History and Other Essays.* Cambridge: Belknap Press of Harvard University Press, 1968.

Gilbert, Felix. *To the Farewell Address: Ideas of Early American Foreign Policy.* Princeton, N.J.: Princeton University Press, 1961.

Gilbert, John H., ed. *The New Era in American Foreign Policy.* New York: St. Martin's Press, 1973.

Gilderhus, Mark T. "An Emerging Synthesis? U.S.–Latin American Relations since the Second World War." *Diplomatic History* 16 (1992): 429–452.

Gleijeses, Piero. *The Dominican Crisis: The 1965 Constitutionalist Revolt and American Intervention.* Baltimore: Johns Hopkins University Press, 1978.

Global Defense: U.S. Military Commitments Abroad. Washington, D.C.: Congressional Quarterly Service, 1969.

Goodman, G.J.W. "Unconventional Warriors." *Esquire,* November 1961, 128–132.

Goodman, Louis W., William M. Leogrande, and Johanna Mendelson Forman. *Political Parties and Democracy in Central America.* Boulder, Colo.: Westview Press, 1990.

Green, David. *The Containment of Latin America: A History of the Myths and Realities of the Good Neighbor Policy.* Chicago: Quadrangle Books, 1971.

Green, Duncan. *Silent Revolution: The Rise of Market Economics in Latin America.* London: Cassell, 1995.

Greene, John Robert. *The Limits of Power: The Nixon and Ford Administrations.* Bloomington: Indiana University Press, 1992.

Goldwert, Marvin. *The Constabulary in the Dominican Republic and Nicaragua: Progeny and Legacy of United States Intervention.* Gainesville: University of Florida Press, 1962.

Gross, Liza. *Handbook of Leftist Guerrilla Groups in Latin American and the Caribbean.* Boulder, Colo.: Westview Press, 1995.

Guevara, Che. *Guerrilla Warfare.* New York: Vintage Books, 1969.

Gwin, Catherine. *U.S. Relations with the World Bank, 1945–1992.* Washington, D.C.: The Brookings Institution, 1994.

Halberstam, David. *The Best and the Brightest.* Greenwich, Conn.: Fawcett, 1969.

Hanson, Simon G. *Dollar Diplomacy Modern Style: Chapters in the Failure of the Alliance for Progress.* Washington, D.C.: Inter-American Press, 1970.

Harnecker, Marta. *Los Cristianos en la Revolucion Sandinista: Del Verticalismo a la Participacion de las Masas.* Buenos Aires: Ediciones al Frente, 1987.

Harrison, Lawrence E. *Underdevelopment Is a State of Mind.* Lanham, Md.: Madison Books, 1985.

Hartz, Louis. *The Liberal Tradition in America: An Interpretation of American Political Thought since the Revolution.* New York: Harcourt Brace, 1952.

Hassler, Warren W. *With Shield and Sword: American Military Affairs, Colonial Times to the Present.* Ames: Iowa State University Press, 1982.

Higgins, Trumbull. *The Perfect Failure: Kennedy, Eisenhower, and the CIA at the Bay of Pigs.* New York: W. W. Norton, 1987.

Hilsman, Roger. *An American Guerrilla: My War Behind Japanese Lines.* Washington, D.C.: Brassey's, 1990.

Hirschman, Albert O. *Journeys toward Progress: Studies of Economic Policy-Making in Latin America.* New York: Twentieth Century Fund, 1963.

———. *Development Projects Observed.* Washington, D.C.: The Brookings Institution, 1967.

———. *A Bias for Hope: Essays on Development and Latin America.* New Haven, Conn.: Yale University Press, 1971.

Hirschman, Albert O., and Richard M. Bird. *Foreign Aid: A Critique and a Proposal.* Princeton, N.J.: Princeton University Press, 1968.

Hodges, Donald C. *Intellectual Foundations of the Nicaraguan Revolution*. Austin: University of Texas Press, 1986.

Hoff, Joan. *Nixon Reconsidered*. New York: Basic Books, 1994.

Holden, Robert H. "Constructing the Limits of State Violence in Central America: Towards a New Research Agenda." *Journal of Latin American Studies* 28 (1996): 435–459.

Horne, Gerald. "American Empire and Cultural Imperialism: A View from the Receiving End." *Diplomatic History* 23 (1999): 463–478.

Huberman, Leo, and Paul M. Sweezy, eds. *Regis Debray and the Latin American Revolution*. New York: Monthly Review Press, 1968.

Humphrey, David C. "NSC Meetings during the Johnson Presidency." *Diplomatic History* 18 (1994): 29–46.

Hunt, Michael H. "Internationalizing U.S. History: A Practical Agenda." *Diplomatic History* 15 (1991): 1–12.

———. "The Long Crisis in U.S. Diplomatic History." *Diplomatic History* 16 (1992): 115–140.

Hunter, John M. "Latin American Integration and the Alliance." *Current History* 53 (1967): 257–265.

Huntington, Samuel P. *The Soldier and the State: The Theory and Politics of Civil–Military Relations*. Cambridge: Belknap Press of Harvard University Press, 1957.

———. *Political Order in Changing Societies*. New Haven, Conn.: Yale University Press, 1968.

Huntington, Samuel P., and Joan M. Nelson. *No Easy Choice: Political Participation in Developing Countries*. Cambridge: Harvard University Press, 1976.

Ikenberry, G. John, David A. Lake, and Michael Mastanduno, eds. *The State and American Foreign Economic Policy*. Ithaca, N.Y.: Cornell University Press, 1988.

Immerman, Richard H. *The CIA in Guatemala: The Foreign Policy of Intervention*. Austin: University of Texas Press, 1982.

Johnson, Edgar A. J., ed. *The Dimensions of Diplomacy*. Baltimore: Johns Hopkins University Press, 1964.

Johnson, Lyndon Baines. *The Vantage Point: Perspectives of the Presidency, 1963–1969*. New York: Popular Library, 1971.

Jones, Alan M., ed. *U.S. Foreign Policy in a Changing World: The Nixon Administration, 1969–1973*. New York: David McKay, 1973.

Jorden, William J. *Panama Odyssey*. Austin: University of Texas Press, 1984.

Kagan, Robert. *A Twilight Struggle: American Power and Nicaragua, 1977–1990*. New York: The Free Press, 1996.

Kaufman, Burton I. *Trade and Aid: Eisenhower's Foreign Economic Policy, 1953–1961*. Baltimore: Johns Hopkins University Press, 1982.

———. "John F. Kennedy as World Leader: A Perspective on the Literature." *Diplomatic History* 17 (1993): 447–470.

Kearns, Doris. *Lyndon Johnson and the American Dream*. New York: Harper and Row, 1976.

Kelly, Francis J. *U.S. Army Special Forces, 1961–1971*. Washington, D.C.: Department of the Army, 1973.

Kennan, George F. *American Diplomacy, 1900–1950*. Chicago: University of Chicago Press, 1951.

Kennedy, Harold T. "The Flood of Imports—How Serious Is It?" *American Import–Export Bulletin* 53 (1963): 603–604.

Kennedy, Paul. *The Rise and Fall of the Great Powers: Economic Change and Military Conflict from 1500 to 2000*. New York: Vintage Books, 1989.

Kimmens, Andrew C., ed. *Nicaragua and the United States*. New York: H. W. Wilson, 1987.

Kirk, John M. *Politics and the Catholic Church in Nicaragua.* Gainesville: University Press of Florida, 1992.

Kissinger, Henry. *The White House Years.* Boston: Little, Brown, 1979.

———. *Diplomacy.* New York: Simon and Schuster, 1994.

Klare, Michael T. *Supplying Repression: U.S. Support for Authoritarian Regimes Abroad.* Washington, D.C.: Institute for Policy Studies, 1977.

Kolko, Gabriel. *Confronting the Third World: United States Foreign Policy, 1945–1980.* New York: Pantheon Books, 1988.

Krenn, Michael L. *The Chains of Interdependence: U.S. Policy toward Central America, 1945–1954.* Armonk, N.Y.: M. E. Sharpe, 1996.

Kunz, Diane B., ed. *The Diplomacy of the Crucial Decade: American Foreign Relations during the 1960's.* New York: Columbia University Press, 1994.

———. *Guns and Butter: America's Cold War Economic Diplomacy.* New York: The Free Press, 1997.

LaFeber, Walter. *The Panama Canal: The Crisis in Historical Perspective.* New York: Oxford University Press, 1978.

———. *Inevitable Revolutions: The United States in Central America.* New York: W. W. Norton, 1984.

Landau, Saul. *The Guerrilla Wars of Central America: Nicaragua, El Salvador & Guatemala.* New York: St. Martin's Press, 1993.

Lethander, Richard W. O. "The Economy of Nicaragua." Ph.D. diss., Duke University, 1968.

Lieuwen, Edwin. *Arms and Politics in Latin America.* New York: Praeger, 1960.

———. *U.S. Policy in Latin America: A Short History.* New York: Praeger, 1967.

Liss, Sheldon B. *Radical Thought in Central America.* Boulder, Colo.: Westview Press, 1991.

Levinson, Jerome, and Juan de Onis. *The Alliance That Lost Its Way: A Critical Report on the Alliance for Progress.* Chicago: Quadrangle Books, 1970.

Loehr, William, David Price, and Satish Raichur. *A Comparison of U.S. and Multilateral Aid Recipients in Latin America, 1957–1971.* London: Sage, 1976.

Loveman, Brian. *The Constitution of Tyranny: Regimes of Exception in Spanish America.* Pittsburgh: University of Pittsburgh Press, 1993.

———. *For la Patria: Politics and the Armed Forces in Latin America.* Wilmington, Del.: Scholarly Resources, 1999.

Loveman, Brian, and Thomas M. Davies, Jr., eds. *The Politics of Anti-Politics: The Military in Latin America.* Lincoln: University of Nebraska Press, 1989.

Lowenthal, Abraham F. "Alliance Rhetoric versus Latin American Reality." *Foreign Affairs* 48 (1970): 494–508.

———. *The Dominican Intervention.* Cambridge: Harvard University Press, 1972.

———, ed. *Exporting Democracy: The United States and Latin America, Themes and Issues.* Baltimore: Johns Hopkins University Press, 1991.

Lyle, Norris B., and Richard A. Calman. *Statistical Abstract of Latin America: 1965.* Berkeley and Los Angeles: University of California Press, 1966.

Lynch, Edward A. *Religion and Politics in Latin America: Liberation Theology and Christian Democracy.* Westport, Conn.: Praeger, 1991.

Lynch, John. *The Spanish American Revolutions, 1808–1826.* New York: W. W. Norton, 1986.

Manger, William, ed. *The Alliance for Progress: A Critical Appraisal.* Washington, D.C.: Public Affairs Press, 1963.

Maritano, Nino, and Antonio H. Obaid. *An Alliance for Progress: The Challenge and the Problem.* Minneapolis: T. S. Denison, 1963.

Massey, Doreen. *Nicaragua*. Philadelphia: Open University Press, 1987.

McCamant, John F. *Development and Assistance in Central America*. New York: Praeger, 1969.

McClelland, Donald H. *The Central American Common Market: Economic Policies, Economic Growth, and Choices for the Future*. New York: Praeger, 1972.

McClintock, Michael. *Instruments of Statecraft: U.S. Guerrilla Warfare, Counter-Insurgency, Counter-Terrorism, 1940–1990*. New York: Pantheon Books, 1992.

———. *The American Connection: State Terror and Popular Resistance in Guatemala*. London: Zed Books, 1985.

McDonald, Forrest. *Novus Ordo Seclorum: The Intellectual Origins of the Constitution*. Lawrence: University of Kansas Press, 1985.

McFarlane, Anthony, and Eduardo Posada-Carbo, eds. *Independence and Revolution in Spanish America: Perspectives and Problems*. London: Institute of Latin American Studies, 1999.

"Men in the Green Berets," *Time*, 2 March 1962, 19–20.

Merk, Frederick. *Manifest Destiny and Mission in American History: A Reinterpretation*. New York: Alfred A. Knopf, 1963.

Miller, Nicola. *Soviet Relations with Latin America, 1959–1987*. New York: Cambridge University Press, 1989.

Millett, Allan R., and Peter Maslowski. *For the Common Defense: A Military History of the United States of America*. New York: The Free Press, 1994.

Millett, Richard L. *Guardians of the Dynasty*. Maryknoll, N.Y.: Orbis Books, 1977.

Millikan, Max F., ed. *Income Stabilization for a Developing Democracy*. New Haven, Conn.: Yale University Press, 1953.

Millikan, Max F., and Walt W. Rostow. *A Proposal: Key to an Effective Foreign Policy*. New York: Harper and Brothers, 1957.

Millis, Walter. *Arms and Men: A Study in American Military History*. New Brunswick, N.J.: Rutgers University Press, 1956.

Moore, Robin. *The Green Berets*. New York: Crown, 1965.

Morales Carazo, Jaime. *Mejor que Somoza cualquier cosa! Revolucion nicaragüense y sandinismo: la otra cara de la moneda*. Mexico: Compañia Editorial, S.A., 1986.

Morley, Morris H. *Washington, Somoza, and the Sandinistas: State and Regime in U.S. Policy toward Nicaragua, 1969–1981*. New York: Cambridge University Press, 1994.

Mulligan, Joseph E. *The Nicaraguan Church and the Revolution*. Kansas City, Mo.: Sheed and Ward, 1991.

Muñoz, Ronaldo. *The God of Christians*. Maryknoll, N.Y.: Orbis Books, 1990.

Nadel, Laurie. *The Great Stream of History: A Biography of Richard M. Nixon*. New York: Atheneum, 1991.

"Nicaragua at the Heart of the Central American Common Market." *Industrial Development*, February 1964, 28–34.

Nixon, Richard M. "Asia after Vietnam." *Foreign Affairs* 46 (1967): 95–125.

———. *United States Foreign Policy for the 1970's: Building for Peace*. New York: Harper and Row, 1971.

———. *The Memoirs of Richard Nixon*. New York: Grosset and Dunlap, 1978.

Novick, Peter. *That Noble Dream: The "Objectivity Question" and the American Historical Profession*. New York: Cambridge University Press, 1988.

Nugent, Jeffrey B. *Economic Integration in Central America: Empirical Investigations*. Baltimore: Johns Hopkins University Press, 1974.

Nunn, Frederick M. *The Time of the Generals: Latin American Professional Militarism in World Perspective*. Lincoln: University of Nebraska Press, 1992.

Nye, Joseph S. "Central American Regional Integration." *International Conciliation* 572 (March 1967): 1–66.

O'Donnell, Guillermo, Philippe C. Schmitter, and Laurence Whitehead, eds. *Transitions from Authoritarian Rule: Comparative Perspectives.* Baltimore: Johns Hopkins University Press, 1986.

Ortega Saavedra, Humberto. *Cincuenta Anos de Lucha Sandinista.* Medellin: Ediciones Hombre Nuevo, 1979.

———. *A diez años de la rendicion total de la guardia somocista.* Managua: Instituto de Historic de Nicaragua, 1989.

Ortner, E. H. "U.S. Special Forces: The Faceless Army." *Popular Science,* August 1961, 56–59.

Packenham, Robert A. *Liberal America and the Third World: Political Ideas in Foreign Aid and Social Science.* Princeton, N.J.: Princeton University Press, 1973.

———. *The Dependency Movement: Scholarship and Politics in Development Studies.* Cambridge: Harvard University Press, 1992.

Painter, David S. "Explaining U.S. Relations with the Third World." *Diplomatic History* 19 (1995): 525–548.

Palmer, Steven. "Carlos Fonseca and the Construction of Sandinismo in Nicaragua." *Latin American Research Review* 23 (1988): 91–109.

Pancake, Frank R. *Military Assistance as an Element of U.S. Foreign Policy in Latin America, 1950–1968.* Ann Arbor, Mich.: University Microfilms, 1975.

Paret, Peter, ed. *Makers of Modern Strategy: From Machiavelli to the Nuclear Age.* Princeton, N.J.: Princeton University Press, 1986.

Pastor, Robert A. *Whirlpool: U.S. Foreign Policy toward Latin America and the Caribbean.* Princeton, N.J.: Princeton University Press, 1992.

Patterson, James T. *Grand Expectations: The United States, 1945–1974.* New York: Oxford University Press, 1996.

Peloso, Vincent C., and Barbara A. Tenenbaum, eds. *Liberals, Politics, and Power: State Formation in Nineteenth-Century Latin America.* Athens: University of Georgia Press, 1996.

Peterson, Peter G. *The United States in a Changing World Economy.* 2 vols. Washington, D.C.: U.S. Government Printing Office, 1971.

Powaski, Ronald E. *The Cold War: The United States and the Soviet Union, 1917–1991.* New York: Oxford University Press, 1998.

Powelson, John P. *Latin America: Today's Economic and Social Revolution.* New York: McGraw-Hill, 1964.

Prados, John. *The Soviet Estimate: U.S. Intelligence Analysis and Russian Military Strength.* New York: Dial Press, 1982.

Prebisch, Raul. *Change and Development—Latin America's Great Task: Report Submitted to the Inter-American Development Bank.* New York: Praeger, 1971.

Rabe, Steven G. "John F. Kennedy and Latin America: The 'Thorough, Accurate, and Reliable Record' (Almost)." *Diplomatic History* 23 (1999): 539–552.

———. *The Most Dangerous Area in the World: John F. Kennedy Confronts Communist Revolution in Latin America.* Chapel Hill: University of North Carolina Press, 1999.

Ramsett, David E. *Regional Industrial Development in Central America: A Case Study of the Integration Industries Scheme.* New York: Praeger, 1969.

Randall, Margaret. *Sandino's Daughters: Testimonies of Nicaraguan Women in Struggle.* New Brunswick, N.J.: Rutgers University Press, 1995.

Rangel, Carlos. *Del Buen Salvaje al Buen Revolucionario.* Caracas, Venezuela: Monte Avila Editores, C.A., 1977.

Ropp, Steven C. "Goal Orientation of Nicaraguan Cadets: Some Applications for the Problems of Structural/Behavioral Projection in Researching the Latin American Military." *Journal of Comparative Administration* 4 (May 1972): 107–116.

Roseberry, William, Lowell Gudmundson, and Mario Samper Kutschbach, eds. *Coffee, Society, and Power in Latin America*. Baltimore: Johns Hopkins University Press, 1995.

Rosenberg, Emily S. *Spreading the American Dream: American Economic and Cultural Expansion, 1890–1945*. New York: Hill and Wang, 1982.

———. *World War I and the Growth of United States Predominance in Latin America*. New York: Garland, 1987.

Rostow, Walt W. *The United States in the World Arena: An Essay in Recent History*. New York: Harper and Row, 1960.

———. *The World Economy: History & Prospect*. Austin: University of Texas Press, 1978.

———. *Eisenhower, Kennedy, and Foreign Aid*. Austin: University of Texas Press, 1985.

Ruddle, Kenneth, and Mukhtar Hamour. *Statistical Abstract of Latin America: 1970*. Los Angeles: University of California Latin American Center, 1971.

Rusk, Dean. *As I Saw It*. New York: W. W. Norton, 1990.

Ryan, John Morris, Robert N. Anderson, Harry R. Bradley, Carl E. Nesus, Robert B. Johnson, Charles W. Hanks, Jr., Gerald F. Croteau, and Cathy C. Council. *Area Handbook for Nicaragua*. Washington, D.C.: U.S. Government Printing Office, 1970.

Saivetz, Carol R., and Sylvia Woodby. *Soviet–Third World Relations*. Boulder, Colo.: Westview Press, 1985.

Sandoval Rodriguez, Isaac. *Las Crises Politicas Latino Americanas y el Militarismo*. Mexico City: Siglo Veintiunos Editores, 1979.

Savage, Charles H., Jr. "After Castro." *America*, 24 November 1962, 1129–1130.

Scheman, L. Ronald, ed. *The Alliance for Progress: A Retrospective*. Westport, Conn.: Praeger, 1988.

Schlesinger, Arthur M., Jr. *A Thousand Days: John F. Kennedy in the White House*. Boston: Houghton Mifflin, 1965.

Schlesinger, Stephen, and Stephen Kinzer. *Bitter Fruit: The Untold Story of the American Coup in Guatemala*. New York: Doubleday, 1982.

Schmitter, Philippe C., ed. *Military Rule in Latin America: Functions, Consequences, and Perspectives*. London: Sage, 1973.

Schneider, Ronald M. "The U.S. in Latin America." *Current History* 48 (1965): 1–8.

Schurman, Franz. *The Foreign Politics of Richard Nixon: The Grand Design*. Berkeley, Calif.: Institute of International Studies, 1987.

Selbin, Eric. *Modern Latin American Revolutions*. Boulder, Colo.: Westview Press, 1991.

Shaw, Royce Q. *Central America: Regional Integration and National Political Development*. Boulder, Colo.: Westview Press, 1978.

Simpson, Charles M. *Inside the Green Berets: The First Thirty Years, A History of the U.S. Army Special Forces*. Novato, Calif.: Presidio Press, 1983.

SIPRI Yearbook of World Armaments and Disarmament, 1968/69. New York: Humanities Press, 1970.

Smith, Peter H. *Talons of the Eagle: Dynamics of U.S.–Latin American Relations*. New York: Oxford University Press, 2000.

Smith, Tony. *Patterns of Imperialism: The United States, Great Britain, and the Late Industrializing World since 1815*. Cambridge, Mass.: Cambridge University Press, 1981.

Sorenson, Theodore C. *Decision-Making in the White House: The Olive Branch or the Arrow*. New York: Columbia University Press, 1963.

Spalding, Rose J. *Capitalists and Revolution in Nicaragua: Opposition and Accommodation, 1979–1993.* Chapel Hill: University of North Carolina Press, 1994.

Squier, E. G. *Nicaragua, Sus Gentes y Paisajes.* Ciudad Universitaria, Costa Rica: Editorial Universitaria Centroamericana, 1970.

Stephanson, Anders. "Commentary: Diplomatic History in the Expanded Field." *Diplomatic History* 22 (1998): 595–604.

Stevens, Robert Warren. *Vain Hopes, Grim Realities: The Economic Consequences of the Vietnam War.* New York: New Viewpoints, 1976.

Strickland, Rennard, and Donal J. Stanton. *A Sourcebook on Economic & Military Assistance.* Muskogee, Okla.: Hoffman Printing Company, 1966.

Szulc, Tad. *Fidel: A Critical Portrait.* New York: Avon Books, 1986.

Taylor Edmisten, Patricia. *Nicaragua Divided: La Prensa and the Chamorro Legacy.* Pensacola: University of West Florida Press, 1990.

Torres-Rivas, Edelberto. *Repression and Resistance: The Struggle for Democracy in Central America.* Boulder, Colo.: Westview Press, 1989.

Tulchin, Joseph S. "Latin America: Focus for U.S. Aid." *Current History* 52 (1966): 28–34.

Valone, Stephen J., ed. *Two Centuries of U.S. Foreign Policy: The Documentary Record.* Westport, Conn.: Praeger, 1995.

Vollman, Sacha. *Quien impondra la democracia?* Mexico City: Centro de Estudios y Documentacion Sociales, A.C., 1965.

Walker, Martin. *The Cold War: A History.* New York: Henry Holt, 1993.

Walker, Thomas W. *The Christian Democratic Movement in Nicaragua.* Tuscon: University of Arizona Press, 1970.

———, ed. *Revolution & Counterrevolution in Nicaragua.* Boulder, Colo.: Westview Press, 1991.

Weaver, Frederick S. *Inside the Volcano: The History and Political Economy of Central America.* Boulder, Colo.: Westview Press, 1994.

Weeks, John. *The Economies of Central America.* New York: Holmes and Meier, 1985.

Wells, Henry, ed. *Nicaragua Election Factbook.* Washington, D.C.. Institute for the Comparative Study of Political Systems, 1967.

Whelan, Joseph G., and Michael J. Dixon. *The Soviet Union in the Third World: Threat to World Peace.* New York: International Defense Publishers, 1986.

Wiarda, Howard J. *Non-Western Theories of Development: Regional Norms versus Global Trends.* Orlando, Fla.: Harcourt Brace, 1999.

Wicker, Tom. *JFK and LBJ: The Influence of Personality upon Politics.* Baltimore: Penguin Books, 1969.

———. *One of Us: Richard Nixon and the American Dream.* New York: Random House, 1991.

Wilkie, James W., ed. *Statistical Abstract of Latin America: 1965.* Los Angeles: UCLA Latin American Center Publications, 1966.

Wilkie, James W., David E. Lorey, and Enrique Ochoa, eds. *Statistical Abstract of Latin America.* Vol. 26. Los Angeles: UCLA Latin American Center Publications, 1988.

Wills, Garry. *Nixon Agonistes: The Crisis of the Self-Made Man.* Boston: Houghton Mifflin, 1970.

Wolpin, Miles D. *Military Aid and Counterrevolution in the Third World.* Lexington, Mass.: Lexington Books, 1972.

Woodward, Ralph Lee. *Nicaragua.* Santa Barbara, Calif.: Clio Press, 1983.

———. *Central America: A Nation Divided.* New York: Oxford University Press, 1985.

Index

ABOUT THE AUTHOR

Michael D. Gambone is an Assistant Professor of History at Kutztown University. Dr. Gambone entered the active duty army in 1985 where he served as an officer in the 82nd Airborne Division at Ft. Bragg, N.C. In 1997, he published his first book, *Eisenhower, Somoza, and the Cold War in Nicaragua, 1953–1961* (Praeger). In 1999, he received a Fulbright to serve as Lecturer in American History at the Japan Woman's University.